'This book combines sophisticated theories of industrial policy with a deep understanding of the policy process, which comes from the author's long experience in policy-making at the highest levels. This unusual combination has resulted in a framework for empirical analysis that is not only fully appreciative of structural dynamics and inter-sectoral linkages but also keenly aware of practical challenges of policy implementation in terms of administrative capabilities, interest group politics, and institutional constraints. A unique, pathbreaking book.'

Ha-Joon Chang, Reader in Economics, University of Cambridge

'Ethiopia is a development miracle in the making, which will provide the inspiration, confidence, and experiences for other African countries, like the Japanese miracle in post WWII to East Asian countries. Dr Arkebe Oqubay's *Made in Africa: Industrial Policy in Ethiopia* is a brilliant book. It provides first-hand insights with academic rigor about how Ethiopia kick started dynamic structural transformation and achieved double-digit growth in the past decade. Anyone concerned about the development in Africa and other poor countries in the world would be wise to read the book.'

Justin Yifu Lin, Professor, Peking University and Former Chief Economist, World Bank

'Solid transformation of the Ethiopian economy will generate its own industry of success attribution, but few will dispute that this book spells out succinctly and beautifully what is changing. There is no special secret as Arkebe rightly demonstrates: industrial policy is about a reform-minded government having a drive to make it happen; but also having the right cocktail of policies that generate the incentives in every front to make success possible. From agro-processing to light industrial production, from textiles to infrastructure servicing, Ethiopia has become a good case study for other countries to emulate. Be it through regulatory and macro incentives, be it through energy-centered investment, it demonstrates the need for coherence and eagerness to learn from other realities, particularly from Asia. A must read for the many Africans engaged in structural transformation.'

Carlos Lopes, UN Undersecretary and UNECA Executive Secretary

'This is a profoundly original book about the Ethiopian development experience which highlights the potential for, and constraints on, industrialization in Africa. It questions conventional wisdom to argue that industrial policy can work even in low-income countries, where the State performs a developmental role and has the space to make its own policy choices. The author recognizes that industrial policy is easier said than done, to focus on implementation as much as analysis, and emphasizes that even if outcomes are mixed there is learning from both successes and failures. This lucid and engaging book is an unusual blend of theory and policy, as Arkebe Oqubay combines careful scholarship with his rich experience as a policy practitioner. It is essential reading for scholars and practitioners in countries that are latecomers to industrialization.'

Deepak Nayyar, Emeritus Professor of Economics, Jawaharlal Nehru University, New Delhi, and Former Vice Chancellor, University of Delhi

'Active and responsive industrial policy, trial-and-error attitude, and great attention to sectoral details proposed in this book are essentially East Asian. As a scholar and policy maker, Dr Arkebe has revealed to us what is going on in the mind-set of Ethiopian leaders, and why the country is growing fast and absorbing a large amount of light manufacturing investment from abroad.'

Kenichi Ohno, Professor, National Graduate Institute for Policy Studies, Tokyo

'This book arrives at a propitious moment. There is a growing recognition of the importance of industrialization in Africa and an expanding consensus on the need for industrial policy but a paucity of studies to map out the terrain of transformation. The volume provides detailed insights into the institutional configuration and political dynamics underlying industrial policy success and failures by an insider closely tied to the center of power in Ethiopia. The book is essential reading for policy makers, academics and students of the political economy of Ethiopian economic policy.'

Howard Stein, Professor School of Public Health, DAAS, University of Michigan

'Arkebe Oqubay is the ultimate insider, yet he offers an admirably detached and balanced assessment of the ups and downs of Ethiopia's industrial policies. His view of industrial policy is a sophisticated one. Successful intervention requires the right political and institutional framework. It demands a deep understanding of market opportunities, of supply-side problems and linkages across activities, and an appreciation of what government can and cannot do. And it depends, most crucially, on the government's capacity to implement the appropriate measures. This book will be essential reading for all those concerned with the process of industrialisation in developing countries.'

John Sutton, Sir John Hicks Professor of Economics, London School of Economics

'*Made in Africa* is a case study of Ethiopia, but far more than a case study. It uses Ethiopia as the centre of a thoughtful and wide-ranging discussion of the literature on the developmental state, industrial policy, and industrialization-at-large, and celebrates the contributions of the more "heterodox" economists such as Hirschman, Rodrik, Amsden, Reinert, and those at the United Nations Conference on Trade and Development (UNCTAD). It is a model of its kind for economists and political scientists working on development issues around the world. What is more, it is beautifully written!'

Robert H. Wade, Professor of Political Economy, Department of International Development, London School of Economics and Political Science, and winner of the Leontief Prize in Economics

Made in Africa

Made in Africa

Industrial Policy in Ethiopia

Arkebe Oqubay

OXFORD
UNIVERSITY PRESS

OXFORD
UNIVERSITY PRESS

Great Clarendon Street, Oxford, OX2 6DP,
United Kingdom

Oxford University Press is a department of the University of Oxford.
It furthers the University's objective of excellence in research, scholarship,
and education by publishing worldwide. Oxford is a registered trade mark of
Oxford University Press in the UK and in certain other countries

First Edition published in 2015
Impression: 3

Published in the United States of America by Oxford University Press
198 Madison Avenue, New York, NY 10016, United States of America

British Library Cataloguing in Publication Data
Data available

Library of Congress Control Number: 2015939040

ISBN 978–0–19–873989–0

Printed in Great Britain by
Clays Ltd, St Ives plc

Contents

Preface

When I spoke previously at the Africa Summit about some of the bright spots and progress that we're seeing in Africa, I think there is no better example than what has been happening in Ethiopia—one of the fastest-growing economies in the world. We have seen enormous progress in a country that once had great difficulty feeding itself. It's now not only leading the pack in terms of agricultural production in the region, but will soon be an exporter potentially not just of agriculture, but also power because of the development that's been taking place there.

President Barack Obama, New York (25 September 2014)[1]

This book is about the 'African Renaissance' as evidenced in the successful development experience of Ethiopia, a country that is in the throes of dramatic political and economic transformation. As President Obama recognizes in his quote above, an African country can break away from dependence on subsistence agriculture and industrialize. The book challenges conventional wisdom on pathways to industrialization. It argues that industrialization requires a strong and development-oriented state with a long-term vision of structural transformation, a highly committed political leadership, and effective transformative institutions. Employing structuralist and political economy perspectives, the book shows that industrial policies can work and indeed thrive in a low-income African country, and that the state can and should play an activist and developmental role. In this process, policymaking independence is a key prerequisite.

For twenty-five years, I have had the privilege of serving in the top leadership of the government of Ethiopia, including as mayor of Addis Ababa and now as special advisor to the prime minister. During those

---

[1] Source: <http://translations.state.gov/st/english/texttrans/2014/09/20140925308885.html>

years, I have had numerous opportunities to participate in difficult policy decisions, and have witnessed the twists and turns of development policy as the government poured immense resources into developing the essential infrastructure and the health and education that are necessary to put Ethiopia, one of the poorest countries in Africa, on a transformational path that will alleviate the abject poverty of millions of its citizens.

Being a member of the highest policymaking circles and developing sectoral policies and strategies is one thing, but reviewing policy outcomes and extracting lessons is another challenge altogether, and requires careful empirical research. This is even more important in view of the country's decision in 2010 to embark on the five-year Growth and Transformation Plan, which departs from earlier plans by focusing on a structural transformation whereby manufacturing industry will steadily lead the economy. This was obviously an enormous challenge for the government. Thus, in 2010, I decided to embark on a research project to review industrial policy in Ethiopia. This book is the outcome of that adventure and of my own desire to contribute to debate on industrial policy and industrialization within a developing country. By the standards of developing countries, the Ethiopian story is worth telling repeatedly, although industrial policy remains very much a work in progress.

It is not possible for anyone to be completely free of bias. Some pronouncements in this book may have been influenced by my direct involvement in Ethiopian politics and policymaking for the past twenty-five years. Nonetheless, I have tried to keep an open mind and a high degree of professionalism in conducting the research, which focuses in the main on three important—and very different—sub-sectors in the economy. This book does not seek to indulge in triumphalism or to deal in sweeping (and all too common) criticisms and generalizations. Rather, the purpose is to explore what may be learnt from failures and successes, and to emphasize and contribute to policy learning. It should also be made clear that, while I am a government minister and have held a range of government positions, the views presented here are personal: they are not expressed on behalf of the government or the other bodies with which I am or have been affiliated.

It is hoped that scholars and practitioners alike interested in industrialization and industrial policy in developing countries, in particular in Africa, will find this book useful. Equally, it is hoped that policymakers in Ethiopia will find the book relevant at a time when there is a shift towards an industry-led development strategy for the country. This will require a fundamental shift in thinking, and the capacity and commitment to climb the steep road ahead. Now is an opportune moment to elucidate the different perspectives, experiences, and challenges, and ideally to provoke further research and dialogue.

Acknowledgements

The book would not have been possible without the support of many organizations and individuals. First and foremost, I would like to thank Professor Christopher Cramer of the School of Oriental and African Studies (SOAS), University of London, for his remarkable intellectual guidance and encouragement throughout the process of researching and writing the book. I am also indebted to Dr Abaraham Tekeste (MOFED) for his encouragement and valuable comments on the drafts. I must thank Professor John Sender, Dr Deborah Johnston, and Dr Carlos Oya at SOAS for their comments on core chapters. I am grateful to the Centre of African Studies (CAS) at SOAS for a postgraduate fieldwork award, and to the Chevening Foundation for its financial support, as well as to Angelica Baschiera of CAS for her administrative support. I would also like to thank Ambassador Greg Dorey, his predecessor Ambassador Norman Ling, Chris Allan, and Barbara Wickham.

In Ethiopia, I am highly indebted to the Office of the Ethiopian Prime Minister for allowing me to take sabbatical leave to work on this book. I am also indebted to the officials of the Ethiopian Ministry of Industry for their full support and for providing me with a work station during my field study. I must also thank all representatives of the firms, organizations, and government agencies for their valuable time and for their readiness to be interviewed, their participation in the survey, and their provision of data. I thank my research assistants, in particular Eyoual Tamrat, Aregawi Gebremedhin, and Tadesse Gurmu, whose dedication and competence has contributed to the quality of the research. Getnet, Hiwot, Simon, and other enumerators participated in the field study. The encouragement and support of Professor Graeme Salaman, Dr Axumite G. Egziabher (UN-HABITAT), Dr Hailemichael Abera (ECSU), and Dr Haileselassie G. Selassie (University of Amsterdam) is greatly appreciated.

The process of publication has benefited from the outstanding guidance and support of Adam Swallow, the commissioning editor of Oxford University Press. Many thanks for this rewarding journey. It has been a joy working with Adam and his team, the production and marketing teams of OUP. I am indebted to Professors Christopher Cramer and Fantu Cheru for taking the time to read the manuscript in full and provide valuable comments before final submission. I am also indebted to the anonymous external reviewers for their very constructive comments, which indeed improved the scholarly quality of the book. And I thank Peter Colenbrander, whose editing work has been remarkable.

Last but not least, I wish to thank my family—my wife Nigisty and our sons, Samuel and Binyam—for their love, encouragement, and support. Nigisty's advice and constant assistance have been invaluable and my hope is that this work will serve as inspiration to our dearest sons. This book is dedicated to them.

Foreword

It is historically unusual for episodes of rapid economic growth to last very long. And it is even more unusual for those growth spells to lead to, and be underpinned by, the kind of structural transformation that makes an initially low-income developing country better equipped to cope with the shocks and constraints of a violently unstable world, while generating jobs and productivity increases that raise the bulk of the population's living standards. Achieving this in a global context in which the incidence of major financial crises has increased, in which international competition is intense and often hostile, and in which commodity prices and global confidence can swing dramatically, is hugely difficult.

While the 'Africa Rising' narrative has become a commonplace in recent years, there have also been concerns about whether rapid growth in many Africa economies is really translating into structural change with widely spread benefits. And in that context, it has become fashionable among economists, who until very recently looked with disdain on the idea, to champion 'industrial policy' in Africa.

It is very encouraging that so many more people now take the idea of industrial policy in Africa seriously. But what, actually, does it mean? What makes an industrial policy—or a strategy of industrialization comprising a whole set of policies—successful in some cases and a failure in others? Is a successful industrial policy more of an art, even a fluke—neatly labelled as a clear policy after the fact, when the fact involved a mixture of strategic hunches about sectoral prospects, ad hoc allocation of protective supports, favourable turns of global demand, and a happenstance combination of bright and driven individuals—or is it genuinely a science that can be learned, copied, and repeated across contexts?

This book will give readers a unique, extraordinary insight into these questions. How many books that are not memoirs or self-help leadership guides, but the product of detailed, primary socioeconomic research, are written by individuals with long experience of political leadership, with years involved in the leadership of a liberation movement that success-fully booted out a totalitarian regime, and with some twenty-five years of high level policymaking behind them? For that is what this book offers.

After I was first in touch with Arkebe, I thought I would try to find out a little more about him. I talked to British Council officials. I talked to an academic who had taught him when he was one of the remarkable cohort of Ethiopian leaders, including the late Prime Minister Meles Zenawi, who had embarked on a distance learning degree programme through the Open University. And I talked to diplomats. They all told me that Arkebe, the former mayor of Addis Ababa, was a highly unusual person. Through our discussions about development economics, about Ethiopia and Africa, and about how one does research, I have gained insights particularly into Ethiopia that would have been difficult to come by in any other way. But I have also seen first-hand some of Arkebe's qualities, qualities that run like a watermark through this book.

Two characteristics in particular shape and colour this work: a frighten-ing work ethic and a taste for the organized close observation and eye for significance that are at the heart of good research. To sit in a position of national authority, with ministerial rank and involved on the boards of various major projects like Ethiopian Airlines (the state-owned enterprise that is now the largest carrier in Africa), or the railway construction programme, but to find time to carry out coalface research and to write, rewrite, and write again the drafts of an academic manuscript must be rather unusual.

But more than the work rate, what struck me, and I think surprised Arkebe himself, was his natural research talent. I can think of quite a few professional academics that don't have this talent. It is a curiosity and modesty motivated, I suppose, by the extreme significance of the research (making something of a mockery of the 'non-academic impact' that UK scholars contort themselves to show every few years in the Research Excellence Framework evaluation of our work). I don't know if he just has a deeply unfair allocation of talents or whether it is about mobilizing a core set of 'transferable skills', but few people surely have been so effective at and passionate about transforming a city as he was when mayor of Addis Ababa; working as a senior advisor to two prime ministers; and doing fieldwork, making site visits, organizing enterprise surveys, and interviewing industrialists across three sectors.

Attentive observation, repeated, reflected upon, is the source of social science insights and other forms of creative enterprise. This book is written with such modesty and intellectual calm that the reader might not always realize—though I hope she/he does—how much passionate observation, as well as extremely hard work, went into the research and analysis.

The product is unique. It presents new empirical material, and the discussion of this material is animated by the experience the author has accumulated and by the urgency of the challenges of structural change. These challenges are also the subject of the Ethiopian government's ambitious Growth and Transformation Plan. And all the sectors addressed in this book—cement, leather, and floriculture—have an important role to play in that plan. The book does not attempt any grandstanding about what in some cases are remarkable episodes of growth, as for example in the rapid expansion of the cut flower export business. Rather, it tries to understand why it is that a single industrial strategy can have such varied outcomes across three sectors. And it emphasizes the obstacles, the constraints, and the difficulties, since while the successes are often impressive, there is obviously a huge amount yet to change in Ethiopia if it is to industrialize.

Arkebe's own experiences probably account for his taste for particular kinds of academic economist. To mangle Keynes's famous quip, this practical man, who does not actually believe himself exempt from intellectual influences, is far from the slave of, but very much inspired by, the ideas of perhaps two defunct economists in particular: Albert Hirschman and Alice Amsden. What distinguishes economists like these (and a few others) from the vast majority of their kind is their deep and direct engagement with observation of the real world, as opposed to doctrinal faith in abstract axioms and the creed of comparative advantage and 'getting prices right'. We were trying to arrange for Alice to visit Addis Ababa, Ethiopia when she died: her irreverence, her deep seriousness, her emphasis on development as a learning process and one that involved finding the right role models, would have been much appreciated.

Here lies the real significance of this book. Many neoclassical economists and international organizations have lately rediscovered the appeal of industrial policy. And it is now very common to read and hear African policymakers advocating industrial policy. But there remains a great deal to understand about what makes for an effective industrial policy in low- and middle-income economies in Africa and elsewhere in the twenty-first century. And there are still ongoing debates. Many mainstream economists taking an interest in industrial policy completely ignore the origins of the insights and arguments they offer—usually because those origins lie in the work of earlier, far less orthodox economists, like Nicolas Kaldor, 'structuralist development economists', and indeed Alice Amsden.

Mainstream proponents (at the moment) of industrial policy also cast their case very much within the framework of neoclassical economics, in terms of 'market failure' and of facilitating the exploitation of current comparative advantage. There continues to be a thick vein of patronizing advice in much of this work, which is rooted in the paternalistic idea that governments of developing countries should not bite off more than they can chew. This book suggests that such advice is often unfounded. It suggests that, much as Albert Hirschman argued in *Development Projects Observed* (1967), governments need to take on problem-rich, technically complex projects, for only by implementing them will they acquire the capacity for further such projects. The targets set out in Ethiopia's Growth and Transformation Plan may be hugely ambitious, but arguably they help create a compulsion (politically a narrow margin for failure) to set in train genuinely transformative developments. This book shows that following through on ambitious industrial policies is far from easy. But it offers insights into the experiences of different sectors, and of policy-making, that are of enormous significance to policymakers elsewhere in Africa and beyond. It makes a contribution to the academic debate. And, hopefully, it offers inspiration for further studies of industrial policy and performance in low-income countries.

Christopher Cramer
Professor of the Political Economy of Development
SOAS, University of London

List of Figures

List of Tables

List of Abbreviations

ADLI	Agricultural development-led industrialization
AfDB	African Development Bank
AGOA	African Growth and Opportunity Act
AU	African Union
CAD	Comparative advantage-defying
CADF	China-African Development Fund
CAF	Comparative advantage-following
CBB	Construction and Business Bank
CBE	Commercial Bank of Ethiopia
CIP	Competitive Industrial Performance Index
CLRI	Centre for Leather Research Industry, Council of Scientific and Industrial Research (India)
COMTRADE	UN Commodity Trade Statistics Database
CSA	Central Statistics Agency (Ethiopia)
DBE	Development Bank of Ethiopia
EABG	East African Business Group
EAL	Ethiopian Airlines
EC	Ethiopian Calendar
ECAE	Ethiopian Conformity Assessment Enterprise
ECBP	Engineering Capacity Building Program (Ethiopia)
EEPCO	Ethiopian Electricity Power Corporation
EFFORT	Endowment for the Rehabilitation of Tigray
EHDA	Ethiopian Horticulture Development Agency
EHPEA	Ethiopian Horticulture Producers and Exporters Association
EIA	Ethiopian Investment Authority
EIB	European Investment Bank
EIG	Endowment investment group

ELI	Export-led industrialization
ELIA	Ethiopian Leather Industry Association
EPRDF	Ethiopian Peoples' Revolutionary Democratic Front
EPZ	Export-processing zone
ERCA	Ethiopian Revenue and Customs Authority
ETB	Ethiopian Birr
EU	European Union
FAO	Food and Agriculture Organization
FDDI	Footwear Design and Development Institute (India)
FDI	Foreign Direct Investment
FDRE	Federal Democratic Republic of Ethiopia
FIA	Federal Investment Agency
GDP	Gross domestic product
GOE	Government of Ethiopia
GTP	Growth and Transformation Plan (2010–14)
GTZ/GIZ	German Technical Cooperation
GVC	Global Value Chain
ha.	Hectare
HFO	Heavy fuel oil
IDC	Industrial Development Cooperation
IDF	Industrial Development Fund
IDSE	Industrial Development Strategy of Ethiopia
IFC	International Finance Corporation
IFIs	International Finance Institutions
IHDP	Integrated Housing Development Programme
IMF	International Monetary Fund
ISI	Import-substitution Industrialization
ISIC	International Standard Industrial Classification (Revision 3.1)
ITC	International Trade Centre
LDC	Least developed country
LIDI	Leather Industry Development Institute
MIDI	Metal Industry Development Institute
MNC	Multinational corporation
MOE	Ministry of Education (Ethiopia)

MOFED	Ministry of Finance and Economic Development (Ethiopia)
MOI	Ministry of Industry (Ethiopia)
MOM	Ministry of Mines (Ethiopia)
MoST	Ministry of Science and Technology (Ethiopia)
MoTI	Ministry of Trade and Industry (Ethiopia)
MSEs	Micro and small enterprises
MUDC	Ministry of Construction and Urban Development (Ethiopia)
MVA	Manufacturing value added
MWUD	Ministry of Works and Urban Development
NBE	National Bank of Ethiopia
NECC	National Export Coordinating Committee (Ethiopia)
NEPAD	New Economic Partnership of African Development
NIC	Newly industrializing country
NIE	Newly industrializing economies
OECD	Organisation for Economic Co-operation and Development
PASDEP	Plan for Accelerated and Sustained Development to End Poverty
PFEA	Public Financial Enterprises Agency (Ethiopia)
PPESA	Privatization and Public Enterprises Supervisory Agency (Ethiopia)
SAP	Structural adjustment programme
SDPRP	Sustainable Development and Poverty Reduction Program
SNNPR	Southern Nations, Nationalities, and Peoples' Region
SOE	State-owned enterprise
SSA	Sub-Saharan Africa
TGE	Transitional Government of Ethiopia (1991–95)
TIDI	Textile Industry Development Industry
TIRET	Endowment Fund for the Rehabilitation of Amahara
TVET	Technical and vocational education training
UCBP	University Capacity Building Programme
UNCTAD	United Nations Conference on Trade and Development
UN-DESA	United Nations Department of Economic and Social Affairs
UNECA	United Nations Economic Commission for Africa
UN-HABITAT	United Nations Human Settlement Program
UNIDO	United Nations Industrial Development Organization
USAID	United States Agency for International Development

USGS	United States Geological Survey
VSK	Vertical Shift Kiln
WB	World Bank
WTO	World Trade Organization

1

Introduction to Industrial Policy in Ethiopia

1.1 The Lion awakes

In March 2014, *Time* magazine published an article entitled 'Forget the BRICS: Meet the PINEs'. PINE is an acronym for the Philippines, Indonesia, Nigeria, and Ethiopia, accounting for some 600 million people. The author notes that for the last fifty years Africa has generally stood on the sidelines as Asia and others in the developing world have made enormous welfare gains. Now, at last, the continent is beginning to make gains. And nowhere is this truer than in Ethiopia. Once synonymous with impoverishment, the country has enjoyed strong management and may be on a new course. The author concludes by musing whether we are not seeing the emergence of Lion economies in Africa, the analogue of Asia's Tigers of the late twentieth century. In the same month, the African Union (AU) and UN Economic Commission for Africa (UNECA) launched a joint annual report at a conference of African finance ministers in Abuja, Nigeria.[1] The ministers and those attending the conference, and the authors of the report, showed strong interest in Ethiopia's attempt at instituting an activist industrial policy.

Ethiopia is Africa's second most populous country and occupies a highly sensitive geopolitical position, and its economic performance does indeed deserve attention. The country has made spectacular leaps on multiple development fronts in recent years. For instance, Ethiopia—whose economy is not mineral dependent—has recorded double-digit economic growth for a decade, quadrupling its gross domestic product (GDP) per

---

[1] See UNECA-AU 2014.

capita.[2] Life expectancy increased by fifteen years from forty-eight years in 1992 to sixty-three years in 2012, and poverty was halved in two decades.[3] This much-discussed performance is partly the result of the country's distinctive development path and bold experiment in industrial policy, which is unlike any other in Africa. Few other countries on the continent have even tried to implement an active 'developmentalist' industrial policy.

Despite hiccoughs and ongoing challenges, Ethiopia's momentum seemingly persists. Indeed, in March 2014, the Ethiopian prime minister inaugurated a new winery and vineyard at Ziway, a rapidly transforming town 160 kilometres south of the capital. The French company Castel, the largest wine producer in Europe, will export most of the output of the new enterprise, and has committed to triple capacity. Of Castel's 750 employees, only one is not Ethiopian. This company has also built three breweries over twelve years, and has the largest share of the growing domestic market. At the opening of the Castel winery, Prime Minister Haile Mariam declared his government's commitment to making Ethiopia the largest wine producer on the continent within a decade, and promised to provide full support to industrialists to this end.[4] This was a serious affirmation, and the government's record in delivering on its promises has so far been good, as seen in the floriculture sector.

A short distance from the Castel winery lies the biggest concentration of flower farms in the country. For instance, floriculture's largest exporter, based in Ziway, employs more than 10,000 workers. In less than a decade, Ethiopia has emerged as one of the leading players in global floriculture. The sector has generated more than one billion dollars in export earnings over seven years, a substantial amount for a new industry by Ethiopian standards.[5] This success is associated with the Ethiopian government's design and

---

[2] The average GDP growth rate for eleven years (2003–14) was 11 per cent, while the annual average growth rates for agriculture, industry, and service sectors were 9 per cent, 13.8 per cent, and 12.2 per cent respectively. The average annual growth rate of industry has increased to 20 per cent during the four years (2011–2014) of Growth and Transformation Plan (MOFED 2014).

[3] The average life expectancy for sub-Saharan Africa was fifty and fifty-six years for years 1992 and 2012 respectively. See World Development Indicators updated on 30 January 2015, and UN-DESA (2013) <http://data.worldbank.org/region/sub-saharan-africa>

[4] Speech of the Prime Minister on 23 March 2014, press release from the Prime Minister's Office.

[5] Ethiopian Revenue and Customs Authority (ERCA 2012a) and the National Export Coordinating Committee (NECC 2012).

execution of a successful industrial policy. Not far along the main road to Addis Ababa, there are a number of new and established tanneries owned by foreign and Ethiopian investors. Closer to Addis Ababa, the eye-catching first industrial park built by a Chinese developer, the Eastern Industrial Zone, dominates a landscape that includes many other warehouses, shops, and factories. All these lie along a road that at the turn of the millennium ran through almost entirely undeveloped country. Within twenty-four months, this industrial zone will have close to 50,000 employees. The world's largest manufacturer of women's shoes, the Huajian Group, started production in January 2012 and currently employs 3,500 people. In the near future, Huajian will build a special zone for footwear production that will employ more than 30,000.[6] Unilever, a leading European manufacturer, is also establishing a factory in this industrial zone.

In the capital, near the ring road, the largest Turkish textile and garment plant employing 8,000 workers is expanding. Many Turkish companies are relocating to Ethiopia, and see the country as the best destination for their investment. According to a representative of the Turkish Federation of Industrial Associations, 'the Ethiopian government not only invites investment, but also provides full support to the firms'.[7] Pittards, a firm from the United Kingdom (UK), established its first glove factory in Ethiopia in January 2012 and exports gloves to Wells Lamont in the United States of America (US), part of Warren Buffett's holding company, and to Japan. In two years, Pittards has expanded production to three factories. According to its young Ethiopian general manager, worker skills and productivity are catching up to international industry standards. In discussing the major obstacles, she highlighted logistics and cumbersome customs procedures, shortage of foreign exchange, acute insufficiency in local financing for expansion, power interruptions, and the supply chain. A globally experienced Korean industrialist also recently pinpointed customs procedures and the slow turnaround at the port of Djibouti as the single most important constraints on doing business in Ethiopia. While many industrialists voice these complaints, most are optimistic these issues will soon be addressed. Many acknowledge the government's efforts

---

[6] <http://www.chinadailyasia.com/business/2014-01/27/content_15115269.html>; See also 'Ethiopia becomes China's China in Global Search for Cheap Labour' <http://www.bloomberg.com/news/2014-07-22/ethiopia-becomes-china-s-china-in-search-for-cheap-labor.html>

[7] Meeting at Prime Minister's Office in April 2014.

in supporting industry, but some warn that the constraints are choking manufacturing.

There are also dramatic changes in infrastructure under way—in power generation, railways, and roads. The Renaissance Dam, the biggest hydropower project in Africa (and the thirteenth or fourteenth largest in the world) and comparable to the Hoover Dam in the US, is being built with finances entirely mobilized from local sources. It is a reflection of and contributor to strong transformative economic growth under tight macroeconomic constraints and a symbol of the government's recognition of the political imperative of transformation. It is also a rallying point for a form of 'nationalism from above' (Anderson 1991) in the context of federalism and an ongoing 'national' issue (Markakis 2011). As the late Ethiopian Prime Minister Meles Zenawi announced, 'No matter how poor we are, in the Ethiopian tradition of resolve, the Ethiopian people will pay any sacrifice.' He continued: 'I have no doubt they will, with one voice, say: "Build the Dam!"' This is just one example of how growth and transformation as a shared national project have been crafted into a 'rhetorical commonplace' (Jackson 2006), helping to shape and justify policy and resource allocations. Moreover, Ethiopia began construction of the largest electric railway network in Africa in 2010. In May 2014, a new toll-based six-lane Addis Ababa–Adama expressway was opened to relieve the intense pressure on the old road to the port at Djibouti.

˙ As already noted, the country has become a destination for investment from Europe and emerging economies, not only China and Turkey, but also India. Deborah Brautigam, writing in *The Guardian* (30 December 2011), summed up differing international perceptions of Ethiopia as follows: 'To the Chinese, Ethiopia, with a fast growing economy and 90 million consumers, looks like good business;...to the West, Ethiopia typically conjures up images of drought and starving children; we want to save Ethiopia.' Brautigam adds that while 'China sees Ethiopia as a land of business opportunities...the African country remains in charge of any deals.' Ethiopia's rapid economic growth and poverty reduction has attracted attention from friends, sceptics, and staunch critics. For instance, a critique by The Economist Intelligence Unit (2012) gives a careful picture of Ethiopia's development path: despite the lack of commercially exploitable hydrocarbons reserves found elsewhere on the continent, Ethiopia has achieved export-driven economic growth rates that are the envy of other African countries. It adds, 'The economic results of this state-led development model have been impressive, and proponents of the difficult-to-define Beijing Consensus have cited Ethiopia as a successful example...Ethiopia has grown more quickly than almost any country on the continent while rejecting the advice from the IMF and others to open up the economy quicker than it would like.'[8]

Although many recognize the recent achievements, few agree on the drivers of growth. An Asian diplomat indicated that the secret has been that 'first, Ethiopia enjoys solid political stability. Second, Ethiopia has found its development path and the government is committed to its implementation. Third, Ethiopia's growing market and big population has been a plus.'[9] On the other hand, Western diplomats and representatives of international finance institutions question Ethiopia's path of economic development, and argue that state-led development is not sustainable and that the state is crowding out the private sector.[10] They recommend slowing growth and arresting public investment as well as rapidly liberalizing financial and telecommunications markets. Ideology has been of no interest to foreign and local industrialists though, and they are busily seizing new investment opportunities.

This rosy picture of a 'rising Ethiopia', however, reveals little about either the actual details of the execution of industrial policy or the full spectrum of challenges faced by low-income countries in general. It does not reflect the daunting task for such countries in industrial catch up and economic transformation. Indeed, given the extraordinary significance of Ethiopian policy and performance, especially in the industrial sector, it is remarkable how little careful empirical work has been done on them. One way to understand the successes of and challenges facing Ethiopia's catch up and transformation is through in-depth study of the leading industrial sub-sectors, for instance, leather, garments, and floriculture, credited with the rapid transformation of the economy over the past decade.

---

[8] <http://country.eiu.com/article.aspx?articleid=659462850&Country=Ethiopia&topic= Economy>.

[9] Discussions with Chinese Ambassador in March 2014.

[10] For instance, <http://www.imf.org/external/pubs/ft/scr/2012/cr12287.pdf>; <http://www. bloomberg.com/news/2013-10-18/imf-says-ethiopian-economic-growth-may-slow-without-policy-shift.html>.

1.2 Has industrial policy's moment arrived in Africa?

Given the dominance of mainstream economic thinking, debate on industrial policy has remained a 'restricted zone' until very recently. In 2011, United Nations Conference on Trade and Development (UNCTAD) and United Nations Industrial Development Organization's (UNIDO) annual report focused on Africa's industrialization, illustrating the challenges it faced. In 2012, a World Bank publication, *Light Manufacturing in Africa,* was commissioned by the former chief economist Justin Lin. This argued that industrialization is possible in Africa, but fell short of supporting industrial policy as the main vehicle in catch up and economic transformation. Peculiarly, it also failed to mention the necessity for an activist 'developmental' state. Two years later, UNECA's economic report suggested that perceptions on African industrialization had started to change, although it appears that perspectives on industrial policies continue to diverge.

Although growth has been uneven among African countries and typically not sustained, more African countries have in recent years experienced longer growth spurts. In some countries, oil, gas, and mineral resources have driven growth and this growth has most often not been inclusive or shared. This trend differs from the East Asian experience of rapid industrialization and economic transformation. Scholars and policymakers are concerned that Africa's growth is insufficient to improve living standards for a rapidly growing population. At a more fundamental level, there are concerns that in many countries policies and political conditions are not in place to sustain rapid growth, to achieve industrialization and economic transformation, and to ensure a more equitable development structure. There are, in short, compelling grounds for debate on African industrialization, structural transformation, and industrial policies.

Is 'Africa rising'? Are 'lions on the move'? Does recent rapid growth in Africa reflect an African version of the Asian Tigers? Perceptions of Africa's economic development have swung dramatically from doom-and-gloom generalizations about a 'growth tragedy' or former UK Prime Minister Tony Blair's 'scar on the conscience of the West' towards a sometimes hyperbolic excitement about recent growth. It is important to examine how far that growth is underpinned by, or is being converted into, deeper, more lasting structural change. Most people agree that such change requires industrialization and rapid technological innovation, which enables countries to move out of subsistence production to more dynamic industrial production. Historically, industrial policy has been central to successful industrialization. However, mainstream thinking has been wary of active industrial policy (see, for example, Ocampo, Rada, and Taylor 2009). Although the idea of industrial policy has become more fashionable recently, it is still unclear what this means in practical terms for Africa. This is the issue this book seeks to address.

1.3 Alternative analytical perspective on late industrialization

The book examines conventional views of and contemporary debate on issues associated with industrial policy. It also deploys an alternative, predominantly structuralist, development economics approach, inflected with political economy, to growth and structural transformation in developing countries and draws on a tradition influenced by Kaldor, Thirlwall, and especially Albert Hirschman. Finally, it makes a novel contribution to current debates. This work is based on the premise that economic performance is the outcome of policies and political economy. Economic transformation and structural change is the essence of economic development. Industrial development, and development of the manufacturing sector in particular, is believed by many (though not all) to be the prime driver of economic transformation and sustained growth (Kaldor 1967; Pasinetti 1981; Thirlwall 2002; Rodrik 2008c; Reinert 2010; Chang 2003a, 2003b; Amsden 2009).

Ocampo et al. (2009: 7) define economic structure as:

> the composition of production activities, the associated patterns of specialization in international trade, the technological capabilities of the economy, including the education level of the labour force, the structure of ownership of factors of production, the nature and development of basic state institutions, and the degree of development and constraints under which certain markets operate (the absence of certain segments of the financial market or the presence of a large under-employed labour force, for example).

According to Hirschman (1958: 6), '[I]n general economic development means transformation rather than creation ex novo: it brings disruption of traditional ways..., in the course of which there have always been many losses; old skills become obsolete, old trades are ruined...'. Structural change can be defined in a simpler way as 'those changes in the composition that are permanent and irreversible' (Pasinetti 1993: 1). This suggests that policies should be designed and measured with the aim of bringing economic transformation and structural change. Because not all sectors have the same economic or change-promoting characteristics, a sectoral approach is called for, which also means that linkage effects should be maximized to generate new activities and induce further investments. It also means that learning and emulation should be enhanced to bring sustained productivity growth in line with international competition (Lall 1992, 2000b, 2003; Reinert 2009; Amsden 1989, 2001). Emulation, moving up the productivity ladder, and advancing towards economic activities with increasing returns are required for successful catch up. Central to this endeavour is the presence of an effective developmental state that invests heavily in physical infrastructure, skills development, and direct credit and other incentives to pioneer firms, so they can succeed in the marketplace.

Many developing countries have been able to achieve rapid economic growth and improve global competitiveness. By contrast, economic growth has lagged in most African countries; or at any rate, it has proven difficult for African countries to convert episodes of rapid growth into growth sustained over twenty or thirty years. Economic development in Africa is of utmost importance to Africans, a daunting challenge to African policymakers, and a black box for researchers. One idea in the literature on growth rates is the 'Africa dummy', a catch-all phrase for the residuals that cannot be 'explained' by other variables in cross-country growth regressions. Various possibilities are then explored or suggested for what may account for this dummy—including geographical variables, ethnolinguistic fractionalization scores, long-run history, institutional development, and so on. However, the Africa dummy literature has been criticized for being analytically, methodologically, and empirically fragile (Jerven 2010a, 2010b, 2011).

1.4 Methodology based on original research

There are three main considerations in setting out the following methodological framework. First, studies on industrial policymaking in sub-Saharan Africa are scant, making it an under-researched topic. This is because such studies have been sidelined as irrelevant and harmful by mainstream orthodoxy and the Washington Consensus since the early 1980s. The lack of research has limited wider appreciation of policy-making, policy learning, and development of policy capabilities. Second, most studies of industrial development in Ethiopia have focused on firm-level quantitative data, which are often incomplete and conflicting. Such data are important in researching an industry's patterns, but fall short of providing a comprehensive picture on policymaking, let alone a political economy perspective. Third, the research approach adopted to date is problematic in that many studies are conducted too quickly, with an overdependence on secondary data only supported by one or two research instruments. This has led to incomplete and, in some situations, misleading findings. Few studies have provided any detail or real depth of understanding of industrial performance and policy in Ethiopia. As a result, the issues are typically frozen in polarized and shallow debates.

These approaches have to be viewed in the context of the aforementioned 'Africa dummy', hopeless 'Afro-pessimism', and the view of Africa as 'exceptional' or homogenous. A typical recent example is the Neopatrimonial School, an over-simplistic view that blames African culture for the 'failure' to reform economic and political systems as prescribed by international financial institutions in the 1980s and 1990s. These incomplete perspectives on Africa have compounded the methodological impediments (Padayachee 2010; Mkandawire 2013) and fail to generate understanding of African social realities. This has undermined data reliability and diminished research outcomes and their usability. Mkandawire (2013: 52) stresses that 'economic policymaking is a highly complex process involving ideas, interests, economic forces and structures' that cannot be reduced to a single explanation. A methodology is needed that recognizes such complexity and considers broader political economy factors rather than simplistic, uniform diagnoses. In the Ethiopian context, scarce availability of research and constraints on data collection compound the methodological problems. Reliable and timely data are not easily available in most organizations in Ethiopia, and many studies are inconsistent as a result.

The research for this book was primarily qualitative, while also drawing on quantitative data (both primary and secondary). A comparative design was adopted, whereby three different sectors were compared within one overarching industrial policy. Based on empirical evidence, this study investigates causal factors and their relationships, but does not pretend to weigh with mathematical precision the relative contribution of specific factors. In view of the limitations of existing data and studies, the study has relied on extensive original data sources and adopted a more comprehensive data-collection system. A census using a qualitative and quantitative questionnaire was conducted in 150 firms, with a 90 per cent response rate. This complemented in-depth and qualitative interviews involving 200 firms, intermediate institutions, government agencies, and policymakers. Site observations of more than fifty factories in differing industries yielded unique insights. A review of some 1,000 primary documents was undertaken, including previously inaccessible documents. Secondary sources were also extensively consulted. The field study involved 1,300 person days, making this the first in-depth study of industrialization and industrial policy in Ethiopia (beyond several rapidly conducted consultancy reports). Appropriate analytical tools have been carefully utilized, generating better understanding and new findings. These are discussed throughout the remaining chapters. The author hopes this project will encourage scholars to undertake more extensive studies. Much of this evidence would have been more difficult, even impossible, for 'outsiders' to assemble.

1.5 Structure of book

The main argument in the book is first, that industrial policy (despite claims to the contrary) can work and indeed thrive even in low-income countries such as Ethiopia. Nonetheless, the book cautions that industrial policymaking is a work in progress in many such countries, and demonstrates the colossal challenge of catching up and industrialization in twenty-first-century Africa. Second, the book argues that the state in developing countries can and must play an activist and developmental role beyond being merely a 'facilitating' actor; that is, being little more than a servant of comparative advantage. Policy independence is an important ingredient. As Mazzucato (2013a: 5–6) highlighted:

> When not taking a leading role, the State becomes a poor imitator of private sector behaviours, rather than a real alternative. It is a key partner of the private sector— and often a more daring one, willing to take the risks that business won't.... The State cannot and should not bow down easily to interest groups who approach it

to seek handouts, rents and unnecessary privileges like tax cuts. It should seek instead for those interest groups to work dynamically with it in its search for growth and technological change.

Third, the book argues that the outcome of industrial policy is typically uneven in different sectors. Overall, what matters for the evolution and effectiveness of industrial policy is the way three factors interact—industrial structure, linkage dynamics, and, broadly, politics/political economy. Fourth, firms from low-income countries face huge challenges in competing in a globalized economy, and more effective industrial policies and instruments that facilitate growth and structural transformation need to be designed and executed.

Based on rigorous and original research in Ethiopia into cement, an import-substitution industry; leather, an export-oriented light industry; and floriculture, the book reviews the constraints on, as well as lessons for, Africa's industrialization and industrial policymaking. The book focuses on the design and implementation of industrial policy in Ethiopia, and on how and why policy outcomes are shaped by different factors in different industries. In view of the renewed interest in industrial policy in Africa and internationally, the book will be a valuable addition to ongoing discussion of the 'African renaissance', and provide arguments and evidence for the possibilities of industrial policy in Africa.

The book is organized into eight chapters. Following this introductory chapter, the second chapter, 'Climbing without Ladders: Industrial Policy and Development', presents a literature review outlining the theoretical framework (structuralist tradition, catch up, political economy), empirical evidence, and the sub-Saharan African context. This chapter also outlines the influence of industrial policy. Such policy has always been a bone of ideological contention, and currently dominant viewpoints are strongly averse to industrial policy in developing countries, and have been better at identifying its failures than its evident successes. The third chapter, 'Setting the Scene: Ethiopia's Industrial Policies and Performance', introduces the main policies and policy instruments developed in Ethiopia in recent years relevant to the selected case studies. This is done both to clarify the context of policymaking in different sectors and to identify national-level patterns in policymaking institutions.

The next three chapters provide sector-specific analyses. Thus, Chapter 4, 'Cementing Development? Uneven Development in an Import-Substitution Industry', explores the cement industry as one of three case studies. Cement production is a strategic import-substituting industry in many countries, driven by growth of the domestic market. The industry has served as a binding agent of economic development and transformation in multiple ways. In Ethiopia, it has undergone major changes in the period under consideration, growing faster than in most developing countries. This chapter examines the industrial structure, linkage effects, policy instruments, and institutions of the sector. In sharp contrast to the overall domination by multinationals of the African cement industry, domestically owned firms continue to dominate the industry in Ethiopia.

Chapter 5, 'Beyond Bloom and Bust? Development and Challenges in Floriculture', discusses the floriculture sector's performance, structure, linkages, and industrialization, and policymaking relating to it. Floriculture shares many characteristics with manufacturing, and this sector has been an economic success story that has attracted international interest and policy debate. It emerged in Ethiopia in 2003 and has since shown sustained growth, making the country the world's fourth-largest cut flower exporter. The chapter offers an alternative explanation for the drivers of growth in the industry, arguing that government policy was critical in this regard. Furthermore, early policies that helped bring about a successful launching became inadequate as the industry matured and encountered new challenges. New policies were thus needed.

Chapter 6, 'Curing an Underperformer? Leather and Leather Products', focuses on the same issues as the previous two chapters, but in relation to leather and leather goods. Unlike cement and floriculture, the performance of this sector has been characterized by erratic and sluggish growth. The puzzle is that there is a century of manufacturing experience and a plentiful endowment of livestock—Ethiopia stands first in Africa, and among the top ten globally in this regard. Industrial policy relating to leather and leather products has been unable to reverse this poor performance, and fully exploit the potential for linkage effects and insertion into the global value chain. However, recent developments have begun to yield more investment, better quality, and more exports of higher-end products. The causes and factors are examined, to derive new insights.

Chapter 7, 'Failing Better: Political Economy and Industrial Policy in Ethiopia', discusses the findings from the case studies more thematically and comparatively, and presents a comprehensive synthesis. Despite growth in all three sectors, outcomes were indeed uneven. As noted earlier, what matters overall is the interaction among industrial structure, linkage dynamics, and politics/political economy. This has significant implications for policymakers.

The last chapter, 'Lessons from Industrial Policy in Twenty-First-Century Africa' briefly draws the empirical contribution and analysis together and highlights some policy and research implications for Africa. Industrial policymaking in Ethiopia is a work in progress, but industrial policies can work and thrive in a low-income African country, and the state can and should play an activist developmental role, with policy independence an important ingredient.[11] However, the book also highlights how great the challenge of catching up and industrialization is for twenty-first-century Africa.

1.6 Conclusion

Few books have been written on the political economy of industrial policy in Africa, even fewer by Africans. This book provides a unique perspective on why policy outcomes have been uneven in different industries, a major challenge to policymakers. It also provides new data and perspectives on the industrial structure of different sectors and firms. Finally, the study is unique and comprehensive in covering the macro- (national policy-making process), meso- (industrial policies in different sectors, institutions, and in-depth industrial structure), and micro-levels. The author, as both researcher and a senior policymaker, reflects on the challenges and lessons of policymaking.

The book is a necessary corrective to the over-aggregated and typically superficial hyperbole on an African economic renaissance. Beyond the restrictive policy guidance by international financial institutions and bilateral donors, and beyond the more recent flag-waving for industrial policy, it is important that the scope and content of industrial policy are informed by empirical evidence and careful, pragmatic analysis. This book shows that low-income developing countries should not simply follow 'comparative advantage', as some would prefer. But equally it shows just

---

[11] This is associated to the broader notion of 'policy space' that refers to the 'various tensions between national policy autonomy, policy effectiveness and international economic integration' UNCTAD (2014: vii). Globalization, market internationalization, and legal agreements (multilateral, regional, and bilateral) create obligations that undermine the scope of national policy.

how difficult pursuing an effective industrial strategy can be (Rodrik 2008a).

Finally, this book highlights how, despite enormous challenges, Africa can catch up, and contests the standard pessimism that Africa is a hopeless continent. The distinguished German political economist, Friedrich List (1841: 123) once said, 'no nation has been so misconstrued and misjudged as respects its future destiny and its national economy as the United States of North America, by theorists as well as by practical men.' Now, the US is the leading economic power of our time. History offers many examples of economic miracles occurring in unexpected places. Indeed, given the role of interventionist states in successful industrialization there, East Asia might have provided a more important lesson for Africa. Even so, the Ethiopian story shows what is possible, and the aspiration of Africans to catch up. With long-term national development vision, highly committed political leadership, and strong institutions, countries can shift from a relatively agrarian to an industrial society.

2

Climbing without Ladders

Industrial Policy and Development

2.1 Introduction

All advanced capitalist nations have used industrial policies and state
interventions to establish their first mover status, to consolidate their
advantages, or to force the pace in catching up on those ahead of them.
Industrial policies have been the rule rather than the exception. The UK
and the US are typical examples of the frontrunners of the nineteenth and
twentieth centuries, with the US having played a successful catch up game
itself. For instance, the eighteenth US president, Ulysses Grant (1868–76),
once pointed out:

> For centuries, England has relied on protection, has carried it to extremes and has
> obtained satisfactory results from it. There is no doubt that it is to this system that
> it owes its present strength. After two centuries, England has found it convenient
> to adopt free trade because it thinks that protection can no longer offer it any-
> thing. Very well then, gentlemen, my knowledge of our country leads me to
> believe that within 200 years, when America has gotten out of protecting all that
> it can offer, it too will adopt free trade (cited in Frank 1967: 164).

And, of course, industrial policy continues to be the rule. As is increasingly
acknowledged, the US owes many of its successes to state support for
technical innovation (Mazzucato 2013a, 2013b).

Current orthodoxy in development economics, however, favours a
minimalist state and short-term intervention. For example, Collier
(2007) argues that 'quite possibly the easiest way for the state to "do no

harm" in this situation is for it to be small, and concentrate on essential public services.' By contrast, commitment to an activist state is virtually a sine qua non for structuralist development economists (Hirschman 1958; Ocampo 2005; Ocampo et al 2009; Chang 1994; and Amsden 1989). For these economists, there is a distinction between tailoring interventions to the elusive idea of 'market failure' and intervening to create and shape market institutions and transactions according to criteria less informed by the quasi-religious faith in competitive perfection displayed by neoclassical economics.

Despite periodic growth episodes, African countries have not succeeded in catching up with advanced capitalist countries. In this context, and after decades of economic stagnation and political instability, Ethiopia has embarked on a course of economic revitalization. The country has adopted home-grown economic policies, experimented with ethnic federalism, and broadly followed a line derived more from pluralist economic traditions than from the 'mono-economics' often regarded as orthodoxy. Arguably, Ethiopia's economic expansion between 2003 and 2014 is attributable to an aspiring developmental state and the adoption of activist economic policies. However, Ethiopia's industrialization and industrial policymaking are still a work-in-progress.

What is industrial policy and what are its foundations and rationale? Can industrial policies and state activism be relevant in the contemporary world? This chapter explores industrial policymaking by outlining theoretical foundations and provides empirical perspectives on industrial policy relevant to understanding the prospects for (and process and outcomes of) such policy in Ethiopia. After introducing the concept, the first part of the chapter discusses the structuralist tradition, classical political economy, and heterodox or pluralist perspectives. Linkage effects, both from industrial and policymaking perspectives, are also highlighted in this chapter. Linkages have direct relevance to policymaking. Just as there is policy learning-by-doing as well as industrial learning-by-doing, so there are linkage-like dynamics in applied industrial policy as well as among economic activities. This idea acknowledges that within the government apparatus, through shifts in one area calling forth new initiatives in other areas or levels of government, bottlenecks and obstacles *may* generate a 'uneven development' of policy capability. The last section of the chapter presents empirical perspectives on Africa.

2.2 Industrial policy

Industrial policy has generated considerable controversy and is vaguely defined, being frequently endowed with different meanings depending on context and the person who defines it (OECD 1975; Johnson 1984; Chang 1994; Rodrik 2008c). One definition is 'a policy aimed at particular industries (and firms as their components) to achieve the outcomes that are perceived by the state to be efficient for the economy as a whole' (Chang 1994: 60). This definition, despite its emphasis on selective targeting, strategic orientation, and efficiency, omits (or keeps implicit) any structural change and the various stages in catching up. Chang's definition resembles Johnson's, which also emphasizes a strategic orientation: 'above all... industrial policy means the infusion of goal-oriented strategic thinking into public economic policy'. For Johnson (1984: 8), industrial policy is 'the initiation and coordination of government activities to leverage upward the productivity and competitiveness of the whole economy and of particular industries in it.'

Others, like Amsden and Chu (2003), Ocampo et al (2009), and UNCTAD-UNIDO (2011), offer definitions more explicitly oriented towards structural change and catching up. According to UNCTAD-UNIDO (2011: 34), industrial policy means:

> ... government measures aimed at improving the competitiveness and capabilities of domestic firms and promoting structural transformation. Industrial policy involves a combination of strategic or selective interventions aimed at propelling specific activities or sectors, functional interventions intended at improving the workings of markets, and horizontal interventions directed at promoting specific activities across sectors.

The emphasis is on 'restructuring of production and trade towards activities with higher technological content' and promoting 'innovative activities that generate domestic spill over' (Ocampo et al. 2009: 152–3). New activities include new industries, new products, new markets, new technologies, and new institutions. While the prime focus is on manufacturing, high value-added products such as horticulture are not excluded (Ocampo et al. 2009). In this definition, industrial policy is viewed as a vehicle for structural change, that is, constant upgrading to higher productivity activities with increasing returns and the centrality of technological development (Amsden 2001; Reinert 2009; Rodrik 2011). This definition calls for an activist state, a perspective rejected by neoclassical orthodoxy, and captures the long-term orientation of industrial policy.

The institutionalist perspective argues that is vital for the state and industrial policy to govern the market (Chang 1994; Wade 1990; Amsden 1989). For instance, Amsden (1989) emphasizes not simply getting relative prices right but 'deliberately getting prices wrong' in order to foster industrialization and structural transformation. Indeed later, Amsden (n.d.) also argued that getting property rights wrong had been equally important in many successful cases of structural change. The mechanisms involve market control, protection of foreign investors, picking winners (*chaebol*, etc.), subsidizing capital, tariff protection, etc. This argument runs contrary to the whole continuum of positions supported by neoclassical economics, from the more extreme neoliberal or 'market fundamentalist' tendency to the more moderate views based on 'market failure' analysis. The core argument in economic orthodoxy is that state intervention and industrial policy distort resource allocation, where optimal outcomes would flow from free markets and free trade regimes (see Bhagwati 1989a, 1989b). Such economists ardently believe that industrial policies only ever cultivate unproductive rent-seeking, and that picking winners is impossible (Krueger 1974, 1980, 1990). Neo-utilitarian and public choice models consider governments to be inherently 'rent-seeking' and view public officials as rational (selfish) maximizers. Free markets, trade openness, economic liberalization, and maximal (rather than optimal) competition on the grounds of comparative advantage are advocated as ideal mechanisms for efficient industrialization. Industrial policies are often also misrepresented or simplified as import-substitution industrialization, or as any form of state intervention (Noland and Pack 2003; Weiss 2013; Peres 2013; Warwick 2013).

This book proposes an operational definition of industrial policy, namely 'a strategy that includes a range of implicit or explicit policy instruments selectively focused on specific industrial sectors for the purpose of shaping structural change in line with a broader national vision and strategy.' The definition clearly underlines the need for selectivity, both in terms of specific industries and targeted interventions, and emphasizes structural changes within the broader framework of the national economy. The following sections explore the theoretical influences on industrial policy, that is, the structuralist perspective, the theory of catch up, infant industry theory, and political economy perspectives.

2.3 Structuralist and catch up perspectives on industrial policy

Industrial policy is primarily underpinned by a structuralist perspective and tradition that upholds the manufacturing sector as a particular engine of growth and driver of structural economic transformation, and as being the best prospect for catching up by late (or late-late) industrializers.

2.3.1 *Structuralist perspectives on industrial policy*

The structuralist approach to economic development holds that economic growth alone does not necessarily produce structural economic transformation and sustained economic development. Economic development is a process of fundamental structural changes and economic transformations embedded in sectoral shifts; sustained productivity increases as a result of constant technological development, accompanied by fundamental shifts in work occupations; and institutional and political economy transformation (Chenery 1960; Chenery, Robinson, and Syrquin 1986; Reinert 2010; Thirlwall 1980, 2002, 2011; Thirlwall and Bazen 1989; Ocampo et al. 2009; Tregenna 2013; and UNCTAD 2011). Structural transformation involves the shift of resources from low to high productivity sectors and activities, and the fostering of a process of reallocation of productive factors among industry, services, and modern agriculture (Ocampo 2008; UNCTAD 2006; Tregenna 2013). This process is characterized by continuous diversification into new economic activities with stronger domestic economic linkages and a higher quality path dependency, and focuses on the development of domestic technological capabilities (Rodrik 2008c).

It is important to clarify the different emphases within the structuralist approach. First, there are the arguments associated especially with Kaldor, whose propositions or growth laws were derived from stylized facts suggesting that manufacturing has special growth-promoting qualities. Second, there is Thirlwall's (2002) view that because rapidly growing developing countries face a structural balance of payments constraint, they need to focus on rapid growth of export revenue. Third, there is what might be called the UNCTAD strain of structuralism drawing on the Prebisch-Singer hypothesis (of a secular decline in the net barter terms of trade for primary commodities vis-à-vis manufactured goods) and its implications. Meanwhile, there are others who argue against relying exclusively on primary commodity exports because of the relative volatility of their export prices. There are also critics of the Prebisch-Singer hypothesis who argue that it has encouraged many years of excessive and damaging export pessimism among the governments of developing countries.

MANUFACTURING AS THE ENGINE OF GROWTH AND TRANSFORMATION

Among advanced countries and newly industrializing countries (NICs), economic growth has been associated with increased income per capita and industrial development (Amsden 2001; Rodrik 2011; McMillan & Rodrik 2011). Tregenna (2008a, 2008b, 2012, 2013) distinguishes between industry and manufacturing, emphasizing that manufacturing specifically has special properties as an engine of growth: 'dynamic economies of scale in manufacturing; strong backward and forward linkages between manufacturing and other sectors of the domestic economy; strong properties of learning-by-doing; innovation and technological progress; and the importance of manufacturing for the balance of payments'. Thirlwall (2002: 41–2) expounds on the strong positive link between manufacturing and growth by referring to Kaldor's growth laws:

> The first law is that there exists a strong causal relation between *the growth of manufacturing output and the growth of GDP*. The second law states that there exists a strong positive causal relation between *the growth of manufacturing output and the growth in productivity* in manufacturing as a result of static and dynamic returns to scale. This is also known as Verdoorn's law. The third law states that there exists a strong positive causal relation between *the rates at which the manufacturing sector expands and the growth of* productivity outside the manufacturing sector because of diminishing returns in agriculture and many petty service activities which supply labour to the industrial sector. [My emphasis]

According to Kaldor (1966, 1967), it is impossible to understand the development process and growth without a *sectoral approach*, and without differentiating between increasing returns in manufacturing and diminishing returns in agriculture and mining (which are land-based). Similarly, Young (1928: 539) emphasized that economic progress partly depends on the increasing returns realized by 'progressive division of labour and specialization of industries'. Young drew on Adam Smith's insight that 'division of labour depends upon the extent of the market, but the extent of the market also depends upon the division of labour'. Historical facts indicate that growth of the manufacturing sector at earlier stages of development depends on the transformation and increased productivity of agriculture, while at later stages it is fed by resources from exports, suggesting the loop between exports and growth (Thirlwall 2002). Ocampo et al. (2009) reinforce this precept by inferring that economic structure and structural transformation is associated with:

> ...the composition of production activities, the associated patterns of specialization in international trade, the technological capabilities of the economy, including the educational level of the labour force, the structure of ownership of factors of production, the nature and development of basic state institutions, and the degree of development and constraints under which certain markets operate... economic development is a process of structural transformation, ...the reallocation of productive factors from traditional agriculture to modern agriculture, industry and services... shifting resources from low-to-high productivity sectors ...a capacity to diversify domestic production structure: that is, to generate new activities, to strengthen economic linkages within a country and to create domestic technological capabilities.

These insights, rooted in economic history, also caution against the pretence that African economies could become advanced capitalist societies without having to pass through a phase of (environmentally often damaging) industrialization. That argument, that industrialization is no longer fundamental to economic development, is also a product of the misinterpretation of experiences in countries such as Singapore, India, and Switzerland. Singapore and Switzerland, in fact, have very high value added manufacturing compared to almost all other countries. And India's much vaunted services-based growth reflects a swing from a trade deficit in services in the early 2000s to a very modest service trade surplus. Further, a huge amount of service sector activity and employment provides services to manufacturing. There is really no convincing evidence that a low-income country can generate sustained rises in living standards without manufacturing. That is why many regard the fall in the share of manufacturing in developing countries, including in Africa, in recent years as 'premature deindustrialization'. This is what Rodrik (2011) refers to as 'growth-reducing structural change'.

THE STRATEGIC IMPORTANCE OF EXPORTS

Some economists emphasize the strategic importance of exports to growth and structural change. For many countries, the export growth rate sets the threshold for a country's rate of growth. The composition of exports is cardinal to industrialization and economic transformation, and can determine future trajectory. Lall (2000b: 1) emphasizes that 'export structures, being path-dependent and difficult to change, have implications for growth and development'. Thirlwall in particular (2002) has argued that sustained growth and structural change in developing countries is threatened by a structural balance of payments constraint, posing critical policy challenges for governments. As a consequence, rapid growth of export earnings sustained over a long time cannot be relied upon if they based exclusively on primary products or low-end exportable products, partly due to the volatility of demand (and prices) for such commodities. Hence, the least developed countries (LDCs) face a steep uphill struggle and, as Thirlwall (1980, 2011) argues, structural balance of payments constraints. The dynamic growth of exports depends on diversified manufacturing goods, with a constant upgrading of the technological features of manufactured goods (Lall 2000b).

Related to this, structural development economists like Raúl Prebisch (1950) associated with the Economic Commission for Latin America and Caribbean (ECLAC) argued earlier that the structure of the world economy is tilted against developing countries. Low-income countries export primary commodities, for which there is a low income elasticity of demand. In Engel's Law, as a person grows richer, they spend a shrinking proportion of their income on basic needs like food, and this is also applicable to countries. Meanwhile, the state of world trade dictates that low-income countries import manufactured items (for which there is a high income elasticity of demand). One consequence of these, and other, structural features of trade and production is that the terms of trade would systematically turn against exporters of primary commodities. Therefore, to protect low-income countries, there is a strong argument for protective trade policies and nurturing infant industry.[1]

2.3.2 Late Development, Catch up, and Industrial Policy

Throughout the history of capitalism, the level of industrial development has been uneven across countries and regions. Empirical evidence

---

[1] For a critique of the empirical record on the disadvantage in the terms of trade for primary commodities vis-à-vis manufactured goods and on the effects this notion has on policymakers and advisers in Africa, see Sender and Smith (1986).

strongly suggests that this unevenness is an essential characteristic of capitalism and industrialization (Gerschenkron 1962; Reinert 2010; Chang 2003a, 2003b; Schwartz 2010). Although all agree on this unevenness, different schools provide differing advice regarding the 'right course' to achieve (industrial) development or catch up. Mainstream economists argue that developing countries should follow the same (imagined) path as the forerunners or advanced industrial countries, and that there is no 'short-cut' to economic development. Others, like the 'preconditions' theorists, argue that some preconditions (such as natural resources, capital and saving, entrepreneurship and managerial abilities, skills or human capital, and institutions) are the key determinants of economic development (Hirschman 1958, 2013; Adelman 2013). However, according to Hirschman (1958), these resources are available in great abundance among a disguised, hidden, unemployed, reserve army of entrepreneurs. Furthermore, the proponents of catch up theories argue that in 'the more backward countries . . . the great spurt of industrial development occurred despite the lack of these *prerequisites*' (Gerschenkron 1962). Gerschenkron argued that latecomers have the advantage of backwardness, as they can be motivated to learn from forerunners. Abramovitz (1994) also emphatically highlights that 'being backward in level of productivity carries a potential for rapid growth'. According to Gerschenkron (1962: 45), however, 'the higher the degree of backwardness, the more discontinuous the development is likely to be'. Further, the implication for structuralist development economists is that the 'advantages of backwardness' do not generate unconditional convergence, but require direct intervention.

Latecomers have a proposed advantage in that they can learn from forerunners (Amsden and Hikino 1994). Latecomers have a compelling reference in the forerunners and their experience, although they have to develop in the face of a formidable competitive pressure from the forerunners. These latecomers are recommended to use institutional innovations to create, mobilize, and concentrate resources with maximum speed and effect. By contrast, forerunners had to develop without any reference point, although they were rewarded with super profits (Shin 1996). The US, a latecomer, was able to catch up with and forge ahead of Britain, the leading industrial economy in the nineteenth century. Germany, France, Sweden, and (later) Finland were also able to catch up in a similar way. The source of the latecomer advantage was the opportunity to follow a more deliberate and less spontaneous process, in the footsteps of the economic giants. Moreover, the process was facilitated by multiple contacts between the latecomer and forerunner. More recently, Japan, Korea, Taiwan, and currently China have been able to catch up without having the full complement of commonly identified prerequisites for advancement.

In response to uneven development, different states tend to follow different development paths that combine a 'Ricardian strategy' and a 'Kaldorian strategy' (Schwartz 2010). The former is based on the export of primary commodities, or even low-cost and low-quality manufactured products, and fundamentally follows comparative advantage. This strategy may be relatively easy to follow, is vulnerable to deteriorations in terms of trade and to highly volatile world market prices, and may not succeed in the end. By contrast, a Kaldorian strategy is export-oriented, based on manufactured products with increasing returns, and maximizes Verdoorn effects. Such a strategy focuses on rapid technological developments and aims to develop competitive advantage. A Kaldorian strategy relies on 'a set of interrelated phenomena like increasing returns to scale, learning by doing, imperfect competition, and economies of speed to generate growth' (Schwartz 2010: 60).

Development is thus about breaking the vicious cycle by focusing on the binding agents, the essential underlying structures, and the strategic issues of development, all of which will allow dispersed, hidden, and unutilized resources to be fully mobilized for development. The pace of development depends not on prerequisites but on the nation's ability and determination to organize for development, which is created in the very process of development (Gerschenkron 1962). One of the state's primary roles is creating the motivation to develop with a basic 'growth perspective', which is rooted in the belief that a society has 'to move forward as it is, in spite of what it is and because of what it is' (Hirschman 1958: 10). 'Such a view', Hirschman wrote in *Development Projects Observed* (1967: 5), 'stresses the importance for development of what a country does and of what it becomes as a result of what it does, and thereby contests the primacy of what it is, that is, of its geography- and history-determined endowment with natural resources, values, institutions, social and political structure, etc.' This can best be done by focusing on clearing blockages and releasing potentials, and aiming at inducement or learning ability as the key link or binding constraint. This, in turn, depends on instilling a 'growth-perspective' or 'the desire for economic growth and the perception of the essential nature of the road leading to it' (Hirschman 1958: 10). Examples of societies that have made advances in particular periods led by just such a growth perspective include South Korea after the Korean War, the US after the American Civil War, Europe after the Second World War—indeed, often but not always after wars. (Although the civil war ended in 1949, China's fastest growth occurred after the adoption of its Openness Policy in 1978). Often but not always, advancement is also closely tied to nationalism or to external and internal threats (Doner, Ritchie, and Slater 2005).

According to Hirschman, 'the complementary effect of investment is therefore the essential mechanism by which new energies are channelled toward the development process', and the process is one 'where one disequilibrium calls forth a development move which in turn leads to a similar equilibrium and so on ad infinitum' (Hirschman 1958: 72). This gives rise to the critical role played by linkage effects and latitudes for performance discussed in the section 2.6 of this chapter. Hirschman (1958) emphatically states that the major obstacle to change is the negative perception or image of change, which thwarts the process of mobilization for development. Such fear of change is often tied to particular interests that are threatened by change. In other words, there is a political economy dimension to this.

2.4 Theory of infant industry in classical political economy

The theory of infant industry can be traced back to Alexander Hamilton (1755–1804). It was he who first proposed this concept, while Friedrich List (1789–1846) is considered to have laid its theoretical foundations (List 1841, 1856; Chang 2003b; Reinert 2009, 2010). The theory is aimed at refuting David Ricardo's (1772–1823) theory of comparative advantage and free trade. According to Ricardo, international trade should be free, with each country specializing in commodities with the least relative costs of production, hence its comparative advantage (Ricardo 2004 [1817]). The Washington Council for International Trade (2013) defines comparative advantage as 'the ability to produce goods at a lower cost, relative to other goods, compared to another country' (www.wcit.org). The comparative argument states that developing countries should produce raw materials and exchange the materials for manufactured goods from the industrial countries. Moreover, it argues that free trade and the market mechanism should be left to function without policy intervention. The theory predicts that this would benefit both industrial economies and agricultural exporters. Essentially, the theory is sensible on its own terms, but desperately static and unrealistic (Singh 2011).

By contrast, the theory of infant industry is based on the assumption that the manufacturing sector should play the key role in the economy, and that its promotion requires jumping ahead of current comparative advantage, thus necessitating protection of infant industries, the use of industrial policies, and an indispensable role for the state. These facets are extensively discussed in the fundamental works of Hamilton (1934) and List (1841). In the early days, when the US was predominantly agrarian and had little industrial base, policymakers did not understand the benefits of manufacturing. President Jefferson maintained that the US should depend on agriculture, as it could rely on European imports for industrial goods (Goodrich 1965). However, Hamilton argued that manufacturing was the key to wealth creation (in contrast to mining, for instance), and that it would also help in the development of agriculture through increased demand, productivity improvements, cheaper supplies of industrial products, and a secured market. Hamilton highlighted the overall benefits in terms of increased labour productivity, full employment, and increasing returns in manufacturing. Like Hamilton, List argued that manufacturing was the primary source of wealth, and a diversified economy based on manufacturing and agriculture has stronger stimuli for growth than an economy based solely on agriculture.

The rationale for protecting infant industry is based on the often prohibitive risks of acquiring finance and new skills, the lack of inducement by entrepreneurs, and the formidable competition from forerunners. The competitive obstacle posed by predominant economies such as Britain was profound and nearly insuperable. List (1827: 32) remarked:

> It takes a long time until the labourers are experienced in the different workmanship and accustomed to it; and until the necessary number for every business is at all times to be had…In the old manufacturing countries, we observe quite the contrary…The old country, as long as it preserves its freedom, its vigour, its political power, will, in a free intercourse, ever keep down a rising manufacturing power….A new country is moreover, the less able to contend against the manufacturing power of the old country, the more the interior market of this old

country is protected by duties, and competition in the new country is supported by drawbacks, and by an absence of duties in the foreign markets.

List contends that 'even if there were not capital and skill enough in the country, they could be drawn from abroad by political measures'. He pointed out that Britain rose to become the leading industrial power by adhering to three mechanisms: 'First, to prefer constantly the importation of productive power to that of commodities; second to maintain and carefully protect the development of productive power; third, to import only raw materials and agricultural products, and to export only manufactured articles' (List 1856: 297). In response to the assertion that protectionism stifles domestic competition and consumer interests, Hamilton argued that once the protected infant industry is able to establish itself, more manufacturers will participate in domestic industry, weakening monopoly and pushing down prices.

The high cost of acquiring new skills and the hesitation by industrialists in the face of perceived risk makes state promotion of infant industry an absolute necessity. The novelty of the industry and the need to build a national industry are the rationale for this support. Both Hamilton and List provide insights into the design of industrial policy. Hamilton emphasizes the importance of understanding the successful instruments countries can use. List distinguishes between inducements and restrictions, between targeted and general instruments, technological transfer, and the importance of a more refined tax system. He contends that the selection of industries should be based on their contribution to the nation's economic and defence interests, and on technological considerations (and even specifies five criteria). Moreover, he recommends the alternating, and sometimes combined use of protection and promotion, and a package for each industry, including incentives for importing locally unavailable raw materials (duty-free privileges) and a bounty for local production of raw materials. The foreseen implementation problems and need for prevention of potential abuse are also stressed.

In his *Report on Manufacturers* (5 December 1791), Hamilton further advocated the importance of inducing foreign capital and investments, foreign technology, and foreign experts and skilled labour to US manufacturing industry. He called for the establishment of a planning board, and the allocation of funds for advancement of technology, rewarding invention, inducing specialists, and importing foreign technologies. This was justified on the grounds that 'in countries where there is great private wealth, much may be effected by voluntary contributions of patriotic individuals; but in a community situated like the United States, the public purse must supply the deficiency of private resources. In what can it be so useful, as in promoting and improving the efforts of industry?' (Hamilton 1934: 276).

List stresses that protecting infant industry 'can be operative for good only so far as it is supported by the progressive civilization and free institutions of a nation, we learn from the decay of Venice, Spain and Portugal, from the relapse of France...and history of England' ([1841] 2005: 132). List links policy effectiveness to 'progressive civilization', which is similar to the widespread political commitment to growth that Hirschman, among others, was interested in (though arguably also foreshadowing the 'preconditions' approach favoured by proponents of the more recent 'good governance agenda'). He also argues that the same policy may be effective in one institutional context but less so in another. In this, he anticipates the arguments of more recent industrial policy advocates and analysts, as well as economic historians like Peter Hall (1987).

Both Hamilton and List argue that infant industry cannot be developed without strong state leadership, maintaining that state intervention emanates from the unqualified sovereign power of the government based on the constitution (Hamilton 1934; List 1841). In his letter to George Washington, Hamilton (1934) notes that:

> ...every power vested in a government is in its nature sovereign, and includes...a right to employ all the means requisite and fairly applicable to the attainment of the ends of such power, and which are not precluded by restrictions and exceptions specified in the Constitution, or not immoral, or not contrary to the essential end of the political society. The principle, in its application to government in general, would be admitted as an axiom...(p. xiii)

List emphasized that the source of state intervention lay in the state's sovereign power and stressed that government 'has not only the right, but also it is its duty, to promote everything which may increase the wealth and power of the nation, if this object cannot be effected by individuals' (Earle 1986: 247; Austin 2009: 81). US industrial policy was based on Hamilton's principles and this policy was evident until the 1950s. Goodrich (1965: vii) confirms that the American government took 'deliberate action to promote industrialisation and economic growth'. The purposeful industrialization of Japan after the 1860s by the Meiji dynasty was based on very much the same belief.

In line with this, Mazzucato (2011, 2013a) argues that 'market failure' (the ideal of perfect competition from which the idea of 'failure' is derived) is a myth, and that the US remains one of the most interventionist of entrepreneurial states. The state has played an active role in creating and shaping new products, new industries, many leading high-tech firms (such as Google, Intel, Apple), and new technologies, such as the internet, biotechnology, nanotechnology, space technology, and most new medicines. *The Economist* (2013: 56) summarizes Mazzucato's views:

> Ms Mazzucato says that the most successful entrepreneurial state can be found in the most unlikely place: the United States. Americans have traditionally been divided between Jeffersonians (who think he governs best who governs least) and Hamiltonians (who favour active government). The secret to the country's success lies, she thinks, in talking like Jeffersonians but acting like Hamiltonians.

Of Britain, O'Brien (1991: 33, cited in Ocampo et al. 2009) argues:

> For more than a century, when the British economy was on its way to maturity as the workshop of the world, its governments were not particularly liberal or wedded ideologically to laissez-faire...the Hanoverian governments...poured millions into strategic objectives which we can see (with hindsight) formed preconditions for the market economy and night-watchman state of Victorian England.

Two centuries after these initial debates, and after the so-called Asian miracle, the debate between orthodox and heterodox scholars continues. A recent exchange between Ha-Joon Chang and Justin Lin on industrial policy typifies the state of the argument in the early twenty-first century. The two development economists differ on the role of the state and whether industrial policy should be based on comparative advantage-following (CAF) or comparative advantage-defying (CAD) principles (Lin and Chang 2009; Lin 2009). Justin Lin, while arguing for a CAF and 'facilitating' state, cautions against efforts to promote *new* comparative advantages, competitive edges, and the constant upgrading of industries. His emphasis is adamantly on 'a *facilitating* state—a state that facilitates the private sector's ability to exploit the country's areas of comparative advantage... the key is to make use of the country's current comparative advantage—not in the factors of production that it may have some day, but in the factors of production that it has now' (Lin and Chang 2009: 2). In contrast, Chang argues that nations should focus on creating and developing their comparative advantages as well as exploiting existing comparative advantage, and he argues for a much more interventionist or *activist* state. Despite the appeal of this approach—based especially on economic history—Chang arguably fails to address how developing countries can effectively deploy most of their available productive forces in the development of a few high-tech industries, given technological backwardness.

Another contribution on the theoretical niceties of comparative advantage and their practical implications for policy comes from Ajit Singh. He (2011: 13) argues that reliance on existing comparative advantage is insufficient and that 'rather than close integration with the world economy, developing countries should seek strategic integration that enables them to integrate up to the point where it is in their interests to do so. This was the strategy followed by the East Asian Miracle countries.' Singh (2011: 13) highlights four areas in which trade openness is beneficial: 'relatively specialized resources', 'diffusion of knowledge', 'sufficient competitive pressure', and in accelerating a Schumpeterian 'process of creative destruction'. This echoes, while going somewhat beyond, Pasinetti's (1981: 259) argument that 'the primary source of international gains is international learning (not international trade), where firms in one country are challenged by lower priced products from abroad. They will either learn how to cut down costs or close down. Some of them, at best, may learn and survive.' Rather than having to choose between mutually exclusive positions (CAF versus CAD), it may be possible to pick up on Singh's more pragmatic and eclectic approach. Such an approach is neatly captured in Schwartz's (2010) analysis, theoretically informed and based on economic history, and introduced above. He argues that many industrializing countries have relied on a *combination* of relying on Ricardian (CAF) practices at an early stage of development and gradually shifting towards Kaldorian (more CAD) strategies (Schwartz 2010). This approach is embedded in dynamic comparative advantage, which is driven by policy to catch up, based on the belief that endowments are endogenous and can be altered (Lall 2005; Johnson 1984). Competitive edge was created by getting involved in new activities (learning by doing), and by continuously adjusting policies to develop new and higher level productive activities that lead to economic transformation (Rodrik 2011; Hirschman

1958; Amsden and Chu 2003). This approach also builds on the belief that technological development is the key determinant of successful industrialization.

2.5 Political economy perspectives and dimensions of industrial policy

Perhaps the key political economy issue is the distribution of particular material interests among groups and the way these can create obstacles to structural change that promotes growth. This section highlights the role of the state and the political aspect of industrial policymaking, and the productive use of rents to accumulate technological capabilities and promote continuous productivity growth. Key issues in industrial policymaking include the complementary relationship between export-led and import-substitution industrialization. Industrial policy also involves the enhancement of policy capabilities, policy instruments, and institutions; and utilizing linkage effects, including the productive use of latitude for performance standards. All of these are discussed below.

2.5.1 *Political economy approach to industrial policy*

An industrial policy is not a technical exercise, but a political process in which political and economic factors interact. Policy formulation, implementation, and outcomes depend on the compatibility of state–society relationships and the political support (or quiescence) of economic actors (Hirschman 1963; Hall 1987; Di John 2009). Understanding the political process, the polity, and the political dimension of each economic policy is likely to be a key determinant of industrial policy outcomes. The state is a political entity and its actions have to be explained within the dominant polity, power balance, or political settlement. Specific social interests drive its actions, and its support is based on the dominant political forces and their interests (Hall 1987; Di John 2009; Hirschman 1963).

According to institutionalist perspectives of political economy, industrial policies are constrained by socioeconomic structures conveyed through political processes and determinants. National economic policies are determined 'first, by what a government is pressed to do and, secondly, by what it can do in the economic sphere . . . the former defines what is desirable in a democracy and the latter defines what is possible' (Hall 1987: 232). The key political determinants are the organization of capital (the relations between finance and industrial capital); of labour (labour markets, organized labour, and labour relations); of the state (the internal organization of state apparatus); of its political economy, which includes electoral practices and political parties; and the nation's position in the international economy (Hall 1987). According to Hall, an institutional political economy approach underscores organizations as key variables in policymaking, which is a political rather than a technical exercise. Policies are responses to pressures from specific social groups, whose interests are significantly influenced by the economic and political structure. Economic policies are often responses to contesting pressures and demands, with major distributive effects (Hall: 1987). For instance, President Jefferson rejected Hamilton's policy proposal, because American manufacturers were too weak to exert meaningful pressure in the early days. The proposal was put into action in 1812, but only after war became imminent and US manufacturers were strong enough to exert pressure (Goodrich 1965). In Latin America, by comparison, given the insignificant share of industrial exports relative to the export of primary products by powerful land aristocrats (Hirschman 1968), manufacturers were in no position to exert enough pressure on the state to adopt favourable policies. The success of a policy ultimately depends on the state's having a clear vision for the sector; the will and capacity to enforce the policy; and the ability to mediate tensions among economic and political actors, while maintaining its autonomy (Cramer 1999a). Cramer (1999a) shows how political factors were one of the key determinants in the industrial processing of primary commodities (or not). It should also be noted that what matters is not the amount of state intervention, but the *type and nature* of state intervention and leadership (Amsden 1989; Chang 1999; Johnson 1982). This perspective is echoed in recent work by Buur (2014), Buur et al. (2012) and associates, including Whitfield (2011) (also see Chapter 7).

In France, state intervention took the form of nationalized state-owned banks and industrial corporations, and the active role of state institutions (Commissariat Général du Plan, CGP; Ecole National d'Administration, ENA; INSEE, the national agency for the collection and analysis of economic data) in planning. In Germany, privately owned investment banks created and guided investments in the railway and steel industries. They also shaped so-called 'cooperative managerial capitalism' (Hall 1987;

Chandler 2004). In Japan, the Ministry of International Trade and Industry (MITI) played a vital role, and bank-corporate organizations (*Zaibatsu*, *Keietsu*) were a key feature, while in Korea the activist state, *chaebol*, and state-owned banks and state-owned enterprises (for instance, the steel manufacturer POSCO) played a significant role in the country's catch up process (Amsden 1989; Johnson 1982).

The developmental state is based on development projects that have the potential to organize society around its vision, and the autonomy (referred to sometimes as 'hard state') to insulate itself against the narrow interests of specific actors and to secure the support of all social forces (Evans 1995; Woo-Cumings 1999). Kohli's 'cohesive capitalism' has some of the attributes of a developmental state (Kohli 2004). In Korea and Taiwan, successful industrialization was supported by land reform that unlocked the potential of rural farmers, secured support, and weakened the forces maintaining the preindustrial status quo (Wade 1990; Amsden 1989). Kohli argues that Japanese reforms and power relationships with local social forces positively influenced the catch up and developmental agenda (Woo-Cumings 1999). This configuration was conducive to industrialization, and demonstrated the difference in the capability of the Japanese state in comparison to Latin America (Kay 2002). Notice should also be taken of the role of horrific war in the dramatic social, political, and institutional change in South Korea. War is a not uncommon precursor of fundamental social change that can be associated with long-run development. Thus Cramer (2006) argues that war has often provided an 'enabling environment' for economic development. Meanwhile, Ocampo et al. (2009) highlight the role of military expenditure in driving the expansion of British capitalism in the late seventeenth and early eighteenth centuries.

2.5.2 Heterodox views on developmental states

The most successful industrial catch up of the twentieth century was in East Asia, most notably in Japan, Korea, and Taiwan, and more recently China. This was spearheaded by what have come to be labelled developmental states. Arguably, many of these developmental interventions were driven by pragmatism and political economy contexts and compulsions, and facilitated by the possibility of experimentation during what Amsden (2007a) has called the First American Empire (1945–79), whose watchword was 'do it your way'.[2] By drawing on the early development insights of economists such as Gerschenkron and Hirschman, a relatively coherent body of analysis of developmental states and their rationales emerged. According to Hirschman:

> If we were to think in terms of a 'binding agent' for development, are we simply not saying that development depends on the ability and determination of a nation and its citizens to organize themselves for development? ... By focusing on determination, for instance, we are taking hold of one of the specific characteristic of the development process in today's underdeveloped countries, namely the fact that they are latecomers. This condition is bound to make their development into a less spontaneous and more deliberate process than was the case in the countries where the process first occurred. (Hirschman 1958: 7–8)

Such a deliberate process of development and catch up cannot be left to market forces, and calls for an activist or developmental state that has a developmental agenda as its central goal.

ORIENTATION AND BASIC FEATURES OF DEVELOPMENTAL STATES

The developmental state has been more formally conceptualized and empirically underpinned by Johnson (1982) in his study of MITI and the Japanese Miracle. Hall (1987) also shows how the postwar French government played a developmental role (as does Meisel 2004). In contrast to states with conventional regulatory regimes, in developmental states the developmental orientation dominates and produces a different business–government relationship. This is further substantiated by other development economists, including Amsden (1989), Wade (1990), Chang (1994), and Evans (1995). Such states are also referred to as hard states and their policies as state development capitalism, although neither illustrates the nature of developmental states accurately. Various other names have been coined by different scholars, such as 'activist state', 'promotional state', Polanyi's 'transformative state', Hirschman's 'mid-wifery' role, and 'plan-rational capitalism' (Polanyi 1944; Hirschman 1958; Johnson 1982). In Johnson's view, 'the issue is not one of state intervention in the economy ... all states intervene in their economies for various reasons ... the question is how the government intervenes and for what purposes' (Johnson 1982: 17–18). From an empirical perspective, it may be sensible to view

---

[2] As opposed to the Second (ongoing) American Empire's motto, 'do it our way'.

the developmental state along a 'predatory-developmental state continuum', with the anti-developmental parasitic state at the one end and the fully transformative and developmental state at the other.

Mkandawire (2010: 59) argues that 'developmental states are not an end in themselves, but an instrument for attaining particular goals—in this case catching up, rapid economic transformation and growth. So what matters is the collective aspiration and intent to develop.' According to Chang (1999), a developmental state takes long-term growth and structural change seriously, manages the inevitable conflicts during the process of such change (with a firm eye on the long-term goals), and engages in institutional adaptation and innovation to achieve those goals. He (Chang 2003a) stresses the state's role as entrepreneur and conflict manager. Zenawi (2012: 169) emphasizes the 'single-minded pursuit of accelerated development', the shared vision of the development project, and autonomy as the basic characteristics of developmental states. Evans (1997) also highlights the necessity of 'embedded autonomy'. He continues that:

> the character of the business community can be reshaped by state policy. . . . In short, either autonomy without embeddedness or embeddedness without autonomy is likely to produce perverse results. Without autonomy, embeddedness becomes capture. Without embeddedness, joint projects that engage the energy and intelligence of business cannot be constructed. The state's contribution to transformation depends on combining the two. (1997: 74)

In the case of almost all late-developers and late-industrializers that succeeded in catching up, the state played a visible transformative role. In the Japanese context, for instance, Johnson (1982: 19) stresses that 'the state itself led the industrialization drive, that is, it took on *developmental* functions'. Kohli (2004: 9) argues that 'the way state power is organized and used has decisively influenced rates and patterns of industrialization in the global periphery.' Cohesive-capitalist states [developmental states] 'have proved to be the most successful agents of deliberate industrialisation in peripheral countries'. It can be concluded that states with the political intent and determination to catch up can play a transformative role.

Developmental states, despite their peculiar nature or orientation, should not be understood as a pure prototype, as no two development paths are identical and none can repeat itself. It is true that the 'developmental state' is a classificatory artifice that, first, tends to be demonstrated by outcomes and, second, gathers under one rubric a wide variety of actual experiences, institutions, and policies. For instance, Hobday (2013: 151–2) identifies great variety among the Asian Tigers in terms of policymaking, capital ownership, industrial structure, and institutional innovation. Most often the developmental state is a post-hoc simplification of what was at the time a less clear-cut, more experimental reality, with many mistakes as well as evident successes. There is also a tendency to use the term loosely and assume that developmental states can be built regardless of the specific country's political economy and history. Doner et al. (2005), for instance, emphasized that threats, resource scarcity, and systemic vulnerability can play a part (Doner et al. 2005; Mkandawire 2001; UNECA-AU 2011). Despite some common views, there is ongoing debate on the context that facilitates the emergence of such states, their viability in Africa, the role played by democracy, etc. These debates revolve around a changed international environment less conducive to developmental states and what some regard as Africa's near-impossible chances to succeed. The neopatrimonialism school argues that African states are unable to develop into developmental states. These views, even when advanced by people considering themselves progressive, reflect what Hirschman (1991) referred to as 'reactionary rhetoric', and in particular the 'futility' and 'perversity' variant of such rhetoric.[3]

THE DEVELOPMENTAL STATES OF
LATE TWENTIETH CENTURY ASIA

The developmental state of the twentieth century has been the object of much study and debate, particularly in relation to the newly industrializing countries (NICs) of Asia. The developmental state associated with NICs exhibits different features that reflect their transformative nature. Based on patterns of development and government behaviour, adherents of the developmental state school have identified the main features of a developmental state. First is the presence of development-obsessed political elites, under fully democratic or authoritarian political systems. While the Korean developmental state, engineered by General Park, was

---

[3] According to the futility thesis, progressive proposals for social change may be accepted as highly desirable but dismissed as impossible. The perversity thesis suggests that similarly agreeable proposals should not be attempted, because they will probably lead to perverse, disagreeable outcomes.

authoritarian, Japan was different, in that a dominant-party system pre-vailed.[4] In Taiwan, despite the Kuomintang's long rule, a multiparty system gradually strengthened. Second, 'the states know what to do and are capable of doing it. There is then a cognitive question and a capacity question' (Herring 1999: 307). This is not dissimilar to Amsden's (n.d.) identification of the importance of the 'right' role model in the industrial policy learning process and of a certain level of skills and knowledge. Having an appropriate role model, but without skilled labour and know-how, cannot be effective; nor can having excellent skills but an entirely inappropriate role model. Such states are purposive and have a 'narrowly-defined national economic goal' or 'national projects', which are infused with nationalism, as was the case with Japan, Korea, and Taiwan. Johnson (1982: 19) adds that 'the very existence of an industrial policy implies a strategic, or goal-oriented, approach to the economy'. Third, such states mobilize the society around the national goals and hegemonic purpose. Under government leadership, a strong alliance between state and indus-trial class or the private sector is built around national goals. Such national and social mobilization requires 'pilot agencies' (such as MITI in Japan and Kuomintang in Taiwan). Although an efficient bureaucracy is indi-cated as one condition, the vitality of institutions is also enhanced during the implementation of the 'national project'. In Peter Evans' interpretation (1995), a bureaucracy that is developmental should be 'embedded' in society, connecting society with the state (what Buur et al. (2012), refer to as an 'embedded and mediating bureaucracy').

Fourth, such states have 'autonomy' and the ability to take decisive political action, which assumes a broad political base that may arise from the legitimacy of the economic growth and transformation. A num-ber of developmental states have implemented land reform, for instance Taiwan, Korea, and Japan, which strengthened their political base, partly by removing or diluting the influence of large landowners, who are typically not well disposed towards industry. Fifth, such states have the political will and capacity to channel developmental rents from less pro-ductive activities to more developmental ones. Wade (1990: xviii) notes that such transfers are 'often in the form of transfers from unproductive groups to productive groups' and 'sometimes in the form of policies to convert unproductive groups into productive ones'. However, one should

---

[4] See also Selwyn (2012) on relationship with labour.

be cautious about the tendency to make neat textbook classifications of developmental states. As Fine (1996) argues, Korea and others did not see themselves as developmental states at the time. The term was invented later and imposes more order and tidiness on the reality than was the case.

Resource mobilization (through domestic saving and revenue collection) and channeling into productive investment was an additional feature. Taxation and the capacity to mobilize resources are believed to indicate state resilience or fragility and reveal the degree of authority and legitimacy (Di John 2006, 2008). Di John (2006: 1) argues that taxation could be the 'principal lens in measuring state capacity, state formation and power relations in a society'. In addition, industrial peace was considered important to rapid industrialization and catch up. National consensus, combined with improved living conditions, appears to maintain industrial peace, though this has sometimes involved brutal pacification rather than liberal consensus. For instance, in Korea, stable industrial relations were maintained through a combination of coercive measures and wage increases following productivity increases. Seguino (2000) argues that the early industrialization of East Asian countries relied on exports produced by a high ratio of women employees, whose wages were artificially repressed.

In conclusion, this section links the older political economy to the idea of the industrial policy embedded in twentieth century developmental states. It also shows that there are varying definitions of what this might entail and a range of features and attributes. The implication is there may be no single blueprint transferable to an African context, but there may be important features to identify and try to adopt and adapt to circumstances on the ground.

2.5.3 Financing Industrialization, Managing Rents, and Supporting Technological Upgrading

Mobilization and apportionment of financial resources during catch up by late developers is a strategic issue. The importance of resource mobilization and the role played by investment or development banks during catch up have long been emphasized in classical works by Gerschenkron (1962) and others. Development banks have long existed, and are considered the flagships or conduits of developmental states (Amsden 2001;

Diamond 1957; Schwartz 2010; Aghion 1999; Diamond and Raghavan 1982; UNCTAD 2008). Ocampo (2008: 132) regards them as 'a major institutional innovation in support of [industrial] policies', and emphatically stresses that development banking is a 'major instrument that has not been limited by international agreements'. In recent years, the Brazilian development bank, BNDES, has become one of the largest such banks in the world.

Development banks are defined as institutions established to 'supply capital and enterprise in order to speed up the process of development', and are seen as catalysts for investment in the private sector (Diamond 1957; Diamond and Raghavan 1982; UNCTAD 2008). Empirical evidence from elsewhere (for instance, Europe, East Asia, and Latin America) reveals the roles played by development banks in industrialization (Diamond 1957; Schwartz 2010; Aghion 1999; Amsden 2001). Although orthodox development economists have typically looked down on such banks, other development economists characterize them as 'flagships', the 'nerve system' or as a 'conduit' for developmental states. The history of development banks shows their diversity of ownership, purpose, and operating patterns, as well as performance (Diamond 1957). BNDES, for example, has played a very different role in Brazil's structural change as compared to South Africa's Industrial Development Corporation. Development banks are also different in their focus on long-term loan capital, in contrast to equity finance or development corporations (Diamond 1957; Diamond and Raghavan 1982; UNCTAD 2008; Amsden 2001; Aghion 1999). In addition, Amsden (2008 1: 11) notes that 'as development banks imposed operating standards on their clients, they themselves tightened their own monitoring skills and procedures'.

In reference to Korea, Amsden (1989, 2001) emphasizes that banks played their role by applying a 'reciprocal control mechanism', by targeting strategic industries, monitoring their loans, imposing export target conditionality, and lending at lower interest rates. This is necessary because rents are to be used to foster learning and catch up, and this depends on disciplining the private sector. Khan and Jomo (2000: 5, 74) define rent as:

> ...an income which is higher than the minimum which an individual or firm would have accepted given alternative opportunities...Rents include not just monopoly profits, but also subsidies and transfers organized through the

political mechanism, illegal transfers organized by private mafias, short-term super-profits made by innovators before competitors imitate their innovations, and so on.... Rent-seeking is the expenditure of resources and effort in creating, maintaining or transferring rents.

Khan and Blankenburg argue that managing rents to promote learning and technological capability depends primarily on political constraints (Khan 2000a, 2000b, 2006; Khan and Blankenburg 2009).

An equally important principle is Amsden's 'reciprocity principle' noted above. Based on the principle of a reciprocal control mechanism, incentives and 'rents' were linked to learning and performance (Amsden 1989). The purpose of rewarding development rent to industrialists in priority sectors is to reduce the disadvantages of competing with well-established industries. Amsden (2008: 108–10) emphatically argues that 'what lay behind successful post-war industrialisation was a monitored system of controls on subsidies. Neither import substitution nor export-led growth were free at all...Performance standards were thus an antidote to abuse and inefficiency in government intervention.' According to Amsden (1990), 'in all late-industrializing countries—Japan, Korea, and Taiwan included—not only have governments failed to get relative prices right, they have deliberately got them wrong in order to stimulate investment and trade'. However, one of the hazards of allocating rents to firms, Amsden indicates, is that the state will be pushed into rent seeking, and firms may not have the incentive to improve their productivity.

Ocampo et al. (2009: 156) also argue that 'incentives should be matched by performance standards' and that these should be 'granted on [a] temporary basis and dynamically adjusted to move forward in the structural transformation process'. Incentives and protection instruments need to be monitored constantly, as their effectiveness in serving industrial policy can fade over time. The allocation of rent, in the form of subsidy, represents the socialization of the risks faced by firms participating in a new industry or producing new products, but has to be linked to performance (Johnson 1982). For instance, South Korea successfully linked incentives to export targets (SaKong and Koh 2010; Studwell 2013; Rhee, Ross-Larson, and Pursell 2010; Amsden 1989; Amsden and Hikino 1994). Most development economists maintain that the East Asian Tigers were more successful than Latin American countries because the former succeeded in disciplining the private sector. In Korea, 'the reciprocity principle...operated in almost every industry' and 'in return for protection of the domestic market, the government required the enterprises to export ... part of their production' (Amsden 2001: 149, 151). This is related to linking incentives to performance, with constant adjustments to new and higher standards; and states had the power and wit to withdraw incentives that were ineffective, that is, incentives were time-bound (Ocampo et al. 2009).

Productive rent management and the reciprocal control mechanism are inseparable from the development of technological capabilities. Such capability is defined as 'the ability to use that capacity efficiently' (Lall 2004). According to Amsden (2001), technological capabilities can be classified into production capabilities, investment capabilities, and innovation capabilities. The emphasis on technological development has increased in the last century with the increased pace of technological progress (Rodrik 2011; Amsden 2001; Lall 1999). Technology and innovation are the key drivers of productivity and economic advancement. Manufacturing has greater scope for contributing to increased productivity, and firms are the main embodiment of this technological advancement. Contrary to the neoclassical assertion that technology is a freely available item, in developing or late industrializing countries, technological supply faces profound constraints. Circumventing them typically takes state intervention.

The most effective industrial policies have had technological development as a central component. The depth and scope of technological development may differ in accordance with the structure of the industry and level of development. Even so, technological development is crucial to industrial diversification and to industrial deepening or upgrading. Interventions include developing technological infrastructure, skills formation, and promoting in-firm technological capabilities (Lall 2004; Amsden 2001; Rodrik 2011). Depending on the context, policies may emphasize 'learning-by-doing', or/and 'innovation' (Amsden 2001).

2.5.4 *Complementary Export-Led (ELI) and Import-Substitution Industrialization (ISI)*

FOCUS ON ELI
Industrial policies and industrialization patterns are often depicted as export-led *or* import-substituting, orientations that are presented as exclusive rather than complementary. Hirschman (1968) objected to this dichotomy, as both strategies are significant and mutually reinforcing.

For most successful late industrializers, ISI has preceded exports, and has continued to grow along with the export industry (Amsden 2009; Lall 2000a; Rodrik 1997; Rodrik 2012).[5] Imports and import substitution are also inseparable, and imports can play a creative role by signalling demand for domestic manufacturing. Imports are also conduits for technological development, as domestic producers may improve the quality of their products to match imported goods. There is a need to strengthen indirect exporters, as these serve as a conduit for exports and domestic production.

Nevertheless, it is important to distinguish the strategic importance of export-oriented industry. The industrialization process has to be eventually oriented towards competition in the international market. Exports will increase the dynamism of ISI by augmenting demand and economies of scale and furnishing the foreign currency requirements of domestic industry. Exports play a key role in tackling market-size limits, improving balance-of-payments, setting high product and productivity standards, and ensuring a sustainable source of capital formation. Exports are the only source of autonomous demand (Thirlwall 2002), and play a key role in disciplining domestic industry and speeding technological development (Lall 2000a). But it has also been recognized that domestic industrialists are often not enthusiastic about embracing international competition, while overvalued exchange rates are often also favourable to domestic ISI industrialists, but can impose structural limitations on the prospects for outward-looking industry (Hirschman 1968; Thirlwall 2002).

Hobday (1995) and Schmitz argue that latecomer firms face two critical challenges: being dislocated from major export markets (marketing gap) and from sources of technology (technological gap). According to Schmitz (2007: 420), 'most developing country firms face the problem of being latecomers: they have to make a rapid transition from patterns of demand and competition typical of a domestic economy, to global standards of competitiveness.' Schmitz (2007: 419) presents this dilemma taxonomically and emphasizes that the key task is combining challenges to firms (setting targets, exposing them to foreign competition in order to have access to support) and supporting firms (access to subsidies, technological

---

[5] Rodrik (2012: 169) highlights that '... the overall record of ISI was in fact rather impressive. Brazil, Mexico, Turkey, and scores of other developing nations in Latin America, the Middle East, and Africa experienced faster rates of economic growth under ISI than at any other time in their economic history.... Industrialization drove this performance'.

support, or protection from foreign competition in the domestic market). Different combinations of support and challenge achieve different outcomes. The Washington Consensus approach offers low support, while posing a high challenge (international openness). An active industrial policy combines high support with high challenge. Protectionism under the old ISI combines high support and low challenge. No policy provides both low support and low challenge. Based on the relative gaps, Schmitz suggests four strategic avenues: first, attracting foreign direct investment (FDI) where marketing and technological gaps are wide; second, integrating into global value chains led by global buyers where marketing gaps are wide but technological gaps are narrow; third, opting for joint ventures and licensing where the marketing gap is narrow and technological gaps are wide; and, finally, exporting domestically designed products where technology and marketing gaps are narrow. Although this approach is helpful in designing export promotion strategies, in reality, the situation is more complex.

ATTRACTING AND MANAGING FDI

Almost all countries use incentives to attract FDI. FDI incentives may be defined as 'measurable advantages accorded to specific enterprises/groups of enterprises by a government to encourage them to behave in a certain manner' (UNCTAD 2000: 11). Technological development, the dynamic effect of domestic capital, and spillover effects can be important in attracting foreign investment (Lall 2000a, 2000b). Foreign investment can be used as a catalyst *'to enable and to embolden a country to set out on the path of unbalanced growth'* (Hirschman 1958: 205, emphasis in original). In addition, it helps by bringing in 'missing' factors of production, and may complement those available locally in the early stages of development of a poor country (Hirschman 1958, 1963). Foreign capital may also serve as a stopgap measure and pressure reliever until the image of domestic investors improves (Hirschman 1958, 1971). To the extent that a sector's or industry's organizational capacity, and the institutionalization of the relationship between that sector or industry and the state are important, it may be that in some cases foreign investors in manufacturing bring greater organizational capacity to a sector (Burr 2014; Buur et al. 2012).

Incentives are secondary to the fundamental determinants such as market size, access to raw materials, availability of skilled labour, and infrastructure development (UNCTAD 2000: 11). This includes tax incentives. According to UNCTAD (2000: 19–23), tax incentives are classified into:

> reduced corporate income tax rate, loss carry forwards, tax holidays, investment allowances, investment tax credits, reduced taxes on dividends and interest paid abroad, preferential treatment of long term capital gains, deductions for qualifying expenses, zero or reduced tariffs, employment-based deductions, tax credits for value additions, tax reductions/credits for foreign hard currency earnings.

Depending on the condition of the latecomer, the role of FDI may be viewed as indispensable, but not necessarily as a supply of capital. For instance, FDI played a relatively small role in Japan and Korea, where domestically owned firms were the key players. FDI played a much more dominant role in Singapore, China, Taiwan, and Vietnam. The political choice was based on the available avenues and on political economy factors. Domestic markets played more dominant roles in Japan's industrialization, and lesser roles in Taiwan and Korea. However, in the long-term, domestically owned enterprises are likely to play a more decisive role in industrialization than foreign-owned firms. They are better motivated to reinvest their profits within the country, easier to control and 'discipline', and arguably are more prone to invest in research and development, to increase local content and local knowledge, and to display better risk-taking and entrepreneurship (Amsden 2007b). The obvious implication is that what matters is less the level and amount of FDI than its composition, where it is directed, whether states succeed in maximizing domestic gains from FDI, and how transfer pricing, employment generation, training, and technical and know-how transfers are managed.

ROLE OF ISI

Many scholars agree that import-substitution is a key transmission belt for promoting industrial development and acquiring foreign technology. One of the main policy issues is how to induce ISI firms to export, and so to become competitive. As noted by Hirschman (1968: 25), 'many industries ... started out producing for the home market and eventually spilled over into foreign market; ... prior, successful acceptance of a manufactured commodity in the home market has even been considered to be a prerequisite for successful exporting.' The possibility of successful exporting also depends on the nature of the economic actors, a 'cohesive, vocal, and highly influential national bourgeoisie' being more effective than traditional importers. Foreign companies with export experience are also likely to invest in the manufacturing sector.

Hirschman (1958) argues that the process of import substitution is dynamic and complex and needs flexible treatment. At the early stages of development, imports serve as a catalyst for domestic industry through demand-formation, demand reconnaissance, and reduction of uncertainty, and by reducing selling prices because of bias against domestic products (Hirschman 1958). With a successful policy, an import will eventually culminate in what Hirschman calls 'import swallowing'. This has to be accompanied by a differently designed protection instruments during the prenatal stage and when the infant industry is born. Hirschman insists that:

> during the prenatal stage, the opposite of the infant industry treatment is called for if the confinement is to be accelerated. In fact, if it is desired to prepare the ground for the creation of a particular industry, then it might be advisable to restrict other imports so as to channel import demand artificially toward the commodity whose eventual domestic production is to be fostered' (Hirschman 1958: 124).

This process will at some point result in 'import-swallowing' and the strengthening of domestic industry (Hirschman 1958: 120–4).

Understanding the dynamics of a specific country's ISI requires identifying the key drivers behind it and its probability of success. According to Hirschman (1968, 1971), there are four distinct origins of ISI: wars, balance-of-payment difficulties, domestic market growth, and official development policy. Import substitution is more likely to succeed and be sustainable when it is driven by expansion of the domestic market. Domestic market growth with a gradual increase of income, coupled with a deliberate policy to identify bottlenecks and promote investment linkages, is likely to lead to successful import substitution. ISI fails when the prime motivation is balance-of-payments constraints or war, Hirschman argued. The failure of import substitution in many Latin American and African countries from the 1960s to the 1990s depended on the weaker drivers behind import substitution than the fact of ISI itself.

2.5.5 *Linkage Effects as Prime Conceptual Framework*

Linkages are a central concept in the history of thought about industrialization, and in the analytical approach adopted in this book. In particular, if linkages matter to the momentum of structural change, then successful industrialization may involve the selection of, and targeting of support to, those sectors and activities likely to have the most, or strongest, linkage effects (Hirschman 1958, 1967, 1986, 1992; Ocampo et al. 2009). According to Hirschman (1981: 76), 'a linkage exists whenever an on-going activity gives rise to economic or other pressures that lead to the taking up of a new activity.' Hirschman (1958) also adds that linkage effects may broadly include the transformation of subsistence goods into commodities, backward linkages (including the development of the means of production), forward linkages, consumption linkages, and fiscal linkages (see also Sender and Smith 1986). Backward linkages involve signalling a lack of—and a potential for—the production of inputs to an existing economic activity. Forward linkages are created where one activity leads to, or compels the initiation of, a new activity that uses the output of the original production as a direct input. Weak linkages among economic activities are typical of underdeveloped economies.

A linkage approach to economic development led Hirschman (1958: 5) to argue, in the fundamental proposition of his unbalanced-growth theory, that 'development depends not so much on finding optimal combinations for given resources and factors of production as on calling forth and enlisting for development purposes resources and abilities that are hidden, scattered, or badly utilized'. A linkage or linkage effect is 'a more or less compelling sequence of investment decisions occurring in the course of industrialization and, more generally, of economic development' (Hirschman 1992: 56). The linkage concept is thus 'devised for a better understanding of the industrialisation process', for 'detecting how one thing leads (fails to lead) to another' (Hirschman 1992: 74). This then leads to a useful policy and investment criterion based on giving priority 'to investments with strong linkage effects', where there is an absolute necessity for 'pressure mechanisms' or 'pacing devices'. Hirschman (1981: 75) emphatically notes that:

> Development is essentially the record of how one thing leads to another, and the linkages are the record of how one thing leads to another from a specific point of view. These on-going activities, because of their characteristics, push or, more modestly, invite some operators to take up new activities...Entrepreneurial decision making in both the private and public sectors is not uniquely determined by the pull of incomes and demand, but is responsive to special push factors, such as the linkages emanating from the product side....the linkage effects of a given

products line [are defined] as investment-generating forces that are set in motion, through input-output relations, when productive facilities that supply inputs to that line or utilized its outputs are inadequate or non-existent. Backward linkages lead to new investment in input supplying facilities, and forward linkages to investment in output-using facilities.

The idea of linkages is clearly related to but not identical with other concepts. Input–output relationships are at the heart of backward and forward linkages, but Hirschman himself was wary of efforts to limit the analytical significance of linkages by reducing it entirely to input–output table measurements, not least because many linkage dynamics are not easily quantified. Linkages have something in common also with the more recently developed idea of supply chains in economic development (and globalization). Whereas supply chains also involve input–output relationships, supply chain analysis tends to emphasize the vertical integration of such chains and, in some iterations, the power relations reaching down through them. Linkages do not always unfold through such explicitly managed chains and can be more spontaneous (and more elusive). Further, while linkages may involve, for example, taking up opportunities for processing domestically available primary commodities or for minerals beneficiation, they are not restricted to this or to a given supply chain. They may operate within or across sectors, opening up the scope of both vertical and horizontal effects.

An example might be the South African firm Bell Equipment. This began in the 1950s, producing equipment for timber and sugarcane cutting, in what was a backward linkage effect from the sugar and forestry sectors. But Bell's experience allowed it to develop the capability, first, and later the ability to identify other possibilities, notably the production of large earth-moving equipment (articulated dump trucks) for the global mining sector. Others, meanwhile, have identified a range of backward, forward, and 'side' linkages deriving from the Finnish timber and forestry industry (see, for instance, Jourdan et al. 2012). These include the development of specialized chemical and biological inputs, machinery and equipment, and specialized services (backward linkages); the production of wood pulp, wood products, including furniture, and construction materials, round wood, and paper and cardboard, including 25 per cent of the world's supply of art paper (forward linkages); and the development of process automation, logistics and marketing, energy production, and environmental industries ('side' linkages). The concept can expand in different directions, and may include fiscal linkages (even the World Bank and International Monetary Fund now advocate greater mobilization of fiscal linkages from resource rents in low-income countries) and spatial linkages where, for example, agriculture can hitch a ride on transport links developed primarily to serve mining or energy mega-projects.

Hirschman (1967: 5) emphasizes that 'some projects and technologies have a special vocation for inducing certain types of learning, attitude change, and institutional reform (and not others).' Stimulating linkages that involve manufacturing may be especially important. This is both because of the special characteristics of manufacturing in the larger growth process (see above) and because, as has often been argued, there are more linkages associated with manufacturing than with, for example, agriculture. This raises a fundamental point about linkages, which is that they do not necessarily unfold automatically in the cumulative causation process envisaged by Hirschman. Rather, linkages typically depend on policy. This can be the macroeconomic policy environment: for example, the compulsion of a potential linkage may be outweighed, for an entrepreneur, by either inflationary uncertainty or foreign exchange shortages or rationing. But there are other more direct ways in which policy matters to unlocking linkage effects. Fiscal linkages from a mining project may be virtually non-existent or significant, depending on the details of contracts between states and mining companies. Local content stipulations in contracts can increase the scope for backward linkages; just as insisting on an obligatory payroll expenditure on research and development can stimulate linkages. Both Chile and Norway have implemented policies on backward linkages from the natural resource sector. By contrast, the demise of the mining research agency COMRO in South Africa shows how policy can undermine or weaken the scope of linkage effects in an economy (for instance, see Jourdan et al. 2012). Even in countries with mineral resources, as in countries without such endowments, steel is often imported at high cost to nascent manufacturing. The costs and scale requirements of a steel industry can undermine the development of a linkage to production. But some countries have reacted to this challenge by establishing state-owned enterprises to produce low-cost steel for the emerging manufacturing sector (including POSCO in Korea, the Japan Iron and Steel Company, CSC in Taiwan, Bao Steel in China, and Rautaruuki in Finland).

An issue complementary to linkages is latitude for failure, another possible source of signalling available to policymakers. Competition is one 'disciplining' mechanism that can help narrow the latitude for failure, although it is rarely close to 'perfect' and may be best thought of in terms of optimal rivalry and competition (e.g., among *chaebol* in Korea) rather than maximal competition. Competition is neither the only nor necessarily the most effective means of promoting learning, adaptation, or productivity. Clearly, the discipline of export competition can narrow the latitude for poor performance in many industries. In the absence of export discipline, policies should promote the intensity of competition and domestic rivalry. Narrow latitude can impel performance, a compulsion to deliver, and put pressure on firms and state institutions. According to Porter (1998, 2008), two central concerns underlie the choice of competitive advantage. The first is the industry in which the firm competes, and the second is its position in the industry. An industry is a group of competing firms producing similar products or services.

The dynamic potential of linkage effects may also not be released because of lock-in or path dependency. According to Mahoney (2000: 507), path dependency 'characterizes specifically those historical sequences in which contingent events set into motion institutional patterns or event chains that have deterministic properties'. Path dependency is a formidable problem because of the deliberate actions of actors to maintain the status quo and to protect their narrow group interests, because of 'cognitive blindness', and because of simple inertia among firms, stakeholders, and government agencies. Again, this serves to emphasize the significance of designing policy that encourages linkage effects rather than waiting for them to unfold automatically.

A final point about a linkage approach and its policy significance is that there can also be employment linkages between different activities. Expanded flower production in a country like Ethiopia (see below, Chapter 5) not only generates direct employment but can stimulate additional employment: indirectly, through, for example, the creation of cardboard packaging plants, logistical services, and cold storage and air freight facilities; and at another remove, through induced demand for labour in the services springing up (bars, hotels, construction, motorized rickshaw transport, etc.). More broadly, indirect employment linkages are a function of productive linkages: induced employment effects are external effects of investment in manufacturing other than these linkages— they are effectively a result of Keynesian multiplier effects (Lavopa and Szirmai 2012). In line with the arguments developed above, manufacturing matters here. Manufacturing generates direct labour demand, and given that most manufacturing is characterized by relatively high productivity, this often means relatively decent jobs at reasonable pay. But it is also known that manufacturing usually has only limited overall employment effects, accounting for a small proportion of total employment. However, the critical feature of manufacturing is that it may have relatively high scope for generating indirect and induced employment across sectors. According to Lavopa and Szirmai (2012: 5), 'the evidence suggests that one job created in manufacturing will create a larger number of jobs in other sectors than one job in any other part of the economy'.

2.6 The African context: why industrial policy and industrialization have failed

2.6.1 *The State of African Economies and the Role of Industry*

Half a century after independence, Africa's industrialization and exports lag far behind the rest of the world. The manufacturing sector in Africa represents 10.5 per cent of GDP, with small and medium-sized firms dominating (UNCTAD-UNIDO 2011). Close to 70 per cent of African manufacturing is resource based and low technology. A significant amount of manufacturing is 'informal' (UNCTAD-UNIDO 2011; Page 2011, 2013; Page and Söderbom 2011). The continent's share of world manufacturing value added (MVA) decreased from 1.2 per cent in 2000 to 1 per cent a decade later (UNCTAD-UNIDO 2011). Primary commodities continue to dominate exports, with overdependence on a few commodities, exposing African countries to vulnerability and external shocks (Cramer 2012; Sender and Smith 1986; UNCTAD-UNIDO 2011; Soludo, Ogbu, and Chang 2004; Lall 2000b). Africa's share of global manufacturing and industrial exports has been persistently insignificant (UNIDO-UNCTAD 2011). Between 2001 and 2006, sub-Saharan Africa's (SSAs) share of manufacturing exports was 0.558 per cent, and only 0.225 per cent when South Africa is excluded (Jomo and Arnim 2012: 511). As Table 2.1 below shows, the low share of manufacturing in the economy indicates low development and lack of structural transformation (Szirmai, Naudé, and Alcorta 2013; Page 2011, 2013).

Table 2.1. Regional structure of production, 1950–2005

Region	1950				2005			
	Agriculture	Industry	Manufacturing	Services	Agriculture	Industry	Manufacturing	Services
Africa	43	22	11	34	28	27	10	45
Asia	49	14	10	36	14	33	22	53
Developing countries	37	22	12	42	16	31	15	53
Advanced economies	16	40	29	45	2	27	16	71

Note: Gross value added as percentage of GDP at current prices, regional average.
Source: Szirmai, Naudé, and Alcorta (2013), Table 1.2, pp. 11–12.

Africa's economies continue to face fundamental structural constraints, including lack of economic diversification, the prevalence of unregulated and often low-productivity economic activities, low productivity in industry and agriculture, and poor infrastructure (World Bank 2010; Commission for Africa 2005). Africa is estimated to lose an estimated 1 per cent of GDP to poor infrastructure alone, which is much higher than in other regions (World Bank 2010). This situation, and a weak regional market, undermine industrial competitiveness. Khan (2012: 439) argues that employment intensity and the labour force participation rate in SSA were much lower than in Asia. Moreover, low saving capacity, weak investment, and limited capital have been additional constraints (UNCTAD-UNIDO 2011).

Since 2000, many African countries have begun to register economic growth, primarily from resource extraction and commodity price booms. This growth continues to be led by the very factors responsible for previous African growth episodes, which did not, however, engender sustained rapid growth and structural change—inward capital flows, cheap capital, and surging commodity prices. Overall, Africa's economic growth has been slower than Asia's or Latin America's, but the continent has also experienced periods of faster economic growth and economic success (Jerven 2010a, 2010b), for example, during its so-called Golden Age (1960–75). Countries such as Botswana and Mauritius more recently, and Côte d'Ivoire in the 1970s, were commended for their somewhat activist industrial policies (Bhowon, Boodhoo, and Chellapermal 2004; Stein 2006; Soludo, Ogbu, and Chang 2004). Supported by cheap borrowing, capital flows, and high commodity prices, these activist states played an important role in achieving economic growth spurts in their countries (Ocampo et al. 2009). However, nowadays African governments are mostly advised against adopting an 'activist' stance on the basis of previous growth collapses. Neopatrimonialism, invoked increasingly since the early 1990s, is said to explain why African states can be neither developmental nor implement activist industrial policies (see Altenburg 2011; Chabal and Daloz 1999). A recent piece of neoclassical advice to African countries has been to focus on factor endowments and light manufacturing industry (Dinh et al. 2012). This counsel tends to come out of an economic tradition that was also at the heart of the Washington Consensus. Yet Africa's slowest growth was recorded precisely during the 1980s and 1990s, the very period when African governments were preoccupied with implementing the Washington Consensus prescriptions.

Recent empirical studies and contributions to the debate on Africa's industrialization highlight the political constraints on, and the acute deficits in, industrial policymaking. Cramer (1999a), drawing on a case study of Mozambican processing of primary commodities, cautions against overgeneralization but highlights that the key constraint on Africa's industrialization has been 'political rather than purely technical or economic… the state lacks the capacity or will to produce a coherent and emphatic analysis and policy package for industrial sectors.' Warren-Rodriguez (2008) highlights that a 'deteriorating policy and economic environment' was the major factor in undermining technological development in Mozambique. As a result, the country failed to optimize its industrial drive through accumulation of technological capabilities and manufacturing skills. 'Wrong policies' have not only led to lack of industrialization, but have in some cases generated deindustrialization (decline in manufacturing share). Tregenna (2008a, 2008b, 2012) provides a comprehensive structuralist explanation based on extensive empirical evidence from South Africa. While emphasizing the 'special characteristics of manufacturing', Tregenna (2008a) highlights recent deindustrialization and the weakness of industrial policymaking in South Africa. Moreover, he (2012) argues that South Africa's dependence on 'domestic demand expansion' as the main source of growth has contributed to weak subsector dynamics, including sluggish technological change. Industrial policy appears to have been unable to effectively promote export capacity and global competitiveness.

Deindustrialization has not been limited to South Africa, but has been a feature of SSA countries at lower levels of development too (Jalilian and

Weiss 1997, 2000), with negative consequences for long-term productive gains. The overall policy environment and structure of African economies in the early twenty-first century remain fundamentally unchanged, although there are some positive departures. For instance, despite limits to Mauritius's transformation and upgrading (the so-called 'Mauritius Miracle', it is one case of successful industrialization and industrial policy (Stiglitz 2011; Rodrik 1997; Bhowon et al. 2004; Ancharaz 2003; Rodrik 2012). (It is surely curious, and linked to the fatalism common to many economists, that the reflex reaction to any remotely successful case of industrialization is to dub it a 'miracle'.) Brautigam and Tania (2009) provide explanations for Mauritius's achievements, highlighting a visionary elite and societal consensus on national vision, transnational networks (such as export-processing zones, EPZs), and systematic vulnerability. Its per capita income rose from $400 in 1968, the year of independence, to about $15,000 in 2012, and the economy diversified from monocrop dependence (sugar) into industrial and services sectors.[6] Mauritius developed EPZs, protection tariffs, and incentives; and innovatively adjusted to changed domestic and international variables. This was accompanied by a positive social and political framework, specifically a sound democratic and welfare system (free education, free health service).

Tregenna more recently (2013) notes that between 2000 and 2007, eleven African countries showed an increased share (at least by 1 per cent) of manufacturing in GDP, eight of which had actually experienced deindustrialization from 1990 to 2000. However, not all industrial policy instruments have been successful across the board. Stein (2012: 322–39), for instance, maintains that despite their wide adoption, EPZs failed in many African countries because they were not part of a broader industrial policy and industrialization drive. He points out that of the 3,500 zones worldwide employing 66 million people in 2006, only ninety-one (2.6 per cent of those in developing countries) existed in twenty SSA countries, employing only about one million people. Most EPZs failed as most were initiated for the short-term goal of benefiting from the African Growth and Opportunity Act (AGOA) or multi-fibre arrangement.

Despite the recent global economic crisis, international factors have been broadly favourable to African countries. These factors include high

---

[6] Unless specified, the currency is in US$ throughout the book.

commodity prices, cheaper borrowing costs, rising foreign investment inflows, increased labour cost in emerging countries, and growing South–South economic ties in investment, trade, and financing. For instance, FDI to Africa has increased fivefold in recent years (AfDB 2011). Brautigam (2011) and Jianhua (2013) highlight the increasing Chinese presence in Africa and its implications for African industrialization. Domestic conditions, such as growing investments in human capital (education and health), political stability, and state institutions have also shown positive developments. Regional cooperation is increasing (AU, NEPAD, and sub-regions), while regional conflicts show a declining trend (HSRG 2012).[7]

2.6.2 African Development and Industrial Policy Literature

A review of African economic development and industrialization raises fundamental issues about analytical perspectives (Sender and Smith 1986; Cramer 1999b; Riddell 1990; Jerven 2011). Most available literature is presumptuous, riddled with gaps, and metes out standard pronouncements. Common diagnoses (for instance, the African 'growth tragedy') and the resultant conclusions are not founded on reliable data or appropriate methodology, and have often reflected political bias. Riddell (1990) stresses how scarce data on industrialization in Africa are, one instance of the larger issue of 'poor numbers' on African economic activity (Jerven 2011). One of the major problems in the African political economy literature is the preoccupation with the source of the 'Africa dummy', a residual in growth equations that cannot be otherwise explained by neoclassical growth models. This quest involves the elaboration of econometric models with ever-expanding variables, most of whose assumptions, data, and technical methodologies are not context appropriate (Jerven 2011; Sender 1999, 2003; Oya 2012). Many of these ingenious statistical exercises, as well as many other analyses, treat the continent as a homogeneous entity, despite the huge diversity between and within its fifty-four countries. This diversity is partly highlighted by the different growth and economic development patterns between states (see, for instance, Sender, Cramer, and Oya 2005). Such an oversimplified approach, however, has led to unrealistic expectations and disappointing outcomes.

---

[7] Human Security Research Group.

The second major problem with existing research on African political economy is myopic Afro-pessimism, as a result of which misrepresentation and ideologically driven bias have significantly clouded reality. This mindset presumes an African growth tragedy and then attributes this to cultural factors and ethnicity, among others (Easterly 2002; Easterly and Levine 1997). This outlook is aggravated by market fundamentalism, which blames state intervention for Africa's underdevelopment and lagging industrialization. It is difficult not to see in this the contempt Hirschman (2008) believed characterized many mono-economic approaches to explaining the state of Africa.

2.6.3 Background to Africa's industrial policymaking

Industrial policymaking has gone through different phases in Africa. The first phase, between the 1960s and 1980s, was driven by vigorous industrial promotion in many countries aiming for self-reliance and import substitution. African nations embarked upon this quest after learning that political independence does not automatically guarantee economic independence and a better quality of life. Nonetheless, this industrialization drive and the resultant economic growth could not be sustained because of balance of payment problems, debt burdens, and the inability to build internationally competitive industries. The final straw was the 1970s oil crises. Poor policies pursued by many African governments during that period—among them, failure to invest in export sectors, neglect of high productivity agriculture, mismanagement of macroeconomic policy and state-owned enterprises—contributed to the crisis.

This period also witnessed some less-than-successful policy experiments, often coloured by populism, such as *Ujamaa* or 'African socialism' in Tanzania. The Zambian mismanagement of copper deposits, war and policy crises in Mozambique, and macroeconomic policy struggles in Ghana and elsewhere are other examples (Kitching 1982; Sender and Smith 1986). Kitching (1982) argued that populist and neo-populist ideology lay behind experiments such as *Ujamaa*, a widely influential initiative that led to a bias in favour of a non-industrial path to development, an option that is not viable in theory or practice. In his book *Manufacturing Africa*, Riddell highlights the neglect of industrialization policy between the 1970s and 1990s, and contrasts this with the focus on Africa's industrial development during the 1960s. These decades were characterized by neglect of the manufacturing sector, the weak structure of manufacturing, low and falling manufactured exports, lack of interlinkages within manufacturing, and weak forward linkages.

The Structural Adjustment Programme (SAP) phase (1980–2000) was characterized by significant policy changes, which resulted in slower industrialization and deindustrialization (Riddell 1990; Padayachee 2010; Tregenna 2013). Most African countries were forced to undertake reforms focused on economic liberalization, privatization, and structural adjustment (Rodrk 2014a). Jomo and Arnim (2012: 511) underline how 'economic liberalisation has brought economic stagnation, de-industrialisation and agricultural decline, rather than structural change induced by productivity gains and stronger domestic demand from increasing incomes'. Industrialization in many countries continued to play a minor role, and the economic reforms promoted by International Financial Institutions (IFIs) did little to promote new industries (Watanabe and Hanatani 2012). Under pressure from the IFIs, most public enterprises were privatized, although this did not lead to significant productivity gains. Trade was liberalized and domestic firms were unable to compete in the international market without protection measures (Riddell 1990). This painful 'adjustment process' also had social costs such as layoffs, and the state's role was weakened.

Agriculture, the traditional economic mainstay, was plagued by problems and failed to increase productivity and transform. Support to farmers and state interventions supposed to improve agricultural productivity were largely ignored (Oya 2010, 2011; Sender 2003; Sender, Oya, and Cramer 2006). Many African countries abandoned industrial policies, and the opening of financial markets to foreign banks weakened domestic capital. There is also evidence of a loss of policy capability (Warren-Rodriguez 2010; Palma 2003, 2009, 2011, 2012). Once these reforms were considered outdated, the poverty reduction strategy and Millennium Development Goals were introduced, also narrowly focusing on social goals and poverty reduction rather than addressing fundamental growth and economic transformation. Indeed, the poverty reduction and social goals are more likely to be achieved through successful economic development and structural changes (Ocampo et al. 2009; Amsden 2009).

Despite the fragmented use of industrial policy instruments, industrial policy has been based on a neoclassical vision of markets. There are two ways in which this may be the case. One is that for a long time, industrial policy has essentially been about *not* interfering in markets, and not promoting industry, etc. The other is the newer neoclassical version, where a moderate effort to facilitate industrialization is accepted, but not more activist and higher risk interventions. Tregenna (2013) underlines the importance of increasing labour productivity in manufacturing, highlighting the dynamic role it played in East Asia. This is a dilemma for many African countries, as low wages are not an advantage until productivity reaches international standards (Schwartz 2010). These observations call for new approaches and policy perspectives that can lead to economic transformation and for more fitting industrial development perspectives for Africa. One of Riddell's conclusions from the case studies in seven African countries is that 'there does not appear to be one particular road to industrialization or mould into which either these or other SSA countries could or should be made to fit' (Riddell 1990: 47). He adds that:

> the long-term prospects for the development and deepening of the manufacturing sector in SSA, in general, and for the seven case-study countries, in particular, will be critically determined by the nature of the policy environment, the incentive system in which manufacturing enterprises operate, and by policies and stimuli targeted specifically at firms within the manufacturing sector (Riddell 1990: 51).

2.7 Summary and Conclusions

The theoretical and conceptual constructs used in this book are summarized as follows. First, mainstream economic theories emphasize that there is no case for active industrial policies and that free markets and trade are superior to interventionism in terms of economic growth. At best, the 'new development economics' (Fine 2006) builds on neoclassical foundations to argue that 'market failures' are fairly widespread and do justify limited corrective state intervention, typically to be tailored to 'state capacity'. From this perspective, even where there is a case for industrial policies (because of market failures or 'imperfections'), there are still grounds for extreme suspicion of state intervention on the basis of rent seeking and political economy considerations. As Mazzucato (2013a: 21) put it: 'Economists willing to admit the State has an important role have often argued so using a specific framework called "market failure". From this perspective the fact that markets are "imperfect" is seen as the exception, which means that the State has a role to play—but *not a very interesting one...*' (my emphasis). Neoclassical economists also typically reject claims that there are sector-specific dynamics in development.

Second, the theory of infant industry has significant policy implications, as it gives prominence to manufacturing and the promotion of new industries. The theory refutes international free trade and posits that protectionist policy is necessary to develop new industries. It also accepts the legitimacy of the state's role in developing these capabilities. These principles and concepts are still relevant in the contemporary world (despite World Trade Organization [WTO] rules, phyto-sanitary standards, etc.).

Third, the structuralist and catch up perspectives provide the basis for industrial policy and a strong rationale for deliberate intervention to generate dynamic gains from industrialization. This perspective also calls for a sectoral approach that is based on manufacturing's greater scope for increasing returns in comparison with mining and agriculture. The dynamics of sectors can be best explained by Hirschman's linkage effects (with varying spillover effects).

Fourth, the role of industrial policies is to 'stimulate the sectors with increasing returns while shifting resources from elsewhere in the economy' and to foster economic transformation by promoting the 'ability of an economy to constantly generate new dynamics' (Ocampo et al. 2009: 10). This perspective also stresses that each country follows its own development path with specific characteristics that are usually not replicable. Industrial policies are basically dependent on the dynamic nature of the state as well as the broader political economy, in particular the relationship of the state with the private sector and other social groups.

Fifth, overall, it is clear that Africa has not been successful to date in industrializing or in industrial policymaking. Furthermore, all the conventional policy prescriptions from the 1980s to 2000s have not achieved structural transformation in Africa. Hence, active industrial policies for achieving this end have to be explored. This book aims to contribute in this regard by using comparative case studies from Ethiopia.

This chapter has also highlighted the dimensions of industrial policy, in particular the strategic orientation towards exports and accumulation of technological capabilities and the productive use of rents through reciprocal control mechanisms and performance standards. In addition to policy capabilities and institutional innovations, linkage effects (including latitude for performance standards) can serve as an important conceptual framework and policy guide. This analytical framework provides the foundation for exploring industrial policy and varying outcomes across three sectors in Ethiopia. A thorough review of the literature on industrial policy over time indicates that all countries can make the transition from agriculture to industry, but the catch up can vary among countries depending on their peculiar national situations, political economy, history, and the international environment.

CLIMBING THE LADDER!

What does this extensive literature review tell us about the challenges of industrial policy and late industrialization, and what are the key drivers? The empirical record discussed above shows clearly that catching up and structural transformation do not depend on 'laissez-faire' and are not easy. As Friedrich List warned, forerunners 'can do nothing wiser than to throw away the ladder' and to 'preach to other nations the benefits of free trade'. This still holds true in the twenty-first century. Despite the importance of the changing global context, the virtues of free trade do not determine the absolute destiny of nations.

As Hirschman emphasized, development is determined neither by scarcity of resources nor by various 'prerequisites'. Structural transformation and catching up go far beyond fixing 'market failures', and depend on a developmental perspective and a transformative state, which are in turn reliant on the political economy of each country. Industrial policies in developing countries should thus address three important aspects that lead to successful catch up: 'innovation in new economic activities or new ways of doing (in a Schumpeterian sense); linkages (Hirschman); and surplus labour (Lewis)' (Ocampo 2007: 1). Countries have to find their own paths of development that reflect their own peculiarities and 'advantages of late development'. What implications does this discussion have for Ethiopia? The following chapters discuss how *climbing the ladder* has been undertaken in twenty-first-century Ethiopia, showing both what is possible and the formidable challenges.

3

Setting the Scene

Ethiopia's Industrial Policies and Performance

Prior experience of manufacturing is regarded by some (for instance, Amsden 2001) as important to the prospects for industrial policy. Ethiopia does have a history of manufacturing, though little is known about the mid-twentieth-century deindustrialization of the country. The British removal of Ethiopian manufacturing equipment and factories built by Italians was justified on grounds that Ethiopia was 'over capitalized' and that 'Ethiopians have no mechanical aptitude'. According to Richard Pankhurst (1996: 43), who chronicled these events:

> the Italian fascist surrender at Gondar, on 27 November 1941, marked the end of the British East African Campaign. Five days later the British military authorities made their first detailed proposals for dismantling of Italian Assets in Ethiopia... Ethiopia at the end of the Italian occupation struck them as better equipped than several long established, but little developed, British colonies or dependencies from which they concluded that the country had been highly, and artificially, industrialised.[1]

This chapter discusses Ethiopia's recent experiences with industrial policies designed to recreate industrial capacity and competitiveness.

Ethiopia is one of the poorest LDCs, although the country has maintained its independence throughout its long history, dating back to the early Aksumite civilization of the first millennium BC. The country was ruled for

---

[1] This episode is also recalled in Michela Wrong's (2005) *I Didn't Do It For You: How the world used and abused a small African nation.*

almost half a century by Emperor Haile Selassie, an absolute monarch who was toppled in 1974 in a popular revolt. A military junta, the Derg, took power in 1975, and established totalitarian rule and a USSR-type command economy. Throughout much of the twentieth century, Ethiopia was identified with famine, conflict, and war, but by the early twenty-first century it was becoming better known for its aspirations to become one of the greatest success stories in Africa. The 1983–85 famine in Ethiopia affected close to eight million people and led to more than 400,000 deaths (some estimates put this figure at one million). It was described by the BBC as 'a biblical famine' and 'the closest thing to hell on earth'.

Less than a decade after the great famine, things started to change. By the early 1990s, the country was emerging from totalitarian rule and three decades of war, and confronted a rapidly declining economy and widespread marginalization of its diverse population as a result of highly centralized Derg rule. Totalitarian rule had ended in 1991 following the defeat of Africa's biggest army by the Ethiopian Peoples' Revolutionary Democratic Front (EPRDF), which led the liberation movement (EPRDF 2011b; Balema 2014). This was followed by a referendum in Eritrea (the first in Africa), which led to Eritrea's peaceful independence. The EPRDF government then established a federal system, and introduced significant administrative and fiscal decentralization. It also pursued an agricultural development-led industrialization (ADLI) strategy, which focused on reducing poverty and stimulating the economy (FDRE 1994, 1996). The strategy assumes that initial take off depends on stimuli from agriculture in terms of growth in demand, supply of foreign exchange for machinery imports, and inputs for factories.

The government has since adopted a Growth and Transformation Plan (GTP) that aims for rapid growth and structural change and the promotion of industry as the leading sector of the economy by 2020 (MOFED 2010). The overriding objective of GTP is to make Ethiopia a lower middle-income country by 2025. This ambitious vision and strategy entails pursuing an appropriate industrial policy, mobilizing the population around the vision, and effective state leadership. Achieving these objectives involves a challenging combination of ideas, policymaking and implementation institutions, and a coalition of interests sufficiently robust to facilitate policy implementation and to lend legitimacy to the state's strategy.

Ethiopia has now been able to reduce the number of people living in poverty from 54 per cent in 1992 to 27 per cent in 2012, while life expectancy has increased from forty-seven to fifty-nine years (by comparison the average across SSA is five years, from fifty to fifty-five) (World Bank 2013). However, these indicators do not tell the whole story, nor are they a strong basis for celebration. There is a need to both extract 'lessons' and acknowledge and engage with the massive challenges and constraints Ethiopia still faces. A constructive approach is to focus on policymaking, on understanding the factors that positively contributed to outcomes, and on emerging challenges in order to sustain the gains made.

3.1 Genesis of Ethiopian industrialization

Ethiopia emerged as a united nation and state in the late nineteenth century, and Ethiopia's industrial development can be traced to the early twentieth century (Zewde 2002a, 2002b). Like other African nations, Ethiopia has gone through stages of industrial development. Manufacturing accounted for about 1.5 per cent of GDP under imperial rule in the 1950s. The sector grew to 5 per cent in the 1970s, and was dominated by foreign owned firms and ISIs.[2] In the 1970s, there were about 300 foreign firms, accounting for more than 75 per cent of the industrial sector. The Confederation of Ethiopian Labour Unions (CELU) had about 50,000 members. The manufacturing sector was limited to the production of consumer goods, and its growth was constrained by the small market size and insignificance of the private sector, as well as its weak forward and backward economic linkages. Land ownership was exploitative and limited to aristocrats, the royal family, and the church. Consequently, agriculture stagnated until the mid-1970s. This was a feudal economic system, rooted in autocratic rule and based on a parasitic aristocracy. The period was characterized by slow economic growth, which led to the popular revolt in 1974 that ended both Haile Selassie's reign (begun in 1934) and the monarchy.

During the Derg period (1974–91), all means of production were put under state control and administered under a socialist economic management system (Balema 2014; Tekeste 2014). Industrialization was guided by a command economy and import substitution, and economic activities were largely designed to support the Derg's war machine. For instance, Asco (a shoe factory) was entirely given over to the production

---

[2] For instance, see CSO and MCIT (1969).

of army boots. Garment and food processing factories had also to service the Derg's 600,000 soldiers. Armament factories were also established, with loans and technical assistance from Eastern Europe and North Korea. ISI was low technology and focused on light industry, as were state-owned enterprises. The policy had an anti-export bias, which also inhibited private sector involvement. Private sector investment, such as it was, was limited to small enterprises such as grain mills. Moreover, labour and population mobility was tightly restricted.

3.1.1 *Industrial policy post-1991: Challenges and opportunities*

The chief aim of this chapter is to outline in detail the process of industrial policymaking in Ethiopia post-1991, in the context of dramatic political changes under the EPRDF-led government. During this period, the government has been heavily engaged in major state-building as a precondition for transforming the country and achieving middle income status by 2025. Phase one covered the period up to 2002. It was a period of transition from war to peace, from command economy to market-based economy, and from totalitarianism towards a more democratic system (Ottaway 1999). The Transitional Government of Ethiopia (TGE), a provisional coalition, introduced a new constitution in 1995. This stipulated a multiparty political system, separation of powers within government, and federalism. Major political changes and economic rehabilitation and restructuring followed. The federal system established followed new political and fiscal models (Balema 2014). The foundations for a market-economy were laid. Recovery and rehabilitation of infrastructure and basic services were undertaken. The revitalization of agriculture was key to political stabilization, the activation of productive forces, and the stimulation of the economy. These policies were also preparing Ethiopia for industrial development. Domestic and foreign investment started to expand slowly. Later, the growth momentum was disrupted by the costly Ethio-Eritrean war of 1999–2000. In addition to the loss of life and physical resources, GDP growth slowed to 1.6 per cent in 2002 and –2.1 per cent in 2003 (MOFED 2010). Thus, although the economy grew at about 5 per cent per annum during this period, this growth was erratic.

The second phase, from 2003 to 2012, is characterized by rapid growth and economic development. Average annual economic growth was 11 per cent between 2004 and 2012, almost double the SSA average for the same period (MOFED 2012a, 2012b). This period featured a clearer national vision, with national strategies and policies in key sectors, which were influenced by East Asian economic growth and developmental practice. The industrial development strategy focused on labour-intensive, export-oriented sectors, such as textiles and leather. Investment promotion became more focused, and Ethiopia attracted more FDI than in years past. The flow of FDI has increased from almost nil in 1992 to more than half a billion dollars in recent years. Corporate governance systems in public enterprises and investments in the commanding heights were further consolidated, while many state-owned enterprises (SOEs) were privatized to strengthen the newly flourishing private sector. Moreover, federalism and decentralization deepened, and new urban development reforms were initiated, increasing industrial and agricultural growth. Support to small farmers grew, including the establishment of market institutions and the development of rural infrastructure. Overall, infrastructure and human development became a national priority.

After 2010, a five-year GTP began to be implemented, with rapid growth in manufacturing and structural transformation of the economy as its central aim. For instance, the target growth rate for manufacturing is 20 per cent per annum. Exports are planned to grow fivefold, with an increased share for industrial exports. The GTP also aims at the development of 2,000 km of railway lines and a fivefold growth in power generation (from 2,000 MW to 10,000 MW) to help the process of transformation. Moreover, the domestic savings rate has to more than double in five years. The GTP emphasizes linkages within the economy, primarily between manufacturing and agriculture, and the creation of a single economic space.

The GDP growth rate has been 10.6, 11.4, and 8.7 per cent in 2010, 2011, and 2012, respectively (MOFED 2013a). Per capita GDP reached about $558 in June 2013 (more than four times higher than in 1991, when it was $120). The ratio of domestic saving to GDP increased from 5.2 per cent in 2010 to 17.2 per cent in 2011. However, bringing down inflation to single-digit figures has been more challenging than government expected. Public investment has also shown significant growth from barely Ethiopian Birr (ETB) 1 billion or $0.2 billion in 1991, to ETB 53 billion in 2011 ($3.5 billion) (MOFED 2012a). Capital expenditure (public investment) was 22 per cent of the total federal budget in the early 1990s and exceeded 56 per cent in 2011. This contrasts starkly with many African countries. Ethiopia's budget allocation has focused on poverty reduction, agricultural development, infrastructure, and human development (MOFED 2013a). Military expenditure had been significantly cut to 1.1 per cent of GDP in 2011, down from 6.5 per cent under the previous regime in 1990. The government has used SOEs to undertake massive investments in energy, telecom, and rail networks (MOFED 2012a, 2013a).

Despite government efforts to put the economy on a high growth path, the share of manufacturing in GDP remains low and the 10 per cent annual growth in national industrial output has not exceeded GDP growth, a necessary condition for change in the composition of the economy. The sector also continues to be characterized by many structural constraints, such as low productivity, low value, and lack of international competitiveness. Export volumes have increased, although the export structure has not fundamentally changed. There has been diversification, but within primary commodities, which has reduced the heavy dependence on coffee (from two-thirds in the 1990s to about one-quarter in 2012). Foreign currency shortages have become pervasive, despite the increased share of exports from 3 per cent of GDP in 1992 to 17 per cent in 2011. This can be contrasted, for instance, with Mauritius's exports, which accounted for 59 per cent of GDP in 2011. Ethiopia's imports of goods and services reached 32 per cent of GDP in 2011, thus highlighting the severity of the balance of payments problem.

One major constraint on rapid growth and catch up is the inability to mobilize resources and concentrate on investment. Resource mobilization requires social mobilization, institutions, culture change, and increased growth dynamics. Ethiopia's gross savings are among the lowest in Africa, despite recent improvements. Arguably, the government's approach appears to resemble the Keynesian perspective, where investment is expected to drive savings up, rather than, or as well as, the other way round. The East Asian developmental states (notably Korea and Taiwan) have been effective in resource mobilization (Amsden 2001; Wade 1990). The powers to levy and collect tax and revenues are defined in the Ethiopian Constitution as well as in various federal and regional proclamations. However, Ethiopia's central government tax revenue as a share of GDP is also among the lowest in Africa. As a result, revenue and tax reform has become a major government priority. Tax reforms include improving the tax information system (introducing sales register

65

machines, automating import–export customs, and assigning tax identification numbers to taxpayers), public tax education and mobilization,
enforcement, and strengthening the tax authority. Despite efforts to
increase awareness of taxpayers' obligations, corruption and contraband
crimes remain major challenges. Progress has been made since 2005, with
government revenues boosted from ETB 11.2 billion in 2006, to ETB 59
billion in 2011, and ETB 84 billion in 2012. Tax revenue has gradually
increased from 5.6 per cent of GDP in 1992 to 11.5 per cent in 2011.[3]

3.2 Patterns of industrial development in Ethiopia

The Ethiopian manufacturing sector has two distinct features. First, there
is a low level of industrialization in terms of the sector's share in GDP,
export earnings, industrial intensity, and competitiveness. Second, the
industrial structure is dominated by small firms and resource-based industries (in particular the food industry), and concentrated around the capital
city. These features are explored below.

3.2.1 *Low industrialization*

Ethiopia's low level of industrialization is well documented by government agencies and in international reviews. Industry is composed of
manufacturing, mining, and construction. First, the share of industry
(13 per cent) and of the manufacturing sector (5 per cent) in the economy
is very low, and has shown little change between 1992 and 2013, even
exhibiting some decline (see Figure 3.1). It is much lower than the 10.5 per
cent average share of manufacturing in the economies of SSA countries
(UNCTAD-UNIDO 2011). In 2009, African industry accounted for 40.7 per
cent of GDP. The corresponding figure for East Africa is 20.3 per cent for
industry and 9.7 per cent for manufacturing.

While manufacturing industry has been growing rapidly, it slightly falls
short of the growth rate of the overall economy (MOFED 1999; Tekeste
2014). The average annual growth rate of the manufacturing industry was
11 per cent between 2004 and 2014, compared to the 10.9 per cent of the

---

[3] The estimated dollar–ETB exchange rate was about ETB 10 in 2006, ETB 16 in 2011, and ETB 18
in 2012.

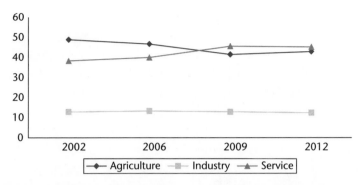

Figure 3.1. Contribution to GDP by economic activity at constant prices

Source: Unpublished data of National Economic Accounts Directorate, MOFED (December 2012 and October 2013)

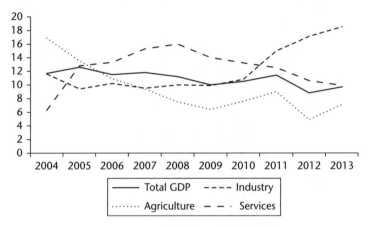

Figure 3.2. Real GDP growth rates 2004–13

Source: MOFED, December 2011 and October 2013

average GDP growth rate during the same period. Recent estimates show that growth of the manufacturing industry has started to accelerate, growing by 13 per cent between 2011 and 2014. This rate of growth is, however, still insufficient to generate the necessary shifts in the structure of the economy, in view of the considerable shares of the agricultural and service sectors (see Figure 3.2).

Second, the share of manufactured goods in Ethiopia's export earnings in recent years has been very low (below 10 per cent), and was based on low technology goods such as leather and leather goods, textiles, and other agro-industry products (see Table 3.1). The export earnings share

Table 3.1. Share of manufactured goods in Ethiopia's export earnings (in $ millions)

	1999	2000	2001	2002	2003	2004	2005	2006	2007	2008	2009	2010	2011	2012
Export earnings (in $ millions)	37	39	84	67	82	75	78	110	109	136	98	89	176	212
Share of manufactured goods (%)	8	8	19	14	15	12	11	11	10	9	7	4	6	7
Growth rate (%)	–	7	116	(20)	22	(9)	5	41	(1)	24	(28)	(9)	97	20

Note: Rounded to nearest single digit

Source: Unpublished data, ERCA (2012a)

of textiles, leather and leather goods, and agroindustry was 51, 40, and 8 per cent respectively in 2011 (ERCA 2012a). This highlights the profound structural problems facing the economy. In SSA countries, the share of manufactured exports in export earnings has decreased in recent years (UNCTAD-UNIDO 2011).

Third, Ethiopia's manufacturing value added (MVA) per capita was only $9 in 2010, in contrast to Egypt's $177 or Mauritius's $522. In UNCTAD/ UNIDO typology (based on five groups, namely forerunners, achievers, catching up, falling behind, and infant stage, that is, below $20 MVA per capita), Ethiopia is in the infant stage of manufacturing. A more comprehensive measure of industrial competitiveness is the Competitive Industrial Performance (CIP) Index (UNCTAD-UNIDO 2011; Lall 1996, 1999). While Ethiopia is considered one of the lowest on the index, it has shown some improvement in ranking in recent years, from 118th in 2005 to 111th in 2009.

3.2.2 Industrial structure

The industrial structure is dominated by smaller firms, and the average size of manufacturing firms is even smaller (Tekeste 2014; Page and Söderbom 2012). Medium and large firms are smaller than in other developing countries (Söderbom 2011). Most firms are concentrated in Addis Ababa and its periphery, the result of historical factors, available infrastructure, and market concentration. The dominant manufacturing industry is the food industry, accounting for more than one-third of the firms and employment in the sector. Insufficient industrial inputs for manufacturing slowed the growth of domestic linkages, as is the case in most sectors.

According to the official 2007 Central Statistics Agency (CSA) survey, close to 40 per cent of small manufacturing enterprises are grain mills, accounting for 50 per cent of employment; 20 per cent were furniture manufacturers; followed by 25 per cent for metal fabrication plants. Most small manufacturers indicate insufficient capital as their biggest problem. Numbers of medium and large firms increased from 1,243 in 2005 to 2,172 in 2011 (CSA 2006, 2012c). Employment also increased from 118,000 in 2005 to 175,000 workers in 2011, primarily in labour-intensive industries such as food products, beverages, and textiles. The first two industries employ about a third of workers in the manufacturing sector. Firms identified market demand as a primary challenge, with newly established enterprises listing infrastructure (electricity, water, and production premises) as a major problem (CSA 2010).

More than 75 per cent of factories are concentrated in the Addis Ababa ring (with 40 per cent in Addis Ababa, 21 per cent in Oromia, 13 per cent in Southern Nations, Nationalities, and Peoples' Region [SNNPR]). Agglomeration economies provide benefits to producers by offering bigger and closer markets, technological spillovers, concentration of services and infrastructure, and consumers (Marshall 1920; Henderson 1974, 2003; World Bank 2008). Thus the spatial logic of industrialization appears to run counter to the dispersion of economic opportunity intended by the federal government.

3.2.3 *Main industrial actors*

Broadly, the key actors are in the private sector, which includes foreign-owned (FDI) and domestically owned firms and firms owned by regional endowment funds. Their relative roles differ from sector to sector. For instance, in banking, food, and leather industries, domestically owned firms dominate the home market, while foreign-owned firms dominate in beverages and floriculture. In some industries, such as cement or construction, both foreign- and domestically owned firms have a significant presence. For industries that require lumpy investment (such as sugar, cement, infrastructure, etc.), government continues to be the major actor.

The first investment law, enacted in 1992, allowed the private sector to be the main industrial actor. Government also charted a privatization programme to encourage the sector's development. The domestic private sector quickly capitalized on the promised benefits, particularly in services, and to some degree in manufacturing and agriculture. By 2009, the share of the private sector in GDP at constant prices was estimated at 90.1 per cent. This sector, of course, includes smallholder agriculture and non-agricultural micro and small businesses. Formal private sector corporations accounted for about 27.3 per cent of GDP in 2009. However, the informal sector is still believed to account for the bulk of private sector activity (Kolli 2010).

Endowment fund–owned enterprises were founded in the mid-1990s, with initial resources provided by the liberation movement for the rehabilitation and development of war-torn regions. These major entities are Endowment for the Rehabilitation of Tigray (EFFORT) and Endowment Fund for the Rehabilitation of Amahara (TIRET) (Vaughan and Gebremichael 2011; Kelsall 2013). Endowment fund–owned conglomerates were established in accordance with Articles 483–515 of the Civil Code of Ethiopia, No. 165 of 1960 (EFFORT 1995). According to Ethiopian law, 'an act of endowment is an act whereby a person destines certain property irrevocably and perpetually to a specific object of general interest' (GOE 1960). These endowment investment groups (EIGs) have primarily invested in large-scale manufacturing sectors, such as cement, textiles, tanneries, breweries, and a malt factory; pharmaceuticals, marble processing, and agro-industries (EFFORT 2010, 2011; Kelsall 2013). For instance, EFFORT founded the second largest cement factory in Ethiopia in 2000. In total, EIGs employ more than 25,000 people in more than twenty enterprises, and their capital outlay is estimated at about $1 billion.

The role of the EIGs was highly controversial during the 1990s and early 2000s, and remains a divisive political issue. The major criticism of EIGs is by IFIs and the international community based on the perception of them as 'parastatals' and the questioning of their party political affiliations (Altenburg 2010, 2013). These critics argue that the entities 'crowd out' private sector opportunities, a view also shared by prominent members of the local chamber of commerce (Altenburg 2010; Vaughan and Gebremichael 2011; Hagmann and Abbink 2012, 2013; Kelsall 2013). An alternative explanation emphasizes the large-scale manufacturing nature of the EIG investments in sectors in which the private sector has shown little interest because of the risks and uncertainties. There is little evidence to confirm that EIGs are party affiliated, in the sense of receiving party donations or special favours. The charge that loan terms for EIGs (from state-owned banks) are uniquely favourable and not subject to the same competition policies as other businesses (Vaughan and Gebremichael 2011) is also not supported by the evidence. In fact, EIGs have fostered industrial development while facing region-specific constraints, such as proximity to the volatile Eritrean border, relatively poor infrastructure, and remoteness from the Addis Ababa market. Thus, EIGs have become major players in Ethiopia's industrial policy and economic transformation (Kelsall 2013). This suggests that EIGs have pioneered long-term value creation, filled gaps where the private sector had been absent, narrowed regional imbalances, and generated employment. Some linkages have been activated by EIG-owned cement, brewery, and agro-processing projects.

Government policy has focused on public investment in a few strategic areas, and government has privatized about 300 enterprises. The central focus of the remaining SOEs is in three broad areas: financial (four corporations in banking and insurance services), utilities and infrastructure (six corporations in electric power; telecommunications; road, air, and sea transport), and large-scale manufacturing investments (three corporations in chemical and cement, metal and industrial engineering, and sugar). Since 2010, the government has established larger conglomerates by merging existing public enterprises and establishing new ones in selected sectors.

In sum, Ethiopia's pattern of industrialization has significant vulnerability, as the export and sectoral composition is not shifting in favour of manufacturing. The major industries are labour-intensive, manufacturing low-value products. Industrial policy needs to move into higher gear, as does structural transformation. Thus, further industrialization is central to the country's path of development.

3.3 Aspiring developmental state

Drawing on discussion in the previous chapter, it is possible to summarize the main characteristics of a developmental state as the exclusive pursuit of development (vision and practice); public mobilization around a grand vision; and state capability, embeddedness, and autonomy. The developmental nature of the Ethiopian government is discussed below.

3.3.1 *Evolution of political process and tenets*

POLITICAL AND IDEOLOGICAL TENETS

The historical roots and political ideals of the ruling party, in power for two decades under a dominant-party multiparty system, have shaped the policies behind the new economic dynamism. EPRDF broadly defines its ideological tenets as 'revolutionary democracy' (EPRDF 2011b; Balema 2014). Its thoughts and strategies, articulated as *Abyotawi* Democracy ('Revolutionary Democracy'), are expounded in speeches, publications, debates, and other communication forums. One sceptical review condemns this cohesive ideology as 'vanguard party rule', and emphasizes that EPRDF's 'condemnation of neo-liberalism is rooted in TPLF Marxist-Leninist origins'. The critique adds that 'the ruling party refused to relinquish command over the economy' and promotes 'a rhetoric that emphasizes *stability* as a precondition for development' (Hagmann and Abbink 2012: 586). The undermining of governance and multiparty politics has been a concern for some scholars, the political opposition, and donors. Some observers argue that this has resulted in a 'monolithic party-state system' dominated by the ruling EPRDF (Clapham 2009; Lefort 2013). Nonetheless, there has been a working relationship with donors and IFIs. Clapham (2009) states: 'Internationally, Ethiopia has had considerable success, presenting itself as a model of "good governance" with donor approval. Having accepted the basic tenets of neoliberalism, it also backed the "global war on terror", giving it scope to promote its own agenda in Somalia, with US backing. Its cardinal problem remains the management of diversity and opposition.' There seems thus to be disagreement among external observers about whether, for instance, the ruling coalition is really in favour of 'neoliberalism', but what is clearer is that, for good or ill, the coalition does not neatly meet the typical criteria for 'good governance'.

WARTIME INTELLECTUAL FORMATION

The developmental orientation of the Ethiopian government has been shaped by many factors, in particular the forging of a wartime coalition when the liberation movement was led by the EPRDF. The liberation movement's origins can be traced back to strongly leftist student activists of the early 1970s. EPRDF emerged as the dominant political and military movement between the mid-1970s and early 1990s. Land reform and the national question were among the main political issues (EPRDF 2011b; de Waal 2012). The values and commitments stemming from the historical experience and intellectual formation of the leadership, in addition to the choice of federalism as a mechanism to manage long-lasting political challenges in Ethiopia, have been key. Furthermore, the desire to maintain independence and the freedom to make mistakes has been a strong theme among the leadership.

The ruling party and government have exhibited a long-term commitment to sustained, rapid, and equitable growth (EPRDF 2011a; 2013a; 2013c; 2013d). Threats of endemic famine and poverty and the risk of

Ethiopia's disintegration under internal and external pressure have all contributed to the commitment to this vision. Increasing political pressure in urban centres has been an important factor for the government's focus on urban economic and governance issues, especially after the 2005 national election. This election and its aftermath were an important wake-up call, perhaps even an internal threat, to the ruling party. The focus on large housing and infrastructure developments and employment programmes in urban centres commenced after, or partly because of, these events.

Considering the widespread and profound poverty in Ethiopia and the country's long history of political fragility and ethnic diversity, the issue of equitable growth has been especially pressing. Regional equity has become the foundation of the polity, institutionalized through a commitment to federalism. According to Clapham (2009), the management of diversity and the difficulty of reconciling 'autonomous systems of power and authority within a common political structure' remain a central challenge for the government (Markakis 2011).

Arguably, this commitment to 'horizontal' equality (Stewart 2002, 2008) may have offered at least a rhetorical counterweight to the clearly accelerating vertical inequality accompanying and encouraged by growth. This is an interesting contrast with Amsden's view that promotion of large concentrated champions was easier in more equal countries like Korea than in, say, South America. In Korea, a homogeneous national identity appears to be a positive factor. In Ethiopia, promoting small businesses and supporting smallholder farms has been preferred to the dominance of a few large firms. This is justified on grounds of increased employment generation and fairer wealth distribution. The focus on agriculture was also warranted by the need to alleviate poverty in the countryside, where more than 80 per cent of people live, and to use agriculture for the initial take off of industrialization.

3.3.2 *Strong developmental orientation in vision and practice*

AN EXCLUSIVE PURSUIT OF DEVELOPMENTAL GOALS

There is strong evidence of developmental state behaviour in Ethiopia, as expressed in the exclusive pursuit of developmental goals. Firstly, the record demonstrates a political commitment to a grand vision. The Ethiopian state has fostered a national project, the 'Ethiopian Renaissance', which lies at the core of public policies. As already noted, the government's medium-term vision is to become a middle-income economy by 2020–25. These public commitments and policy statements may be nothing more than that, and many governments make rhetorical commitments that do not correspond to reality. What is more important is whether the rhetoric is matched by the behaviour of developmental states and translated into meaningful interventions in investment, resource allocation, policy implementation, and outcomes such as rates of growth of key indicators and structural change. The government has been directly and aggressively investing in infrastructure development and human resource development towards this end. For instance, its interventions to increase electricity generation capacity, expand railways and roads (over 90,000 kilometres of roads, including universal access to rural roads), and create capacity to train half a million university students amply demonstrate its developmental orientation (MOFED 2010).

Ethiopia has sustained double-digit economic growth, in particular between 2003 and 2013, without relying on a resource boom (such as oil or minerals).[4] It is recognized as having one of the ten fastest growing non-oil economies. The government has reduced the country's famine vulnerability and improved its capacity to feed its growing population (UN-DESA 2007; CSA 2013). The number of people living below the poverty line has declined by half. Enrolment in primary schools has increased from below 20 per cent in the early 1990s to about 95.3 per cent in 2013. In 2012, the total student population in all levels exceeds 30 million.

The government has emphasized the essential role of an activist state in the process of catching up, a role further necessitated by the strong determination and vision to develop Ethiopia. This developmental orientation is home-grown and based on specific conditions in Ethiopia, although emulating forerunners has also played a role (for instance, Germany's technical and vocational education and training [TVET] and university system, Japan's Kaizen production system, China's industrial parks). Ethiopia's rich history of independence and civilization and its mimetic interest in finding East Asian role models have served as sources of inspiration.

---

[4] See also CSA Statistical abstracts including (CSA 2001, 2002, 2007, 2008, 2010, and 2011b), CSO (1983), and CSO (1987).

3.3.4 *Building from scratch: State capability and embedded autonomy*

STATE CAPABILITY

Another developmental characteristic is the somewhat imprecise idea of the capability of the state. The bureaucracy from the dictatorial regime of the Derg was politically hostile to the new EPRDF-led government, having been used as an instrument for war mobilization, and having served both the command economy and predatory ends. The state machinery at the time was ill-suited to serving the new political leadership's developmental goals. The bureaucracy of the newly established federal state had to be rebuilt. This implied massive bureaucratic transformation in terms of political indoctrination (with the philosophy of the new government) and instilling professional capabilities. The civil service reform programme was thus initiated in the late 1990s to this end; but it was not selective in its focus and did not succeed in generating the required transformation. Arguably, the party's organizational capability was strong and may have compensated for the perceived deficiency of the bureaucracy in the short term.

INHERITED CAPACITY OF PRIVATE AGENTS

Although the old private sector barely survived under the Derg, some of its participants managed to seize the opportunity to invest in many sectors after the introduction of the market economic system in 1991. Nonetheless, the low level of infrastructure and human development undermined the profitability of productive investment and instead encouraged unproductive and rent-seeking activities among all actors, including public officials and the private sector. In this, both push and pull factors interplay. On the one hand, some of the businesses such as trading have been speculative, earning super profits and evading tax; while this has not been the case in some productive activities such as manufacturing. On the other hand, the private sector faces differing and unequal constraints across sectors. And given existing constraints, incentives push businesses and entrepreneurs to invest more in short-term activities: they are not 'compelled' by incentive structures and institutions to do things differently. It is not that they are inherently good or bad, or weak or strong. What is needed is a policy setting that incentivizes and maximizes the dynamism of the private sector in Ethiopia.

EMBEDDED AUTONOMY

Another developmental characteristic is the embedded autonomy of the state. Embeddedness comes with acceptance and, hence, legitimacy. Autonomy is also about avoiding capture by specific interests and maintaining policy independence. Ocampo et al. (2009: 155) suggest that the 'the nature of the partnership [between state and private sector] will vary from country to country, depending on the characteristics of both the private sector agents and the state' and the purpose should be 'mutual learning'. The government and the political party leadership in Ethiopia have been careful to maintain autonomy and distance from the private sector, although this has been uneven among sectors. Such distance obviously limits mutual learning and achieving in an environment of high rent seeking by both civil servants and the private sector, and requires political commitment and skillful management. The distance here may have hindered the institutionalized interaction between state and productive private sector identified by Buur et al. (2012) as critical to productive expansion, though this has changed in some Ethiopian sectors, as later chapters show.

During the liberation struggle and post-1991 period, the rural population continued to offer political support, guaranteeing the legitimacy of the ruling party. However, as the economy diversifies and new and powerful social actors with a vested interest in the economy emerge, state autonomy becomes ever more critical. In a country where rent seeking is widespread, the state and the private sector are disposed to be locked into a state of mutual suspicion and mistrust. This lack of trust has been an obstacle to a durable state–business relationship. In this context, maintaining the balance between state autonomy and developing trust remains challenging. Structural factors such as intense foreign exchange constraints have combined with political history to add urgency—and hostility—to these fraught relationships in some cases. In one respect, this also shows the inability of government policy to shape private sector behaviour (though later chapters show how state–business relationships have sometimes evolved in more productive ways).

POLICY INDEPENDENCE

In addition, the government withstood pressures from IFIs and their shareholders and has kept important parts of the economy under state ownership. This includes the power company (EEPCO), telecom (Ethio

Telecom), the railway company, and banks. These SOEs were used to advance broader developmental objectives and industrial policies. The political wrangling between the Ethiopian government and the IFIs is documented by Stiglitz (2002: 32),

> When I arrived in 1997, Meles was engaged in a heated dispute with the IMF, and the Fund had suspended its lending program...Ethiopia resisted the IMF's demand that it "open" its banking system, for good reason. The Ethiopian banking system was seemingly quite efficient...The IMF was unhappy, simply because it believed interest rates should be freely determined by international market forces, whether those markets were or were not competitive.

This is an example of how pressures combined with ideas to generate particular ways of addressing difficult challenges. Liberalization of the banking sector, it has been argued, might have detrimental political consequences, considering the low levels of capacity of domestic banks and the government's insufficient regulatory capacity. The government's approach to privatization also differed from what IFIs prescribed. The above developmental state construct also influenced the government's attitude towards FDI. Government FDI policy has entailed an open policy in most sectors, with the exception of banking and certain businesses (e.g., security).

One interesting aspect has been the growth of pressure from foreign experts. This is not always in the form of heavy-handed IMF or World Bank demands or insistent pressure from bilateral donors and governments. Sometimes, it is far more subtle and in the guise of supportive offers of help and advice, arguably designed to adjust the parameters of policy design and to introduce new or rival 'rhetorical common places' into discourse and thinking among Ethiopian policymakers.

3.3.5 *Foundations of policymaking in Ethiopia: Strategy, institutions, practices*

In broad terms, industrial development in Ethiopia between 1992 and 2013 has been shaped by major political changes, shifts in economic policies, and the political economy factors outlined in Chapter 1. The organizational structure through which policy is designed, implemented, adapted, stalled, and clogged was moulded within and is being changed by this broader context. This and subsequent sections of this chapter map the economic interests and principal agents, the policymaking framework, policy instruments, and institutions shaping industrial policy in Ethiopia. No such comprehensive overview has existed prior to this research, to the best of the author's knowledge. Moreover, this mapping exercise minimizes the need for repetition in the three case studies in Chapters 4–6.

The mapping of industrial policy instruments and institutions may also further elucidate the circumstances by identifying patterns or striking features, especially those which have a bearing on the research. As the narrative and analysis in this and subsequent chapters show, anti-fragility was the dominant characteristic: there were successes, failures, and remarkable changes and adaptation under threat. Anti-fragility applies to phenomena that benefit from stressors, volatility, and threats, and that gain strength and reduce fragility (Taleb 2012). Industrial policy instruments have evolved from their rudimentary beginnings into more coherent and complementary toolkits, and from the generic to the more targeted. On the other hand, institutional mismatches (rules failing to regulate in the ways intended) and persistent institutional constraints have been significant and have undermined the effectiveness of policy. Chapters 4–6 develop and compare these issues through specific sectoral examples.

INDUSTRIAL DEVELOPMENT STRATEGY OF ETHIOPIA
Within the broader ADLI, the Industrial Development Strategy of Ethiopia (IDSE) is the basis for the country's industrial policies. ADLI became the country's development strategy in 1994. IDSE has been the ruling party's guiding document since 2000, although it became an official document only in August 2002. The industrial development strategy aims at promoting industrial development that is export-oriented, agriculture-led, and focused on employment generation through labour-intensive industries. It emphasizes the need for all-round support to industrialists, and promoting an environment conducive to private sector expansion through macroeconomic stability, infrastructure provision, and access to loans. Also highlighted is human resource development, improving the regulatory environment and justice system, and combating a rent-seeking political economy. The strategy gives due attention to the development of medium and large-scale manufacturing firms, particularly in priority industries such as garments and textiles, agro-processing, meat processing, leather and leather products, and construction.

Central to the strategy is the development of small enterprises. The commitment to micro and small enterprises (MSEs) is the political and ideological corollary of commitment to small farmers. But in adopting this approach, government is setting itself up for the huge challenge of coordinating and leading large numbers of dispersed investors, producers, and traders. Indeed, the government has found it immensely difficult to deliver on commitments to numerous, widely scattered small farmers and businesses. This challenge is further compounded by resource and institutional constraints, as well as the low level of industrialization and insufficient industrial experience.

To conclude, the key features are that the IDSE policy document was originally based on the ruling party's white paper, and it is one of the main documents used for indoctrination and training within the party, the civil service, MSEs, technical-vocational institutes, and universities. Second, the document has not been supported by research and updated in light of changing circumstances and perspectives. Third, it has not been fully supported by any sector- or industry-based comprehensive strategy.

SECTOR DEVELOPMENT PROGRAMMES AND FIVE-YEAR DEVELOPMENT PLANS

Planning is considered one of the tools of industrial policy and it is used with different levels of emphasis. In Ethiopia, the industrial development strategy was translated into medium-term five-year development plans, including the Sustainable Development and Poverty Reduction Program (SDPRP, 2002–05), a Plan for Accelerated and Sustained Development to End Poverty (PASDEP, 2005–10), and GTP (2010–15). The distinctly bold GTP reflects, first, the government's ambition to pursue rapid industrialization and structural economic transformation. Its target for the annual growth rate in manufacturing was set at 20 per cent, while total export earnings were to increase fivefold. These targets are extremely high compared to experience elsewhere. Second, in terms of sectoral transformation, the share of industry in GDP was to increase from 12.9 per cent in 2009–10 to 15.6 per cent in 2014–15. GTP also called for a related shift in infrastructure development. For instance, electricity generation was to increase from 2,000 to 10,000 MW, and a new railway network was to be developed. Third, the priority industries were expanded to include textiles and garments, leather and leather products, sugar and sugar-related products, cement, metal and engineering, chemicals, pharmaceuticals, and agro-processing (MOFED 2010; KOICA 2013).

Ambitious plans can arise from positive intentions to force the pace of change (if the plans are shared and reinforced by incentives, sanctions, and accountability systems), or from lack of data and poor analysis. Where key agents and interest groups are not involved in the process, it can become especially easy to blame them for failures to achieve targets. Where there are repeated setbacks in achieving targets, then the tendency to pay lip service to plans will become more apparent. The planning process should clearly define boundaries and content, as there are different interpretations of plans. Almost all countries use planning. What differs is the purposes and instruments. Central planning has been used in command and socialist economies, while indicative development plans have been extensively used in Korea, Taiwan, Japan, and France, among others. Many institutional and historical factors influence the boundaries and content of specific indicative plans. The evidence from Ethiopia suggests that its planning process has been subject to precisely these challenges. For instance, SDPRP, PASDEP, and GTP are not uniform in content or approach (MOFED 2002, 2006, 2010). Moreover, there have been repeated cases of agencies blaming others, often sidetracking committee meetings in the process. Evidence of lack of reliable data and analyses include, for instance, exaggerated targets for the cement industry and low targets for alluvial gold mining. The absence of sufficient data and sectoral understanding makes such digressions unavoidable. In short, there can be no effective industrial policy without state capacity to gather reliable data across economic sectors and to deploy the requisite analytical capacity to translate evidence into concrete policies and to closely monitor outcomes.

POLICYMAKING HIERARCHY AND CONSTITUTIONAL FRAMEWORK

The policymaking framework emanates from the Ethiopian Constitution (which was endorsed on 8 December 1994, and came into force on 21 August 1995). The new Constitution stipulates that the federal government and states have legislative, executive, and judicial powers (FDRE 1995). The highest federal authority, the House of Peoples Representatives, ratifies proclamations, basic policies, and budgets, while the Council of Ministers approves regulations, policies, and executive directives,

- FDRE Constitution (at federal level)
- State Constitutions (at regional or state level)

- Proclamation (endorsed by the House of Representatives/ Parliament)
- Regulations (endorsed by Council of Ministers)
- Policies

- Five-year plans (House of Representatives and Council of Ministers)
- Executive directives (Council of Ministers or Ministries)
- Annual plans and budget (Parliament and Council of Ministers)

- Ministerial directirves (Ministries)
- Operational guidelines and manuals (Ministries and agencies)

Figure 3.3. Policymaking hierarchies in Ethiopia

which are acted upon by ministries (see Figure 3.3). The Constitution also stipulates the need for public participation in policymaking processes. Regional governments (states) and local administrations play important roles in implementing industrial policies by, for instance, providing land to businesses and promoting MSEs (FDRE 2012). This entails increased institutional complexity and calls for more effective coordination among government hierarchies in order to implement an effective industrial policy. By contrast, Korea, Taiwan, and China have centralized unitary systems, which have helped them in pursuing industrial policy. The challenge for the Ethiopian government is to ensure that the policies and goals set at the federal level are implemented with the same conviction locally and regionally.

3.4 Industrial financing: Policies and instruments

3.4.1 *Ethiopian banking policy and constraints*

Despite pressure from the IMF and World Bank on Ethiopia to liberalize its financial sector (see BBC, 'Ethiopia hits out at IMF', 1 September 2003), as well as diplomatic pressure from individual countries, foreign banks are not allowed to operate in Ethiopia. The government intends to continue with this policy until domestic banks achieve the required financial, managerial, and technological capacity to compete against international banks, and until institutions are developed to regulate giant foreign financial institutions. 'Intrinsic financial fragility' and vulnerability, and high dependence on foreign capital expose LDCs to external shocks (UNCTAD 2011). Palma (2003) argues emphatically that 'developing countries should avoid opening up their capital market' in order to avoid crises. Grabel (2003) notes the need for financial architecture that harnesses economic development and equity, and warns against uncontrolled surges of international private capital. UNCTAD (2011) also advocates a regional developmental framework in which regional and sub-regional development banks play a positive role (UNCTAD 2011; Grabel 2003; dos Santos 2011).

Ethiopian policy also emphasizes the key role of state-owned banks, in particular policy banks, in supporting the government's industrial policies. The regulatory arrangements, on the other hand, have two dimensions. The National Bank of Ethiopia (NBE), the central bank of the country, regulates the financial sector as a whole. In addition, the Public Financial Enterprises Agency (PFEA) was established to supervise state-owned banks and financial institutions, including the Commercial Bank of Ethiopia (CBE) and the Development Bank of Ethiopia (DBE).

Because of this policy framework, the main actors in Ethiopian banking are the government and the domestic private sector. State-owned banks continue to dominate the Ethiopian banking industry, with 40 per cent coverage of branches and 60 per cent of the capital base. While CBE spearheads trade support (working capital and international banking services), DBE provides long-term loans to priority sectors at subsidized rates (CBE 2011, 2012). CBE was established in 1970, and had 209 branches in 2012, while DBE has thirty-two. State-owned banks combined had 273 branches and private banks 408 branches. Another state-owned bank, the Construction and Business Bank (CBB) established in 1983 for mortgage financing, continues to exist but has little influence in the sector. The policies pursued by the previous regime meant there was not a single private bank until 1991. Following the opening up of the economy in the 1990s, however, there has been rapid growth of private banks. In 2012, there were sixteen privately owned domestic banks. In addition, there are micro-finance institutions that focus on supporting smallholder farmers and urban MSEs. Lending rates have remained relatively stable throughout the period (between 7.5 per cent and 14 per cent).

Nonetheless, the financial industry in Ethiopia remains underdeveloped (EEA 2013) in terms of capital, savings, and institutional capacity. Specifically, the constraints and weaknesses of the banking sector are: capital constraints due to low domestic saving; the banks' tendency to focus on short-term lending to the service sector rather than long-term financing of, in particular, manufacturing; the limited coverage of banking services; weak institutional capacity; and slow pace of modernization (NBE 2011; MOFED 2010). Recent policies to increase the level of savings and investment include expansion of banking outlets and improving coverage, sale of bonds (in particular, in relation to the Renaissance Dam), savings for housing programme, and increasing saving rates (MOFED 2013a).

3.4.2 *DBE as prime policy bank*

DBE was established in 1908 and was the only development bank that financed long-term industrial and agricultural projects. The government aims to use DBE as a policy bank to advance industrial policies, as indicated in its industrial development strategy. DBE's policy directive specifies that the bank should 'provide medium and long-term loans for investment projects, which are engaged in agriculture, agro-processing and manufacturing industries, preferably export focused' (DBE 2012a). The two criteria for funding eligibility are 'diligence or KYC (know your customer) assessment to identify the integrity of the borrower' and appraisal of 'the feasibility study submitted by the applicant'. DBE's interest rate is lower than that of commercial banks and market interest rates, entailing a subsidy of between 2.5 and 5 per cent. The bank requires a minimum equity contribution of 30 per cent. Loan processing times have decreased over time, although not to the satisfaction of clients. Sole responsibility for deciding on loans rests with the bank's president, while the board of director's responsibilities are confined to policy decisions and to overseeing bank performance. Before 2005, the board was involved in loan approval, which resulted in conflicts of interests and lax accountability. The Ministry of Finance and Economic Development (MOFED) and Ministry of Industry (MOI) have indirect influence in prioritizing loans.

Since 2005, DBE loan policies, procedures, and terms have been brought into line with government priorities. Reforming the bank took longer than expected and was not completed until very recently. In 2012, two-thirds of DBE loans were channelled to the manufacturing sector, while 23 per cent went to agriculture. The major beneficiaries in manufacturing were textiles (30 per cent), and non-metallic industries, primarily cement (20 per cent). Industrial crops and floriculture were the key loan beneficiaries in agriculture. In terms of concentration, 83 per cent of loans were disbursed to fifty industrial projects in textiles, cement, and sugar (DBE 2012b). Thus, DBE is serving the government's industrial policy by promoting industrial and agricultural development.

Despite the recent operational changes, DBE has been constrained in supporting rapid industrialization in a number of ways. First, DBE's role is restricted by its limited capital base and by its 'single borrower limit'. Second, bureaucratic inefficiencies and rigid application of standards have undermined DBE's role in effectively supporting industrial policy. This has arisen from the difficulty of balancing transparency and efficiency. Many firms in the leather, floriculture, and cement sectors complained about delays in processing loans and the lack of efficiency and flexibility in procedures. By contrast, the government and DBE's board, wishing to ensure accountability and transparency, strictly follow procedure. Third, DBE faces information asymmetry problems, that is, insufficient knowledge of industries and difficulty in approving borrowers based on their past record. Finally, the bank's limited institutional and human resource capacity has also undermined its effectiveness.

3.4.3 *CBE's active role in industrial financing*

CBE has played an indispensable role in promoting exports and industrial development. Experience elsewhere shows that commercial banks may play a partial role in investment financing, either through specialized subsidiaries or co-financing (Aghion 1999; Schwartz 2010; Diamond 1957). Since CBE's capital base was much bigger than DBE's, it co-financed large-scale industrial projects such as sugar and cement projects. Until 2005, the bank's loans were not in line with government policy, and between 2000 and 2005 it accumulated bad loans because of laxity in loan terms. The result in 2003 was that 52 per cent of loans were non-performing. Recently, thanks to more effective management, this percentage has decreased significantly, and the bank has made changes to its portfolio in line with government policy. This involved shifting from the profitable import and domestic trade towards financing exports, agriculture, and manufacturing. Consequently, CBE's lending to manufacturing and agriculture increased to 25 and 23 per cent respectively after 2002. Its lending to domestic trade declined to 10 per cent, while the import–export trade accounted for 30 per cent of lending in 2011. Its share of export financing increased from mere 17 per cent in 2008 to more than 80 per cent in 2012, reaching $1 billion. While CBE has furnished working capital to manufacturers, as well as providing an international banking service, in practice the bank discriminates against manufacturing, as it does not recognize machinery as collateral, but favours buildings instead.

CBE has also provided long-term loans of more than ETB 15 billion for the government-sponsored housing programme, and more than ETB 3 billion for capacity building in the construction industry (MUDC 2013). Coordination between CBE and DBE has been strengthened, thereby apparently augmenting the implementation of industrial policy. It seems that CBE has, in part, played the role of a development bank. According to its president, a major constraint for the bank is inadequate institutional capacity in terms of sectoral knowledge and experience.

3.4.4 Supplementary financing instruments

Resource mobilization through domestic savings and domestic revenue mobilization, and channelling these resources into productive investment are also features of developmental states. The government has, in addition, used other industrial financing instruments. It established an Industrial Development Fund (IDF), intended to finance expansion projects by public enterprises. This has allowed government to mobilize part of the profits of SOEs and use them to finance very high priority projects. Allocation decisions are made by MOFED and MOI based on the country's five-year plan. Public enterprises can retain a maximum of only 15 per cent of corporate income and can reinvest in productivity, technology, and governance capabilities. This funding scheme has been an innovative and important trade-off, allowing investments in priority areas upon approval by the respective boards, and improving enterprise performance.

The government has also permitted the channelling of external loans for investments by public enterprises. This includes loans for expansion projects by Mugher Cement, Sugar Development Corporation, and

Ethiopian Airlines (EAL). In addition, government has allowed promoters of large-scale, mainly FDI projects, to access external loans from international funding agencies. For example, Derba Cement received loans from the African Development Bank (AfDB), European Investment Bank (EIB), and International Finance Corporation (IFC). More recently, the government made compulsory the buying of a 27 per cent central bank bill (the NBE Bill) by private banks, which is then used by DBE for long-term lending and investment in priority sectors. This has been a contentious issue for private banks, NBE, and IFIs, on the grounds that the arrangement favours public projects. There is an element of truth in this, as loans to the private sector diminished after 2011 due to the strain of financing new infrastructure projects. These initiatives indicate the gap between long-term investment requirements and the government's quest for alternative financing without opening up the banking sector to foreign banks. This experience of policymaking thus shows not only successes, but also fragility and adaptation under threat.

In conclusion, as discussion in the following chapters will highlight, the following findings can be underscored. First, a key feature of industrial financing has been the banks' lack of knowledge of the industries they finance, the slow and bureaucratic process of financing, deficiencies in prioritizing and selecting prospective industries, and low institutional capacity. Monitoring effectiveness differs by sector, and loans were less linked to economic performance. The banks were mainly concerned with timely loan repayment, rather than driving long-term performance. Second, government was reluctant to privatize banks and to admit foreign banks, a major bone of contention with IFIs, bilateral agencies, and other countries. Third, government did not use the banks effectively as policy banks, at least initially, and loans were not targeted at industrialization. Fourth, this improved after 2004–05, and all government banks were reoriented to follow government policies and priorities. DBE and CBE have now effectively become policy banks and been instrumental in providing long-term working capital to some key sectors. Fifth, the government even sought to influence the behaviour of private banks (focused on trade and short-term loans) and used indirect instruments to channel resources for financing long-term priority investments. Lastly, the gap between credit supply and demand in priority industries remains huge, indicating that banks need to give more attention to deposit mobilization.

3.5 Investment and export promotion

3.5.1 *Investment promotion instruments and organs*

Foreign investment was welcomed in all sectors, with the exception of telecommunications and finance. Since 2004, the Ethiopian government has targeted Turkey, India, and China as sources of FDI in manufacturing. Combined with increased labour cost in these countries, this targeted investment promotion has had positive results. The country's improved economic performance, expanding domestic market, and cheap labour were key attractions. In addition, the Netherlands government has provided incentives to floriculture firms that invest in Ethiopia, while China has supported the establishment of an industrial park (for instance, through the China-Africa Development Fund) as part of 'China Goes Global Policy' (World Bank 2012a; Brautigam 2011). The building of new industrial parks (for example, the Eastern Industrial Zone in Dukem, the first in Ethiopia) has attracted more investments from China (MOI 2012c). The share of Chinese investment in manufacturing, mostly by private sector investors, amounted to 83 per cent of registered FDI certificates (FIA 2012a). Most of the Chinese SOEs are involved in construction works (hydropower projects, railway and road construction) and providing equipment for private and government projects (including cement manufacturers and the Ethio-Telecom SOE). China has also become a partner in financing infrastructure and in project execution (Brautigam 2011). Exim banks in China, as well as Turkey, India, and Egypt have provided support. Between 2004 and 2010, FDI flow to Ethiopia was 2 per cent of the country's GDP, much lower than in most Asian countries. The equivalent flow in Vietnam was 5.7 per cent (2000–10); in China, 3.9 per cent (1991–2010); and in South East Asia, 4.5 per cent (World Bank 2012a). However, the volume of investment in Ethiopia has grown rapidly since 2005. In floriculture, FDI comes mainly from Europe, Israel, and India. In breweries, West European companies are visible, while in the cement industry, textiles, and leather and leather products, Chinese, Indian, and Turkish companies dominate (NECC 2012).

Guiding FDI towards industrial exports, the development of technological and marketing capabilities, and increasing local content continues to be a key challenge. Experience in Asia and elsewhere shows that FDI does not necessarily bring net positive effects, and strengthening the indigenous private sector is vital from a long-term perspective (Amsden 2009).

INVESTMENT INCENTIVES

To create an incentive structure, incentives must be designed, granted, and implemented, and there must be follow-up on compliance (UNCTAD 2000: 23). Incentives that included exemption from customs duty on capital goods and related spare parts, and a two to five-year tax holiday on profits were provided. The latter may be extended for two years for investments in remote regions and for exporters who export more than 50 per cent of their output. Investors are also entitled to 'carry forward losses' and to use a preferred depreciation system, accelerated or straight-line. The incentives were uniform in that they applied to most sectors, rather than just some. The domestic private sector was quick to respond by investing in many areas, including manufacturing. However, the incentives and institutional supports were insufficient to direct the private sector into priority manufacturing areas, into value addition, and into technologically advanced activities.

GENESIS OF INVESTMENT ADMINISTRATION

In view of the low levels of industrialization and private sector development, and the intense competition worldwide to attract investment, designing appropriate policies and incentives to attract foreign investment has become paramount. In 1992, the first investment office was established to promote and facilitate domestic and foreign investment. It was an autonomous body led by a board of investment and chaired by the prime minister (FIA 2012b). The board had fifteen members, including the Ministers of Finance, Trade, Industry, Agriculture, and Foreign Affairs, the NBE Governor, Commissioner of Science and Technology, and the Secretary of the Chamber of Commerce. The Minister of Planning and Economic Development (the current MOFED) deputized as chairperson. In the same year, the proclamation was amended and directed regional states on how to organize their own investment offices under regional enactments. In 1996, the investment office was re-established as the Ethiopian Investment Authority (EIA) with additional powers. It had a seven-member board, again chaired by the prime minister. The notion of a 'one-stop' service was also adopted, although it became evident that this concept was not fully understood, so that significant adjustment at federal and regional levels was needed. Institutional tensions among federal, regional, and local agencies have undermined the effectiveness of the one-stop service, for instance, in the provision of land for investment.

In 2002, the EIA was rebaptized as the Federal Investment Commission and in 2006 it became the Federal Investment Agency (FIA). This was accountable to the Ministry of Trade and Industry and was led by a new board of investment, comprising government officials and private sector representatives and chaired by the Minister of Trade and Industry. In reality, the private sector representatives were handpicked to represent the industrial associations. With the restructuring of the cabinet in 2010, the agency was made accountable to MOI.

A review of board of investment minutes (2008–12) shows that of a total of 446 decisions, 75 per cent related to duty-free privileges. Another 8 per cent related to VAT and excise duty exemptions (FIA 2012c). Only seventeen decisions and consultations (8 per cent) focused on amendments to various directives. This finding indicates that, first, the highest political leadership (the board of investment) did not focus on institutional constraints and development of the agency's institutional capacity. The repeated cosmetic changes to the institution serve as additional evidence of this deficiency. Second, this finding also highlights the vague lines of accountability between board and management team. The management executive should have made the most of these decisions, but a lack of delegation hampered efficient service delivery. Third, the finding also indicates that executive directives lacked clarity, thereby creating transparency loopholes. The latest changes under a new proclamation in 2013 specify expanded responsibility for the agency, including 'one-stop service' and 'investment after-care'.

CONSTRAINTS AND CHALLENGES

First, frequent revisions to and weak implementation of investment policies (for instance, of one-stop service) have undermined the incentive effect, contributing to a largely piecemeal approach and insufficient learning. Nevertheless, unlike the export-trade duty schemes, which were not revised for a long period, these revisions do imply some learning. Second, investment incentives were intended to encourage investment in remote regions and to support equitable regional growth. Despite some improvement in investment flows into major regions, investments continue to concentrate on Addis Ababa and Central Oromia. The economies of agglomeration appear to dictate the spatial distribution of economic activities. There is thus a constant tension between equitable regional growth and the reality of economic agglomeration, between interlocking economic logics and the pressures of politics. Investment promotion is thus in a major quandary (Schwartz 2010; Henderson 2003; Marshall 1920).

Third, recent shifts in investment policy favour selected industries in the manufacturing sector and the domestic private sector. Manufacturing was accorded more generous incentives than other sectors, while incentives for established industries (tanneries, cement etc.) were reduced (KOICA 2013). The development of industrial parks was given priority in investment law. According to a proclamation ratified in September 2012:

> ...the encouragement and expansion of investment, especially in the *manufacturing* sector, has become necessary...to strengthen...domestic production capacity;...further increase the inflow of capital and speed up the transfer of *technology* into the country;...enhance and promote the *equitable distribution* of investment among regions; put in place a system of *supervision* to ensure that permits and incentives granted to investors are used for the intended purposes;.... the system of *administration of investment* needs to be transparent and efficient... the establishment of *industrial development* zones helps, by creating enabling and competitive conditions, to interrelate manufacturing sectors based on value creation as well as to attract and expand investment.... [my emphasis]

Because of lack of effective control, there were many instances of abuse of incentives by investors. These included abuse of duty-free privileges, including selling duty-free vehicles and goods for hotel and touring operations at market prices, and the transfer and resale of land given under concessional terms (see various Ethiopian Revenue and Customs Authority [ERCA] and FIA reports).

In summary, the investment agency has not been effective and is largely without 'teeth'. It was reduced to compiling data on the number of investment licences and capital, and providing investment certificates. The tendency was to measure investment success by total registered capital rather than actual outcome.

3.5.2 *Export promotion and trade protection*

Development economists and economic historians have emphasized export-led industrialization as a strategy for catching up (Studwell 2013; Wade [1990] 2004; Amsden 1989; Thirlwall 2002; Ocampo et al. 2009). What matters is not openness per se, but the manner of an economy's insertion into international markets (Ocampo et al. 2009). Export promotion is vital not only to generating foreign exchange and for balance of payments (see Chapter 2), but also for pushing the productivity and competitiveness of a national economy. Ethiopian industrial policy documents emphasize export-led industrialization, and refer to the success of the East Asian experience (FDRE 2002).

EXCHANGE RATE AND ALLOCATION INSTRUMENTS

A stable exchange rate is part of a state's macroeconomic policy for sustained industrialization (FDRE 2002). Since 1992, the value of the ETB has been constantly adjusted to narrow the disequilibrium. There is indeed an argument for aiming at an undervalued currency to underpin export performance (Ocampo, Rada, and Taylor 2009). Under the Derg's command economy, exchange rates remained unadjusted, resulting in an overvalued currency, with a powerful anti-export bias (Tekeste 2014). It remained at ETB 2.07 against the dollar for almost seventeen years (1975–91). Contrary to IFI prescriptions for full liberalization, the current government adopted a managed floating system, which narrowed the gap between the official and parallel market. A weekly auction of exchange rates is conducted among local banks, and the central bank intervenes to influence rates and reduce volatility. In 2010, the local currency was devalued by about 20 per cent (Figure 3.4). The uneven effects of the exchange rate on cement, floriculture, and leather and leather products industries are discussed in Chapters 4–6.

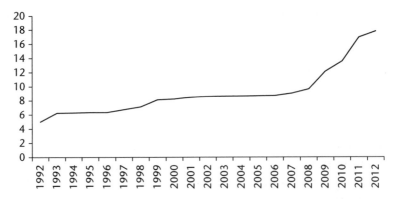

Figure 3.4. ETB–US$ exchange rate (July monthly average), 1992–2012
Source: National Bank of Ethiopia, Research Department, 30 November 2012

FOREIGN CURRENCY RETENTION

The foreign currency retention scheme was introduced in 1996 by the National Bank of Ethiopia (Tekeste 2014; NBE 2013). In terms of the directive, eligible exporters can retain up to 30 per cent of foreign currency earnings, and exporters need to open two foreign currency retention accounts for this purpose. The account holder can use 10 per cent with no time limit for various purposes, such as the import of goods and export promotion. Moreover, the holder is free to sell the remaining 20 per cent within one month. This system was extensively applied and not difficult to administer. As the country's foreign currency reserves were limited, there were persistent shortages and the central bank made allocations based on government priorities. This instrument was used in periods of critical shortages; and often, prioritization suffered from subjectivity that caused dissatisfaction, and malpractice in banks. The complaints were from international contractors (because of delayed payment), investors (repatriation of profits), importers, exporters, and investors alike.

EXPORT PROMOTION AND TRADE DUTY INSTRUMENTS

Multiple export promotion schemes, such as duty-drawback, voucher schemes, and bonded warehouses, were used to reduce the pressure of increased working capital requirements and to relieve bottlenecks in trade facilitation and logistics. These schemes may be broadly classified into *pre-export* incentives (voucher systems, bonded warehouse), and *post-export* incentives (duty-drawback). Under these schemes, the export sector was exempted customs and indirect taxes such as VAT, customs duty, and withholding taxes upon submission of the necessary documents. The administration of the export promotion schemes is rife with problems. First, MOI and other bodies have never developed reliable and timely input–output data, a basic requirement for the system. The burden of preparing these data was transferred to manufacturing firms, who had neither the time nor capacity to undertake the task. Second, the system was not supported by online services and automation to speed up processing. This problem was exacerbated by lack of coordination among government offices. Processing involves different government offices such as the MOI, the ERCA, FIA, NBE, banks, and shipping agencies. On top of this, there was a lack of trained personnel, weak supervision, and corrupt practices. Third, domestic firms supplying to exporters were unable to benefit from this system, due to deficient design and implementation. The system, moreover, failed to improve over time. Manufacturers, the supposed key beneficiaries, were not involved in the design and implementation processes. Finally, this system was further weakened by lack of awareness and anti-export and anti-manufacturing biases among different levels of government agency. Chapters 4–5 will further explore how these instruments failed to support industrial policy.

EXPORT TARGET-SETTING AND MONITORING

Developmental states have used industrial policy in a visible way to discipline the private sector by providing rents that are linked to performance. An export target-setting system has been used to review monthly export performance since 2010. Experience in Korea and Taiwan shows that export discipline and monitoring was instrumental in export-led industrialization. The export target-setting instrument has, however, been largely ineffective in Ethiopia, thanks to the passive engagement of exporters, and, in part, the government's inability to provide the support required to operationalize targets. Target-setting requires a comprehensive approach and shared commitment (or compulsion) involving both government and industrialist. In addition, an export award was endorsed in a regulation, but was ineffective and did not have the intended outcome. No effort was made to target industrialists for the award, rather than all exporters. The scheme was discontinued after some recipients of the award were charged with tax evasion and other illegal activities.

DIMINISHING ROLE OF IMPORT TARIFFS

Tariffs are used to protect domestic production against import competition, although their application has diminished over time. Trade liberalization waves since the mid-1980s, structural adjustment reforms in Africa, and the requirements of the World Trade Organization (WTO) accession have shaped the rules of international trade. Ethiopia began trade liberalization under the auspices of the IMF and World Bank in the early 1990s. Tariff reduction was one of the components of this liberalization. The government has adopted a *gradual approach*, in which seven major revisions have been made to customs tariffs between 1993 and 2011. The upper tariff rate decreased from 230 per cent before 1993 to 35 per cent in 2011, while tariff bands decreased from twenty-three to six (MOFED 2011a, 2012c; ERCA 2012b). The simple average tariff rate decreased from 41.6 per cent in 1992 to 20 per cent in 2011, while the weighted average rate decreased from 79.1 to 17.5 per cent in the same period. Import bans were used in exceptional cases, notably cement; and were used to discourage the export of raw materials, for instance, raw hides and skins in 2012 (MOFED 2013b). Nevertheless, Ethiopia's tariffs in 2012 were still higher than those in many SSA countries. Ethiopia, as a WTO applicant, is expected to further reduce its tariffs.

3.6 State as direct economic actor and privatization

3.6.1 Direct role of state as economic actor

Contrary to mainstream viewpoints, activist states use SOEs as direct producers and industrial players with multiple goals (see also Chapters 2 and 7). Ownership structure has no relationship to inferior performance or bureaucratic inefficiencies, and SOEs can play a key role in catch up (Chang and Singh 1997; Chandler 2004; Chandler et al. 1997; Nolan 2012; Amsden 1989). Direct participation in economic activities has been cardinal to the government's industrial policy in Ethiopia, and may have been influenced by many factors (FDRE 2002; EPRDF 2011c; EPRDF 2013e). First, the low level of industrialization in Ethiopia and the limited capacity of the domestic private sector (in terms of long-term, high-risk, and large-scale investments) require an active government role to supplement the small private sector in accelerating economic growth. Prior to 1991, the private sector had been prohibited from engaging in industry. Second, given the low level of infrastructural and human resource development, widespread market failures, as well as enduring perceptions of political risk, the private sector is more likely to invest in areas of quick return, rather than in productive sectors essential to long-term development. This has necessitated a selective government presence in strategic areas by establishing SOEs, where necessary, in joint developments with foreign investors. The ideological underpinnings of this policy appear to be rooted in the government's developmental perspective, which underscores the state's key and active role during catch up (EPRDF 2011b). In addition, Ethiopia has a long history of SOEs dating back to the pre-1974 imperial period and the Derg regime (1974–91). This history may have shaped a domestic political outlook that is not hostile to this policy approach. However, this is difficult to ascertain and evidence.

Recent policy has focused on rationalizing major public enterprises by merging them into new entities. For instance, Metal Engineering Corporation (METEC) was founded in 2011 from former defence engineering plants. A new Ethiopian Shipping and Logistics Corporation (ESLC), established in 2012, is a merger of Ethiopian Shipping Lines, Ethiopian Maritime and Transit Enterprise, and the Dry Port Enterprise. A new Chemical Industry Corporation (CIC) will focus on fertilizer, chemical, and cement enterprises. However, it is not clear whether this reflects a coherent policy focused on the development of national champions as key drivers of industrialization.

3.6.2 Privatization as complementary policy

Since 1980, privatization became the most generally prescribed cure for the ills of SOEs worldwide (Cramer 1999c).[5] This was based on the ideological belief that government is a problem and should play a minimal role (Stiglitz 1998; Cramer 1999c; Bayliss 2006; Bayliss and Fine 2008). Privatization became part of the IFIs' structural adjustment programmes (SAPs) that were imposed on almost all African countries as a precondition for accessing loans. According to Stiglitz (1998), privatization should not be seen as an end, and regulatory mechanisms should be put in place for a positive outcome. The justifications for privatization included operational improvement, efficient allocation of resources, reduced government spending on SOEs, strengthening the capital market and FDI inflows, and technology and skills transfers. Ethiopia's privatization strategy diverged from IFI prescriptions and was the subject of intense dispute. Late Prime Minister Zenawi (BBC 2003) remarked that 'the IMF has been pressing the government to sell these state firms, but we resisted these measures which would have resulted in the collapse of our business'. This opposition has been recorded often enough.[6] In terms of institutional

---

[5] *In Private Island: Why Britain Now Belongs to Someone Else*, James Meek (2014) reveals how privatization was carried out assiduously across many sectors in UK without bringing about economic dynamism. Rodrik (2012, 151) highlights that 'privatization would have been the conventional route, but it was ruled out by the Chinese Communist Party's ideology', and China's economic miracle after the 1980s is hard to deny.

[6] For instance, see BBC (1 September 2003) 'Ethiopia hits out at IMF'; AFP (31 August 2003) 'Ethiopia rejects proposal to privatize loss-making state firms'; <https://brian.carnell.com/articles/2003/ethiopia-and-the-international-monetary-fund-at-loggerheads-over-privatization/> 'Ethiopia and the IMF at Loggerheads Over Privatization'.

development, privatization proceeded through a taskforce under the prime minister's office, assisted by multiple technical teams. An autonomous agency, the Ethiopian Privatization Agency, was established in 1994, and was led by a board of directors appointed by the prime minister. Another agency, the Public Enterprises Supervisory Agency, was also established to supervise the public enterprises that were made autonomous. Faced with operational ineffectiveness and labour instability, both agencies were later reorganized as one agency, the Privatization and Public Enterprises Supervisory Agency (PPESA). Under the Derg's command economy, all enterprises were structured as bureaucratic corporations. The Federal Democratic Republic of Ethiopia (FDRE) Proclamation 25/1992 disbanded these corporations, and public enterprises were to be independent legal entities organized as profit centres, and to be led by their own boards of management appointed by the PPESA (FDRE 1992).

Several conclusions can be drawn from Ethiopia's privatization programme. First, in parallel with privatization, government has also continued to invest, solely or in partnership, in areas where it believes the market system would not invest. Saigon-Dima Textiles is an example of the joint development between the government and Turkish investors, which was initiated by the Turkish Party. The government has pursued a gradual and pragmatic approach. This is consistent with Janos Kornai's argument that privatization is 'the prime economic task of a change of economic system', and that a gradualist approach leads to organic development of the private sector, by encouraging new domestic private sector investors to enter (Lindbeck 2007; Kornai 1990). Some now argue that it was too slow (it took two decades), reflecting lack of government commitment to privatization and of private sector development. This conviction is further underscored by the government's embarkation in recent years upon large-scale investments in sugar, fertilizer production, metal, and engineering. The sequencing of the privatization programme was arguably logical, given institutional capacity, the objective of promoting the domestic private sector, and building confidence/credibility. Privatization began with smaller firms (such as those in retailing), later advancing to bigger firms as experience was gained. This sequencing was similar to that adopted by Mozambique and Zambia (Cramer 1999c, 2000).

Second, the lack of domestic private sector capacity in terms of motivation, finance, and managerial capacity to buy about-to-be-privatized firms posed a major problem. The government deliberately used the

Table 3.2. Summary of privatized firms and buyer profile

Period	Privatized firms		Revenue (million ETB)		Yearly privatized firms	Revenue per firm (million ETB)
	Firms	In %	Revenue	In %		
Phase 1 (1994–2001)	230	73	3,100	24	29	13.5
Phase 2 (2002–2011)	82	27	9,600	76	8	117
Total	312	100	12,800	100	17	41

Profile of buyers

Buyer profile	No. of firms	Share in %
Domestic buyers	264	85
Foreign buyers	31	15
Total	295	100

Source: Unpublished data of PPESA (2012)

privatization programme to foster domestic businesses. Preferential requirements were specified, and many auctions targeted only the domestic private sector. As a result, 85 per cent of firms privatized were sold to domestic buyers (see Table 3.2). The outcome was expected to be even better, particularly in terms of the domestic private sector's buying some of the large-scale enterprises. However, the sector's weak response eventually led to more opening up of privatization to foreign firms. Consequently, foreign buyers bought many large enterprises. For instance, three breweries (Meta, Harar, and Bedele) were sold to two European firms (Diageo and Heineken) for about $400 million in 2012. Government revised the less favourable valuation method, and extended payment times. Domestically owned firms were allowed to pay up to 65 per cent within five years, and foreign buyers up to 50 per cent within three. The interest rate for delayed payment was to be based on NBE's saving rate ceiling.

Third, transparency and accountability were as important as outcome, thereby arguably narrowing the scope for abuse of resources and corruption. About three-quarters of the firms were transferred through open tender and auction. Regional endowment funds bought no major privatized enterprise, and there is no evidence of widespread gains by government officials or politically connected individuals (Kelsall 2013). In 2000, two ministers were implicated in corruption related to privatization, and jailed.[7] This is described more fully in Chapter 5. Lack of institutional

---

[7] See also World Bank (2012b).

capacity (in the form of weak coordination among government offices, shortages of skilled personnel, lack of appropriate valuation method and effective promotion), was a major constraint. The use of external experience and expertise appears to have been limited, and the process shows learning by doing. This problem was bigger particularly in the early phases of privatization, but was less costly as the focus was on smaller firms.

3.7 Coordination and sectoral organs

3.7.1 National Export Coordination Committee (NECC)

List (1856) emphasizes that a nation's effective political economy is dependent on the strength of its institutions. Institutions have played critical roles in industrialization, and have in turn evolved because of the catching up strategies adopted (Amsden 1989; Rhee et al. 2010). In the Ethiopian context, a particular set of institutional mechanisms was developed, including the National Export Coordination Committee (NECC), MOI and its affiliated institutes, and SOEs such as DBE. The following analysis is based on a few selected institutions.

NECC was established in 2003 after the endorsement of the new industrial development strategy in 2002. Its precursors included the Export Promotion Board (1995–98) and the Ethiopian Export Agency (1998–2002), which had been largely ineffective (FDRE 1998a, 1998b). The NECC's aims and mandates are promoting exports and improving coordination among government institutions. It is chaired by the prime minister and is composed of representatives of relevant government ministries. Membership was limited to fewer than fifteen, although recently it has exceeded twenty-five.

NECC meeting agendas have included performance reviews (monthly targets and actual performance) of the overall export sector and each ministry. Discussion has been based on the report of each relevant ministry and agency, and focuses on constraints requiring decisions. Between 2003 and 2012, NECC had ninety meetings. Monthly meetings have rarely been cancelled, have always been chaired by the prime minister, and usually take almost a day. Where necessary, difficult decisions were made by the prime minister, the highest executive decision-maker. Decision-making was improved by the presence of most of the key actors, and generally issues were discussed until consensus was reached. Partly thanks to NECC's leadership, exports grew on average by about 22 per cent per annum between 2006 and 2012. During the same period, merchandise export earnings more than tripled from US$1 billion to US$3.2 billion. The NECC has continued to function effectively since the death of its founding chair, Prime Minister Meles Zenawi, who is recognized as the architect of the country's industrial development strategy (EPRDF 2013b).

The Korean parallel is the National Export Promotion Meeting established in 1961 and chaired by the Korean president, General Park, which met on a monthly basis. It had 172 members, including thirty-six cabinet ministers and state ministers, fifty presidential and ministerial staff, fifty representatives of firms and industrial associations, eight bank representatives, and nine representatives of universities and research institutions. Its name later changed to National Trade Promotion Meeting. Its sole aim was export promotion, and to this end monthly targets were set and decisions, characterized by pragmatism and flexibility, and were made on the spot (Rhee et al. 2010). Rhee et al. attribute its effectiveness to the capable and effective bureaucracy, which provided current and dependable information; the alliance between the state and industry; and the obsession and single-minded focus on exports as prime driver of the economic growth. Through the meetings, government intentions were conveyed to firms and industries, incentives were negotiated, and information relevant to government decisions was received. Overall, the meetings served as a vehicle for the national export promotion campaign and to unify the export sector. Because of an almost fanatical export discipline that linked export growth to the nation's survival, exports increased from $60 million in 1961 to $22 billion in 1982. This process was assisted by a 'reciprocal control mechanism', which combined operationalized targets, accountability and sanctions, and performance standards (Chang 1994; Amsden 1989; Studwell 2013).

Despite the Ethiopian NECC's important role in expanding export earnings, its achievements fall far short of the targets. Several factors have contributed to this. First, NECC has had a narrow composition. For instance, important government institutions, such as CBE, DBE, EAL, and institutes responsible for key export industries were not included. Their participation might have improved the decisions, coordination, and implementation. Industrialists and their industrial associations were also not represented on NECC. Had they been, the committee would have been better informed about industrial constraints and opportunities and better positioned to make sound decisions. Moreover, industries could have better understood government intentions and priorities, and helped operationalize targets and associated sanctions. This would have contributed to greater trust and a stronger partnership between government and industry. Industrialist involvement would, of course, give rise to technical and political questions about which industrialists to include, and the mechanisms needed to ensure this marriage did not lead to political hijacking by particular interest groups. In addition, sector-level dialogue platforms needed strengthening, to allow for deliberation between government and intermediary institutions. A political choice should also be made to balance 'autonomy' and 'embeddedness' (Evans 1995).

Second, limiting NECC's agenda to direct export issues led to the neglect of other manufacturing industries, thereby undermining the complementarities between export and import-substitution industries. For most successful late industrializers, import substitution has preceded exports, and continues to grow along with the export industry (Amsden 2001, 2007a). Arguably, this neglect, together with emerging political pressures from vested interests, contributed to the slow growth of Ethiopia's import-substitution industries.

Third, many NECC discussions focused on operational issues, often arising from weak accountability systems (NECC 2012). The sub-committee structure was intended to promote operational coordination among NECC members, but failed in this role. NECC could have focused only on major coordination failures had most of the more routine coordination problems been tackled at sectoral, regional, or local levels. This underscores the importance of effective accountability, with sanctions for those who do not deliver.

Fourth, a major obstacle to effective export target setting was the limited supply response of the Ethiopian economy, determined by its productive capacity. This structural rigidity has significant implications for export development. For NECC's close monitoring of progress in export expansion to work, it has to have a well-operationalized target. Such targets have to take account of the supply capacity of the domestic economy (and hence reflect individual firm's targets) and the support required to meet the targets (credit, logistics, land, etc.). This was clearly lacking in Ethiopia. Therefore, simply setting targets (and even imposing sanctions for undershooting) may be necessary, but is insufficient. Targets also need to be closely tied to analytical capability, a key area in which there has been too little development in recent years. These issues are explored further in subsequent chapters.

3.7.2 Institutes: Organizational key to developing industries

MINISTRY OF INDUSTRY AS FOCAL AGENCY

The focal ministry and lead agency in the manufacturing sector is MOI. There are also specialized institutes that oversee and support specific industries (such as leather and leather products, textiles and garments, basic metals and engineering), and agencies with specific mandates (such as privatization, supervision of public enterprises). These are part and parcel of a strategy to develop and improve the institutional interactions between the state and specific sectors and industries (Buur et al. 2012). MOI has been through a string of restructuring exercises almost every five years, after each election. Factors such as the ministry's structure at different periods, the weight of political appointees (in particular, in improving coordination with other federal and regional government institutions), and access to the prime minister have influenced the ministry's effectiveness. MOI has been largely unable to function as the lead agency for industrialization due to its limited mandates and lack of political influence over other institutions. This deficiency was raised on different occasions in NECC, as MOI tended to bring coordination problems and constraints to NECC, rather than itself effectively coordinating.

INSTITUTES AS ARCHETYPES FOR DEVELOPING
SPECIFIC INDUSTRIES

Since 2009, autonomous institutes have been adopted as the main institution to lead and develop key industries. The three institutes established were the Leather Industry Development Institute (LIDI), Textile Industry Development Institute (TIDI), and the Metal Industry Development Institute (MIDI). These institutes were initially used for export-oriented industries, but later also supported import-substitution. They were introduced after many failed attempts to use directorates within the regular bureaucracy. Recently, there have been efforts to expand the 'institute' approach to other sectors. Although belated, the institutes (for leather, textiles, and metal industries) and an agency (for horticulture) have been instrumental in channelling supports to their respective industries and firms. They have also helped by dealing with bureaucratic inertia, organizing the incentive structure, and strengthening government–industry information flows and collective learning. These institutes have been overloaded with administrative and facilitation tasks because of the major bureaucratic obstacles in many government offices, a major constraint facing firms. Company owners and managers argue that public service delivery and facilitating trade and customs are more important than training and technological support. The bureaucratic nightmare in government offices is evidence of leadership failure, as the ultimate responsibility lies with the political leadership. Unless this challenge is addressed satisfactorily, the institutes will not be able to focus on developing the technological capabilities of firms. Moreover, the institutes themselves suffer from a shortage of capable staff and insufficient understanding of industrial policy, the industries, and related issues. They also lack the passion to push the industry policy. A twinning programme has been instituted between sectoral institutes and international organizations, apparently with promising results. However, research collaboration between institutes and universities remains weak. These issues are further explored in the following three chapters.

3.8 Summary and conclusions

Ethiopia has embarked on industrial development after a history of inadequate industrialization from the mid-1950s to the early 1990s, based on ISI that failed to bring rapid growth and structural transformation. In the 1990s, the government focused on postwar recovery, economic and political reforms (including federalism), and the creation of a multiparty polity. The Ethiopian government has certainly engaged in policy experiments and largely maintained its autonomy. This is partly because of the degree of legitimacy it achieved throughout the war and war-to-peace transition. Partly also, it is because of the government's foresight in crafting and using the country's geopolitical significance. Economic growth has been impressive, although structural transformation lags far behind.

This chapter suggests that Ethiopia in recent years has exhibited features of a 'developmental state'. It has also suggested that there is a strong case, based on economic history and structuralist development economics, for such a developmental state, in particular, for an activist focus on industrialization. The proof of the pudding, however, lies in the detailed evidence of policy implementation and performance in manufacturing overall and in particular sectors. Manufacturing to date has played an almost insignificant role in the Ethiopian economy, including employment creation and export earnings. However, there may yet be significant implications from recent manufacturing policies and performance for future directions. This book has been motivated precisely by this history and reasoning and its aim is to observe and analyse in detail the performance of, challenges to, and industrial policy experiments of the activist developmental state. More broadly, the book aims to explore the wider feasibility and rationale for an activist state in applying industrial policy in SSA.

4

Cementing Development? Uneven Development in an Import-Substitution Industry

4.1 Introduction

There has been a dramatic transformation in the use and especially production of cement in Ethiopia over the past hundred years or so. Imported Portland cement was used during the construction of the Ethio-Djibouti railway between 1904 and 1917. The Italians, during the invasion of 1938, built the Diredawa Cement Factory, with a yearly capacity of 30,000 tons. In the mid-1960s, the Ethiopian government built two cement plants at Massawa (in Eritrea) and Addis Ababa, with a combined annual output of 150,000 tons. Two production lines (with an installed capacity of 600,000 tons of clinker per annum) were built at Mugher between 1984 and 1991. All state-owned factories were managed by Mugher Cement Enterprise from the mid-1980s.

After a long period of sluggish development prior to the 1990s, the Ethiopian cement industry recorded impressive growth between 2000 and 2012. Installed capacity in the industry rose from 800,000 tons in 1999 to 10 million tons in 2012 (MOI 2012b; MOI 2013). The average annual growth rate for cement production was more than twice that of Africa or the globe during this period. By the end of 2012, the number of firms had increased from a single SOE to sixteen firms. New firms upgraded their technologies and exploited economies of scale. The cement industry has undergone major changes throughout this period, and it appears that Ethiopia is likely to become one of the top three cement producers in Africa. With the existing growth forecast and 300 kg per capita consumption per annum, domestic demand could reach 36 million tons in 2020. Average global cement consumption per capita was 390 kg in 2012 (MOI 2012b). In sharp contrast to the overall African cement industry, where multinationals dominate, domestically owned firms are the leading players in Ethiopia.

Government industrial policies have shaped the cement industry's development through direct and indirect interventions. Direct support including subsidized long-term investment loans, investment promotion incentives, and access to the mining resources required as inputs. On the demand side, the government's large-scale housing and infrastructure development programmes, combined with the expansion of private sector construction, has led to a building boom since 2005 (MOFED 2012b). This became the prime driver of growth in the cement industry. Nevertheless, the process was also fraught with difficulties. The government did not make timely interventions in the face of new challenges, and lacked a realistic long-term strategy for the industry. Consequently, it failed to prevent and contain cyclical crises in the industry. The country faced critical shortages and was compelled to import cement between 2006 and 2011, while in 2012 firms had excess capacity and surplus production. The industry also suffered from lack of competitiveness and low productivity. Moreover, domestic technological capability remained at a relatively low level.

Different methodological tools—including surveys, interviews, site visits, and document reviews—have been used to provide the evidence and insights and enable further exploration of these issues in this chapter. Where appropriate, the experiences of other countries (such as China, India, and Korea) with established cement industries have been drawn upon. The quantitative and qualitative survey was a quasi-census of all sixteen firms in the cement industry. In addition, qualitative and in-depth interviews with forty individuals in twenty-eight establishments were undertaken. Site visits to twelve cement factories provided additional insights. A review of hundreds of documents was conducted, including primary and secondary sources. In addition, detailed historical and current data from the two major cement factories (which produced 100 per cent of Ethiopian output until 2007) were consulted. Where possible, this chapter uses data updated to mid-2013, thereby enabling a better grasp of ongoing trends within the industry. The International Standard Industrial Classification (ISIC) and US Geological Survey (USGS) definitions have been adopted to allow cross-country comparisons and matching against surveys conducted by the Central Statistics Authority (CSA) of Ethiopia.

The chapter reaches the following conclusions. First, the state provided support to the cement industry in many ways, including massive policy-induced industrial expansion through direct support to the sector, and to the construction industry as a whole. Second, some of these policies were more effective than others and the sector has absorbed a large share of very scarce resources. Some policies were perhaps 'over-designed'—they added little to the main investment stimulus, the rapid expansion of the market. Third, arguably indirect policies, notably government investment in housing and infrastructure, were more effective than some of the direct support. There have been trade-offs (foregoing fiscal revenue to create incentives; facilitating the import of inputs versus supporting the export sector through devaluation) and learning experiences. The tensions/trade-offs are particularly noteworthy: foreign exchange constraints and allocation of scarce resources to promote an important industry, as well as the mixed results of policy.

The following sections analyse the sector's performance, followed by discussion of the emerging industrial structure of Ethiopia's cement industry. Then, linkages and industrial development are addressed. The last section discusses policies and related instruments, institutions, and the policymaking process.

4.2 Sector performance

4.2.1 *Output growth patterns*

Between 2006 and 2010, the Ethiopian cement industry grew on average by 12.4 per cent per annum, which was twice the world's and Africa's average growth of 4.5 per cent (Figure 4.1).There was a more than tenfold increase in annual cement output from the 237,000 tons in 1991–92 to more than 3 million tons in 2010. Growth in output was steady throughout the period, with the exception of a surge in 2000 due to the commissioning of a second factory, which doubled output. Cement output also experienced another surge in 2012, after the commissioning of new factories and expansion projects. Due to spurts in investment and long gestation periods, the cement industry often experiences uneven annual rates of growth.

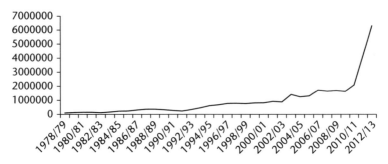

Figure 4.1. Production (in tons), 1978–2013

Source: CSA, Report on Large and Medium Scale Manufacturing and Electricity Industries Survey, 1978/79-2010/11; MUDC July 2013

Table 4.1. Comparison of growth rate and rank

Description	Average annual growth rate		2013 Installed (million tons)	2012 production	
	Growth rate (%)	Years		Actual (tons)	Ranking
International comparison					
World	4.5	2006–2010		3,700	
China	10.7	1998–2010		2,150	1st Globally
African comparison					
Africa: total	4.5	2006–2010		140	
South Africa	1.8	2006–2010		13	1st SSA
Nigeria	14.2	2006–2010	35	5.4	2nd SSA
Ethiopia	12.4	2006–2010	12.2	4.2	3rd SSA
Kenya	10.8	2006–2011		4.1	4th SSA

Source: Own computation from USGS (2010a, 2010b, 2011a, 2011b) and CSA (2012)

As of 2013, installed production capacity in Ethiopia exceeded 10 million tons per year. This improved the country's ranking from the fifteenth largest cement producer in SSA before 2000 to the third behind South Africa and Nigeria. East Africa's cement industry has shown faster growth after 2005 than other African regions. Nigeria and Kenya have similarly witnessed fast growth (Table 4.1). However, Ethiopia's per capita cement consumption (69 kg in 2012) still lags the average per capita consumption of developing countries. In 2012, the per capita consumption of China, Vietnam, India, and Africa was 1,500 kg, 700 kg, 200 kg, and 150 kg respectively. This estimate is based on United Nations Department of Economic and Social Affairs's (UN-DESA) population figures; and exports have not been deducted as they are considered insignificant.

4.2.2 *Employment growth patterns*

As the cement industry is capital intensive, its direct contribution to employment is limited. Personnel in cement factories increased from 1,648 in 1992 to 7,233 in 2012 (Figure 4.2). The average wage in the cement industry is higher by 122 per cent than in the leather and leather goods sector. In 2011, the average monthly wage in the latter industry was ETB 965 for male workers and ETB 864.43 for female. The cement industry's average wage was ETB 1,835. Despite these higher wages, labour costs in cement factories account for 3.5 per cent of total production costs.

On the other hand, the cement sector has generated significant employment through forward linkages to downstream cement product manufacturers (concrete products and ready-mix cement). As part of its drive to create jobs and build capacity in the construction industry, government has promoted small enterprises in the cement products subsector since 2003. The cement and cement products industry together accounted for 10 per cent of total recorded manufacturing employment in 2011, thus highlighting the indirect employment-generation effects of cement production. There are also small unrecorded enterprises producing cement-based products for households, which employ many people. This puts the cement industry in second place after the food and beverage industry and ahead of such labour-intensive sectors as textiles and leather (Table 4.2). It is worth recalling that the employment created in the construction industry has not been included here, as the direction of linkage is primarily backwards from the construction industry to cement, not the reverse. Nonetheless, to the extent that the expansion of a domestic cement

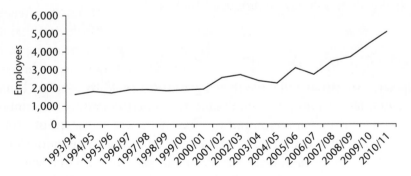

Figure 4.2. Total employees in the cement sector, 1993–2011

Source: CSA, Reports on Surveys on Manufacturing Sector from 1993 to 2011

Table 4.2. Annual growth rate of cement industry, 2006–11 (in per cent)

	2006–07	2007–08	2009–10	2010–11	Average annual growth rate (%)
Total manufacturing	5.2	13	24.7	(1)	4.2
Cement industry	26.6	7	21.1	4.3	14.7
Cement products industry	70	20	(10)	(17)	15.7

Source: CSA Survey on Manufacturing and Electricity (2012)

Table 4.3. Personnel composition and profile in cement and leather/leather goods sectors

Variables or ratios	Cement	Leather	Variance in %
Female: total employees	13.4	46.3	28.9
Professional staff: total employees	8.2	4.3	190.7
Technologists-engineering: professional staff	42	22.2	189.2
Technicians: total employees	16.3	6.5	250.8
Expatriates: total employees	7.9	4.5	175.6
Production: support staff	89:11	77:23	115.6

Source: Oqubay (2012)

industry has been fundamental to the continued expansion of construction in the country, cement may be argued to play an employment-generation role significantly greater than what is captured in direct employment data for the industry and in statistics covering forward-linked enterprises.

The scaling down of regional housing development programmes is a major reason for the slower growth in the cement products industry in 2009–10 and 2010–11. Cement enterprises rely less on female employees (below 15 per cent), and use twice as many higher professional and technologically skilled personnel than more labour-intensive industries such as leather and related products (Table 4.3).

4.2.3 *Capacity utilization and cost efficiency*

Capacity utilization and cost efficiency in the form of the cost per ton of cement offer clear insights into the industry's performance. The former is the achievable maximum output without increasing the unit cost. In the cement industry, capacity utilization is measured either in terms of clinker production, which is directly related to kiln capacity, or of cement production. Cement plant and equipment manufacturers usually specify the maximum attainable capacity of cement factories for benchmarking.

Table 4.4. Capacity utilization in Messebo and Mugher Cement

Year	Mugher (in %)		Messebo (in %)	
	Cement	Clinker	Cement	Clinker
2000–2002	105.26	101.18	33.61	34.80
2003–2005	106.25	101.41	101.74	83.73
2006–2008	92.19	96.09	139.03	109.53
2009–2011	69.01	67.97	101.14	80.85

Source: Own computation based on Messebo and Mugher data (2012)

Moreover, in terms of cost efficiency and productivity, the key determinants are capital productivity and capacity. Due to the capital-intensive nature of the industry, and high fixed costs, labour plays a marginal role in total productivity.

Table 4.4 shows the pattern of capacity utilization. Although Mugher Cement Enterprise (MCE) enjoys a proximity advantage over Messebo Cement Plc (MCP) to the major of Addis Ababa market (90 km vs. 870 km), Messebo exhibited better performance in terms of cost efficiency and capacity utilization. This was because of advantages in plant technology and a more responsive management. Capacity utilization in the first few years following commissioning are usually low. Between 2006 and 2010, capacity utilization increased as market demand rose (Table 4.4). Power shortages are the major factor that reducing achievable capacity utilization. After 2011, with the entry of new firms into the industry and improvement in the electricity supply, excess production capacity in cement was created. The domestic market failed to expand to match increased productive capacity. Six firms were operating below 50 per cent of capacity, four firms at between 60 and 80 per cent, and only four reached 80 per cent capacity. Messebo and Mugher have operated at higher capacity in 2011–12, and between 50 and 60 per cent in 2012–13, and produced/sold 2.15 million tons. This variance in capacity utilization is associated with the excess production capacity of factories. In the survey, the firms identified fierce competition for a limited market as the main reasons for low capacity utilization. The firms also indicated uncertainty and seasonality of demand as their prime concerns.

The second related performance parameter is productive efficiency (cost efficiency), which shows the ability to produce a ton of clinker or cement with the least possible inputs and resources. Energy efficiency can be an

Table 4.5. Energy and cost efficiency (Mugher and Messebo)

Year	Share of energy of the total cost (%)		Energy cost per ton cement (ETB)	
	Mugher	Messebo	Mugher	Messebo
2000–2002	55.80	18.14	171.43	223.22
2003–2005	49.46	33.56	197.50	216.54
2006–2008	60.47	48.61	333.97	322.52
2009–2011	67.95	44.86	692.47	299.81

Source: Mugher and Messebo Data (2012)

important proxy for measuring productive efficiency, since energy is the major cost component in cement production. Energy has increasingly become the most important cost component, given global fuel scarcity and related price increases. The cost per ton of cement should be contrasted with best industrial practices and industrial benchmarks. Energy efficiency in Ethiopia during 2000–11 was much lower than the accepted industrial norm (Table 4.5). Mugher's cost of energy per ton exceeded $50 in 2009–11. Messebo has eventually reduced its cost by a third by shifting to coal. There has been no national energy savings programme, unlike in Asian countries such as Japan, China, and India. According to studies on energy efficiency, energy savings benchmarks can help reduce consumption by up to 15–25 per cent (World Bank 2009a; UNCTAD-UNIDO 2011). Energy accounts for 40 per cent of manufacturing costs in India, and coal accounts for up to half of the energy costs (CSTEP 2012). Until recently, the competitive pressure in Ethiopia was low (low rivalry among domestic firms, weak pressure from imports, and less pressure to export), which has weakened the motivation to improve performance and productivity. The cost efficiency of small firms that use Vertical Shift Kiln (VSK) technology was higher than those using rotary kilns, and unit costs decreased with bigger kiln capacity. In general, factories have cut their energy costs from ETB 240 in 2011 to ETB 180 in 2012.

These characteristics and the trends in the Ethiopian cement industry have policy implications for managing demand, developing technological capability, increasing capacity utilization, and raising energy efficiency. Without investment in energy-efficient technology and raising productivity, the competitiveness of the Ethiopian cement industry may be eroded further.

4.3 Industrial structure of the cement industry

4.3.1 *Global trends*

This section discusses the technical and economic characteristics of the cement industry, its shifting structure, the roles of cement manufacturers, and the implications for the political economy. The industry has undergone structural shifts, particularly since 2008. Because of improvements in process technology, economies of scale have increased: for instance, kiln size doubled in terms of clinker output.

GLOBAL CEMENT INDUSTRY
Global cement production has shown a constant annual growth rate of about 5 per cent from the 1970s. After that date, growth has shifted to emerging economies in Asia, including Japan, Korea, China, and India. In 2011, total global production reached 3.7 billion tons of cement (USGS 2013). There were 2,360 integrated cement factories and 750 independent grinding plants globally. China's share is 1,000 integrated plants and 350 grinding plants (excluding obsolete factories). Currently, Asia is the biggest player, contributing more than 70 per cent of production and consumption (see Table 4.6). The share of emerging economies has increased to about three-quarters of total production. China is the world's biggest cement producer and consumer, with about 60 per cent of world production (USGS 2013).

Given the product's low value–high volume characteristics and the global abundance of the necessary raw materials, cement is usually characterized as a non-tradable commodity. Although shipping and mass transport advances have enhanced its portability and tradability, less than 10 per cent of output was traded globally during the last decade

Table 4.6. Global cement production outlook (2012), in million tons

Country	Amount	Share (%)	Country	Amount	Share (%)
World	3,700	100			
China	2,150	58.1	Iran	65	1.8
India	250	6.8	Turkey	60	1.6
USA	74	2	Russia	60	1.6
Brazil	70	1.9	Japan	52	1.4
Vietnam	65	1.8	Korea (Rep)	49	1.3

Source: USGS (2013)

113

(Selim and Salem 2010; COMTRADE 2012). In 2010, the international trade in cement was 5 per cent, a volume of 151 million tons (67 per cent through seaborne trade). This was 8 per cent less than the 2007 figure. The top five exporters were Turkey (19 million tons), China (17 million tons), Thailand (14 million tons), Japan, and Pakistan (10 million each). The dominant producers and consumers in the global market were multi-national corporations such as La Farge (French), Holcim (Swiss), Heidelberg Cement (German), Italcemento (Italian), CEMEX (Mexican), and CNBM (Chinese), which between them produced about one billion tons of cement in 2012. In terms of technological advancement and equipment manufacturing, West European manufacturers dominated the industry during the twentieth century. Currently, China is the dominant player, accounting for the manufacture of more than 40 per cent of global cement equipment (China Cement Association 2013). This global shift has shaped the technology used in Ethiopian industry. While almost all large cement factories sourced their technology from Europe until 2000, China has over the last decade become the source of such technology in Ethiopia. For instance, Sinoma International and CNBC supplied large-scale cement manufacturers in Ethiopia (Mugher and Dangote, and Messebo and Derba respectively), thereby lowering investment layout and making production relatively cheaper.

Africa's share of global cement production was less than 5 per cent in 2011, and the cement industry was dominated by multinationals (USGS 2010a, 2010b, 2011a, 2011b, World Bank 2009a, 2009b; Wu 2004). In 2011, annual cement production in Africa reached 150 million tons, which were produced in 190 plants in more than thirty countries. Only a quarter of these plants were integrated plants, producing clinker and cement. The biggest producers were the North African countries Egypt, Algeria, Morocco, Tunisia, and Libya, which accounted for more than half of total African production (USGS 2010b). This was not exclusively driven by growing domestic demand, but also partly by stricter environmental regulations in Europe that forced firms to relocate to North Africa (Selim and Salem 2010). Recently, the regional share of East and West Africa has increased, while North Africa's share declined relatively. This stemmed from the political situation in North Africa since 2011, and increased investment in SSA countries such as Nigeria and Ethiopia. Four multi-nationals, La Farge (fifteen factories), Holcim (seven factories), Heidelberg Cement (eleven factories) and Italcemento dominate the African cement industry, with the bulk of their production concentrated in North Africa (Imara 2011). These multinationals produced close to half of African output in 2011. Currently, a new player, Nigerian-owned Dangote Industries, has increased its presence in many African countries, including Ethiopia. The efficiency and productivity of the African cement industry is low compared to the performance of the industry elsewhere (World Bank 2009a, 2009b).

4.3.2 Performance latitude, economic, and technological characteristics

ECONOMIC AND TECHNOLOGICAL CHARACTERISTICS

Given its technological and economic characteristics, three features of cement production are particularly significant in low-income countries like Ethiopia. First, the capital intensity and economies of scale, as well as the strategic significance of cement in a period of rapid growth and structural change in a very low-income economy, created a build-up of pressure that called for active involvement by the state. In particular, the size of the investment required has put considerable pressure on DBE, the country's only investment bank. Second, the nature of production and economies of scale and scope have necessitated the rapid acquisition of effective organizational capabilities. Unlike the family firms that can thrive in leather or floriculture, success in larger cement firms has required salaried managers and professionals with technical skills. Evidence from elsewhere (Chandler 2004; Amsden 1989) suggests that large national enterprises may play a greater role in creating capabilities transferable to other industries. Third, the cement industry has a narrow latitude for failure. Demanding performance standards play a positive role in the implementation of industrial policy. As the evidence reviewed in this chapter shows, however, a narrow latitude for failure does not prevent inefficiencies and mistakes in industrial policy.

ECONOMIES OF SCALE AND SCOPE

The economies of scale and scope differ from industry to industry and are related to the specific production process used by firms (Chandler 2004). According to Drucker (1999), the commonest production processes are the 'unique product production process, mass production (flexible and rigid), and continuous production'. Continuous process (flow) production systems are operated in the cement industry, among others. Techno-logical progress shapes the nature of the production process. For instance, early cement plants were small and used VSK, in contrast to modern cement production using bigger rotary kilns. The cement industry's con-tinuous process depends on the uninterrupted flow of inputs such as energy and raw materials. This places serious demands on electricity providers, fuel logistics, and the organization of inputs and throughput. It also determines the nature of distribution and marketing of goods.

The large-scale nature of the industry acts as a major barrier to entry and exit. With increased scale, unit costs of production diminish. Hence, certainty of market demand is both a prerequisite and an advantage. This is why, particularly in developing countries, the government is better placed to invest in such large-scale undertakings. This is in line with what Hamilton highlights, that 'to produce the desirable changes as early as may be expedient may therefore require the incitement and patronage of government' (Hamilton 1934: 204).

During the different development phases of Ethiopia's cement industry, kiln size has increased and technology (automation, process) has improved, bringing significant increases in factory capacity and capital investment (see Table 4.7).

In the Ethiopian case, the Mugher SOE and a factory in Tigray owned by EFFORT, the regional endowment fund, were the pioneers and first movers in the cement industry. They played the lead role, taking risks,

Table 4.7. Economies of scale and capital intensity in the Ethiopian cement industry

Factories	Period	Technology	Capital investment
1st generation (Massawa, Diredawa, Addis Ababa cement plants)	1960s	Small scale; Rotary kilns: 100 tons per day (TPD); Annual capacity: 30,000–150,000 tons	Below ETB 10 million
2nd generation (Mugher-Line 1 and Line 2)	1980s	Large scale; Rotary kilns: 2 X 1,000 TPD Annual capacity: 850,000 tons	Below ETB 300 million
3rd generation (Messebo)	2000	Large scale; Rotary kilns: 2000 TPD Annual capacity: 850,000 tons	ETB 1,200 million
4th generation (Mugher, Messebo, National, Derba and Dangote)	2010	Large scale; Rotary kilns: 3,000 TPD; 5,000 TPD Annual capacity: 1.4 million tons each; 2.5 million tons each	$120–351 million

Source: Own summary (based on firms' documents and interviews)

and absorbing or facilitating externalities. After seeing the growing demand and generous returns, many private businesses began to invest in the industry. Of course, there were private sector investments in mini-cement plants between 2005 and 2011. Rather than being based on a long-term business development strategy, these investments were made to exploit the excessive rents created by shortages in the domestic market. Despite skyrocketing cement prices, the huge capital requirements of such projects is another factor preventing the private sector from making immediate investment decisions. Thus, the private sector was (understandably) slower to comprehend the full significance of investing in the cement industry in Ethiopia. Consequently, the government and the endowment fund, although themselves rather late starters, played a pioneering role in terms of investing at the appropriate scale.

In terms of economies of scope, large cement factories were forced to integrate their activities vertically. For instance, in distribution and sales, they relied on their own marketing and sales force (except the mini-cement plants) rather than using external wholesale or retail outlets. Likewise, they relied on their own or closely affiliated transport facilities (for instance Messebo and Derba). One of the most critical inputs is packaging, and most enterprises have established their own packaging factories (for instance, Mugher, Messebo, and Derba). In terms of energy inputs, some factories have engaged in coal mining (Messebo, Derba, National Cement, Abyssinia), although this was still at an early stage at the time of this research. Almost all cement manufacturers have their own quarries for mining limestone and related inputs. This shows the significant dynamics in terms of economies of scale and scope.

NARROW LATITUDE FOR POOR PERFORMANCE
The latitude for failure in production depends primarily on the intrinsic technological characteristics of the production process of an industry. Hirschman (1967: 87) emphasizes that the lack of latitude for failure or, positively, 'the presence of discipline', imposes 'propensities and pressures to which the decision makers themselves are subject'. His popular example is the airline industry, where developing countries have the potential to develop successful airlines due to the narrow latitude involved. In this industry, due to safety requirements, the space for operating at a sub-standard level is limited. Safety and other features of cement production have indeed imposed pressures on decision-makers. The

product's perishability exerts additional pressure on production and distribution. The shelf-life of cement is 120–180 days. Moreover, seasonality and uncertainty of demand adds to the pressure exerted by the perishability effect, as the rainy season (June to September) is the slack period for construction in Ethiopia. Demand uncertainty is the basic feature of cement and other similar industries, creating cyclical swings due to the long gestation period. This implies that caution and long-term focus are essential in decision-making.

Consistency of quality is an unconditional requirement for cement manufacturers, because of the safety considerations for buildings and construction works. Ensuring consistent product requires laboratory facilities in large cement factories, and also in mini-cement plants. As cement is used for various purposes and concrete specifications depend on geology, weather, topography, and building codes, constant research into product development is critical to the industry's growth. And environmental protection is also becoming important, as the cement industry is a major polluter.

4.3.3 Changing structure of the industry and political economy dimensions

SHIFTS IN OWNERSHIP STRUCTURE

A major structural shift has occurred in the cement industry in the past two decades. In terms of ownership, the industry has shifted from a state-owned monopoly (Mugher) until 2000 towards private sector domination. Mugher accounted for two-thirds of cement production in 2000, decreasing to a quarter in 2011–12. Another ownership dimension of the Ethiopian cement industry concerns the role of domestic firms. Two local cement manufacturers (Mugher and Messebo) dominated the industry until 2005, accounting for about 95 per cent of the country's cement production. This ownership structure appears to be the outcome of deliberate industrial policy. The fact that Mugher survived the privatization programme was due to the government's decision to maintain a presence in the industry. Likewise, Messebo was one of the first of EFFORT's investments.

Two interesting developments in the domestic private sector were the emergence of National Cement from the old, small, privatized firm, Diredawa Cement, which was acquired by East African Business Group

(EABG); and the establishment of Habesha Cement, promoted by former managers of the Mugher SOE. In 2002, EABG negotiated for and bought a small, abandoned state-owned cement mill in Diredawa (built by the Italians in 1938) and upgraded the plant into a 150,000-ton capacity facility. EABG then commissioned a study on a large-scale cement factory with a capacity of 1.4 million tons. The factory was in the commissioning stage in mid-2013. The owner of EABG is Ethiopian, a third generation industrialist who has built an industrial zone and a food processing complex. Neither Habesha's promoters nor EABG had political ties to the state or ruling party. Habesha initiated the project, mobilized equity from more than 16,000 shareholders (the highest number of shareholders in large-scale manufacturing), attracted two South African partners, and secured loans from DBE. This is a striking example of entrepreneurial dynamism in the private sector.

Likewise, other domestic businesses entered into joint venture arrangements. Ture Business group (which had imported Chinese equipment for more than thirty years) entered into a joint venture with two Chinese private manufacturers. The joint venture established a cement-grinding factory in Addis Ababa and two small cement plants in Diredawa. Currently, domestically owned firms continue to account for about half of total installed capacity in the industry. This contrasts starkly with the situation elsewhere in Africa, where multinational corporations (MNCs) dominate (Global Cement 2012). The foreign firms operating in Ethiopia are not traditional multinationals. Among foreign investors in the cement industry, the Chinese are dominant, with seven firms, followed by Indians. A Saudi tycoon owns the biggest plant, Derba Cement, which is part of the largest conglomerate in Ethiopia, Midroc Group, which is owned by Sheik Mohamed Al Amoudi, an Ethiopian by birth. Another major investor is Dangote, whose plant was still under construction when this research was carried out. Foreign-owned firms together account for the other half of installed capacity in Ethiopia's cement industry.

CHANGING COMPETITIVE STRUCTURE
Competition was virtually nonexistent when the two state-owned cement manufacturers dominated the cement industry. Mugher Cement had a full monopoly until 2000, when Messebo Cement began operations in northern Ethiopia. The Messebo plant was built between 1998 and 2000, and has a capacity of 850,000 tons of Pozolana Portland Cement (PPC).

Mugher had an advantage in terms of proximity to the main market around Addis Ababa, and the first mover advantage in acquiring skills, but also a steeper learning curve. After 2005, mini-cement plants sprung up, but their market share has never exceeded 10 per cent, and they have had an insignificant influence in shaping the cement industry.

After 2011, there was a shift to an oligopolistic market structure. A key milestone was the increased production due to new entrants and expansion at two factories. Derba Cement (the largest firm so far in the industry, with installed production capacity of 2.5 million tons), East Cement (with installed capacity of 700,000 tons), and expansion projects of Mugher and Messebo (additional capacity of 2.8 million tons) became operational more or less simultaneously in 2011. The market will become more competitive as projects under construction come on stream in 2015. In addition to sales promotions, transport and credit facilities are increasingly being offered to customers by cement manufacturers (Nazret 2010) to win market share.

INTERPLAY OF INDUSTRIAL STRUCTURE AND
GOVERNMENT POLICY

Against this backdrop, it is important to examine the political dimension of this changing competitive structure. Porter's generic analytical framework is moderately useful in addressing features of industrial structure, policy, and performance as they change over time. However, a word of caution is needed: his framework tends to undermine the pivotal role of the state, resulting in a deceptive separation of market and state and a restricted focus (Aktouf 2004, 2005).

According to Porter (2008: 80), 'industry structure grows out of a set of economic and technical characteristics that determine the strength of each competitive force'. The five underlying forces that determine the evolving industrial structure are the: threat of new entrants; bargaining power of buyers; threat of substitute products; bargaining power of suppliers; and domestic rivalry among existing competitors (see Table 4.8). Porter adds that the relative pressure of each factor and their relationship are context-specific: they vary by industry and across time. Likewise, an industry's development may involve a shift driven from inside the industry or from outside. More importantly, government policies affect each of these five forces. In view of this framework, it is noteworthy to assess the underlying changes in Ethiopia's cement industry and the effects of government policy.

Table 4.8. Interplay of shifting industrial structure and government policy

Five competitive forces	Policy intervention	Shifts and outcomes
Threat of new entrants:	Cement industry has high entry and exit barriers due to economies of scale and high capital requirements. The government policy included: a) Long-term loans made available for capital investment; b) Providing investment incentives to mitigate risks and induce new players; c) Mining resources close to the market made available to firms; d) Foreign currency allocated on preferential basis; e) Government involvement directly through SOE and quasi-public enterprises; f) FDI barred since the end of 2013; opportunity for loans for new entrants narrowed.	a) High entry barrier was overcome; Number of players increased to sixteen, primarily FDI and domestic private sector; b) Significant increase in total production capacity; c) Technology and equipment modernized, with increased kiln capacity; d) The gate for newcomers has now been closed as FDI participation is restricted and finance is temporarily unavailable. e) Mugher continued to be an active industrial player with 20 per cent market share (currently has an installed capacity of 2.3 million tons); f) The privatization of Diredawa cement factory induced new private investment of 1.4 million tons.
Bargaining power of buyers	a) Government was the biggest buyer (above 50 per cent or two-thirds share between 2005 and 2013); b) Shortage (2006–2011) and buyers bargaining position was weak. Hence, high price and delay; c) Import of cement during shortages; d) Regulation of market during shortages (allocation, price, etc.)	a) Construction boom acted as key driver of the cement industry until 2011; b) Demand failed to cope with the supply and excess capacity; c) Buyer's bargaining position increased; cement price decreased and availability improved; d) Seasonality, market uncertainty, product perishability push the industry to improve e) Government's action to stimulate demand (domestic and export) required;
Threat of substitute products	Alternative inputs (steel etc.) not extensively available; a) Government introduced the use of agro stone (substitute) in government projects, with modest success.	a) Insignificant impact in reducing demand; b) Limited scope for substituting concrete in the long-term.
Bargaining power of suppliers	Transport and energy are key supplies. Government: a) supplies heavy-fuel oil, coal, pet coke, and electricity to all firms; b) Transport cost increased and shortage increased firms' margins. Government imported 1,200 trucks for cement transport, and allowed firms to own transport fleet;	a) Supply of inputs at subsidized rate;[1] b) Affected by the firms' technological choices (kiln types and capacity, distance from sources);[2] c) Transportation cost affected by distance from main market and fleet availability; d) Backward and forward integration opportunities are observed.

(continued)

Table 4.8. *Continued*

Five competitive forces	Policy intervention	Shifts and outcomes
	c) Packaging materials: major factories own packaging factory.[3]	
Rivalry among existing competitors	a) Competitive edge of firms differed. No scope for specialization; b) Price competition driven primarily by price as product is homogenous.	Derba followed aggressive price war; Mugher was still in 'sleep mode'; Messebo aggressively worked on efficiency improvement (production process and energy use) and transport optimization. National cement has focused on markets in neighbouring countries, reducing its investment cost, and selling clinker to mini-cement plants. Mini-cement plants were surviving by focusing on market niches.

Notes: [1] Mugher, Messebo, and Derba have their own packing factory and sell packaging material to others. Messebo uses the permanent transport fleet of a sister company. Derba has imported 700 heavy trucks. National Cement was importing trucks. Currently, there is a shortage of freight transporters and often reliability is a problem. This, and the existence of incentives (duty-free import of vehicles for own transport service), have influenced the decision by cement factories to operate their own transport fleets.

[2] HFO and coal are imported by government, and the administrative costs are absorbed. Private petroleum distributors barely add to their profit margins. Although official data are not available, the subsidy is estimated to exceed 10 per cent.

[3] In terms of kiln type, rotary kilns consume less energy than VSKs; bigger capacity kilns consume less energy than smaller kilns; factories with coal conversion technology benefited by using coal (cheaper than HFO) to power the kiln. Thus, the supply has a varied effect on firms, depending on their technology choices and scale of production.

Source: Own summary (based on collected data and analysis)

It is possible to observe from this matrix that these patterns have significant implications for industry, cement manufacturers, and government policy. First, in an increasingly diversified sector, government leverage and ability to guide the industry has not decreased substantially. Such means as guiding Mugher and influencing other firms (such as Messebo, National Cement, and Derba), procuring cement from foreign markets, supplying inputs, and becoming the single major buyer have been used. Although new institutional mechanisms (such as the role of the industrial association) will evolve, the presence of domestic firms (which have good working relations with government) will allow government to lead the sector.

Second, the new competitive environment could be used by government to improve the sector's long-term competitiveness regionally and internationally, by directing it towards exports through incentives, restrictions, and enforcement, and through support schemes that focus on improving productivity and quality. Clearly, also, stimulation of the domestic market requires definite government intervention. Current low capacity utilization and the resultant risk of bankruptcy have significant implications for financial health of DBE, an indispensable component of industrial policy in Ethiopia.

Third, the cement industry is a classic oligopoly, where a few firms dominate (Chandler 2004). This can be measured by weighing the 'four-firm' concentration ratio by measuring the market share of the four largest firms. In 2012, the concentration ratio was 75 per cent, meaning that the 'big four' (Derba 2.5 million tons, Messebo 2.3 million tons, Mugher 2.3 million tons, East Cement 700,000 tons) had installed capacity to supply three-quarters of the market. Total installed capacity of the overall cement industry was 10 million tons (excluding National Cement and Ethio-Cement, which were not operational). This domination could lead to restrictive trade practices through collusion, market-sharing arrangements, raising prices, or curtailing production. Experiences elsewhere provide extensive examples of such practices. The US cement industry (1930 and beyond), the Indian cement industry, Pakistan, and South Africa are some examples. Conditions that lead to anti-competitive behaviour and, to an extent, cartel formation, are high market concentration, excess capacity, high entry and exit barriers, a collusive history in the industry, and the role of the industrial association. Most of these factors appear to fit the Ethiopian cement industry well. Thus, new industrial policies are now required to prevent undesirable oligopolistic outcomes in the industry. With the 'right competition policies' and government guidance, the oligopolistic market could be turned to more efficient ends, including lower prices, better quality, and higher productivity. For instance, in 2011, the per-ton cement price in China and Vietnam, both low-cost producers, was $53 and $62 respectively. Brazil and the US were medium-cost producers ($91–$92), while SSA countries were high-cost producers (Nigeria $223, Angola $250, Ethiopia $175 for Ordinary Portland Cement [OPC]). Mugher's price per ton was ETB 2,900 (dollar exchange rate was ETB 16.5).

4.4 Cement-construction infrastructure linkages

4.4.1 Construction–cement linkage

This sub-section highlights the powerful linkages and feedback loops between construction and the cement industry in Ethiopia. The Ethiopian construction industry grew by about 13 per cent per annum between 2004 and 2011, exceeding the annual GDP growth rate of nearly 11 per cent. Its share of the economy expanded from 4.2 per cent in 2000 to 5.8 per cent in 2011. The building sub-sector has multiple socioeconomic impacts. First, it employs hundreds of thousands of unskilled and skilled workers, thereby helping reduce urban unemployment (World Bank 2009c). According to a CSA survey on construction in 2008–09, there were 1,384 construction firms (Grade 1–6), which employed 252,977 people at peak times and 171,965 during the slack season. In addition, the producers of construction materials employed 86,279 persons. This figure may be much higher since not all smaller firms are registered. According to MOFED (2012a), the Integrated Housing Development Programme (IHDP) and urban road construction programme employed 193,000 and 373,800 workers respectively in 2011. Second, it supports and accelerates industrialization through cheaper and timely construction of factories. Third, it contributes to the economical expansion of social infrastructure. Fourth, it stimulates the manufacture of building materials. Fifth, it contributes to wealth creation, housing and property development, and promotes savings and the development of the financial sector. The construction industry can also play a significant role in generating foreign exchange.

4.4.2 Policy learning through housing development programme

The government-sponsored IHDP demonstrates construction sector/ cement industry dynamics rather well. This programme is part of broader urban development and is designed to redress the housing shortage, which is also a hot political issue for most residents, particularly in Addis Ababa. In the capital, there was an estimated backlog of 450,000 houses in 2005 (AACG 2003), which has increased since because of population growth and rural-to-urban migration (UN HABITAT 2010). The mounting demand for houses necessitated the massive construction of public housing through IHDP.

The United Nations Human Settlement Program (UN HABITAT 2010) concludes that the programme is unique in being 'large-scale and pro-poor; an integrated approach to housing, slum prevention and economic development'; as well as in creating 'access to home ownership'. The report added that 'the IHDP is not just a housing programme, but a wealth generation programme through low-cost housing... In light of Ethiopia's uncoordinated and inefficient housing sector, the Integrated Housing Development Programme has provided a highly successful tool for affordable housing delivery at large scale.' The IHDP has gone through three phases: pioneering the programme in Addis Ababa, scaling up, and a subsequent scaling down. After successful completion of the pilot project, IHDP went on to construct more than 30,000 houses in Addis Ababa in the first year. An autonomous agency staffed with a committed and qualified management team was established. The technical assistance of an international agency (German Technical Cooperation, GTZ-IS) was sought for the pilot project, and the city government paid for its services. Discussions with the public were conducted and 453,000 applicants registered for the programme. The programme's popularity and experience gained during the first phase in Addis Ababa prompted the government to replicate it in other regional towns. IHDP's cement consumption exceeded half a million tons per year, amounting to more than a quarter of production capacity in the country.

The second phase included the scaling up of the housing programme at national level. The programme was one of the key priorities in the PASDEP five-year national development plan, which called for the building of up to 900,000 houses through both IHDP and private sector initiatives. Regional institutions were established in four states and in selected towns. The Ministry of Works and Urban Development (MWUD) spearheaded the programme.

Other government-sponsored building projects included the construction of thirty-two public universities, more than 1,000 health centres, and housing projects for new sugar projects. Financial resources and foreign exchange were earmarked for IHDP. Through it, more than 150,000 houses were built in sixty-five towns. The cement requirement reached one million tons per annum, accounting for about half the country's production capacity. IHDP, together with other public infrastructure programmes and private real estate investments, created excess domestic demand for cement. Cement imports thus became necessary (see Table 4.9). In 2011–12, the national programme was scaled back. Meanwhile, high housing demand in Addis Ababa continues. Potential homeowners interested in public housing have reached one million (947,376 registered in 2013 out of which 42 per cent are female). The housing programme involves several contribution schemes, whereby beneficiaries can contribute 10, 20, or 40 per cent to reflect and encourage saving.

Table 4.9. Cement imports 2006–11 (in tons)

Importer	2006	2007	2008	2009	2010/11	Total
Private	306,829	694,362	839,242	–	–	1,840,433
Government	–	11,000	335,147	821,547	650,000	1,817,694
Total	306,829	705,362	1,174,389	821,547	650,000	3,658,127

Source: MOI (2012b) and MWUD (2010, 2013) (Unpublished)

LINKAGE EFFECTS TO BUILDING MATERIALS MANUFACTURE

The construction boom has boosted the local manufacture of building materials. Consequently, the first glass factory, ten steel factories (mainly rebar manufacturers), and fifteen cement factories were built between 2004 and 2012. In the meantime, the construction industry suffered until domestic cement manufacturers could catch up with growing demand. Capacity constraints delayed projects by more than a year and construction costs increased by about 15 per cent (MWUD 2013). The government used various instruments to tackle cement shortages and regulate the market (price controls, cement allocations, import permits, and direct imports by government). The government also intensified quality controls to curb the sale of sub-standard cement, which had become a serious concern. It also increased transportation capacity. Although the effects were limited until local cement production matched demand in 2012, these measures did enable partial containment of price hikes created by the cement shortage.

4.4.3 Capacity building and modernization of the construction industry

A deliberate decision was taken to use public construction programmes to enhance domestic construction capacity. The housing development programme is typical of how government develops the capacity of domestic contractors, consultants, and small enterprises. The shortage of building contractors was a critical bottleneck in the housing programme. Modular, standardized, and economical housing designs, and the innovative application of a sub-contracting model fuelled participation by small and medium contractors. Government eased the entry barrier by revising the contractors' licensing requirements to encourage participation by new and young professionals. It also supported new construction firms with government-financed training packages, collateral-free loans, and direct access to government building contracts. As a result, the number of contractors increased fivefold to more than 2,500. The number of contracting firms with owners with engineering backgrounds also increased, improving the technical capacities of the firms (MWUD 2009).

Likewise, the housing programme promoted the development of domestic architectural and engineering firms. New architects and engineers were registered as consultants, thereby allowing consulting firms to undertake design, contract administration, and supervision. The increase in contractors and consultants has intensified competition, changing the landscape of the construction industry. About 3,000 items of construction and transport machinery were also imported under a government-sponsored and subsidized programme to develop contractor and transport capacity. This included some 1,200 heavy-duty vehicles, 1,000 tippers, 500 wheel-loaders, and more than 150 other pieces of machinery. The investment required a loan facility of ETB 3 billion. Government arranged collateral-free loans, with a debt ratio of up to 70 per cent. It took a lead in carefully preparing specifications and making bulk purchases, thereby saving half the investment cost (MWUD 2010). As this package was designed and implemented with the participation of construction firms, it helped to boost industry capacity. According to one firm, government intervention in procurement has increased its annual savings by up to ETB 30 million. Another advantage associated with these programmes was the University Capacity Building Programme (UCBP), which was fully financed by the government with technical support from GTZ. Local contractors, consultants, project managers, and small enterprises were supported through the construction of thirteen universities. The development of standardized, modular, and economical housing technology also improved cost efficiency in the construction sector. According to UN HABITAT (2010: vii), 'the programme has also built the capacity of the construction sector, addressed . . . existing slums and . . . been a significant generator of employment.'

From a policymaking perspective, a different kind of 'narrow political margin for failure', especially after the 2005 elections, shaped policy design and influenced the effectiveness of implementation. The ruling party won the 2005 national election but lost Addis Ababa. In 2007, it was able to win the local election in Addis. These elections revealed the fragility of the government's political base and policies in urban areas

(Simon 2011; EPRDF 2013c). It was a milestone for the ruling party, prompting it to come up with comprehensive urban economic, social, and governance packages (MWUD 2007). Youth frustration at the lack of employment was critical, making the housing programme and the development of micro/small enterprises central to urban development programmes. Government interventions to develop the construction industry and improve cement transportation were both policy- and politics-induced. These linkages were not fostered sooner, since the direct effect of the transportation bottleneck was not felt. Transport shortages were a critical obstacle to the politically important housing programme. This underscored the linkage dynamics and compelled federal and regional government agencies to act collectively to improve coordination. Private sector collaboration and participation was also key to the success of the programme (in construction, building material manufacturing, and transportation). In a way, this demonstrates a propensity for 'anti-fragility' (Taleb 2012) in Ethiopian policymaking, that is, the ability to resolve conflicts and policy contradictions, sometimes pre-empting them before a crisis emerges. This anti-fragility had significant effects in developing the cement industry.

4.4.4 *Infrastructure development: energy and transport*

Infrastructure development is a key determinant of manufacturing sector growth. In particular, the large-scale cement industry depends on the growth of infrastructure. Cement manufacturers unanimously agree on this. The cement industry in turn contributes to infrastructure growth through added demand for improved services (to address shortages of power, disruptions, and quality issues); and by manufacturing industrial goods used in construction. Energy supply and bulk transport services are the most critical inputs for the cement industry. In fact, the cement industry and power sector interlock.

The Ethiopian government has invested massively in the development of roads. For instance, in 2013 the federal government allocated 27 per cent of its budget to roads. In addition, in 2010 Ethiopia began construction of an extensive electrified railway network covering more than 5,000 km. This network has eight corridors, including corridors to Djibouti, Kenya, Sudan, and South Sudan. The project costs more than $15 billion, with China, India, Turkey, and Brazil (in process) providing part of the financing.

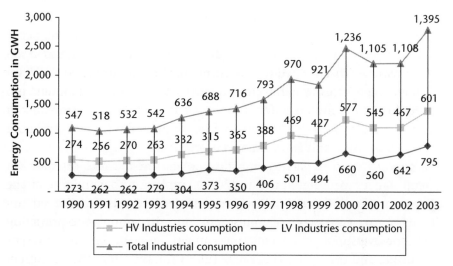

Figure 4.3. Growth of industrial energy consumption (in Ethiopian Calendar)
Source: EEPCO 2012

In addition to inputs such as coal, heavy fuel oil (HFO), and pet coke, the uninterrupted supply of electricity is a necessary condition for cement manufacture. In Ethiopia, electricity generation increased from 370 MW in 1992 to more than 2,179 MW in 2011 (Figure 4.3). With the completion of fourteen ongoing projects, generation capacity will increase nearly fivefold to 10,000 MW (EEPCO 2012). Ethiopia's electricity tariffs are cheaper than those in many African countries, including Mauritius (by 35 per cent), Kenya (37 per cent), and Uganda (66 per cent). Ethiopia also has huge hydropower capacity, one of the cheapest and cleanest sources of energy. This power could be exported to neighbouring countries, contributing to regional economic integration.

4.4.5 Summary

The observations above on the development of linkages underscore a number of points on the role of policy. First, incentives seem to have had an effect on investment, particularly duty-free importation, tax holidays, repatriation of generated profits in foreign exchange, and provision of land and quarries, etc. It is highly unlikely investments would have been forthcoming without these incentives. Yet they were not sufficient on their own. Market demand had also to expand to trigger investment in the cement industry. Government incentives—or 'intermediate assets'—were also costly. For instance, significant long-term industrial financing had to be provided because of the gigantic scale of the new projects in the cement sector. This drained the government's limited capital (and foreign exchange) resources, which were also needed to support other industries. It should also be emphasized that the use of a public development bank to support industrial policy is rare in SSA, though such banks are more common in Asian and Latin American countries.

Second, there is an art to adjusting policies in the face of changing circumstances. Amsden and Chu (2003) emphasize that the role of the state changes as industrial policies are upgraded to meet changing requirements during each stage of industrialization. In light of the prevailing domestic oversupply of cement, government has abandoned investment incentives and even prohibited new FDI in the industry. The incentives may have outlasted their usefulness through time. However, prohibiting investment in the industry altogether has been overhasty. Such decisions might be justifiable if all the relevant information was available. The potential effect of this rash decision is compounded when we consider that cement exports were not given serious consideration. Structuralist perspectives highlight the strategic importance of exports to growth and economic transformation: exporting is the only 'true component' that comes from outside the economic system, where demand is therefore autonomous and can cover required imports, such as capital goods crucial to growth (Thirlwall 2002). Moreover, the current state of the industry seems to bring larger issues to the forefront. On one hand, a strong interest group emerged as a result of the promotion of the cement industry, and the industry's strategic importance in the growth of the construction sector and indirect employment creation increased. On the other, there is a question about the strategic primacy of the sector, given its limited contribution to foreign exchange earnings and dependence on imported machinery. Will the power of the interest group or simple policy inertia prevent flexibility or adjustments in the selection of strategic priorities? It is clear that powerful foreign industrial interests have moved into Ethiopian cement, and it may be difficult to resist their control, given international cartels, economies of scale, and technological advantages. The critical question is whether this matters at this stage. What is the thinking on this? What are the institutional mechanisms? The government still has

Mugher and Messebo to guide the industry, and its role as a major consumer of cement gives it some advantages in influencing the industry. Yet, the industry clearly requires new policies and institutions.

This sector shows that in an age of privatization, the Ethiopian government has not simply held on to some SOEs but actively sought to use them as key tools in industrial strategy. Governments play a central role by developing innovative institutions that overcome market barriers and mobilize and concentrate capital investment. The main role of institutions in latecomer states is as 'functional substitutes' to mobilize resources and to deploy them to capital-intensive projects. Reflecting this developmental approach is the government's decision not to privatize but expand Mugher Cement between 2006 and 2011 with an investment outlay of $150 million, thereby tripling the company's capacity to 2.3 million tons and ensuring it a 20 per cent market share in Ethiopia. Moreover, the Council of Ministers has agreed to restructure Mugher into a much bigger conglomerate, the Ethiopian Chemical Corporation, which would produce building materials, fertilizers, and chemical products. Messebo Cement was EFFORT's first industrial project and EFFORT has also expanded Messebo's capacity to 2.3 million tons. This strategy is fully in line with government policy, and its investment focused on the northern region of Tigray. Again, this affirms government's interest in maintaining its presence and playing a direct role in the industry.

Moreover, fundamental to the growth of the cement industry was the growth of the construction industry. The latter, in turn, was shaped by government policy. Current demand constraints could put the industry in a precarious position. Broader policies that stimulate domestic demand through the expansion of construction and (more modest) promotion of exports, are necessary for the sustained growth of the cement industry. Policies that foster productivity improvements in line with global benchmarks are also critical. In addition, we are witnessing the growing importance of large corporations, which are playing a role as national champions in the development of the industry. The Ethiopian manufacturing sector is dominated by small and medium enterprises, and historically large corporations have played an insignificant role. In view of increased economic globalization, economies of scale, and the 'global business revolution' (Nolan 2003, 2012), developing countries (including Ethiopia) also need larger corporate entities.

4.5 Industrial policy in the cement industry

This section reviews government policies and policy instruments in the industry more broadly, and focuses on direct instruments. There is no evidence to suggest selective targeting prior to 2002. Nevertheless, the cement industry was positioned as a priority in the IDSE of 2002 (FDRE 2002) and the PASDEP and GTP five-year plans. According to the latter: 'This result [the gap between actual production of 1.7 million tons and the PASDEP target of 4.7 million tons] suggests the need to increase the production and supply capacity of cement in order to meet the needs of the fast growing construction industry' (MOFED 2012b).

4.5.1 Investment promotion and incentives

The investment promotion policy in the cement industry involves FDI and domestic actors, incentives, and access to mining resources. Since the first investment proclamation of 1992, the sector has been open to foreign investors. However, it was only after domestic consumption expanded to create excess demand that FDI entered the sector. The incentives to investors included a tax holiday on profits of up to three years, and a loss carry-forward benefit. Investors could import equipment and machinery and up to 15 per cent of spare parts duty-free. Moreover, expatriates were exempted from income tax for two years. In September 2012, a new law was passed reserving investment in cement production to domestic investors. It also reduced the investment incentives, in particular the profit-tax holiday. In general, this move reflects the diminishing relevance of investment incentives to the cement industry.

Third, government facilitated access to factory land and quarries for limestone, gypsum, clay, and pumice, among others. Factory land was made available at giveaway prices (between ETB 10 and 25 per square metre, depending on location) on long-term lease arrangements. In most cases, the price of land barely exceeded the cost of compensation to the relocated farmers. The quarries were also available nearby (mostly within a radius of 25 km), in particular for clay and limestone, which account for 80 per cent of inputs. The federal Ministry of Mines (MOM) provides exploration and mining licences to foreign investors, while domestic investors get them from regional mining agencies. A total of twenty-seven mining licences and thirty-eight exploration licences were given (at a very low rate) during this period (MOM 2012). Government royalties per cubic metre of limestone, clay, gypsum, and pumice are ETB 4.29, ETB 4.01, ETB 7.50, and ETB 12.48 respectively (Mugher 2013). The major input into OPC is limestone and pumice.

Fourth, the government is the sole provider of electricity, and this energy-intensive industry has enjoyed tariffs that are among the lowest in SSA and other developing countries. The tariff was $0.043 per kilowatt hour (KWH) in 2008, compared to $0.02–0.46 in SSA, and $0.05–0.1 in other developing countries (UNCTAD-UNIDO 2011; Mugher 2013; EEPCO 2012). The recent tariff is $0.039 per KWH, and Ethiopia entirely relies on renewable energy, in particular hydropower.

Investment promotion has attracted more than 100 investors into the sector, especially after 2003 (Table 4.10). Only 2 per cent of the investment was registered before 2002, while the investment flow became significant after the construction boom and cement shortage became evident. By July 2012, the number of investors involved in actual implementation and operational phases exceeded twenty. Twelve of these were mini-cement plants (with less than half a million tons annual production capacity and using VSK), while the remainder were medium and large cement factories.

The incentives have eased the financial burden on investors and improved their profitability by reducing investment costs. This was a significant advantage, since cement factories have to operate at reduced capacity for the first few years of production. Nonetheless, expansion of the domestic market was the prime reason for investing in the sector. In addition to political stability, the growth of the domestic cement market was the most important factor in the increased investment after 2002. Prior to that date, the domestic market was weak and investment in the industry was low. By 2012, according to the CEO of Pretoria Portland,

Table 4.10. Summary of investment certificates for cement industry

Period	Cement manufacture		Cement products manufacture		Total	
	Firms	%	Firms	%	Firms	%
1992–2002 (ten years)	2	2	40	22	42	11
2003–2012 (ten years)	101	98	239	78	340	89
1992–2012	103	100	279	100	382	100

Source: Own computation from unpublished FIA data, August 2012

South Africa's major cement manufacturer, 'the country's current investment plans, combined with one of the fastest growing cement demands in Africa, makes us extremely confident about the sustainability and growth of this investment.'[1]

It is difficult to weigh the value of the substantial resources committed by government, in a context of extreme macroeconomic constraint and the relatively high opportunity cost of subsidizing this industry, vis-à-vis the effect of the stimulus. Cement production would probably have expanded, perhaps at a slower rate, without such intervention, and with the foreign-dominated ownership common to low-income countries. The government's policy represents a classic, centralized use of rent to encourage the strategic development of a sector, but at the risk of rent dissipation among mini-plants, eventual oversupply, drain on foreign exchange, etc.

Another issue relates to the GTP, which targeted tenfold growth in five years. This proved to be grossly unrealistic, and was not founded on a careful market study by government. In 2012, new and existing cement factories faced market problems, and they had to operate below one-third of capacity. Government decided to halt new investment and to suspend or slow projects that were at an early stage. Questions arise as to whether this was necessary in the absence of full knowledge of the cement market, and such a decision should be based on a longer term perspective. It is also noteworthy that implementation of the investment policies was relatively easy, and required no complex administrative capacity.

4.5.2 Industrial financing of cement industry

Cement requires large investment outlays and long-term financing. The government has used three, apparently successful, financing instruments to support the industry. The major mechanism was long-term DBE loans, and when necessary, co-financing through CBE. In addition, government used industrial development financing for Mugher Cement, and foreign equity and debt financing for foreign investors.

---

[1] <http://www.cemnet.com/News/story/150263/south-africa-s-ppc-invests-in-ethiopian-cement-firm.html>.

DBE INVESTMENT FINANCING

The main source of long-term financing was DBE. It provided fifteen-year loans at a subsidized interest rate (about 5 per cent), and financed up to 70 per cent of the investment requirement without collateral. In terms of allocation, cement was a top priority (DBE 2009, 2012a). A quarter of loans for manufacturing were directed to the cement industry (Table 4.11). Moreover, half of the six largest borrowers and a third of loans exceeding the single-borrower limit were in cement. DBE has so far financed Messebo, Derba, National Cement, and Habesha, which have a total capacity of 7.5 million tons. CBE has participated in co-financing, providing working capital and an international banking service (opening letter of credit). It has also acted as a channel for Exim Bank of China loans to Mugher Cement. The major constraints were the difficulty borrowers had in mobilizing their equity satisfactorily, the single-borrower limit, and the banks' capacity to mobilize sufficient resources.

INDUSTRIAL DEVELOPMENT FUND AND FOREIGN EQUITY FINANCING

The Industrial Development Fund (IDF) was designed to finance SOE expansion, and to be replenished from the profits of public enterprises. All public enterprises can retain a maximum of 15 per cent of corporate incomes. Mugher Cement Enterprise has benefited from this scheme, receiving ETB 700 million. Some foreign-owned investments have

Table 4.11. Industrial sub-sector loans above 1 per cent of total portfolio (in ETB)

Manufacturing sub-sectors	No. of loans	Total portfolio including comm. bal.	Total portfolio excluding comm. bal.	% share from total loan portfolio with comm. bal.
Textile industry	32	4,994,845,112	3,618,933,985	29.56
Non-metallic manufacture: Cement	16	3,816,033,665	3,261,478,706	22.59
Chemicals and chemical product industry	22	668,583,821	530,628,318	3.96
Leather and leather products industry	21	465,425,456	412,883,257	2.75
Food industry	214	458,803,339	431,980,303	2.72
Beverage industry	7	410,370,887	381,208,559	2.43
Total	312	10,814,062,280	8,637,113,128	64.01

Note: Commitment balance means loans approved but not disbursed fully or partly. Such balance is always there for projects under implementation.

Source: DBE (2012b), loan portfolio concentration report, 31 December 2011

accessed foreign loans that occasionally need government clearance or consent. The International Finance Corporation (IFC), African Development Bank (AfDB), and European Investment Bank (EIB) participated in financing Derba Cement. The China-African Development Fund (CADF), Exim Bank of China, and the South African Industrial Development Cooperation (IDC) were additional participants.

FOREIGN EXCHANGE

The major devaluation in June 2010 of the ETB had a negative effect on cement production. This was due to its coincidence with project implementation, and the heavy dependence on imported heavy machinery. The cost increase amounted to some 20–25 per cent. Firms state that it disrupted their cash flows, increased investment costs, and forced renegotiation of loans. This is a typical dilemma in industrial policy, where governments choose a specific policy critical to the survival and growth of one industry, but which has the opposite effect on another.

4.5.3 Mixed results in skills development

Clearly, government has played a central role in the development of this sector as a major buyer and direct industrial player. It helped kick-start the industry. It helped stabilize the market-stabilizing role. What has been less remarked upon is the fact that the cement SOEs helped accelerate growth by generating positive external economies in terms of expertise, experience, knowledge, and skill. New cement projects used the expertise of ex-SOE staff during project implementation and to operate. As the CEO of Pretoria Portland remarked of Habesha: 'I have been impressed with the professionalism of Habesha management and their advisors. They have significant experience in the cement industry and we have already built great relationships.' SOEs also assisted by way of training, laboratory testing, etc. for newly established factories.

However, there have been serious missed opportunities in technological and skills development. In many developing countries, the cement industry is considered an intermediate or heavy industry, with large economies of scale and capital intensity, and requiring professional management. Project design, implementation, and operation are complex, requiring investment capabilities. A number of countries have used this industry as a springboard for late industrialization and to develop their technological capabilities. Korea is one such, with Hyundai in particular reckoned a success. Hyundai not only successfully pioneered the local cement industry, but also used exports for developing technological capabilities in the 1960s. Chung Ju-yung, founder and, until his death in 2001, chairman, established the first cement plants in the early 1960s, before diversifying into the motor industry (late 1960s), heavy industry (including the biggest shipbuilding yard, at Ulsan), electronics, aerospace, defence, steel, etc. The investment capability developed during the construction of the cement factories was transferred to construction works and to building cement projects on a turnkey basis (Amsden 1989; Studwell 2013).

In China, after the late 1980s the growth of the cement industry was integrated into a strategy to increase asset concentration and economies of scale. More importantly, China developed the capacity to design cement plants and manufacture equipment, and enhanced its capacity to build cement factories on a turnkey basis and to undertake innovative research in the cement industry. The two largest Chinese technology and machinery suppliers are CNBC and Sinoma International. They have increased economical kiln capacity to 10,000 tons per day (the biggest size currently). All the major new cement factories in Ethiopia are being built by Chinese manufacturers including Derba Cement, Messebo Cement, Mugher Cement, National Cement, and Dangote. The growing domestic market, coupled with appropriate policy, enabled China to become the powerhouse of the global cement industry. In Ethiopia, the government arguably missed an opportunity to use the growing domestic market to develop the country's technological capability, although there were pioneering examples from which government and industry could have drawn positive lessons (see below).

DEVELOPMENT OF INVESTMENT CAPABILITIES

One case that demonstrates the role of the government in the development of technological capabilities is investment capability. According to Amsden (2001), technological capability requires production capability, investment capability, and innovation capability. Investment capability involves personal training, pre-investment feasibility studies, project management, project engineering, procurement, embodiment in physical capital, and operational start-up. Investment capability is critical to reducing project costs and time and to meeting project aims. It can also improve a firm's future competitiveness and productivity. Such capacity enables future projects to be effectively managed, and enhances the country's domestic capacity to implement major projects.

Both Korea and Japan used various policy instruments to develop technological capabilities, such as local content requirements, guidance in selection of technology, prohibiting turnkey projects, giving preference to the breaking down of technologies, equipment, and activities. In Ethiopia, development of technological capabilities was not pursued. First, there was no local content requirement to encourage local manufacturing. As the major financier of the cement projects, the government had the influence to insist on this requirement.

Second, almost all major projects (Derba, Messebo, and Mugher) adopted a turnkey approach, and were unable to develop their investment capabilities. The incentives and instruments were not designed to promote learning (technological capabilities) and learning rents were not made available. National Cement adopted a non-turnkey approach. The owner established his own project office and hired a foreign consulting firm. He sub-contracted the civil and electro-mechanical work to a Chinese contractor and procured equipment from China. He claims to have saved a quarter of the investment cost by this means. He is also involved in developing a coal mine with other partners: this is at an early stage. In a different context, Messebo built its first factory without adopting a turnkey model, and completed construction within twenty-four months (1998–2000). It also used a local industrial equipment manufacturer to manufacture some machinery locally, which also reduced costs (for instance, transportation). A local consulting firm (in a joint venture with an Indian firm) also supervised the project. During the second-phase expansion of Messebo (2008–11), which used a turnkey model, project execution took about thirty months, thereby showing that the turnkey mode does not necessarily guarantee success. Project promoters of many mini-cement plants also built the factories themselves without adopting the turnkey approach. Where they did use that approach, they did so primarily to avoid delays and minimize risks (see Table 4.12). This vividly illustrates how the lack of appropriate policy and institutions to promote technological capabilities leads to failure in developing a critical industry. Knowledge acquired and experiences gained even through isolated initiatives were lost (for example, a local equipment manufacturer, MIE, which developed some experience in manufacturing cement-making equipment in 1998–99 did not sustain its first initiative).

Table 4.12. Turnkey model choice

Response	Frequency	Per cent
To minimize risk	3	23.1
To optimized project investment	2	15.4
To avoid delay	4	30.8
Lack of experience in cement industry	3	23.1
To make easy project management	1	7.7
Total	13	100

Note: Some responses are tallied more than once.
Source: Oqubay (2012)

Third, government failed to guide the selection of technology, and firms did not benefit from collective action, which would have been more favourable to government. Because of this, project execution took longer, with increased costs; and domestic project-execution capacity did not develop. One example of the failure to guide technology selection is the missed opportunity to introduce coal conversion technology, which is related to the introduction of coal as a source of fuel. Even the state-owned Mugher firm failed to incorporate this technology during its expansion. Contrary to the neoclassical assertion that technology is a freely available shelf item, in developing or late-industrializing countries, technological supply is plagued by profound constraints. It typically takes state interventions to circumvent these constraints. Such interventions include developing technological infrastructure, skill formation, and promoting in-firm technological capabilities (Lall 2003; Amsden 2001; Rodrik 2011). Choice of kiln capacity could have been improved with collective action and state guidance. Similarly, government guidance would have helped mini-cement plants improve technology imports. Instead, they imported inefficient, poor-quality equipment, which frequently broke down. Downtime was high and plants operated at less than a third of capacity. Joint support in technology selection could also have promoted an association of mini-cement plant investors.

Government's failure in this respect lies primarily in the lack of long-term perspective on the cement industry and of a clear institutional and policy framework for building technological capability. There was no comprehensive plan focused on the long-range development of the industry, other than the general five-year plan. The latter was mainly concerned with increasing output, not technological development or improving the industry's productivity and competiveness. This also relates to the lack of emphasis on technological guidance. The presence of a strong agency to lead the sector and of an industrial association might have helped.

4.6 Industrial policymaking: Policy instruments and institutions

It is hoped that the wide-ranging aspects of policymaking raised in preceding sections provide a comprehensive perspective on the political economy of the Ethiopian cement industry. Additional issues, in particular institutions and industrial policy, policy responses to energy use, and industry regulations are examined in this section. Discussion of these issues may provide additional insights into policymaking.

4.6.1 *Institutions and industrial policy in cement industry*

In several ways, bureaucratic constraints and coordination difficulties have weakened policy effectiveness.

INTERMEDIARY INSTITUTIONS
There was and is no association of cement manufacturers. Dialogue between government and manufacturers was not institutionally supported, and infrequent and informal consultations were the norm. This is puzzling, given the role of industrial associations in many countries. Seemingly, however, this did not significantly constrain the growth of the sector for many reasons. First, the SOE had a monopoly until 2000, and until 2005 there were only two firms, both closely affiliated with government. Therefore, they enjoyed direct and indirect access to policymakers and government agencies. It also seems government tolerated the firms, and collected rent on their monopolistic position. This policy was driven by the government's interest in expanding the sector and minimizing DBE's risk (cement manufacturers had to repay loans acquired before 2000 and new loans for expansion). The companies' profit margins exceeded 20 per cent throughout the period. The large size and influence of the major players (private and public) seems to have facilitated their direct access to policymakers and government agencies after 2005.

COORDINATING AND SUPPORT INSTITUTIONS

Multiple institutions are involved in implementing industrial policy in this sector, such as DBE, MOI (through FIA and the Chemical Directorate), MWUD, MOM, and MOFED. In addition, service providers, in particular the Ethiopian Electricity Power Coroporation (EEPCO), played a key role in the sector's development. The Ethiopian Petroleum Corporation (EPC) also played a role as the sole provider of HFO throughout this period, and in 2012, of coal imports. Moreover, influenced by experience in the export sector, in 2011 a high-level National Committee for Import Substitution, Construction, and Employment Creation (NCISEC) was established. Chaired by the late prime minister, its members included MOI and Ministry of Construction and Urban Development (MUDC, MWUD's successor), among others. The committee took important decisions in relation to the cement industry, such as making the use of coal compulsory. In contrast to the NECC, it was, however, far from successful. Apparently, there is insufficient clarity on the body's role and agenda. Some of the topics related to export activity fall under NECC, while others fall under infrastructure development (another committee). The decision was made in late 2012 to incorporate import-substitution industries (cement and steel, pharmaceuticals, food processing, and beverages) into the NECC agenda. This will allow for better coordination and a clearer focus on the manufacturing sector.

The Chemical Directorate of the Ministry of Industry serves this sector as well as pharmaceutical and other chemical projects, and has a staff of sixteen junior professionals. This team lacked the skills and knowledge to support the cement industry. This has mattered in particular in market/demand analysis and forecasts, as well as in project implementation, including the introduction of coal conversion. Recently, government, recognizing the institutional gap, has established a new institute for the building materials, manufacturing, and chemical industries.

Firms indicate that dealing with government offices was a major hindrance, although with fewer implications than for sectors where smaller firms dominate (Table 4.13). Despite this, most firms maintain that horizontal coordination among federal agencies was better than vertical coordination among federal, regional, and local administrations. The small number of players in the industry, the size of the firms, and the established contacts with government were probably important. In addition, cement plants require less service from the public administration

Table 4.13. Management time spent in handling government-related issues

Management time (%)	Number of firms	Per cent
≤15	5	31.25
16–30	6	37.50
>30	5	31.25
Total	16	100.00

Source: Oqubay (2012)

than export-oriented sectors, which require customs clearance, import and export permits, tax refunds, etc.

4.6.2 Policy response in energy provision and energy efficiency

For the energy-intense cement industry, energy is a strategic issue. A key issue for the industry is energy utilization and the efficient burning of raw materials. This is the single biggest cost to cement factories. It also has a significant effect on foreign currency savings. Thus, the cement industry is dependent on the continuous flow of energy, which affects the quality and cost of the products. The sector cannot expand where the energy infrastructure is inadequate or the power supply unreliable. Despite the government's commitment to invest in energy infrastructure, the energy supply continues to be a binding constraint on the cement industry. Globally, cement factories use coal as the major fuel source. For instance, in the US, coal's share is 67 per cent, followed by 14 per cent for pet coke and 1 per cent for HFO. Energy costs amount to only 25–30 per cent in developed countries, but are as high as 50 per cent in developing countries. Ethiopia's industrial energy intensity (measured by ton of oil equivalent per $1,000 of MVA) rose by 65 per cent between 1990 and 2008 (from 1.989 in 1990 to 3.275 in 2008). Vietnam, China, and Pakistan reduced their energy costs by 17, 65, and 28 per cent respectively in 2008 (Vietnam 0.928, China 0.791, and Pakistan 0.953).

Energy costs include the cost of electricity and of burning materials. In terms of electricity, 94 per cent of firms surveyed confirmed they were adversely affected by power interruptions. About three-quarters of firms stated that power shortages had significantly affected them, particularly during plant construction. Moreover, 90 per cent of firms emphasized that the electricity supply had a delaying effect on the commissioning of cement plants. Lost production days due to power shortages and

Table 4.14. Lost revenue due to power shortages (Mugher Cement Factory)

Year	Lost production days	Lost production and revenue	
		In tons	In ETB
1998	9	20,160	9,160,704
1999	7	15,680	7,124,992
2000	27	60,480	30,149,280
2001	1	1,859	986,943
2002	8	17,920	10,571,008
2003	13	29,120	17,177,888
2004	1	2,016	1,383,379
2005	0.3	717	492,005
2006	0.3	650	663,910
2007	0.3	605	617,947
2008	45	100,800	156,240,000
2009	119	266,963	517,240,812
2010	42	93,542	190,591,825
2011	97	217,280	638,803,200
2012	5	11,021	23,695,150
Total	375	838,813	1,604,899,043

Note: Lost revenue is based on ex-factory. 2012 involves only nine months.
Source: Mugher Cement Enterprise records (2012). Figures are rounded.

disruptions range from 60 to 400 working days. Table 4.14 shows that revenues lost by a cement SOE to power shortages were significant.

The National Committee on Import Substitution, Construction, and Employment Creation decided that cement factories must shift to pet coke and gradually to coal. The decision focused on the use of imported coal and an ultimate shift to domestic coal. This policy was driven by foreign currency savings rather than full appreciation of linkage dynamics. A comprehensive policy package could have led to the development of a strong coal mining industry. Before this policy decision was made, a study was conducted by experts from EPC, which was to import coal and pet coke (replacing the HFO imports), MOM, MOI, and cement firms. This effort by government to make a study and engage stakeholders was positive, but it also shows that policymaking was ad hoc. But which agency is responsible for energy provision and efficiency and can champion them? Most survey respondents agree that energy is the biggest component of their costs and support coal conversion. However, they are concerned the change was initiated without sufficient preparation.

Factories that had bought new plants prior to this decision (including the SOE), were not advised to procure coal conversion technology. This lack of guidance suggests either government shortsightedness or complacency in directing technological capabilities during procurement and project implementation, especially as thermal energy is the norm in most cement-producing countries.

This lack of planning and agency could be one reason the coal conversion policy has faced impediments during implementation. Despite favourable attitudes, only a few firms readily adopted the technology. Thus, although government imported coal for cement firms, half of them needed extra finance and time (12–18 months) to equip their factories with the conversion technology. Mugher's higher energy costs are related to older plants and the use of HFO rather than coal. When this survey was conducted, anthracite was not being imported for mini-cement plants.

In sum, the government's commitment and plan to develop the electricity sector was an important strategic response that facilitated growth and expansion in the cement industry. It is impossible to imagine this growth without development of the energy sector. In addition, with political commitment and the right policies, it should have led to successful backward linkages to the local coal industry. It should be noted that in this case industrial policymaking failed by not inducing new activities and industries. The initiative to introduce coal use was not taken by the lead agency or MOI, but by some of the individuals involved. Even then, government did not pick up the issue, or persistently pursue its implementation.

4.6.3 Coping with market challenges: Shortages and excess capacity

The cement industry has faced recurrent vicissitudes over the last two decades. The market was more or less stable until 2004. However, both market and government were caught by surprise when critical shortages of cement occurred in 2005, which lasted until 2010. Again, both market and government appeared ill-prepared when the industry suddenly experienced excess supply and productive capacity in 2011. The policy responses are documented below. Four instruments were used: price control, product allocation, import licences, and direct imports by government.

PRICE CONTROL

Price control was enforced to stabilize the price of cement. For instance, the SOE had to get government approval for any price increases during the period 1992–2005. After 2005, MoTI introduced a price control mechanism for Messebo and Mugher factories during the period of shortage. More than twenty price increments were approved between 2005 and 2010. The price control did not focus on the small cement plants, whose market share was only 10 per cent. Price controls helped to contain costs on government projects, but did nurture rent-seeking in various forms. Cement traders exploited the shortages and benefited through speculation. Various administrative measures were taken, but had limited results. The two cement factories used every loophole to gain an unfair advantage from these practices. One cement factory sold in retail outlets at a higher price through its sister company. Cement was also resold at higher prices, resulting in two parallel markets. Various forms of leakage were widely reported (MWUD 2009). Price control was lifted in 2011, when production exceeded demand.

PRODUCT ALLOCATION

Allocation of cement products was prioritized: the first priority was the housing development programme; second were the infrastructure programmes; and third private sector firms, in particular major manufacturers. Allocation was also necessary to optimize transport costs: allocations were based on proximity. MWUD, which coordinated all housing and building projects (2006–10), made allocation decisions. Allocations gave rise to contention and controversy, as supply and demand never matched. While this policy helped direct critical input to priority public and private construction projects, it prompted rent-seeking activities too. For example, some contractors and businesses that received priority allocations resold the cement at higher prices (MWUD 2009). This is one of the commonest rent seeking practices, whereby people collect rent from their permits without paying a penny,[2] and is a good example of the economic behaviour identified in Kornai's (1980) work on shortage economies (see also Lindbeck 2007).

---

[2] In Amharic, የስሚንቶ የአየር በአየር ንግድ

IMPORT PERMITS

When demand outstripped domestic production, the government decided to import cement for the first time. The cement industry had always been protected by an import ban rather than an import tariff. Government first gave an import licence to a single corporation, which seemed to have the institutional capacity, finance, and foreign exchange and had close ties with the ruling party. To the embarrassment of the government, this initiative ended in fiasco when the corporation failed to import on time. Then, under a new directive, import licences were issued to those engaged in trade and construction on a *franco-valuta* basis.[3] *Franco-valuta* can have an indirect impact on the foreign currency market. In the face of increased black market activity, a normal process of opening a letter of credit replaced the *franco-valuta* arrangement. Even this stratagem proved ineffective, given the difficulty of controlling the importers' source of foreign exchange, and was abandoned.

DIRECT IMPORTS

The government, persuaded by increased requests for import licences, finally made the political decision to directly import cement through MWUD. Sufficient foreign currency was allocated on a priority basis. MWUD set up a logistics project office to implement this scheme. Later, the project office became an important mechanism for capacity building among transporters and construction firms. All the government agencies involved, including MOFED, MoTI, the Ethiopian Revenue and Customs Authority (ERCA), Ethiopian Standards and Quality Authority (ESQA), Ethiopian Shipping Lines (ESL), and CBE enhanced their coordination efforts under the ministry. Contact with the international cement trade following the decision to import was an eye-opener for government and the domestic construction industry. Sourcing cement from Pakistan proved the best procurement strategy. For instance, the Karachi free on board (FOB) price of Pakistani cement was $53 per ton, and landed cost at Djibouti $80 in 2010. The cement price in Ethiopia had surpassed ETB 3,000 ($200 based on 2010 exchange rates), although this figure had dropped to $100–120 in 2013. This price disparity between imported and domestic cement does raise questions about the decision to back

---

[3] *Franco-valuta* means using one's own foreign exchange to import cement, as opposed to the ordinary practice of using official foreign currency.

this sector, given the large volume of scarce resources allocated to it. But the dynamics are more important and complex, and the price is gradually dropping. For the first time, government was also able to gain experience in handling and shipping a perishable commodity. The coal-use norm in Pakistan appears to add to the pressure on government to adopt this technique. Imports were allocated primarily to government projects, and were sold through the government wholesale agency, MEWIT. The agency was not known for its high performance, but played its designated role thanks to close supervision by MWUD. The transport shortage was solved by importing more than 1,200 heavy trucks, which were allocated to transport operators under an open bid system.

In 2011, government and cement manufacturers were again taken by surprise by the excess capacity, accentuated by the fact that all major factories commenced production at the same time. Government was not prepared to give guidance through export promotion or by stimulating the domestic market. Its immediate response was to ban new investments, suspend investment loans, and slow ongoing projects in the early stages of construction. The decision was an immediate reaction based on nervousness, rather than on comprehensive understanding of market conditions. This experience shows that industrial policy in Ethiopia is a work in progress. What has been unique in Ethiopia is the willingness of government to change course when things go wrong without having to incur additional transaction costs.

4.7 Conclusions

This chapter has shown, first, that the cement industry has responded to rapid growth in the construction industry. Despite some mismatches with demand, the Ethiopian cement industry has now grown such that Ethiopia has become the third largest cement producer in SSA. This is mainly attributable to public policy (incentives, credit, housing and infrastructure development, etc.). The tensions/trade-offs are noteworthy, in particular between foreign exchange constraints and the allocation of scarce resources to promote an important industry, as well as the mixed results of policy.

Second, shifts in the industrial structure are marked by an ownership pattern that is dominated by domestic public and quasi-public enterprises, and is different from the patterns in other SSA countries. Domestic firms still play an important part, although the role of FDI has increased. This pattern is partly the result of deliberate policy choice.

Third, the incentives yielded different outcomes, some more effective than others. Incentives alone are not sufficient, but when the key factor—demand—reached or exceeded a certain level, the incentives triggered investment in cement to such an extent that the government had to abandon them. Indirect policies in housing and infrastructure development played crucial roles in the expansion of domestic demand and, consequently, the cement industry.

Fourth, there have been no deliberate, comprehensive policies to develop the technological capabilities of the industry and individual firms. Such efforts as there were, were fragmented, short-lived, and ineffective. Moreover, the failure of policies to enhance domestic competition and expose firms to exporting appears to have contributed to the low competitiveness and productivity of the Ethiopian cement industry.

Nonetheless, the cement industry has performed as a binding agent, albeit flawed, of economic development and transformation in multiple ways. The evidence suggests that the industry has been a partial *transformational* player in economic development. This industry has the potential to positively influence the development of heavy industry. The organizational capabilities of emerging large corporations have the potential to make them national champions. Government policies were the key drivers of the transformation of the cement industry, and its expansion was not based on factor endowments.

The research has clarified how very mixed the cement industry's experience has been: it has been hugely important, experienced some notable successes, and signalled the importance of the state. It has demonstrated synergies among industrial and other public policies, the interplay between economic and political factors, the dynamics of policymaking, and the significance of the narrow latitude for poor performance. While the success of government policies is evident, there have also been failures, and hence fragility, which have slowed sustained growth. Adaptability and learning were inherent, once again showing the anti-fragility of Ethiopian policymaking.

5

Beyond Bloom and Bust? Development and Challenges in Floriculture

5.1 Introduction and overview

Floriculture tells a story similar to that of the cement industry, but adds to it in ways that help reveal both the achievements and reasons for the unevenness of industrial policy outcomes in Ethiopia. The economic success of this sector has attracted international interest and debate (*The Economist*, 7 February 2008 and 8 April 2009; Reuters, 2 March 2009; Mano and Aya 2011; Gebreeyesus and Iizuka 2010; Rodrik 2008b). Floriculture resembles manufacturing more than traditional agriculture (UNCTAD-UNIDO 2011). It emerged in 2004 and has since shown sustained growth. Virtually the entire output of the sector in Ethiopia is destined for export markets, markets characterized by intense international competition. Europe is the major outlet, with the Netherlands the main hub and destination. Flowers imported into the European Union (EU) must meet technical requirements, including MPS (environmental sustainability certification for floriculture) and Global GAP, which focuses on good agricultural practices. Product variety, quality, consistency, and vase time are important considerations. Floriculture production is mainly clustered around Addis Ababa because of better infrastructure and logistics. FDI has played a key role in this sector, facilitating the spread of technological know-how and penetration into international markets.

Since 2004, floriculture has generated close to $1billion in export earnings, making Ethiopia a major global player in the sector (EHDA 2012a; UNCTAD-UNIDO 2011). Moreover, it has created direct employment for about 40,000 people, higher than the combined employment in the cement and leather sectors. It has also been a springboard into new exportable goods such as vegetables, fruits, and herbs, thereby creating more jobs and export revenues (EHDA 2011a, 2011c, 2012a). The government is working to make more land available for expansion beyond the existing 1,500 ha.

Many agree that Ethiopian floriculture has indeed been successful, although the explanations for this success diverge. One widely shared explanation has been 'comparative advantage', which emphasizes natural endowments as the key determinant, rather than policies or the role of the state (Lin 2009; Dinh et al. 2012; Singh 2011). Although endowments are important, this line of reasoning fails to explain why a strong sector did not emerge earlier in Ethiopia, or in neighbouring African countries with similar endowments. It also fails to explain why the Netherlands, a high-income industrial country, continues to be the industry's leader despite its lack of cheap labour and natural endowments.

Another explanation associates the success with the 'discovery process' and private sector activism (Rodrik 2004). Although collective learning may have played a major role, there is no convincing reason to assume that this was the sole or prime factor. Moreover, the collective learning and activism was mutual, involving state and private sector agents, rather than unilateral. For instance, the establishment of the industrial association, which has played an active role in the development of this sector, was partly initiated and facilitated by government. The government's readiness to make bold policy decisions and political commitments to develop this sector was equally important. Thus, the discovery process theory does not fully capture the actual development of Ethiopia's floriculture industry.

Patrimonialism has also been advanced to explain the sector's growth. In essence, growth flows from clientelism nurtured by the ruling party/government. This study shows, however, that not a single firm was owned by government or party officials, and investment opportunities were open to all interested parties regardless of politics or networks. Another less prevalent explanation emphasizes the role of the 'Dutch trio actors'. This narrative suggests, tacitly, that the success of the sector in Ethiopia is entirely due to the role played by three external actors, namely Dutch FDI; Dutch market structures, in particular the flower auction centres; and Dutch development cooperation (Melese and Helmsing 2010). This may partly be true, but the argument fails to recognize that these factors are not unique to Ethiopia. Implicitly, this view disregards internal dynamics as the key drivers of industrialization and exaggerates the role of external forces in African economic development.

Contrary to these arguments, an alternative explanation credits much of the success to state activism and industrial policy. For instance, UNCTAD and UNIDO, in their 2011 report on African industrial development, state that 'there are also cases in Africa where industrial policy has led to success in either developing new export products or adding value to existing products. For instance, in Ethiopia, state activism played a critical role in the successful development of the cut flower industry' (UNCTAD-UNIDO 2011: 63). This view rejects the absolute determinism of factor endowment and is associated with the structuralist tradition and the political economy perspective, which emphasize the state's role in economic development. It also recognizes that political processes, interests, and constraints determine the choice and outcome of economic policies.

To examine these arguments and provide a more nuanced explanation, this chapter presents a detailed analysis of the floriculture industry in Ethiopia and offers a more comprehensive explanation of the drivers of its growth. The chapter argues that government policy was critical to nurturing and expanding floriculture. The rise of this new industry can be better understood by exploring the interplay between policymaking and institutions, and the dynamics of industrial structure and interest groups. Analytically, the chapter draws especially on Hirschman's concept of linkage effects. As a subsidiary approach, Rodrik's view of industrial policy as a discovery process is adopted. The booming floriculture sector is a classic demonstration of how unemployed labour, underutilized local entrepreneurial potential, and natural endowments can be mobilized for economic development.

Given natural endowments such as favourable altitude, water supplies, and temperatures; and fertile soils, cheap labour, and proximity to Europe (relative to Kenya, Tanzania, and Zambia), comparative advantage has certainly been important. But static comparative advantage is only one element in the rapid expansion of the sector. The evidence presented in this chapter suggests it may not even have been the dominant factor. Rather other factors, notably an activist state applying an industrial policy to the sector, have been at least equally important.

A number of insights can be derived. First, the government's commitment to developing this sector was evident in the concerted use of policy instruments that were exceptionally clear and coherent. This phenomenon is sometimes loosely referred to as 'political will', but the chapter concludes with a better understanding of this commitment. It also demonstrates how a politically well-designed and implemented industrial policy can lead to the development of a new industry that would otherwise have been unlikely to emerge under a laissez-faire regime. Second, the collective learning of the state and industry was also impressive, showing that the industry 'picked the state' while the state 'picked the firms'. Learning was not without problems, but in the floriculture sector, the benefits outweighed the costs. Third, this process was aided by investors with the necessary technology and international market connections, thereby easing the learning process. Fourth, this sector benefited from the narrow latitude for poor performance as defined by the technological nature of the production process. Export discipline was crucial to survival as there is very little domestic demand for flowers. This situation served to catalyse the evolution of performance standards and policy interventions. Fifth, the policies that helped initiate a successful take-off became inadequate to the challenges of the industry as it grew, thereby necessitating appropriate new policies.

This chapter's main theme is the causes and drivers of this growth (the 'why'), which also includes the growth and realization of linkage potential, and what this reveals about policy effectiveness. The study was chiefly based on qualitative research, whose design was linked to a preliminary quantitative survey of sixty-two of the sixty-nine firms in the sector. Semi-structured and in-depth qualitative interviews were then conducted with thirty participants, including firm owners and managers and heads of government agencies. Site visits were made to flower farms, packaging factories, and the airfreight terminal. Document reviews were carried out, covering the Ethiopian Horticulture Development Agency (EHDA), the lead agency of the sector, and the NECC, the national spearhead in the export sector. Content analysis and decision tracing were used in these reviews.

5.2 High growth in floriculture

The most important indicators of growth in the floriculture sector are its export performance, employment patterns, and productivity trends. In particular, the sector's significance for Ethiopia lies in its easing of balance of payments constraints, and its potential to create job opportunities for a large, unskilled and semi-skilled labour force in conditions of widespread unemployment in rural and small towns. Where data are available, performance is compared to performance in other countries and other sectors.

5.2.1 Rapid export growth

The floriculture industry continues to be almost exclusively export oriented, and the export trade determines the survival and growth of the sector and is the key indicator of the sector's international competiveness. Export performance is presented in terms of growth, diversification, and volatility.

EXPORT GROWTH

Floriculture was almost nonexistent in Ethiopia before 2004. Immediately after its establishment, exports grew rapidly (Figure 5.1). Cut flower exports increased from three tons in 2003–04 to more than 50,000 tons in 2011–12, with export earnings rising from $0.32 million to about $200 million. The average annual growth rate was an astronomical 400 per cent, which was unmatched in the country's history. For instance, the annual average growth of the overall exports sector in the same period was 22.6 per cent, and earnings from manufactured exports were less than 16 per cent. The horticultural sector is broadly divided into floriculture

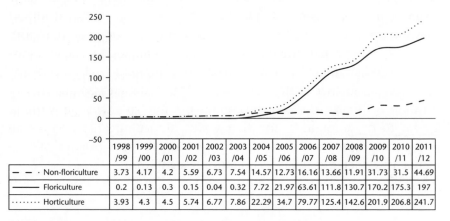

	1998 /99	1999 /00	2000 /01	2001 /02	2002 /03	2003 /04	2004 /05	2005 /06	2006 /07	2007 /08	2008 /09	2009 /10	2010 /11	2011 /12
— — · Non-floriculture	3.73	4.17	4.2	5.59	6.73	7.54	14.57	12.73	16.16	13.66	11.91	31.73	31.5	44.69
——— Floriculture	0.2	0.13	0.3	0.15	0.04	0.32	7.72	21.97	63.61	111.8	130.7	170.2	175.3	197
········· Horticulture	3.93	4.3	4.5	5.74	6.77	7.86	22.29	34.7	79.77	125.4	142.6	201.9	206.8	241.7

Figure 5.1. Export value of floriculture and horticulture, 1999–2012 (in $ million)
Source: Unpublished data from ERCA Planning Department, October 2012

Table 5.1. Floriculture exports, 2004–12 (value, volume, growth rate)

Year	In value ($ millions)		Volume (millions kg)		Comparators: growth rate of value (%)		
	Amount	Growth rate (%)	Amount	Growth rate (%)	All Exports	Manufactured	Vegetable/ fruit
2004	0.32	700.00	0.03	169.76	21.16	(8.95)	12.14
2005	7.72	2,312.50	2.73	10,265.28	10.41	4.56	93.17
2006	21.97	184.59	6.23	128.94	40.09	41.26	(12.68)
2007	63.61	189.53	13.60	117.72	14.64	(0.60)	26.98
2008	111.76	75.70	22.40	64.71	28.52	23.82	(15.48)
2009	130.70	16.95	29.17	30.20	(1.18)	(27.85)	(12.81)
2010	170.20	30.22	35.96	23.28	38.03	(8.59)	166.38
2011	175.28	2.98	41.56	15.58	37.40	97.16	(0.72)
2012	196.97	12.37	46.79	12.60	14.77	20.35	(41.91)
Average annual growth rate (%)		392		1,203	22.65	15.68	33.21

Source: ERCA Planning Department, October 2012

and food horticulture, comprising vegetables, herbs, and fruit. During this period, the growth of non-floriculture horticultural exports was less than 33 per cent. Within the horticultural sector, floriculture dominates, with an 83 per cent share of total horticultural export earnings.

Within a decade, cut flowers became one of the top five export products, accounting for more than 6 per cent of merchandise export earnings. Between 2004 and 2012, the industry has earned close to $1 billion (Table 5.1). Sometimes it is argued that its contribution to net foreign exchange earnings was minimal, as the industry consumes huge amounts of foreign exchange. This is a valid statement, but account needs to be taken of the contingent role played by the sector in increased import substitution through the local production of inputs, and in air transport. The latter exceeds half the total cost, as flowers are high-value and low-volume products that rely heavily on efficient airfreight services. With the increased dominance of the state-owned EAL, and increased import substitution of inputs, the concerns about net foreign exchange earnings appear to be unfounded. In other words, floriculture has become an increasingly important contributor to Ethiopia's tight balance of payments. It is, therefore, macroeconomically significant.

EXPORT DIVERSIFICATION

Export diversification is an important feature of sustainable growth and structural change, especially if it is dominated by high-value goods, such as manufactured goods and modern agricultural products. In terms of export diversification, the share of floriculture in export earnings increased from mere 0.05 per cent in 2004 to more than 6.2 per cent in 2011, making it the fifth largest source of foreign exchange. The share of vegetables, fruit, and herbs was constant during this period. Ethiopia's mono-crop dependence on coffee exports has decreased as a result, declining from 60 per cent in 1998 to 26 per cent in 2011.

DESTINATION AND PRICE PATTERNS

Europe absorbs more than 94 per cent of Ethiopia's floriculture exports, distantly followed by the Middle East (2.5 per cent of exports), and Asia/US (2 per cent). The main export destinations are the Netherlands, which accounts for 85 per cent of floriculture export earnings, and Germany, 5 per cent. The price patterns were robust compared to the volatile export prices for other primary commodities. For instance, the price of coffee has always been volatile and decreased by 31 per cent in 2012–13. In terms of floriculture's export earnings in 2013, the biggest six players were Sher-Ethiopia, AQ Roses, Red Fox Ethiopia, Herburg Roses, Ziway Roses, and Linssen Roses, which combined had a 58 per cent share of export earnings.

In sum, floriculture has shown strong growth and had a significant impact on export diversification. It should also be noted that the rate of growth slowed in 2011 and 2012. The cause was neither low demand nor competition from other countries. On the contrary, the global market is favourable, most existing farms are seeking to expand, and new growers are looking to invest. The key challenges will be examined later.

5.2.2 Substantial employment generation

Employment generation is another important indicator of policy outcomes. First, the floriculture industry is labour-intensive and dependent on specific skills. Second, employment creation is one of the central aims of the industrial development strategy as well as the floriculture sector. In view of high youth unemployment in urban centres and high population growth, the job creation agenda has increased in prominence. Ethiopia is the second most populous country in Africa (85 million in 2012, and population growth of 2.6 per cent), and more than 2 million people are added annually (CSA 2011).

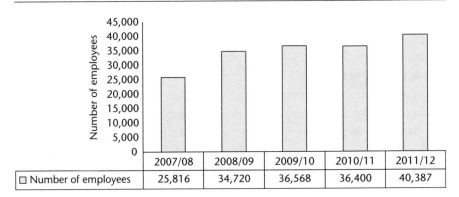

Figure 5.2. Number of employees in floriculture, 2007–12
Source: DLV, Quantitative Unified Information, and EHDA 2012a

In 2007, employment in floriculture stood at about 25,000, rising to 40,000 in 2011, an increase of more than 55 per cent (Figure 5.2). According to EHDA, employment in the flower industry grew to 50,484 in 2012 (EHDA, 2012b). This trend becomes even more significant when both the direct and indirect employment created is considered. Floriculture also generated indirect jobs through the associated expansion of horticulture. Overall, the horticulture sector employed 183,804 people in 2012 (EHDA 2012a), mostly (133,320) in non-floriculture horticulture. In general, the employment contribution of this sector, which deploys twenty persons per ha. is impressive compared to other agricultural activities (traditional smallholder farms or mechanized commercial farms) and the overall manufacturing sector, which currently employs less than 175,000 people. The leather and leather industry and the cement industry together employ fewer than 30,000 workers.

SOCIAL DIMENSION
The above employment creation shows the sector's strong contribution to poverty-reduction. This is consistent with findings by Cramer, Sender, Johnston, and Oya (forthcoming) that floriculture has a positive effect on poverty reduction and direct and indirect employment. It also contributes to social equity by employing predominantly female workers, who account for more than 75 per cent of the workforce. More than 95 per cent of employees were between the ages of eighteen and twenty-nine, and according to forty-one of the responding firms (89 per cent of respondents), more than 90 per cent of employees were recruited from the region

in which the farms are located. Both these factors add to the sector's social and political significance.

Most workers (76 per cent) were permanent, only 14 per cent were on contract, and 9 per cent were temporary. On most farms workers are unionized. Above 93 per cent are production workers with only 7 per cent engaged in administrative and support activities, indicating the pressure for production efficiency. Most of the workers are semi-skilled and unskilled, with only 1.5 per cent professional staff (of whom only one-tenth were technologists) and below 2 per cent technicians. This highlights the lesser technological depth compared to manufacturing, such as in the cement industry.

The labour issue has become a serious challenge to the industry, and for government intervention. Recently, many of the farms (especially those around Addis Ababa) have faced major problems in retaining experienced workers. Indeed, this is an issue of wider concern, which has been given frequent attention in the media, including a series of TV programmes. Meetings on the issue during 2013 were addressed by the prime minister. Many garment factories around Addis Ababa and employment agencies are targeting employees in the floriculture industry. The farms have been easy and attractive targets for recruitment, since the farm workers are judged to have better skills and a better work ethic.

This continues to be a major problem. For instance, between June 2012 and May 2013, more than 1,350 workers (mostly with three years of experience) left five firms, mostly for the Middle East. Of these, 74 per cent were from Sher-Ethiopia (in Ziway and Koka), 8.3 per cent from Redfox Ethiopia, 7.4 per cent from Ethiopia Cutting Plc., and 10.9 per cent from Lafto Rose, ET Highland, and Dugda. Sher-Ethiopia lost 1,000 workers in five months (EHDA 2013). On average, the five cut-flower farms worst affected lost 272 workers per month. Consequently, many farms were working below capacity, and it usually takes five to six months to train staff to a minimum level of output. This challenge required a comprehensive response by government and the industry association, although by mid-2013 they had been unable to reverse this trend. Thus on 17 April of that year, the former EHPEA chair reported 'the shortage of women workers continued to be a serious constraint on ET Highland Flora and all other flower farms' (Oqubay 2012), a finding confirmed by other observers.[1]

---

[1] In late 2013, many Ethiopian migrants returned from Saudi Arabia because of 'permit'-related charges.

While it may be true that employees in floriculture are targeted for their skill and discipline, it also may be that young women are using such employment as a stepping stone. They seek work on the farms to save some money (to pay employment agents, transport, and associated costs), get to know Addis and its periphery, network with experienced migrants, reach out to employment agents, and finally leave for factories and the Gulf. This is natural in any labour market, and floriculture employers have to adapt. This leads to a second point. Given high urban unemployment and huge rural underemployment, this turnover may not be entirely undesirable, in line with Lewis's theory of the unlimited supply of excess labour. However, even though basic employment in the greenhouses is not highly skilled, there are frictions and costs associated with this turnover, and employers in some areas (for example, near Bisheftu, east of Addis Ababa) claim that the labour market is tightening. From one perspective, this illustrates the strong positive externalities of the floriculture industry. If other employers have a preference for women with flower sector experience, floriculture employers are effectively subsidizing the development of a capitalist labour force that is available to other employers. From another, it raises a policy challenge as the industry matures and faces stiffer competition and higher labour costs. While government can help to create the right conditions, the onus is on the industry itself to develop a dynamic comparative advantage if it wishes to remain competitive. Such a predicament is not unique to floriculture: all industrial sectors go through a similar process of change, adaptation, and in the worst case, decline. Firms that innovate survive, those that don't die out unceremoniously—such is the nature of capitalist development.

5.2.3 *Productivity: Key challenge and work in progress*

Coping with international productivity levels is critical for developing countries in order to exploit their comparative advantage in having a cheap and trainable labour force (Schwartz 2010). Productivity growth depends upon many factors, such as the pace and level of learning, as well as on government support in socializing risks. The major productivity indicators in this sector include labour productivity (stems cut per labour-hour), yield (stems) per ha., investment per ha., cost per stem, and profitability per worker.

The closest comparator for measuring productivity in Ethiopia is Kenya. According to earlier data from Global Development Solutions (GDS) in 2006, marketable stems per ha. were higher and total cost per stem was lower in Kenya. The selling price of an Ethiopian flower was higher due to the variety (type) and ecological factors. The discrepancy in productivity was caused by the gap in learning in the latecomer Ethiopian floriculture industry, and a slower pace of productivity improvement. Nonetheless, between 2006 and 2012, Ethiopian floriculture showed increases in productivity (Table 5.2). The marketable stems per ha. increased by more than 9 per cent, and the farming cost per stem decreased by the same per cent. Quantitative information from 2012 (DLV 2012) gives the yield per ha. as 2.03 million stems. Many Ethiopian firms visit Kenyan farms, indicating proactive learning by copying from more experienced establishments. Many firm owners stated that the gap has been narrowing lately due to learning by doing and the resultant accumulation of industry experience, which is essential given the intensity of international competition.

It was also observed that learning by doing in floriculture was relatively quicker than in other industries. Workers got used to the discipline of work and agricultural professionals acquired skills rapidly. Tens and probably hundreds of agricultural graduates (from Hawasa, Jima, and Haremaya universities) have replaced expatriates from India and Kenya as production managers on many farms. For instance, the biggest firm (Sher-Ethiopia) and second biggest (Linssen Rose) had no foreign employees in 2012.

Table 5.2. Benchmarking rose production in Ethiopia and Kenya

	Unit of measurement	Ethiopia 2006	Kenya 2006	Ethiopia 2012	Kenya 2012
Production (farm) cost ha.	$	63,334	81,134	63,131	85,000
Plants/ha.	Number	65,000	80,000	75,000	75,000
Yield per ha. (Stems/ha.)	Number	1,685,000	2,300,000	1,850,000	2,000,000
Loss rates	Per cent	2	5	2.5	2
Marketable stems/ha.	Number	1,651,000	2,180,000	1,803,750	1,960,000
Farming cost/stem	¢	3.84	3.50	3.5	4
Post-harvest, transport, marketing	¢	11.66	8.60	12.35	13
Total cost/stem	¢	15.50	12.10	15.85	17
Sales price/stem	¢	18.3	14.40	19.2	21

Source: The 2006 data are adopted from Melese and Helmsing (as adopted from GDS 2006). Data represent running costs and exclude set-up costs. The 2012 data are based on EHPEA's data on average performing firms in Kenya and Ethiopia.

5.3 Industrial structure of floriculture

The industrial structure and economic and technological characteristics of floriculture differ significantly from traditional agricultural activities and share many of the characteristics of the manufacturing sector. Industrial structure refers to technological and economic characteristics, market structure, and international positioning (Hirschman 1967; Chandler 2004; Evans 1995). Labour-intensive industries are typically characterized by fewer and smaller economies of scale and scope. Industrial structure is an important determinant of sectoral performance in particular contexts and is a constraint on (but also sometimes facilitator of) government policy. Hence, understanding industrial structure is a key factor in the design and outcome of industrial policy.

5.3.1 *Firm ownership and corporate structure*

There were sixty-nine active firms in this sector in 2012, all privately owned. Foreign firms accounted for 63 per cent (thirty-nine firms), domestically owned firms for 26 per cent (sixteen firms), and the remaining seven firms were jointly owned. Almost all foreign-owned firms had prior experience in the industry before coming to Ethiopia. Of these firms, 32 per cent were from the Netherlands, 17 per cent from India, and 12 per cent from Israel. The biggest such firm, Sher-Ethiopia, was among the first to invest in Ethiopia.

Among domestic firms, 71 per cent (fifteen firms) were owned by local investors, while the remainder were owned by members of the Ethiopian diaspora. This diaspora is estimated to be more than one million, with the highest concentration in the US (up to half a million) and the Middle East. Most domestically owned firms were new entrants, and had different backgrounds (Table 5.3). This finding differs from the observations in the *Enterprise Map of Ethiopia*, which generalizes that most successful business people in different industries had prior trading experience (Sutton and Kellow 2010). The current study proves that this was not true of most of them. For example, one successful firm is owned by a member of the Ethiopian diaspora, a professional educated in the UK, who had worked for several organizations, including the Bank of England. When he wanted to enter the business, he studied the industry, secured a soft loan from the state-owned bank (in less than six months), and

Table 5.3. Owner employment background/work experience

Background	Number of firms	Share in %
Same industry (floriculture)	32	56.1
New entrant	11	19.3
Trade	8	14.0
Manufacturing	5	8.8
Trade and manufacturing	1	1.7
Total	57	100

Source: Oqubay (2012)

received land around Bisheftu. Sometimes the distinction between diaspora and domestic is not clear-cut: he is also from a four-generation *Merkato* family (involved in trading). Another self-made Ethiopian entrepreneur started as a shoe shiner, later became a shop owner, and currently owns a general trading house. He worked hard, became literate, and he earned his BA in management through evening classes. Before he decided to invest in this sector (along with his partner), he too studied the industry, including visits to foreign-owned firms and Dutch auction centres. He secured loans in less than half a year and acquired land. He employed a highly paid farm manager (Indian), and has a regular weekly management meeting at the farm. Both these firms have performed well. Among those firms that failed, some were owned by people who were also engaged in the import trade and had shown little inclination to learn about and manage their flower farms. They regarded flowers as a supplementary or side business.

Ownership most often took the form of family businesses, and family experience played a critical role in the industry. Among foreign firms, 42 per cent have businesses in other countries, with 20 per cent in Holland and 12 per cent in Kenya. Unlike the cement industry, medium-sized firms dominate in floriculture. Owner-managers manage close to 73 per cent of farms. More than 55 per cent of managers have prior experience in the sector. The key decision-makers in 83 per cent of firms (out of sixty firms) were owner/family members, and only seventeen were managed by a corporate manager and board of directors (Oqubay 2012). Other studies show that flower farms in many countries (including the Netherlands) are family owned, and predominantly small and medium in size (CBI 2002, 2013; Melese and Helmsing 2010; Nico 1998). Their size allows them the advantage of fast and flexible decisions, reduced overheads, and a hands-on management style. Although conceptions of size vary from country to country, farms of less than 25 ha. are considered medium-sized in this book.

The total area in Ethiopia under flower farms increased from 922 ha. in 2008 to 1,500 ha. in 2012. During this period, foreign-owned firms increased their land holdings from 615 ha. to 1,101 ha., and their share of flower-producing land from 67 to 76 per cent. Land developed by domestically owned firms increased from 56 ha. to 104 ha., accounting for barely 7 per cent. Land held by jointly owned firms has been limited to 237 ha., with their share declining from 27 per cent to 16.5 per cent in the same period. As regards farm size, there is no variation between domestic and foreign-owned firms. Between 2005 and 2011, the domestically owned firms' share of exports was very limited and decreased from 25 per cent in 2008 to 13.3 per cent in 2012. In terms of volume, it decreased from 20 per cent to less than 10 per cent in the same period. Raising domestic firms' share in production and export, and transfers of technology, should be an important priority of industrial policy for this sector.

5.3.2 *Market and competitive intensity*

Understanding market structure and competitiveness is important to comprehending the underlying pattern in the floriculture sector in Ethiopia. The global floriculture market in 2009 stood at €26.2 billion (Table 5.4). Europe had the highest share (€11 billion), followed by Asia (€7.6 billion), and North America (about €5.5 billion) (FloraHolland 2010, 2012, 2014). During the financial crises of 2007–09, market growth in Europe and the Americas was stable, while Asia showed a modest growth of 10 per cent (FloraHolland 2010, 2014). According to International Trade Centre (ITC) and UN Commodity Trade Statistics (COMTRADE), in 2011 the world export leader in cut flowers was the Netherlands, with 53.7 per cent of the total, worth more than €3.2 billion. Following far behind were Colombia (€858 million, 13.5 per cent), Ecuador (€393 million, 7.35 per cent), Kenya (6.5 per cent), and Ethiopia (1.83 per cent). In 2010, Kenya exported 117,000 tons, worth €0.5 billion (MilcoRikken 2011), while Ethiopia exported 50,000 tons, generating €146 million. Although the scope for growth in the flower market seems modest, these figures show that Ethiopia has considerable opportunity to increase its share of the world market.

Table 5.4. Global production in floriculture (in million euros), 2007–09

Year	Total production value	Africa value	South America value	North America value	Asia value	Middle East value	Value in Europe
2007	24,356	504	1,450	4,059	6,891	220	11,232
2008	24,395	594	1,382	3,998	6,865	220	11,337
2009	26,196	634	1,441	5,450	7,608	220	10,843

Source: FloraHolland, 2010

MAJOR MARKETS AND DESTINATIONS

Markets are classified broadly as auction markets and direct markets. There are auction markets in Amsterdam, Dubai, and Germany. The biggest is FloraHolland, with 4,000 employees, a €4.35 billion turnover, and 12.4 billion products traded in 2013 (FloraHolland 2014). Close to 80 per cent of Ethiopian cut flowers are sold on Dutch auction markets. Direct sales are through supermarkets and niche markets. Other major destinations are Germany, the UK, France, Italy, Belgium, and recently Russia (EHDA 2012c). The major flower products are roses, cuttings, carnations, *gypso-phillia*, *hypericum*, and *eryngium*. Prices are usually higher during winter, when European farms are less productive, and around events such as Valentine's Day or the New Year. Buyers look for bigger volume transactions and competitive prices, indicating their increasing bargaining power (CBI 2013). This also underscores the competitive pressures to increase productivity and operate at lower costs with thin profit margins.

AIR TRANSPORT

Most cut flowers have a high value–weight ratio, and are very perishable. Flowers are consumed throughout the year, and must respond to varying consumer requirements through time. Thus, the industry depends on air transport and cold-chain logistics throughout the value chain. Air transport fees account for more than half the total cost of the product (EHDA 2012b, 2011b), and combined with marketing account for up to 75 per cent of total costs. Frequency and timeliness of flights and other logistical arrangements are of utmost importance in meeting orders on time and ensuring that flowers arrive fresh to maximize vase time. The strategic importance and role of EAL becomes clear from this perspective (see Section 5.4 below).

PRICE-DRIVEN COMPETITION

International trade patterns for flowers are significantly affected by their perishability and by air transport services. Income levels and the state of the global economy affect consumption and price patterns. The 2008 recession slowed the growth of the international trade, and prices declined by 5–10 per cent from 2002 to 2012. Big-headed roses, especially from Ecuador and the Netherlands, are the priciest, and small-headed roses the cheapest. Big-headed roses from Kenya and Ethiopia are in the medium price range, with those from Uganda, Tanzania, and Zimbabwe at the lower end. Hybridization and breed development are significant factors in improving prices, productivity, and market share. Dutch breeders are the leaders in the field, and usually earn up to 2 per cent in royalty fees for a limited number of years.

COMPETITIVE INTENSITY

The major competitors in the European and American rose markets were Colombia, Ecuador, Kenya, Ethiopia, Israel, Uganda, Tanzania, and Zimbabwe. Major flower-growing countries in the developed world were downsizing under the pressure of high labour costs, increased energy costs, and land scarcity. Floriculture has also been downsized in Zimbabwe due to political factors and lack of price competitiveness. Uganda and Tanzania are facing major competitive challenges because of higher production costs. Kenyan floriculture is vibrant and has nearly fifty years of experience behind it. Kenya's flower farms cover 3,000 ha., while Ecuador's covered 6,000 ha. in 2012. By contrast, Ethiopian floriculture is only a decade old and has grown rapidly to make the country the fifth largest exporter in the world and the second largest exporter in Africa (Table 5.5). This only came about through an active industrial policy. However, the

Table 5.5. Exporter rankings in world floriculture (2010)

Country	Export volume in '000 tons	Export value in million €
Netherlands	639	3,151
Columbia	220	858
Kenya	117	500
Ecuador	102	393
Ethiopia	50	146

Source: Rikken (2011)

growth of the industry has begun to slow in 2012 and 2013, suggesting the need for new policies.

5.3.3 *Technological characteristics of floriculture*

Technological factors shape ownership type, production management, and economies of scale and scope.

VALUE CHAIN IN FLORICULTURE

Effective and intensive management of the value chain requires an integrated approach from farm to final point of purchase. The perishability and limited vase time of the product, and production uncertainties, create a greater need for such management by owners. Almost all owners have to be at their farms most of the week and in constant communication with agents and customers. For instance, the (Dutch) owner of the biggest firm spends two weeks at his Ziway farm in Ethiopia, and two weeks in Holland to manage his business there. Moreover, his son is permanently based at Ziway. The owner of the second biggest firm and his son are always at their farm near Addis Alem. This reflects the narrow latitude for poor performance in floriculture.

ECONOMY OF SCALE AND SCOPE

Floriculture is even more labour-intensive than traditional farms in Ethiopia. Also, in comparison with smallholder farming or other commercial farms, it requires more capital, for greenhouses, irrigation, and cool chain infrastructure. An investment of $300,000 to $500,000 is required per ha. According to the survey undertaken for this book, forty-five of the sixty-two firms had invested more than ETB 3.5 billion in total, of which close to 58 per cent was spent on land development, greenhouses, and buildings, while 17 per cent was for the purchase of machinery, equipment, and vehicles. In a way, floriculture is also technology-intensive, as it is dependent on developing new varietals (which requires extensive research and development), sustained propagation, and a skill-intensive production process. Many farms in Holland are used for breeding and hybridization, and use sophisticated technology for maximizing productivity.

Most of the farms in Ethiopia average less than 20 ha. Indeed, 47 per cent of firms have plots of 11–20 ha., and one-quarter held allotments of less than under 10 ha. Only 20 per cent of the firms held more than 21 ha.

Sher-Ethiopia is unique in owning or leasing 350 ha. of developed land (with greenhouses and irrigation facilities).

NARROW LATITUDE FOR POOR PERFORMANCE

The product is perishable: according to one grower, sixty days of effort can be lost in minutes. It requires maximum care throughout the year. The implications of perishability are clear throughout the value chain from farm to market. Vase time is affected by the time span of the value chain. Cold-truck transport and coldroom storage at airports and during flights are crucial. Hygienic and phytosanitary requirements are strict and may affect trade, placing significant pressure on firms. Phytosanitary procedures involve the inspection, testing, surveys, and treatment related to plant quarantine

Timely delivery, high quality, competitive pricing, and product variety are critical to success. These factors make for a narrow latitude for poor performance, dramatically narrower than, for example, Ethiopian textile, garment, and leather/leather products. Firms are under constant pressure, and their narrow latitude for poor performance also affects the support industry (such as packaging producers), air transporters, logistics and transit companies, EHDA, and other regulatory bodies.

These features are compounded by the technological uncertainties found in floriculture. It is these, rather than process technology, capacity utilization, or demand uncertainty that are the key drivers of a flower firm's competitiveness. Flower farms, despite their greenhouse and irrigation technology, are dependent on water supply, wind patterns, weather changes, etc. The production process is permeated by significant uncertainty. Intensive management, knowledge, experience, and often subtle adjustments are called for, meaning that flower farms can seldom be run as a side business, as some persons seem to have imagined.

5.3.4 Summary

It is clear that the particular features and structure of the floriculture sector have analytical and policy significance. First, floriculture is highly competitive and exclusively export-oriented, which has compelled firms to make maximum efforts to survive and thrive. This has served as a positive pressure to complement government policies. Second, the management-intensiveness of the business, product perishability, production uncertainties, and intense international competition have powerful implications for policy. Effectively, they translate a narrow margin for error in production and distribution into a narrow margin for policy failure. Because of this, there may be particular scope in this sector for policy learning, with potential (but not automatic) linkages to policymaking in other sectors. Just as employers in other sectors appear to prefer workers with floriculture experience, so too is there an emerging demand in government for officials with knowledge and experience of developing and adjusting policy interventions in the flower sector.

Third, the industry has been dominated by FDI. The primary role of FDI is technology, market access, and a 'demonstration effect', rather than as a source of capital. Local entrants agree on the importance of FDI, and working relations are friendly. A significant number of local firms have so far survived the competition. This issue will be further discussed later in the chapter.

Fourth, medium-size, family-owned firms dominate the industry. This means that knowledge and technology is less codified and 'learning by doing' plays a critical role.

Fifth, the nature of the product and markets is such that air transport is a critical component of competitive advantage in terms of cost, quality, and timely delivery. This has significant implications for the services provided by air carriers. Finally, the backward and forward linkage effects to activities and other mechanisms provide wide opportunities for the development of new industries, products, and processes. Nevertheless, realizing this potential calls for appropriate industrial policies and related instruments.

5.4 Linkages and industrial development: Value-chain spin-offs from floriculture

This section discusses the new industries and spin-off enterprises aligned with the floriculture sector: packaging, air cargo, and new growth corridors. Linkage effects, even apparently obvious ones, do not always manifest themselves. It therefore makes sense to think of linkage potential and to pay attention to factors that advance or even compel such investment decisions. In other words, linkages are not always automatic. Unlike the cement sector, where the major cost is energy, floriculture's major costs are air transport, fertilizer and chemicals, packaging, and labour (Table 5.6).

Table 5.6. Cost components of floriculture

	Cost in millions (ETB)	Share in per cent	Source
Airfreight	961	55.2	Mainly domestic (EAL)
Fertilizer & chemicals	311	17.8	Imported
Labour	182.6	10.4	Local
Packaging materials	171	9.8	Domestic manufacture
Total cost	1,748		

Source: Oqubay (2012) based on forty firms

These components can be categorized as locally manufactured inputs, imported inputs, utilities and distribution, and labour and related services. For instance, in 2011 packaging accounted for 98 per cent of locally manufactured inputs and fertilizer and chemicals for 90 per cent of imported inputs. Airfreight accounted for 92 per cent of service and utilities costs. This input and output mapping helps us to understand linkages.

5.4.1 *Backward linkages and value-chain spin-off: The packaging industry*

This section explores linkages by relying on Hirschman's concept of linkage effects (1958, 1981, and 1992). The floriculture sector has been constrained by underdeveloped domestic inputs and a weak support industry. According to recent studies, up to 80 per cent of inputs were imported, sharply undermining corporate competitiveness because of longer delivery times, increased costs, and higher working capital needs. Moreover, importation involved the loss of hard-earned foreign currency and of the opportunity to generate employment and build the country's productive capacity. Input–output analysis reveals that packaging materials are one of the three major input costs (35.5 per cent) in the industry. Packaging is a basic input as it is non-substitutable, and has a major value addition and marketing effect. It also affects the quality of flowers, space utilization, and airfreight charges. Packaging materials cost ETB 171 million (out of a total of ETB 482 million for the three inputs), accounting for up to 10 per cent of overall production costs. Packaging materials were imported in huge quantity (more than ETB 100 million or $7.5 million) in 2011, and doubling in 2012 (EHDA 2012d, 2012e).

With the right industrial policy, imports can serve to develop new industries in accordance with '*the gradual swallowing of manufactured imports'* hypothesis, a process 'in which the growth of imports induces domestic production' (Hirschman 1958: 110, emphasis added). Hirschman (1958) stresses the creative function of imports in stimulating new comparative advantage. He argues that 'traditional theory could hardly be expected to see a connection that could also be formulated as follows: countries tend to develop a comparative advantage in the articles they import ... We have stressed here the *"creative"* role imports can play in the development process, a role that has been almost entirely overlooked' (Hirschman 1958: 113). This involves value-chain creation, with further expansion of employment, and strengthening backward and forward linkages. The packaging industry in Ethiopia demonstrates this notion. With the development of the flower industry, consumption of packaging articles reached a certain threshold, making their local manufacture economically feasible. This in turn induced investment in the packaging industry.

By the end of 2012, there were sixteen firms, with an installed capacity of about 75,000 tons, supplying corrugated boxes for flowers. This process was accelerated by strong public support. EHDA, jointly with the Ethiopian Conformity Assessment Enterprise (ECAE) and Ethiopian Standards Agency (ESA), established standards for these articles. EHDA played an active and leading role in the development of the packaging industry, further strengthening floriculture's support industries (EHDA 2012d, 2012e).

To induce the packaging industry, many policy measures were taken. In short, the evolution of this direct linkage was policy-dependent. These measures consisted of both incentives and sanctions to enhance the competitiveness of the flower industry. First, the investment incentives relevant to floriculture were applied to the packaging industry to make it competitive with imported items. Factory gate prices were also negotiated and agreed. Second, standards were set and the producers were given technical support to meet them. To enforce compliance with quality standards, factories were shortlisted, thereby accelerating the process. Gradually, the quality of the domestic manufactured products improved, which encouraged floriculture firms and other horticulture exporters to use them. This has saved significant foreign currency, and built up local manufacturing capacity.

Unlike in the floriculture industry, Ethiopians dominated the packaging industry, accounting for 60 per cent of factories and 75 per cent of installed capacity. The main challenge is lack of locally available raw materials, due to the underdeveloped state of the pulp and paper industry. It is often argued (for instance Khan, 2011) that *ex ante* incentives and intermediate assets are inefficient because they can be swallowed up and still not perform, but that *ex post* incentives are much more effective. Although this may often be true, the packaging experience suggests that *ex ante* incentives can be effective. What is important is putting in place appropriate and easily implementable control mechanisms. Administering *ex ante* incentives can, however, be tricky and may fail to induce the necessary action by economic actors. One example is the duty drawback scheme in the flower and leather sectors, which became impossible to implement and consequently failed to motivate firms.

5.4.2 *Air cargo and the state-owned airline's developmental role*

Floriculture cannot flourish without a reliable and competitive airline industry. Until recently in Ethiopia, no such partner has been able to meet floriculture's requirements for frequency, cost competitiveness, and service quality. This is because of the losses airlines can incur as a result of the occasional variations in the volume of flowers. Many airlines participated occasionally, but were not sufficiently reliable in terms of frequency and cost. EAL, the state-owned national carrier founded in 1945, has been the flagship passenger carrier of Ethiopia. Despite intensified international competition that bankrupted other airlines, EAL has expanded, modernized its fleet, and upgraded its infrastructure. It trains pilots, technicians, and other staff, and provides overhaul services for itself and other airlines at its maintenance centre. As part of its initiative to modernize its cargo fleet, it has acquired Boeing 777s and is the first African airline to own the Boeing 787 Dreamliner. EAL's success mirrors Hirschman's hypothesis of how the narrow latitude for poor performance can help developing countries to build a successful airline. The experience of EAL also refutes conventional neoliberal criticisms of SOEs.

AIR CARGO CHALLENGES

Cold chain management on farms, in the form of refrigerated vehicles, and at airport cold storage facilities was a binding constraint, particularly in the early days of floriculture. Irregular flights were another major problem. EAL has played a critical role in reversing this situation, to the extent of operating at a loss. EAL, EHDA, the Ethiopian Horticulture

Table 5.7. Perishable lift capacity on freighter flights, 2009–12 (in kg)

	2009	2010	2011	2012	2009–12 (average)
Monthly average	2,130,411	2,863,439	2,984,180	4,467,010	2,804,332
Annual total	25,570,411	34,361,265	35,810,164	38,866,096	33,651,982
Annual growth rate		+34%	+4.2%	+8.5%	+52%

Source: EAL (2012)

Producers and Exporters Association (EHPEA), and other regulating bodies jointly paved the way for EAL's crucial intervention. The state's motives for playing an additional role through the EAL correlate with Hirschman's (1981: 80) finding that 'it is also possible, that the state, as a result of having intervened successfully in one sector of the economy, will acquire the *capability* and the *appetite* to tackle advances for other sectors or for the economy in general'.

The development of the floriculture industry put significant pressure on EAL in many ways. Historically, cargo transport was a secondary EAL operation. With pressure mounting to support the floriculture industry, government and EAL resolutely seized the opportunity to develop an air cargo business. This required long-term, multibillion dollar investments in aircraft and infrastructure. Thirty-five new aircraft, including Boeing 777s for flower transport, were ordered in 2009, and additional aircraft were leased as a temporary solution. Lift capacity for perishables grew by 52 per cent between 2009 and 2012, reaching 40,000 tons a year in 2012 (Table 5.7).

STRATEGIC RESPONSE
EAL's experience in this regard is a classic example of how a government can use a public enterprise to support industrial policy and industrial development (Amsden 1989; Chang and Singh 1997). The strategic importance of perishable cargo has been incorporated into EAL's strategy as set out in its *Vision 2025*. EAL's freight capacity increased fivefold from 37,000 tons in 2003 to 181,000 tons in 2012, and the airline plans to increase its annual cargo capacity to 710,000 tons by 2025 (EAL 2012). Fleet size will increase to ten Boeing 777 and seven 757 freighters at a cost of about $2 billion. A new provisional cold storage facility was built at Bole international airport's cargo terminal in 2013 to meet the demands of floriculture firms and address the cold storage bottleneck. Similar cold storage facilities were built by government in Mekelle, Bahirdar, and

Table 5.8. Government fuel subsidy for floriculture (2008–09)

Period	Original price	New price	Variance	30% variance
April 2008	5.16	8.64	+3.48	1.04
May 2008	5.16	9.66	+4.50	1.35
June 2008	5.16	11.01	+5.85	1.75
July 2008	5.16	11.13	+5.97	1.79
August 2008	5.16	11.05	+5.89	1.77
September 2008	5.16	9.41	+4.25	1.28
October 2008	5.16	8.48	+3.32	1.00
November 2008	5.16	7.84	+2.68	0.80
December 2008	5.16	6.99	+1.83	0.55
January 2009	–	6.27	+1.11	0.33

Note: EAL's 30 per cent subsidy is not included

Source: MoTI (14 April 2008)

Diredawa to serve newly developing horticulture clusters. By 2020, the capacity of the Bole cargo terminal will have increased to 1.2 million tons.

A challenging moment for EAL and the floriculture industry was the more than doubling of fuel prices in 2008–09. Such increases have obviously to be passed on by airlines to the end user. The challenge for the Ethiopian government and EAL was how to ensure the survival of the floriculture sector, given that airfreight accounts for more than 50 per cent of its production costs. At its meeting in January 2008, the Council of Ministers took the difficult and bold decision to subsidize 30 per cent of the cost increase (Table 5.8). Another 30 per cent of the increased cost was subsidized by EAL.

This decision to subsidize a third of the fuel cost increases was difficult politically, in view of the government's earlier decision to end subsidies on fuel for transport, factories, or homes. It also raises concerns that such subsidies could be a bad precedent. But, if many floriculture firms had gone bankrupt, large lay-offs would have resulted and the new industry would have been doomed. The experience is clear evidence of the importance of an industrial policy in Ethiopia, where state activism and the role of SOEs have been critical in a situation of systemic market imperfection. It also shows concretely how governments can play an effective coordination role.

5.4.3 *Propagating the model: horticulture and new growth corridors*

Linkages can involve not only new spin-off businesses but also new geographic areas. Hirschman (1981: 76–7) maintains that 'with the

Table 5.9. Performance of non-floriculture, 2008–12

Year	Developed land (ha.)	Employees	Export volume (in 000s ton)	Export (in million $)
2008	1,124	–	41,120	18.53
2009	1,665	33,300	39,830	17.41
2010	1,841	36,820	66,410	31.86
2011	5,214	62,570	93,010	40.00
2012	11,110	133,320	123,600	53.15

Source: EHDA Statistical Bulletin Issue 01, October 2012

broader linkage concept, a new activity could also be defined as one that yields the same product as before but is carried on in a *new place* [emphasis added]'. The evidence suggests that while new activities have been induced in the horticulture sector, regional diversification was limited. Recently, non-floriculture (vegetables, fruits, herbs) has rapidly expanded, engaging thirty-two firms. In 2012, it generated more than $53 million in export earnings, and employed 133,000 people on 12,552 ha. of land (Table 5.9).

Close to 90 per cent of non-floriculture farms are concentrated around Addis Ababa and in central Ethiopia, where the flower farms are clustered. Three factors have contributed to the growth of this sector. First, floriculture firms have diversified into other horticulture activities, as is evident from the fact that half of the thirty-two horticultural firms were originally engaged in flower farming. Second, the linkage has mainly been generated by the flower sector due to its externalities and spill-over effects (technological diffusion, management skills, technical staff), as both sectors require similar expertise. Despite additional incentives provided by regional governments (for instance, by providing land freely, which has attracted fifteen firms), only four firms are operating in Amhara and Tigray. This starkly demonstrates the fact that policy instruments can be less effective in countering economic agglomeration and is in line with the observations on Ethiopia's cut flower industry by Mano and Suzuki (2011).

Third, institutional arrangements have positively induced these linkage effects. For instance, the lead government agency EHDA, the sectoral association EHPEA, and the NECC have focused on the whole horticulture sector (not just floriculture). The presence of linkage dynamics from the floriculture industry seems real. It is also noteworthy that the non-floriculture sector has a greater employment-creation potential than the flower sector. It also has much larger potential in the domestic market. Moreover, it appears to have much greater potential linkages with small-holder farming (for instance, through outgrower schemes). Due to wider latitude for poor performance, the participation of domestically owned firms is much higher (43 per cent in contrast to 25 per cent in flowers).

In conclusion, although floriculture may be weaker than leather and leather products in terms of backward linkages, its linkage dynamics have been exploited and promoted through more effective policies. In the next chapter, a direct comparative analysis between floriculture and leather is developed.

5.5 Discovering 'new' sources of growth: Rise of floriculture

ADLI (Agricultural development-led industrialization), adopted as the country's development strategy in 1995, acknowledged agriculture as the engine of economic growth. It focused on smallholder farms, labour-intensive activities, and export promotion. The importance of high-value agricultural products and labour-intensive industries was also stressed. Nonetheless, it did not become evident that floriculture was one of the priority sectors until 2002.

5.5.1 *Genesis of a new industry*

During the Derg regime (1975–91), the Upper Awash State Farm and ET Fruit (both state-owned commercial farms) were producing flowers on 160 ha. of land, and a few flowers were exported to Europe, amounting to a few tens of thousands of dollars. These were summer flowers, and were not based on greenhouse production. In the late 1990s, a new summer-flower farm was started by Ethio-Flora (owned by an Ethiopian investor) on a 5 ha. plot in Ziway. In 2000, Meskel Flower (owned by a member of the diaspora) was the first to inaugurate a rose farm in a greenhouse on 5 ha. at Ziway rented from farmers. Ethio-Dream, ET-Highland, and Golden Rose followed between 2001 and 2003. These pioneering firms secured no government support in terms of financing or land. There were no com-prehensive guidelines and the sector encountered many challenges.

In 2004, these five small domestically owned flower farms established EHPEA to lobby the government to address these issues. This far-sighted action, which drew on Kenyan experience, was the exception in the Ethiopian private sector at the time. EHPEA managed to persuade government to establish a lead agency. Following these small local firms, large and foreign firms entered the industry. Thus, it is not always FDI and large firms that play the pioneering role. Encouraging firms to take such a role is an important characteristic of industrial policy. To what extent, then, did government specially reward pioneer firms?

From 2003 until EHDA was established as the lead agency in 2008, MOI (through the Ethiopian Export Promotion Agency) provided support to this sector. In 2004, NECC was established to coordinate and lead the overall export sector. It played a vital role in addressing many of the constraints the firms faced. This demonstrates the state's political commitment and the ability of the top political leadership to pick and make winners. Government opted to 'pick' the whole sector, and NECC made it a priority. Land on state-owned farms in Oromia region, within 200 kms of Addis Ababa, was made available to the industry.

FROM LATENT TO POLICY-LED COMPETITIVE ADVANTAGE

Most flower growers have a background in floriculture in Holland, Kenya, Ecuador, India, or Israel. According to most of them, their decision to invest in Ethiopia was based on natural endowments (land, altitude, water, and soil), cheap labour, and government investment incentives. Affordable land was a key factor in attracting investors from other flower-growing countries such as Kenya, and was a consequence of government policy. Land leases in Ethiopia were cheaper than in Kenya. Annual lease prices for Grade 1 land (in Sebeta, Bisheftu etc.) ranged between ETB 1.23 and 4.01 per square metre, and for Grade 2 land between ETB 1.01 and 3.01. Second, geographic location or distance to the main European market compared to other competitors (such as Kenya, Zimbabwe, and Ecuador) was another advantage, in view of the effect of air transport as a key cost. Third, the availability of cheap and trainable labour ($1.0 per day in Ethiopia vis-à-vis $2.50 in Kenya) was an important advantage in a labour-intensive industry. However, these endowments did not translate into competitive advantage until the right policy and accumulation of capability were in place. Investment interest materialized when all the necessary supports (such as investment finance) were provided at the right time and at the required scale. Natural endowments can be more than compensated for by developing technological capability, as witness the Dutch floriculture industry. The Dutch are global leaders in floriculture production and international trade, despite the high cost of labour and energy, harsh winters, and being at sea level. They built the industry by making it more technology-intensive, supported by the required clustering, infrastructure, logistics, and trade facilitation.

5.5.2 Inducing change in a new industry: Investment, export promotion, and other instruments

INVESTMENT PROMOTION

The key investment promotion policies involved attracting FDI and domestic firms to the sector and related incentives. The latter included a profit tax holiday of up to five years, and provisions for loss rescheduling. In addition, duty-free privileges on all capital goods and related spare parts (up to 15 per cent of the value of capital goods) and construction materials were provided. According to FIA data (2012), 314 projects in the industry were given investment certificates until 2012. In terms of execution, only 32 per cent of licensed projects were in operation, 14 per cent were in the implementation phase, and the remaining 46 per cent were in a pre-implementation phase. Only twenty-seven investment projects (a mere 9 per cent) were registered between 1992 and 2001. Investment interest increased after 2002, with peak of seventy-five projects in 2008 (Table 5.10). This number gradually decreased after 2008, falling below a third of the growth in 2003–08. This highlights the difficulty government faces in coping with the growth of the sector, in particular in providing serviced land and finance.

FDI increased due to targeted promotion of Dutch firms, which was supported by a Dutch government initiative as part of the Dutch development cooperation programme. Following a successful Dutch trade

Table 5.10. Investment certificates in floriculture, 1992–2011

Period	Number	Share from total (%)	Average firms per year
1992–2011	315	100	15.7
1992–2002	27	8.6	2.45
2003–2011	288	91.4	32
2003–2008	249	79.1	41.5
2009–2011	39	12.4	13

Source: FIA (2012a)

mission in 2004, the Dutch government encouraged Dutch firms to invest in Ethiopia. These firms benefited from Dutch grants covering up to 60 per cent of initial investment. Stricter environmental and spatial planning regulations, the narrow scope for domestic expansion, and rising production costs acted as push factors in Holland (Melese and Helmsing 2010). The investment incentives offered by the Ethiopian government were also very attractive. In addition to soft loans, serviced land was available on favourable lease terms, and land stock (under government control) was readily available.

In sum, the investment incentives were relatively straightforward and did not require elaborate administration. For instance, three-quarters of the firms surveyed confirmed that there were no implementation problems with the profit-tax holiday. The floriculture sector clearly represents a sizeable net benefit to the Ethiopian economy, in terms of foreign exchange and especially employment, as well as in less quantifiable 'soft technology' transfers and the development of industrial enterprise capabilities. But rather than unfolding as an inherent comparative advantage, these effects are the result of sustained and significant government intervention; and, in the case of Dutch foreign investment, of a double subsidy from both Dutch and Ethiopian governments. This deviates from Justin Lin's propositions on comparative advantage and Rodrik's industrial policy as a discovery process. Nonetheless, as the following sub-section shows, not all government support was as straightforward.

EXPORT PROMOTION AND DEVALUATION
Export promotion policy included several instruments (see Chapter 3). In August 2010, government used exchange rate policy to promote export competitiveness by sharply devaluing the ETB. Survey results indicate this policy has helped floriculture firms, which are 100 per cent exporters. These actors appreciate its effectiveness, and the fact that the measure did not require the cumbersome government procedures associated with other incentives. Many firms utilized their profits for additional expansion, and the ratio of imported inputs in the total cost structure is relatively modest and can be covered from their retention accounts.

Sixty-two per cent of firms surveyed indicated that the voucher system had significant implementation problems, while an almost identical percentage asserted that the VAT and duty-drawback have had similar difficulties. More than 55 per cent of firms believed that export retention directives were equally problematic. However, 68 per cent of firms indicated that the customs branch at Bole airport and EAL provided satisfactory service. In general, as observed in leather and leather products, export promotion instruments were not fully effective. The main reason is that they were ineffectively coordinated and inefficiently executed by the bureaucracy.

5.5.3 Industrial financing of floriculture

The prime source of long-term investment financing was the state-owned DBE. This bank provided financing at a subsidized interest rate without any collateral requirement, and the loan covered 70 per cent of the investment project (DBE 2012a). The DBE president remarked that 'in the absence of collateral, the loans to this sector held significant risk to the bank, considering the *perishability* of the product' (Oqubay 2012). Yet, nearly ETB 1.2 billion was given out as loans to almost two-thirds of floriculture firms. Private banks provided limited loans to some firms, following in the tracks of DBE. In 2012, more than 84 per cent (some ETB 1 billion) of DBE's total loans were good-performing (Table 5.11). The average loan was ETB 29 million, while the maximum was ETB 149 million and the minimum ETB 6 million. Outstanding loans in 2012 were below ETB 200 million, fairly modest arrears in relation to total loans provided. Only ten floriculture firms faced foreclosure, their arrears amounting to ETB 120 million. Seven of these firms were domestically owned, two were foreign-owned, and one was jointly owned. In June 2013, all the bankrupt firms were transferred to third parties. Studies by the bank, confirmed by firms, show that the causes were poor management, lack of knowledge of the floriculture sector and skills (selection of

Table 5.11. DBE loan performance in floriculture (in million ETB), 2007–11

	Amount
Number of firms	40
Total approved loans	1,167
Average loan size	29
Maximum loan size	149
Minimum loan size	6
Good performing loans	981
Outstanding loans	199
Arrears	243

Source: DBE (2012c)

varieties, farming methods, marketing), and the failure to use expertise. For instance, some of the firms overinvested in non-essential facilities, focused on low-value flowers, and depended solely on auction markets. Additional factors included disagreements among shareholders or promoters, and poor screening by banks.

In summary, lack of management and experience in the industry, and lack of decision-making capability and policy execution on the side of DBE were the major factors behind arrears and foreclosure (DBE 2012c). Nevertheless, the government used its policy bank to promote the industry and it is unlikely that the industry would have received such huge loans in the absence of DBE. Empirical evidence from elsewhere (for instance, Korea and Taiwan) confirms the role development banks play during catch up (Amsden 2001; Ocampo et al. 2009; Wade 1990, among others).

In this author's survey (Oqubay 2012), about 83 per cent of firms confirmed that DBE's support was satisfactory, the highest rating for any federal institution. There were also major problems. The first shortcoming was DBE's lack of knowledge about the floriculture industry. This affected screening, appraisal, loan decisions, and loan monitoring. Second, DBE's policies, standards, and terms were rigidly designed and inflexibly executed. For instance, one loan proposal was rejected, even though the project was the most economical (about $250,000 per ha. investment). DBE refused it because the firm proposed to use wood to build greenhouses and traditional *chicka* (mud) to construct storage buildings. In other words, this firm was 'too cheap' in comparison with higher priced investment proposals relying on technologies and materials regarded by industry experts as unnecessarily costly. Such comparability became a major challenge for the bank, which had to ensure transparency and consistency of decisions.

A survey commissioned by the Dutch embassy confirms that commercial banks not only charged higher interest rates but also that loan amounts were inadequate (Royal Netherlands Embassy 2012). It added that the 'process for obtaining a loan is long and very thorough' and expressed concern about abuse of attractive loans. In May 2012, one of the successful flower firms complained that DBE would only accept 30:70 equity:loan ratios (even when proposals contained ratios more favourable to it). The firm's owner also complained that DBE refused to accept early loan repayment. Some investors, who had used their own capital in order to speed-up the project, were rejected when they requested loans from DBE, as the bank's rigid procedures would not allow this. One of the firms whose proposal was dismissed had a successful track record in the industry in Ecuador. There have been renewed efforts by DBE to address these shortcomings.

APPLICATION OF RECIPROCAL CONTROL MECHANISM

A key dimension of industrial policies is the principle of reciprocity, though this is really a euphemism for the state's disciplining of capitalist enterprises that it supports with incentives. This issue has important implications for improving standards and the use of rents for productive ends (Amsden 1989; Khan and Jomo 2000). For instance, in land provision, if a firm did not start operations on time or if it misused the land, the latter was taken back and given to other investors. The risks and leakages associated with an inadequate 'reciprocal control mechanism' appear to be not too significant. This is because of a combination of positive factors such as the high competitiveness of the export sector. Moreover, given the perishability of the product, established export channels, and limited domestic demand, leakage was not as serious a concern as it is for export commodities such as coffee and *chat*. Nonetheless, although DBE had loan access criteria and a monitoring scheme focused on timely loan repayment, these were not enough to shape the behaviour of actors. The incentives were not sufficiently linked to performance or the reciprocity principle, although the government coped over time. In the early stages, there were instances of over-invoicing for equipment purchases, which DBE, new to the industry, was in no position to control. NBE has been exercising strict control over the repatriation of export earnings, and recently the DBE has been nominated as the focal agency to administer the firms' export transactions. Due to the sensitivity and high-risk nature of these loans, DBE took swift measures. It commissioned a study of all farms, classified the firms into three groups, and took exemplary steps by taking over two foreign and two domestic farms. The categories included firms with management problems, ethical problems, and firms which have a prospect of recovery. Their purpose was to influence the firms' behaviour.[2] It also rescheduled the loans for most firms affected by the economic recession in 2007–08.

[2] Interview with DBE president in May 2012.

5.5.4 *Provision of affordable land, infrastructure, and logistics*

Land is publically owned in Ethiopia, and the government provided land to investors on long-term leases and at low prices within 160 km of Bole airport terminal. Close to 1,500 ha. was being used for floriculture by 2012 (see Table 5.12). The cost of land was below $10 per square metre in 2008 in Ethiopia, compared to $30–40 in Kenya. According to one company's annual report, land comprised about 1 per cent of total costs in 2011. Initially, firms were given land that was formerly part of state farms. Later, allocations became more difficult as land had to be provided from farmed land or by regional administrations, often by means of complicated procedures. Two-thirds of the firms surveyed reported problems in acquiring land. Delays in handing over land and escalating lease prices became major obstacles to the expansion of the sector. Moreover, land provision was in some regions hampered by weak political commitment and rent seeking at different levels of the administration. Surveys by the Dutch embassy in 2010, 2011, and 2012 show that corruption has increased, particularly in lower level government offices and local administrations. More recently, efforts were being made to establish a land bank under the EHDA. Lease terms are favourable as firms can pay on an annual basis over twenty-five to thirty years (EHDA 2012b; EHPEA 2007).

Most of the farms are close to urban centres, so the infrastructure constraint has not been binding. However, disruptions to electricity supplies were a major complaint, especially as greenhouse temperatures have to be controlled. Most firms also complain that the provision of other infrastructure had implementation problems. Almost all of them (85 per cent) stated that this was especially true of logistics services. Moreover,

Table 5.12. Land development and utilization

Year		FDI	Domestic	Joint	Total
2007/08	Ha.	615.6	56.5	249.9	922.0
	Share (%)	66.8	6.1	27.1	100.0
2008/09	Ha.	840.2	62.2	337.5	1,240.0
	Share (%)	67.8	5.0	27.2	100.0
2009/10	Ha.	886.0	72.6	347.4	1,306.0
	Share (%)	67.8	5.6	26.6	100.0
2010/11	Ha.	963.0	86.0	251.0	1,300.0
	Share (%)	74.1	6.6	19.3	100.0
2011/12	Ha.	1,100.9	103.9	237.6	1,442.40
	Share (%)	76.3	7.2	16.5	100.0

Source: EHDA Report to NECC (2012b)

two-thirds of firms believed that the services provided by ESL and the Ethiopian Electric Power Corporation (EEPCO) were poor. Clearly, there is significant room for improvement.

5.5.5 Summary

Above all, a growth perspective, appropriate policies, the political commitment to execute, and learning capability appear to be the key factors in exploiting comparative advantage to develop a competitive new industry. However, the key findings are threefold. First, the outcomes were a product of endowments, institutions, enterprise, experiment, and learning: they were produced by policy, but also by politics. Industrial policy involved multiple instruments, which were coherent and compatible with the country's broader development strategy. This policy and related instruments were constantly improved, and created a conducive and supportive environment for the industry. These policy instruments were also assisted by 'push factors' (for instance, Dutch government policy to encourage Dutch companies to invest in Ethiopia and support them).

Second, implementation of policy was often inadequate as a result of lack of capacity and coordination gaps among government agencies. In addition, a lack of long-term vision and its translation into plans has become an impediment to sustained growth of the industry. Actors in the sector appeared complacent about the achievements to date and future prospects.

Third, adequate reciprocal control mechanisms were not put in place. This deficiency did not lead to unintended results in terms of performance or rent seeking, as it was offset by the narrow latitude for poor performance in a dynamic market. The role of credit policy and public development banks in industrial development needs to be underlined.

Fourth, mistakes were made (for instance, leading to some bankruptcies) in policy execution. However, the evidence suggests there have been net positive gains and that any sector-wide cost–benefit analysis needs to take account of dynamic and often unpredictable features rather than applying a rigid, narrow, and static perspective. It should be emphasized that the benefits of the development of a competitive flower industry outweigh the costs, since overall the policy helped generate new industries with multiple long-term benefits.

Finally, this story shows that even with such costs, active industrial policies are significantly better than laissez-faire policies, which had hitherto failed to induce the development of the industry. Government has gradually learned lessons and shown the ability to cope (as in the management of bankrupt firms) in managing rents and disciplining industrialists.

5.6 Policymaking and policy organizations

The research shows that the outcomes of industrial policies depend not only on policy content, but also on the complementarity and coherence of industrial policy instruments. More importantly, the outcome depends on effective institutions, coordination, and collective learning by government and economic actors.

5.6.1 *Specialized institutional support to a new industry*

Chapter 3 sketched the overall coordinating institutions, lead agencies, and intermediary institutions. The establishment of EHDA as lead agency to develop the horticulture sector was an important innovation. The agency's aims are 'to ensure the fast and sustainable growth of horticulture production and productivity; to facilitate the export of diversified horticulture products that meet international food safety standards; and to coordinate the development of supporting services' (FDRE 2008b: 2–4). In discharging these multiple duties and responsibilities, the agency is expected to collaborate and coordinate its activities with EHPEA, the industrial association for floriculture. The agency became fully functional within six months, and a director general was appointed. The organizational structure was designed around the core activities of sector development, technological capabilities, and market development. EHDA was also made a member of NECC.

Working visits and study tours by government officials and industry actors were made to Kenya, Ecuador, and the Netherlands. Benchmarks, codes of practice, and standards have been frequently referred to and applied with the close collaboration of the Dutch embassy. This suggests policy learning and evident improvements in policy capabilities. Such learning opportunities, including learning by copying or from models, are known to be important in catch up by developing countries (Amsden

1989, 2001). Second, open dialogue between government and the industrial association was also effective, although it was not supported by a systematic institutional structure, such as Japan's deliberation forums (see Johnson 1982).

More than 70 per cent of the firms surveyed are convinced that EHDA works closely with economic actors in the sector. Nevertheless, only 53 per cent believe that EHDA has played a significant role in developing the sector, hinting at higher expectations of EHDA, or at least highlighting the difficulty for those involved of neatly distinguishing the factors that influence outcomes. Moreover, 57 per cent of firms believe EHDA focuses more on regulating than on supporting firms. In addition, about a quarter of firms state that EHDA lacks appropriate knowledge of the industry. In sum, EHDA needs to improve its institutional capacity and shift towards providing effective support to floriculture, especially in the industry's next stage.

5.6.2 Effective institutional coordination and policy coherence

The key coordinating institution in the overall export sector is the NECC. Among banks, DBE is the key institution for industrial financing, with EAL its counterpart in providing air transportation and air cargo facilities. NBE and Ethiopian Revenue and Customs Authority (ERCA) are the regulatory bodies for export activities and the repatriation of foreign currency. A critical intermediary is the EHPEA.

NECC

NECC made floriculture one of its top priorities from 2004 to 2011. Its coordinating role was impressive, particularly before EHDA's establishment. Once EHDA was in place, it became part of NECC, providing a platform for identifying and discussing constraints and securing government agency support. Since 2004, NECC has discussed 365 issues during eighty meetings. Among the four categories of issues, the least discussed are linkage effects (18 per cent), followed by logistics and market issues (23 per cent), and firms and capacity building (27 per cent), while the incentive package was the most discussed issue (32 per cent). Among the single issues, the most discussed are investment and export incentives, land and infrastructure, industrial financing, capacity building, and the cold chain logistics system. Although this breakdown hints at priorities and the comprehensiveness of the issues, it does not give relative weighting to the topics.

PERSISTENT COORDINATION DRAWBACKS

Implementation of industrial policies is usually dependent on the active support and facilitation of multiple agencies, and the development of an appropriate institutional web for the coordination of efforts was an expensive process. Organizations involved include government agencies and intermediary institutions, and there is also public–private dialogue. Coordination remains a major failure, along with (and because of) bureaucratic inertia and low government agency capacity. The floriculture industry is affected by federal, regional, and local levels of government. Forty-seven per cent of floriculture firms reported loose coordination among federal institutions, while 54 per cent noted that coordination among federal, regional, and local administrations was even worse. However, 60 per cent rated the support of regional states favourably. These firms strongly recommended that coordination obstacles among government institutions be resolved. Close to two-thirds of the firms were satisfied there is dialogue between government and economic actors, but recommended a more regular and institutionalized dialogue forum and emphasized the need for greater consultation and communication. Moreover, they complained of the frequent revisions to government directives without sufficient consultation with industry. They also stressed the need for one-stop public service and enhancing government officers' knowledge of the industry. This points to the need for a stronger 'business–government' dialogue.

Most firms complained that bureaucratic obstacles were so great that management teams and owners spent significant time in handling government-related affairs: a quarter spend more than 30 per cent of their time on this, and an additional 41 per cent spent 16–30 per cent. In short, coordination remains incomplete and stands out as a binding constraint. The strength of these views reflects the size and family ownership of the firms and the nature of the industry: the firms cannot afford to spend time on bureaucratic issues.

INTERMEDIARY INSTITUTIONS AND
INDUSTRY–GOVERNMENT DIALOGUE

Intermediary institutions play a key role in all industries, not least this one. The Netherlands, Ecuador, and Kenya have well-developed associations that actively lobby for the industry and market and technological development. Kenya, for instance, has a developed horticulture industry of about 300 firms. The Horticulture Crops Development Authority, established in the 1970s, has a headquarters and twenty-four branches. The Ethiopian counterpart is EHDA, which has no branch offices. Kenya's Product Health Inspection Service (KPHIS) provides a high standard of phytosanitary service with laboratories at Nairobi airport. Kenya also has an industrial association (Fresh Produce Exporters Association of Kenya [FPEAK]) for the sector, established in the 1970s and comprising 121 members, of whom forty-nine are in floriculture. In the Netherlands, floriculture firms have a strong association as well as world-renowned auction facilities. The Ecuadorian industry association also plays an active role in market development.

Survey results indicate that nearly 91 per cent of the firms in the sector belong to EHPEA, a much higher percentage than for other Ethiopian industrial associations. As regards EHPEA, 90 per cent of firms think it plays an important role in knowledge transfer and training, and almost three-quarters agree that it lobbies government and promotes investment. This is positive, especially in relation to the other industrial associations in Ethiopia. About 80 per cent of firms agree that the Dutch embassy plays a positive role in sector development.

As regards unions, almost all workers are unionized. Unions negotiate with employers about salary and working conditions, although they are weakened by the constant influx of labour. Labour–employer relationships differ from firm to firm.

5.6.3 Policymaking

Three government directives in 2011–12 are selected to demonstrate the policymaking process and divergent political views and interests. These are NBE's new export directive, the new cargo directive, and new packaging standards. Together, these examples highlight the complexity and tensions underlying simplistic ideas regarding 'political will'. Unless policymaking is transparent and participatory, mutual suspicion between government and private sector will be reinforced. The 'political will' to act weakens where transparency and participation in decision-making threatens the interests of powerful groups benefiting from the status-quo. Lack of 'political will' and state capture are two sides of the same coin.

NEW EXPORT DIRECTIVE

NBE and EHDA prepared a new NBE export directive in 2012. Firms were consulted and the draft discussed, and the directive was implemented within a short time of preparation. The unit of measurement in floriculture was changed from stem to weight. Moreover, the amount to be repatriated was to be based on average auction prices. During the survey, 69 per cent of firms believed the new directive was unnecessary and the consultation was unsatisfactory. In addition, 71 per cent insisted that the preparation time was too short. On the effect of the policy on firms, 59 per cent indicated it was significantly negative. Among firms listed as delinquent, more than half stated they were wrongly included on the list due to errors and lack of coordination among government offices (DBE, NBE, ERCA). About 16 per cent blamed their inclusion on delays caused between buyers' and corresponding banks.

Differences in the interpretation of the directive (whether related to free on board [FOB] or cost, insurance, and freight [CIF]) persisted until mid-2013. This problem was compounded by the over-restrictive implementation of export directives for many years. The current NBE export directive applies rigid controls to foreign currency repatriation rather than a more flexible, balanced approach that promotes exports and repatriation (NBE 2012a). Firms suggest that the current monthly export permits and the acceptable margins ought to be reviewed. NBE claims that exporters do not repatriate foreign currency earnings on time or indeed in full. For instance, on 1 June 2012, NBE instructed banks not to issue export permits for the month to ninety-nine flower growers. However, non-compliance with the existing export directive does not necessarily arise from deceitful practices by exporters. As experience elsewhere shows, intense balance of payments constraints can on occasion cause government to be overly strict with exporters, to the extent that 'the goose that lays the golden egg' is killed.

NEW PACKAGING STANDARDS

EHDA and related government agencies worked with the industry to develop a local packaging capacity and to improve quality. Almost all firms agreed this project was necessary, but insisted that consultation was inadequate and preparation time too short. Due to instructions to buy from the limited number of factories that complied with the specified standard, 77 per cent of firms mentioned they incurred higher costs. The majority (54 per cent) acknowledge this requirement helped reduce damage to perishable goods. The firms also recommended that more manufacturers become involved in packaging to reduce prices, and insisted that obligatory requirements be lifted.

NEW CARGO DIRECTIVE

A new directive on air transport was introduced in 2012. Intermediary logistics firms were dropped and a direct contract between EAL and each firm was inaugurated. Two-thirds of firms supported the new directive, but again complained about the insufficiency of consultation and preparation time. Firms demanded more transport options, improved handling at the airport, and reduced freight costs. This book was written shortly after the introduction of this directive, but additional feedback (after the new provisional cold storage became operational) showed increased satisfaction with EAL service.

5.6.4 Emerging challenges

OVERRELIANCE ON FDI

FDI's role in floriculture has been positive not only in terms of export earnings, employment, and linkages, but also in terms of the sector's very development. Even owners of domestic firms acknowledge this. Survey results indicated that more than two-thirds of domestic firms regard FDI as positive in both know-how transfer (87.5 per cent) and market access (69 per cent) (Table 5.13).

Externalities and spill-over effects have been positive, as domestic firms found the opportunity to learn from farms in their vicinity, or from Dutch auction centres and Kenyan farms. Such learning opportunities were in

Table 5.13. Domestically owned firms' views on FDI

Responses	Technology and know-how transfer		Market access development		On FDI contribution	
	No. of firms	%	No. of Firms	%	No. of Firms	%
Important	11	68.75	7	43.7	12	75
Moderate	3	18.75	4	25	4	25
Little	2	12.5	5	31.2	–	–
Total	16	100	16	100	16	100

Source: Oqubay (2012). Response rate is 90 per cent

most cases initially facilitated by foreign-owned firms. Such firms facilitated introductions to Dutch breeders, and to logistics suppliers, and foreign marketing infrastructure. The clustering of farms eased and encouraged learning by doing and copying. It also allowed the ample supply of skilled human resources (farm supervisors, technicians, and semi-skilled workers). Recently, most foreign-owned firms use only Ethiopian staff, including as farm managers. This FDI dominance raises eyebrows, however, as it makes the sector reliant on foreign actors, with associated long-term risks.

Heavy dependence on foreign investment, limited strategic negotiation with foreign investors, and limited direct linkages between foreign and domestic firms highlight some of the limitations of industrial policy in this sector. It also shows how government has been quite timid in its efforts to maximize domestic firm governance, technological know-how, and other benefits in the sector. First, there have been repeated complaints that foreign-owned firms are making a lesser financial contribution to the country by over-invoicing overseas costs and declaring lower selling prices (through subsidiaries or sister companies). This arguably highlights the leakage of foreign exchange from the country. Second, Dutch breeders usually sell their new and high earning breeds primarily to the foreign-owned firms. Third, some of the foreign firms (due to their dominant size, logistical advantages, market access, economies of scale) secure excessive rents by exploiting their local monopoly. In addition, there is ample evidence that foreign-owned firms were less enthusiastic about government interventions to address market inefficiencies (for instance, in packaging or airfreight). There are also associated risks of a footloose industry, which in one case appear to be real. One (anonymous) firm told the author it had decided to expand its farm in Kenya in 2012 rather than in Ethiopia. Thus, while the role of foreign-owned firms was largely positive, it poses a fundamental challenge that requires an effective policy response for the promotion of domestic actors.

DEVELOPING STRONG DOMESTICALLY OWNED FIRMS
The issue of developing the domestic private sector was raised at the second meeting of the NECC in February 2004, but was given no prominence in the Growth and Transformation Plan, 2010–15. Such domestic firms as have survived, have so far shown good, if uneven, progress

Table 5.14. Benchmarks of International Capacity Building Programme

	International benchmark	Very good	Good	Poor
Productivity (stem)	8 kg per m^2	0	4	14
Waste in bush management	≤5%	7	7	4
Fertilizer optimality	100%	3	4	11
Cool chain management	2–3° C	9	9	0
Cool chain management	15° C	11	7	0
Human resource utilization	10 per ha	0	2	16

Source: Own computation based on EHDA data (2012b)

(Table 5.14). This positive outcome was attributed to the joint efforts of both government and industry.

This author's survey (Oqubay 2012) results show that there has been progress in cool chain management and bush management, while productivity (the highest was only 6.3 kg/square metre, with fifteen persons per ha.) lags. The availability of horticulture professionals has improved over time, with many of them replacing expatriates from Kenya and India. Research and development into seed varieties or farm practices, and the expansion of propagation facilities, appear to be at rudimentary levels, and an appropriate policy response appears to be lacking. Various standards and certifications have been introduced in the industry and most firms are participating and increasingly complying. This project has benefited from the support of the Dutch embassy, which has sponsored the use of experts. Such standards include MPS-A, MPS-SQ, Global Gap Certification, Codes of Good Practice, and Integrated Pesticide Management (IPM). However, there are differences in the levels firms have been able to achieve. For instance, fourteen firms were gaining bronze MPS certification, while three had already achieved silver certification.

Another major concern is the decreasing role of domestically owned firms. Due to the potential benefits, their share should be expanded, and supports should enable this. Reversing the current trend requires a strategic response. In addition, domestic firms still use intermediaries rather than dealing with their final customers and focus on low-value varietals. The key challenges of involving new and the right type of domestic entrant and of speeding up learning and catching up remain. Moreover, the size of the sector could be increased to strengthen its international competitiveness and fully exploit its potential for employment generation.

EMERGING CHALLENGES IN THE GROWTH STAGE

The floriculture sector has been at an incipient stage until recently, facing problems specific to that stage. For instance, land, industrial finance, air transport by EAL, and incentive packages played critical roles during this stage. Although these instruments may continue to be important during the growth stage, they may not be sufficient. The growth stage has its own unique constraints and challenges and they demand appropriate policy. For instance, technological and marketing upgrading could be critical. Productivity levels in Ethiopia are far behind industry benchmarks, and need to catch up with Kenya and Ecuador, and also the Netherlands. Maximizing the potential of existing and new linkages is critical. This requires policy adjustments focused on new strategic issues, and developing more appropriate institutions.

It should be noted here that there are two distinct aspects: the expansion of new projects and of existing firms. So far, only 1,500 ha. have been developed. For firms to expand, critical support in terms of land, credit, and cargo transport should be provided. Second, different policies and institutions are required to address the evolving role of domestic firms, technology, skills, productivity, market diversification, etc.

5.7 Conclusion

The Ethiopian floriculture sector has shown rapid development in terms of foreign exchange earnings, export diversification, employment generation, and linkage effects. A range of policies and institutions were applied, and the evidence suggests they were largely effective. Implementation has been better than in other sectors, and support institutions have been relatively effective. Despite this progress, the full potential of the sector has not been realized because of implementation constraints and emerging challenges.

Second, the industry's narrow latitude for poor performance helped shape the behaviour of interest groups in the sector and complemented policy interventions. Linkage effects were multifaceted, including backward linkages (packaging products), forward linkages (air transport and cold chain logistics), horizontal growth of horticulture, development of new corridors, and other spill-over effects. Ethiopian floriculture has indeed fostered linkages and stimulated economic development through various mechanisms.

Third, the industry was first 'pioneered' by small domestic firms. Other firms, particularly foreign firms, followed suit. This is in sharp contrast to the widely held view that FDI and large firms play the pioneering role.

Fourth, FDI nonetheless played a key role by contributing to technological development and market access. Foreign-owned firms are predominantly medium-sized, family-owned enterprises with prior experience in the sector. Despite continued government support, the domestically owned firms' share has been limited. Ethiopians are increasingly filling farm management and other technical positions. This calls for further indigenizing the sector in terms of ownership and human resources.

Fifth, the policymaking process followed a distinctive path (as it is not widely applied in other industries in Ethiopia) of collective learning and discovery. The story shows that not only has government picked and made winners, but the 'winners' have also picked the government. The government, through multiple agencies such as the NECC, EHDA, DBE, and EAL, has played key and exceptional roles in developing the sector. Intermediary institutions, in particular Ethiopian Horticulture Producers and Exporters Association (EHPEA), were also active in promoting floriculture.

In sum, the central role of the state in developing the sector through appropriate policy and institutions, and the presence of active industrialists, firms, and a sectoral association were key success factors. While the transformative potential of this sector is immense, the process of achieving this also offers substantial learning opportunities for government and other economic actors. For the record, the findings also show that there are multiple shortcomings in industrial policy. Examples include the inability to sustain the growth of the sector after 2008, the lack of technological deepening, and inadequate participation by domestically owned firms.

At first glance, floriculture, with its rapid expansion, seems to evidence the huge success of an activist state in designing and applying industrial policy. The clarity and consistency of this policy seems to point to a strong political commitment to it. However, the findings suggest that there is more to this sector's experience than a neat 'success or failure' or indeed 'comparative advantage versus activist state' dichotomy. The relatively successful sectoral performance was neither a simple product of well-designed policy nor achieved in spite of industrial policy. Instead, the following themes emerge.

First, the notion of 'political will' is of itself unhelpful, especially when it suggests an abstract ('autonomous') and coherent commitment acting on a sector. Rather, 'political will', or sustained commitment to a clear strategy, is endogenous to the political economy of a sector (and to the array of other sectors, institutions, and interlocking interests). In the example of Ethiopian floriculture, and especially in comparison with other sectors covered in the book, the evidence suggests that policy was especially effective because of the relatively small (and recent) set of interest groups. This simplified communications and relations between government and sector interests. However, as the sector has evolved and new interests and challenges have developed, these relations have become more complex and the cracks in policy coherence have become more evident.

Second, while it is clear there have been significant successes in sector performance and in policy effectiveness, the success on both counts is far from unmitigated. The research highlights a number of problems for the industry and serious weaknesses in policy design and implementation. It is as much from these shortcomings as from the successes that scholars and policymakers can learn.

Third, this circumstance underscores the need for industrial policy to be sector-specific: what works for cement may not work for floriculture. Policies that were appropriate at one stage may have to be adapted later. Understanding the interplay of linkages, political economy, and industrial structure does offer the potential for effective policymaking.

Fourth, the research highlights the significance of learning by making policy, of the dynamic emergence of new and shifting challenges, and to some extent of unanticipated consequences that provoke varying responses over time. This makes it virtually impossible, at least in the absence of a highly detailed understanding of political economy and industrial structure, to predict the outcome of industrial strategies. One cannot, that is, 'read off' likely success or failure from generalized models, be they inspired by laissez-faire or structuralist development economics.

A final word: government–business dialogue or the collective learning of state and industry is essential to industrial policy's success, but only succeeds if the state plays a leading and activist role. Mazzucato's quote below beautifully encapsulates the spirit of Ethiopia's industrial policy in the floriculture sector:

> When not taking a leading role, the State becomes a poor imitator of private sector behaviours, rather than a real alternative. It is a key partner of the private sector—and often a more daring one, willing to take the risks that business won't. . . . The State cannot and should not bow down easily to interest groups who approach it to seek handouts, rents and unnecessary privileges like tax cuts. It should seek instead for those interest groups to work dynamically with it in its search for growth and technological change. (2013a: 5–6)

6

Curing an Underperformer? Leather and Leather Products

6.1 Overview and perspectives

The Ethiopian leather and leather products industry has existed since the 1920s and dominated the country's limited manufactured exports until the 1990s. Almost all firms in this sector were originally owned by foreigners, mainly Armenians. The first shoe factory, Darmar, was founded in 1927, and the first tannery (Asco) was established in 1925. Growth has historically been slow, and lower-end products dominated the product mix. Export earnings amounted to merely tens of millions of dollars, with close to 95 per cent of such earnings coming from semi-finished hides and skins, and the balance from finished leather and leather products (ERCA 2012a). In 2011, Africa's export earnings from this sector accounted for about 1 per cent of global export value, and Ethiopia's share of Africa's export earnings was less than 1 per cent. Ethiopia's share of African footwear production was less than 0.3 per cent in 2011 (FAO 2011). The African export market is entirely dominated by Tunisia (61 per cent) and Morocco (37.5 per cent). In terms of exports of semi-finished and finished leather, Ethiopia stood second to Nigeria (40 per cent), and was followed by Kenya (17 per cent).

The main puzzle is that even with prolonged manufacturing experience and plentiful livestock resources, performance in Ethiopia has been persistently poor. This sector suffered from inertia and path dependency that arguably acted as a brake on policy changes. Evidence also suggests that obvious linkage effects from the rich endowment of primary input materials are far from automatic.

A number of explanations are offered for this poor performance, but they are generally unsatisfactory. Several of these will be familiar to the reader from earlier chapters. The first standard explanation relates to factor endowment, in terms of which Ethiopia and other African countries should focus entirely on leather and leather products, given abundant cheap labour and livestock. Ethiopia's livestock population ranks sixth in the world and first in Africa, and the country possesses a quarter of Africa's cattle. Its goat and sheep population is the second biggest on the continent, and respectively the eighth and tenth largest worldwide (FAO 2011). Yet the sector has underperformed. Although natural endowment is an important consideration in policymaking, this argument fails to recognize that sector development and exploitation of advantages are shaped by effective policy choices and institutional adjustments. This is better demonstrated by comparing the sluggish growth of the leather sector in Ethiopia with Italy's leadership in the industry. Italy, an industrialized country with higher labour costs and shortages of raw materials, continues to be the industry's leader and biggest exporter (exporting more leather products than the total exports of all developing countries bar China). Italy has maintained its position by constantly enhancing its technological leadership and competitive edge. Thus, the endowment factor is inadequate in explaining the circumstances of Ethiopia's leather and leather products industry.

Another explanatory approach relates to the GVC. Its proponents argue that the division of labour is determined by a country's position in the GVC. Schmitz (2004: 1) argues that, 'the upgrading prospects of local enterprises differ according to the type of GVC they feed into' (see also Gereffi and Fernandez-Stark 2011; Kaplinsky 2005; Humphrey and Schmitz 2004). Although the GVC literature is useful in understanding the industry, it does have serious limitations. To the extent that it sometimes places the weight of 'structuring' and influence on core industrialized countries, it risks inculcating a kind of fatalism with regard to developing-country agency (thus echoing dependency theory). It also diverts attention from the arguably more important issues of domestic policy, in which the interaction between political economy factors and GVCs features prominently.

In contrast to these explanations, a political economy and structuralist perspective (discussed in earlier chapters) may provide a much sounder explanation. In particular, the political constraints on policymaking and institutions, and the role played by various interest groups and their relations with the state, can open a new avenue of analysis. In addition, Hirschman's linkage approach (1958, 1981, and 1992) offers a sensible conceptual framework for understanding linkage dynamics in terms of potential, and converting this potential into material outcomes. Guided by this perspective, this study uses extensive primary and secondary data. The analysis is based on disaggregation of the industry into subsectors, namely the tanning sub-industry or the manufacture of leather, and the leather products sub-industry, comprising the manufacture of footwear, gloves, jackets, belts, and other accessories. As with the other sectors in this study, the key research tools were a quasi-census survey covering the whole industry (the fifty-seven respondents represented almost 90 per cent of firms in the sector); qualitative and in-depth interviews (seventy-five interviews); site visits and observations in factories (mainly tanneries and leather products); and document reviews. The industry classification is based on the International Standards of Industrial Classification, Revision 4 (hereafter ISIC). The statistical data of CSA, FAO, International Trade Centre (ITC),[1] and UN COMTRADE have been used for historical and comparative purposes.[2]

The research yielded the following main insights. First, by comparison with floriculture or cement, the industry's growth in terms of output, exports, and employment has been sluggish. Thanks mainly to inappropriate policies, the sector has underperformed badly. Industrial policy in the leather and leather goods sector has long been unable to improve performance or to fully exploit linkage potential and insertion into the GVC. However, matters have started to change very recently.

Second, one of the main reasons for underperformance is the lack of effective policy response to the challenges of raw material supply. This industry is material-intensive, so a reliable supply of low-cost and good-quality raw materials is the key determinant of its growth. Input analysis reveals that material costs amount to more than 70 per cent of production costs. Despite the comparative advantage suggested by abundant herds and flocks, the sector experienced shortages, rising prices, and low-quality inputs (hides and skins for tanneries, finished leather for leather

---

[1] For example ITC (2012).
[2] CSA list of firms involved in 2012 survey of manufacturing was referred to investigate active firms.

products). For instance, prices more than tripled between 2009 and 2011, and quality deteriorated from 1991 to 2012 (FAO 2009; LIDI 2012d; ELIA 2012). The principal failure here has been the lack of a consistent and effective policy that works for the large number of scattered rural producers. This is despite of a political commitment to small producers and the high priority afforded the industry in the GTP.

Third, interests within the industry have been contradictory, contributing to the disappointing performance. At least until recently, tannery owners dominated the industry but have shown little interest in technological upgrading of the sector. This has been compounded by an inadequate policy response (for instance, in supporting value addition and introducing a multi-modal transport system) and inappropriate institutions (notably, the absence of institutions for inputs). This failure to invest in industrial upgrading has meant the sector has fallen prey to a buyer-driven GVC (Schmitz 2004). This situation may not preclude local initiatives to accelerate upgrading, but does present policy challenges.

Fourth, as shown below, recent developments have begun to yield more investment, better quality, and more exports of higher-end products. In the 1990s, the shoe sub-industry was on the verge of extinction in the face of stiff competition, in particular from China. However, it has been able to survive and improve its market share in the domestic market. Nevertheless, the evidence is still too thin to give rise to unbridled optimism about this sub-industry, since there are still contradictory interests (for instance, around path dependency and the low value trap) that are poorly managed by the state, and the fundamental input supply problem remains unresolved.

6.2 Sector performance and policy outcomes

The industrial development strategy emphasizes the integrated development of animal resources, meat processing, and the leather and leather products industries. Development of animal resources is underscored as the cornerstone of the meat and leather sectors. The strategy further highlights the aim to develop local capacity to export finished leather by improving the quality and productive capacity of existing tanneries as well as through new investments. Also emphasized by the strategy is the employment-creation potential of the leather goods sub-sector and the need to enhance production capabilities by developing and managing human resources, improving input supply, and by gradually developing a domestic input and accessories industry. In reviewing this sector's performance, it is relevant to assess the effectiveness of industrial policies over the past two decades. As this sector is export-oriented and labour-intensive, appropriate performance indicators are output, exports, employment, and labour productivity.

6.2.1 Output growth

Volume trends have been erratic, with periods of expansion followed by substantial declines and then rapid recovery (Figure 6.1). Production volumes in the tanning sub-sector, measured in square feet, increased on average by 20.6 per cent per annum between 1992 and 2011. The footwear sub-sector, on the other hand, grew on average by about 13 per cent per annum in the same period. Nevertheless, these average growth rates conceal significant fluctuations. Tanning production was close to 101 million square feet in 1992; declined to about 70.2 million square feet by 2000; and bounced back to145.7 million square feet in 2001. It then continued to decline before it reached a new peak in 2009, at over 160 million square feet. Growth in the sub-sector appears to have declined again in recent years.

Likewise, the average growth rates for footwear mask fluctuations. Some 874,000 pairs of shoes were manufactured in 1992. Production generally

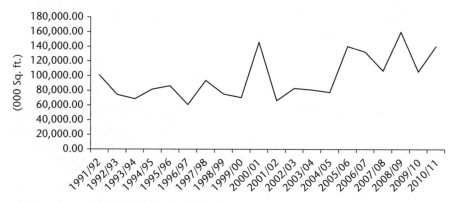

Figure 6.1. Total production of semi-finished and finished leather by volume, 1992–2011

Source: Own computation based on CSA Report of Surveys on manufacturing, 1992–2012

continued to increase in subsequent years, reaching a new peak of close to 1.6 million pairs in 2000. Production then plummeted to 846,000 pairs of shoes in 2005, even fewer than in 1992. Thereafter, production recovered, rising to some 2.2 million pairs in 2011. This figure is minuscule in comparison with Africa's total output (91 million pairs) or the world's (4.4 billion pairs) in 2010. Morocco alone exported 29.3 million pairs and Tunisia 25.1 million pairs in that year.

6.2.2 Export performance

EXPORT VOLUME AND EXPORT EARNINGS
The leather and leather products industry has been a significant source of export revenue for Ethiopia for many decades. The export performance of the leather industry is consistent with the production performance of the industry described above. Although export earnings increased on average, they have experienced significant fluctuations over the years. Leather and leather products exports from 1999 to 2012 totalled more than $1 billion. Although this figure seems large, it becomes less striking given the century-long existence of the sector and the country's acknowledged potential in this sector. Ethiopia's share of the global market and of the African market is almost nonexistent.

Export revenue between 1999 and 2011 showed significant instability and variability. For instance, exports by the leather sector ranged between 3,000 tons in 2011 and 16,000 tons in 2007. Export earnings were $60 million in 2004 but only $56 million in 2010 (ERCA 2012a; LIDI 2012g). There was, moreover, a significant gap in actual export revenues and targets during 2002–12 (Figure 6.2). Actual performance fell below 50 per cent of target performance, possibly because of shortcomings in planning and implementation. This mismatch highlights both the government's desire to develop the industry and its inability to do so. On the other hand, there is no real evidence on the magnitude of transfer pricing/ under-invoicing, tax avoidance/capital flight, or smuggling.

Because of the industry's relatively slow growth, between 1999 and 2012 its share of total earnings declined from 7 to 3.5 per cent, and its share of manufactured export earnings decreased from 86 to 52 per cent. Moreover, this decline is not the result of exceptionally performance by other sectors.

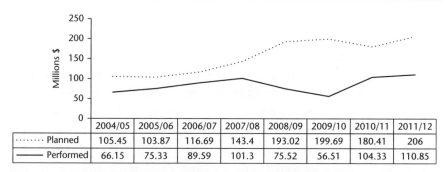

	2004/05	2005/06	2006/07	2007/08	2008/09	2009/10	2010/11	2011/12
········ Planned	105.45	103.87	116.69	143.4	193.02	199.69	180.41	206
—— Performed	66.15	75.33	89.59	101.3	75.52	56.51	104.33	110.85

Figure 6.2. Export target and performance of leather sector (in million $)
Source: Own computation based on unpublished LIDI data, December 2012

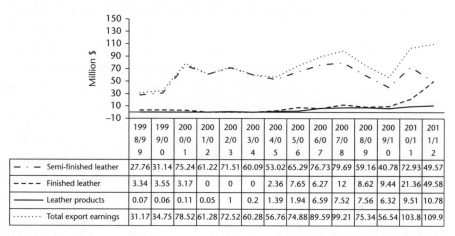

	1998/99	1999/00	2000/01	2001/02	2002/03	2003/04	2004/05	2005/06	2006/07	2007/08	2008/09	2009/10	2010/11	2011/12
— · — Semi-finished leather	27.76	31.14	75.24	61.22	71.51	60.09	53.02	65.29	76.73	79.69	59.16	40.78	72.93	49.57
– – – Finished leather	3.34	3.55	3.17	0	0	0	2.36	7.65	6.27	12	8.62	9.44	21.36	49.58
—— Leather products	0.07	0.06	0.11	0.05	1	0.2	1.39	1.94	6.59	7.52	7.56	6.32	9.51	10.78
········ Total export earnings	31.17	34.75	78.52	61.28	72.52	60.28	56.76	74.88	89.59	99.21	75.34	56.54	103.8	109.9

Figure 6.3. Share of semi-finished and finished leather (based on export earnings), 1999–2012
Source: Own computation based on unpublished data from ERCA, October 2012

The transition to higher-value added leather and leather products exports was *slow*, and has only recently begun (Figure 6.3). There was a modest increase in the export share of finished leather after 2006. In 2011, it reached close to $50 million (1,357 tons) and leather products exports reached $11 million (586 tons). Exports of raw hides and skins dropped significantly (from 15,000 tons to 5,000 tons) after 2009, following the government's export ban on crust (LIDI 2011). Nonetheless, overall export revenue for the industry has increased, thanks to the shifts towards value-added products. Export earnings from raw hides and skins were $5.3 per kg in 1999, while earnings from processed and value-added leather and leather products increased 4.7 times to $25 per kg in 2012 (LIDI

2012g). However, not all tanneries could upgrade their product mix, so the increase in total earnings was unevenly spread.

Comparison with other developing countries in this regard is instructive, and Vietnam is an appropriate comparator for many reasons. It has the same population size as Ethiopia and made the transition from a centrally planned economy after 1986. Vietnam, which was never on the global leather and footwear map, has since recorded impressive growth to become one of the top five leather and footwear exporters in the world. In 2000, its leather and footwear exports exceeded $1 billion, and by 2007 they surpassed $4 billion. They have recently topped $10 billion. Between 2007 and 2011, shoe exports increased by 164 per cent and bag exports by 2,005 per cent (LEFASO 2012). The industry contributes 10 per cent of total export earnings, and leather products are the sixth most important export commodity. The sector employs more than 650,000 workers, about 10 per cent of national employment. Major trade partners are the EU (accounting for 48 per cent) and US (30 per cent), and the country also exports to East Europe, Brazil, and China.

EXPORT DESTINATIONS

Ethiopia's exports of leather and leather products are concentrated on a few destinations. The top ten destinations in 2011 were Italy (32 per cent), China (22 per cent), India (14 per cent), Hong Kong (12 per cent), UK (10 per cent), Indonesia (2 per cent), Germany (2 per cent), Turkey, Romania, and Thailand (ERCA 2012a). Nonetheless, changes are happening. In 2009, Western European countries absorbed more than 55 per cent of the total exports in the sector, while Asia's share was below 37 per cent. By 2011, these shares stood at 43 per cent and 51 per cent respectively. This increased trade between Asia and Ethiopia seems to be caused by increased Chinese and Indian investment in the sector. While Italy, a traditional trading partner, is still the single largest buyer (one-third of Ethiopian exports), the shares of China, India, and the UK have shown some increase. Although diversification has its own benefits, existing evidence is insufficient to show advantages in terms of price or technological or skills development.

INDUSTRY CONCENTRATION

In the exports of crust and finished leather, the top five exporters, accounting for 56 per cent of the total, were Ethiopian Tannery (a privatized firm owned by Pittards, a UK company), 15 per cent; ELICO (a privatized firm currently owned by the Midroc Group), 12 per cent; followed by China-Africa Tannery (11 per cent), COLBA, and DIRE (which are locally owned), 9 per cent each. In shoe exports, German-owned ARA (29 per cent) and four local firms dominated in 2012. Lately, changes have come to the leather products sub-sector with the advent of new players such as Huajian, the largest Chinese manufacturer of ladies' shoes. So far, industrial concentration in Ethiopia is much lower than in Vietnam, where five firms account for about 70 per cent of exports (GIZ 2009). With increased FDI in this sector, however, concentration in Ethiopia is expected to increase.

COMPETITIVE EDGE

Poor quality also contributed significantly to weak export performance. The industry is incapable of timely exports of good quality products at competitive prices. Customer orientation and competitive spirit were below the desired level. Respondents cited the poor quality of raw materials and lack of skilled personnel as the main causes for this. Lack of cost competitiveness was primarily due to shortages and the high prices of raw hides and skins. As Table 6.1 starkly shows, material inputs account for about 85 per cent of production costs in both leather and leather products. Hides and skins or finished leather accounted for 66–70 per cent of production costs. This finding on inputs as binding constraints is in line with the World Bank's study (Dinh et al. 2012) and Cramer's (1999d) observations. By 2014, the crisis in the raw material sector for leather remained fundamentally unresolved.

Table 6.1. Major inputs in tanning and leather products

Major inputs	Leather sub-industry (in %)		Leather products sub-industry (in %)	
	2010	2011	2010	2011
Local raw materials and semi-processed inputs	60.6	66.4	44.8	70.6
Imported raw materials and semi-processed inputs	24.5	26.9	31.6	16.2
Utilities, transportation, and logistics	11.2	4.2	3.2	3.3
Labour and related service	3.7	2.5	20.3	9.9
Total	100	100	100	100

Source: Oqubay (2012)

6.2.3 *Employment generation*

This industry is labour-intensive, especially the leather products sub-industry, which also employs more female workers (about 46 per cent of the total workforce) than the tanning sub-industry. According to CSA Survey Reports (1991–2012), annual average employment growth in the leather and leather products industry is 4.54 per cent. Between 1992 and 2003 the workforce grew by only 1.04 per cent to 7,352 (CSA 1993, 2012c). An annual average growth rate of 3 per cent was recorded between 2003 and 2007, while it doubled between 2007 and 2012 because of new investments. The number of firms seeking investment certificates increased from eighty-seven in the fifteen years after 1992 to 133 firms between 2007 and 2011. However, actual investment did not exhibit such high rates of growth.

Total employment in the fifty-seven medium and large firms sampled was 15,443 in 2012. More than 57 per cent were permanent workers, 20 per cent were on contract, and the remainder were temporary. By contrast, permanent employees accounted for more than 70 per cent of the workforce in the cement industry and 76 per cent in floriculture.

6.2.4 *Labour productivity and capacity utilization*

LABOUR PRODUCTIVITY TRENDS

Labour productivity is measured as production per person per day, where production is in terms of square feet in tanneries, and pairs per day in footwear. For leather garments, reliable data were unavailable. Many existing leather products manufacturers do not specialize in leather garments, and only produce them in small quantities. Data on footwear had to be disaggregated into leather and non-leather footwear (canvas, rubber, plastic). Labour productivity trends in leather footwear show that the sub-sector has remained stagnant for a very long time. As Figure 6.4 illustrates, it declined following liberalization in the early and mid-1990s and has never recovered. Production per person was 1.00 pairs per day in 1993, 1.17 pairs in 2002, and 1.06 pairs in 2011. Compared to other countries, current labour productivity in the leather footwear sub-industry is low. Intra-country productivity comparisons have their own drawbacks, as many variables distort the comparison. However, approximate average productivity in men's leather shoes was 6 pairs in China, 4 pairs in

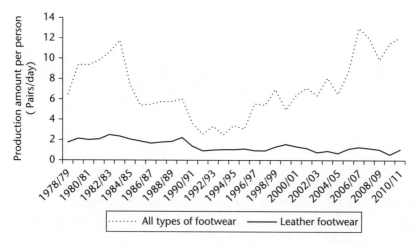

Figure 6.4. Labour productivity in footwear, 1979–2011

Source: Own computation based on CSA Report on Large and Medium Scale Manufacturing and Electricity Industries Survey, 1978–2012

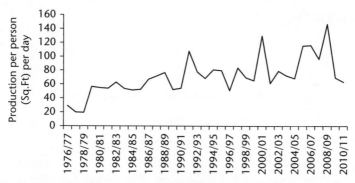

Figure 6.5. Labour productivity in tanning, 1977–2011

Source: Own computation based on CSA Survey of Manufacturing, 1978–2012

Vietnam and India, 3.3–3.5 pairs in South Africa, and according to recent observation by India's Footwear Design and Development Institute (FDDI), 3–3.5 pairs in Ethiopia (FDDI 2012).

Tanneries appear to perform better, but labour productivity has been highly erratic (Figure 6.5). The production per person was 77.85 square feet per day in 1993, 61.32 square feet in 2002, and 63.64 square feet in 2011. At times, however, labour productivity has doubled, as in 2001 and 2009.

CAPACITY UTILIZATION

Another indicator of efficiency and productivity is utilization of installed capacity. There can be biases in this indicator if it is not measured properly. Survey results show that the sector suffers from low capacity utilization. According to the survey for this study, more than two-thirds of firms operated below 60 per cent of capacity (Table 6.2). The main reported causes for this were raw materials shortages, delays in input supply, market or demand problems, lack of working capital, and lack of skilled workers.

The tannery sub-industry, which is more capital intensive, has very low capacity utilization: only 67 per cent for soaking and 57 per cent for finishing. Moreover, the ratio of finishing to soaking capacity for sheep and goatskins was 68 per cent (Table 6.3).

In sum, it is clear that the overall leather sector has a long way to go to meet the GTP's target output of $500 million by 2015. Employment has remained below 20,000, insignificant in comparison with the 650,000 employed in this sector in Vietnam. China's five million workers in the sector underscore the employment scope of this sector.

Table 6.2. Capacity utilization of firms (whole sector)

Capacity utilization (%)	Number of firms	Per cent
<20	6	13.0
20–40	12	26.1
41–60	12	26.1
61–80	12	26.1
>80	4	8.7
Total	46	100

Source: Oqubay (2012)

Table 6.3. Capacity utilization of tanneries (2011)

Product type	Soaking capacity utilization (%)	Finishing capacity utilization (%)	Ratio of finishing to soaking capacity (%)
Sheep and goat skins	70.63	57.87	68.17
Cattle hides	57.29	54.80	93.33
Total	66.53	56.82	74.83

Source: Own computation based on unpublished LIDI data, October 2012

6.3 Industrial structure, economic, and technological characteristics

This analysis of the structure of the leather and leather products industry of Ethiopia is based primarily on the quasi-census conducted by the author (Oqubay 2012). The results highlight the dominance of small and medium firms, the low entry and exit barriers, and the wide latitude for performance.

6.3.1 Industrial structure of the Ethiopian leather and leather goods industry

GEOGRAPHICAL CONCENTRATION OF FIRMS
AND INDUSTRIAL CLUSTER

Industrial clusters are 'the geographical concentration or localization of enterprises producing similar or closely related goods in a small area' (Sonobe and Otsuka 2006). Marshall's (1920) pioneering work states that agglomeration economies provide the advantage of information spill-over, division of labour and specialization, and labour market development. Porter (1998), for his part, emphatically highlights the role of industrial clusters in many industries: 'A nation's competitive advantage in industries is often geographically concentrated. Geographic concentration is important to the genesis of competitive advantage, and it amplifies the forces that upgrade and sustain an advantage... Government policy has an important role in nurturing and reinforcing clusters'.

The Ethiopian leather and leather products industry comprises sixty-five medium- and large-sized firms clustered in and around Addis Ababa. Fifty-six per cent (thirty-two firms) are in Addis Ababa, 36 per cent in Oromia (seventeen firms), and 11 per cent in each of Amhara and Tigray (six firms each). Other than Addis Ababa, Mojo, a rapidly growing industrial and transport hub on the Addis–Djibouti corridor, had the highest concentration of tanneries. Of the firms outside Addis Ababa, more than 70 per cent lay within a 200-km radius. Historically, all the old tanneries and shoe factories were established along rivers in Addis Ababa and Mojo because of the local availability of skilled labour, because Addis Ababa is also the biggest domestic market in Ethiopia, and because of better infrastructure and services. Similar agglomerations have been observed in Brazil, China, Italy, and Vietnam, a strong indication of the role of industrial clusters in the leather products industry. Although there have been recent efforts in Ethiopia to encourage cluster development, this is at an early stage and requires further study.

SIZE OF FIRMS

According to CSA survey data (2012b), the average size of manufacturing firms in 2010 was eighty-one persons, while 149 persons were employed per firm in the leather and leather products industry. This trend appears to be associated with the firms' origins as SOEs, which were larger than privately owned enterprises. Some of the new FDI-owned firms are, however, much bigger than the privatized SOEs. For instance, Huajian had 1,200 workers in 2012. Moreover, Vietnamese factories on average employ four times as many workers as their Ethiopian counterparts (GIZ 2009; LEFASO 2004, 2012). One of the largest footwear manufacturers in Vietnam (owned by the Taiwanese Chin Luh Group, which is the major manufacturer for Nike) employs 24,000 workers and manufactures 20 million pairs of shoes per annum. While the subcontract production system is not present in Ethiopia, 70 per cent of firms in Vietnam operate on this basis.

OWNERSHIP AND CORPORATE STRUCTURE

SOEs dominated the sector until the first decade of the new millennium. All large firms were owned by the state under the Derg regime's command economy. The leather and leather products industry was opened to private investment following the transition to a market-led economy in the early 1990s. By 2012, all nine of these SOEs had been fully privatized, and two-thirds of them had been bought by domestic private firms. Unlike in cement and floriculture, Ethiopian nationals now dominate the leather and leather products sector. This was not a direct result of government policy, since the investment law opened the sector to FDI. Again unlike floriculture, the Ethiopian diaspora has played an insignificant role in the leather industry, investing in only four firms. About three-quarters of the sector's businesses are sole proprietorships or private limited companies, while 'share companies' have little presence. Nearly two-thirds of the firms surveyed agreed that they were 'family-businesses'. Moreover, the general managers of these firms were family members, owner-managers, or partner-managers, a pattern reminiscent of floriculture, in which 72 per cent are owner-managers.

Of the total number of firms in the industry in 2011, foreign-owned firms accounted for 23 per cent in the leather manufacturing sub-industry and 28 per cent in leather products (footwear and gloves). Foreign-owned firms produced less than 25 per cent of the leather, and around 30 per cent of leather products, and accounted for about 35 per cent of leather exports and 55 per cent of leather products exports. Thus, foreign investors are more active in leather products and oriented towards exports. Domestically owned firms sold 38 per cent of tannery output and 68 per cent of footwear production to the local market. The origin of FDI was less concentrated, with China, the UK, and a Chinese–Italian joint venture each having a 21 per cent share, and India a 14 per cent share.

In Vietnam, by comparison, FDI plays a more important role (45 per cent), and state-owned firms have a presence, albeit diminishing, in footwear production. In 2009, the sector had 465 medium and large footwear manufacturers and forty-two tanneries. Domestically owned firms accounted for 50 per cent (256 firms), while seventeen firms were jointly owned, and six were SOEs. The balance were foreign owned (GIZ 2009; LEFASO 2012). In 2004, FDI accounted for 44 per cent of footwear; domestically owned firms 28 per cent; SOEs 21 per cent; and jointly owned companies 6.5 per cent.

6.3.2 *Economic and technological characteristics of the industry*

TECHNOLOGICAL CHARACTERISTICS AND LATITUDE
FOR POOR PERFORMANCE

The leather and leather products industry has distinctive technological and economic characteristics. It is classified as light industry and labour-intensive. Based on technological intensity, Lall (2000b, 2003) classifies leather production as low technology (LT-1). The production process is product-driven, and depends on labour skills and variable market orders. Economies of scale and scope are smaller in leather and leather products than in industries such as cement. However, there is an increasing trend towards concentration.

Given the limited capital requirements and the divisibility and low-tech nature of the machinery, barriers to entry are low. However, entry into international markets, driven by fashion houses and global retail chains, is very competitive (Schmitz 1999; Schmitz and Knorringa 2000; Gereffi 1994; Gereffi, Humphrey, and Sturgeon 2005). Delivery times are becoming shorter and product varieties are increasing, while cost-competitiveness is stiffening. The latitude for poor performance is therefore narrower in leather products, and the competitive pressures facing Ethiopian leather products manufacturers are stronger than for tanneries. The latter have wide latitude for poor performance in comparison not only with leather products, but also industries such as cement or floriculture. This is in line with the argument 'that export structures, being path-dependent and difficult to change, have implications for growth and development. Low technology products tend to grow the slowest and technology intensive products the fastest' (Lall 2000b: 1). This may imply the need for a top-down approach, where the leather products industry becomes stronger and pulls the tanning sub-industry up (UNIDO 2012). This is also in line with capitalist globalization in all industries after the 1970s, including the dominance in this sector of global actors such as Nike, Adidas, Reebok, and Puma (Nolan 2012). These four brands dominate the $75 billion global athletic footwear market and have a 20 per cent market share. The GVC in this sector is characterized by increasing buyer dominance (UNECA-AU 2013; Gereffi et al. 2005; Schmitz and Knorringa 2000; Kaplinsky and Morris 2000; Schmitz 2007).

The key stages in the leather and leather products value chain are the recovery and supply of hides and skins, their conversion into semi-processed and finished leather, the manufacture of leather products, and marketing. The sector is material-intensive, and has much stronger backward linkages, especially with agriculture. In terms of linkages 'calling forth' activities, it may be worth establishing a sequence here: the industry was created because of the existence of the livestock sector, which implies a forward linkage from livestock. As the leather sector develops, it has the potential to stimulate huge livestock production (productivity and quality) through a backward linkage. This shows there is the potential for a 'feedback loop'. However, this is not evident in Ethiopia due to the leather products industry's lack of dynamism. In addition, agriculture (specifically, livestock) is vulnerable to drought and variable rainfall, thus constituting immense 'supply side' technological uncertainty. This has significant implications for policy design in the leather sector in terms of institutional support, extension and veterinary services, credit, access to grazing and watering facilities, fodder cultivation, post-slaughter care, and marketing. Moreover, livestock owners and leather producers, on account of their dispersal, lack of organization, and sometimes conflicting interests, are poorly placed to bring pressure to bear on government. This is relevant to government policy commitments and concerted effort.

Another key dynamic relevant to policy in the leather sector is the pressure to improve environmental compliance. Tanning has significant environmental effects, including air, water, and ground contamination. Leather substitutes are expanding, while buyers and regulators are increasingly insisting on strict environmental protection and the application of eco-friendly labels, such as LITE standards (Low Impact to Environment) and Leather Working Group. A current major issue is the lobbying to ban the use of chrome in tanning. This represents a significant challenge, as chrome is very economical and is used by nearly 80 per cent of the world's tanneries. Decreased applications of salt are also being strongly encouraged. Furthermore, traceability is becoming important, as is the tracking of carbon footprints. And at the same time as the leather industry is being pressured by buyers and others to improve its environmental compliance and promote its environmental image, it is under constant pressure to reduce production costs and expand the fashion range (FAO 2008; Kaplinsky 2005; OECD 1976).

TECHNICAL CAPACITY AND STAFF COMPOSITION

A firm's competiveness and productivity is largely driven by its pace and scale of learning, and one aspect of the technical capacity of firms is staff composition, specifically the extent of the professional and technical core. The number of professionals in fifty-two firms was 440, or 2 per cent of the total workforce, while the share of technical experts and engineers was below a quarter of total professional staff (or 1 per cent of overall employees). This is believed to be very low. Moreover, only 4 per cent of all workers have technical or vocational training. In view of the industry's skilled worker shortage and low retention levels, firms may have less motivation to invest in skills development.

6.3.3 Market structure and international competition

GLOBAL MARKET STRUCTURE

The global market for leather and leather products was $60 billion in 2011 (FAO 2011). Growth of the leather products sub-sector is determined by the global economic situation and consumer demand. On the other hand, the leather sub-sector's growth is determined by demand from the leather products industry, and production in the meat and dairy industries (FAO 2008; OECD 1976).[3] In terms of global footwear production, China is the leader, dwarfing all countries with 42 per cent of world production and employing five million workers (FAO 2011). The Chinese footwear sub-industry is the biggest employer in the world (China Leather Industry Association 2012). Vietnam, Brazil, and India follow far behind in global exports of footwear. While Italy leads in higher-end products, China, India, and Brazil are focused on the lower end.[4]

The main source of hides and skins for China, Europe, and the Far East has been the US. The US exports some 750,000 tons of bovine hides and skins per year, while China is the biggest importer of bovine hides and skins (FAO 2013). Brazil's annual domestic consumption of hides and skins stood at 12 million in 2011. Brazil has 213 million head of cattle (14 per cent share of the world's cattle population), an increase of 23 per cent in ten years. This remarkable growth is attributed to Brazilian policy and the Brazilian leather promotion agency's initiatives to improve sustainability, quality, innovation, and creativity.

6.3.4 Summary

In reviewing the Ethiopian leather and leather products sector, certain features stand out. First, small and medium, mostly family-owned, firms dominate both sub-sectors. Economies of scale and scope are low, as are entry and exit barriers. Because the sector is not demand-constrained, there is the opportunity to engage more firms. The firms' limitations suggest the need for increased support from government agencies; marketing, research, and development institutions; and industrial associations. Learning from Brazilian and Vietnamese experience may be important. Second, as a labour-intensive industry, labour productivity plays a central role, implying a need to focus on developing production capability. The dominance of high productivity and low cost countries

---

[3] The global leather market showed sustained growth between 1981 and 2006, from $13 to $60 billion, but was slowed by the 2008 global economic crisis (FAO 2008). Of the total sales, the hides and skins segment, tanning, and leather footwear accounted for 12, 30, and 58 per cent respectively in 2007 (FAO 2008).

[4] Brazil has one of the fastest growing leather goods sectors in terms of exports and production. Brazil's export earnings increased from $700 million in 2000 to more than $2.2 billion (352,222 tons) in 2011. This shows that this is not a 'demand constrained' sector, but one in which new competitors have expanded to take larger slices of the global market.

(such as China, Vietnam, and India) and the increased buyers' bargaining position in the GVC pose formidable challenges for entrants like Ethiopia. Industrial clusters, which have played important roles in Italy, China, and Brazil, could do the same in Ethiopia.

Third, the latitude for poor performance is wide, implying that policy effectiveness is hampered by the lack of inherent pressure in the production process. Firms prefer to sell on the domestic market rather than in the more competitive export market. Moreover, the small size and limited capital base of the domestic firms limits the scope of specialization, and the firms view diversifying to other business as a better option to mitigate their business risks. This implies, arguably, the need for innovative policymaking and institutional arrangements. Relatively, the leather products sub-industry exerts greater pressure of export discipline.

Fourth, just as energy is critical to cement, and air transport to floriculture, the input supply issue is a binding constraint on this industry. This is due to the material intensity of the product. In view of the factor endowments of Ethiopia, which also became a key factor in attracting investment, the key policy challenge will be addressing this binding constraint. With these premises, the following sections review the policy and institutional responses of the government.

6.4 Linkages, path dependence, and industrialization

6.4.1 *Path dependence and low value trap in leather and leather products industry*

Path dependence 'characterises...those historical sequences in which contingent events set into motion institutional patterns or event chains that have deterministic properties' (Mahoney 2000). Path dependence is locked in and hard to escape (Vergne and Durand 2010). The Ethiopian leather and leather products industry has experienced path dependence in the form of a low value trap. This dependence has been reinforced by many factors. First, pressures from the GVC have been less acutely felt, as Ethiopian leather and leather product output is based on tanneries. Footwear production and exports have lagged leather production. The tanning industry was dependent on raw hide and skin exports until 1975, and on semi-finished leather exports until December 2011. Under the command economy (1975–91), government was forced to prohibit hide and skin exports in order to secure supplies for nationalized state-owned firms that were experiencing shortages of, and high prices for, raw materials. Evidence suggests this intervention was not made with a view to upgrading the industry.[5]

Until 2007, the main export was wet-blue and pickle. It was only in that year that the government imposed a high tax to discourage exports of low-end semi-finished leather and encourage exports of crust. After 2011, crust exports were also discouraged by a high export tax, and exporting finished leather was promoted. Despite these interventions, the sector faces major challenges in terms of value addition, localization of inputs (local content is below 60 per cent), industry upgrading, and product design and development (Oqubay 2012). This stands in contrast to Vietnam, which has managed to break into the GVC, competing primarily on cost (against China and others) after liberalization of the centrally planned economy in the late 1980s. It is now the second largest manufacturer of footwear in the world.

Second, exports of semi-finished leather suited the Ethiopian tanneries because they only had to deal with a limited number of European tanneries (unlike the footwear and other leather products manufacturers). This reduced buyer uncertainty and facilitated good relationships with higher value leather manufacturers. The prices of semi-finished leather were stable between 1991 and 2008, and the trend changed only after the end of 2008 because of falling retailer demand. For instance, in the US hide prices decreased by more than 50 per cent in 2009 (FAO 2008). Changes in consumption patterns for leather products do not directly transfer to crust level manufacture. The purchasers of finished leather are leather products manufacturers, who put heavy pressure on leather processors and insist on stringent specifications, costs, delivery times, and quality. The logistics of acquiring chemical inputs is more complex and requires more working capital. After the oil price hike in 2008, operating costs in Ethiopia increased as chemical costs rose. This situation further worsened when raw hide and skin prices increased threefold on the local market between 2009 and 2012 due to the establishment of new—mostly

---

[5] The decision was also partly influenced by the Derg's need to produce boots for its soldiers under extreme balance of payments constraints.

foreign-owned—tanneries. As a result, tanneries came under increasing pressure and the leather products industry was hard hit.

Third, with rising demand for leather footwear, the tanneries and footwear industry were able to sell profitably on local markets. In this they were assisted by the increased price of imported leather footwear because of devaluation. This strengthened the dominance of family-owned firms, some of which had also been involved in footwear manufacture. Those who invested in tanneries after 1992 were hides and skins traders, some of whom saw manufacturing as an extension of their hides and skins trade. They also regarded their monopoly of the supply of raw inputs as advantageous and were not interested in the government's (half-hearted) efforts to improve the supply of raw hides and skins. Instead, they considered that the status quo offered better advantages in terms of access to raw materials, price, and quality.

Fourth, the historical evolution and composition of the Ethiopian Leather Industries Association (ELIA) further consolidated the tanneries' position. Tannery interests shaped the association's activities as well as how government was lobbied. Eight firms, all tanneries, originally founded ELIA in 1994. In 2012, ELIA's membership reached thirty-nine, of which 61 per cent were tanneries, and tannery owners also owned some of the twelve footwear manufacturers. The firms do not share cohesive aims and seem to wish to avoid competition. For instance, they effectively lobbied to prevent new foreign firms from investing in tanneries, as predicted by Hirschman in *The Political Economy of Import-Substituting Industrialization in Latin America* (1968). This policy decision was made on a provisional basis in 2012, and became part of the new investment code. In the absence of a stronger reciprocal control mechanism, the organizational capacity of these private sector investors seems likely to consolidate industry path dependence rather than to break it.

Fifth, the low value trap and path dependence involves professionals and management as well. Most managers and professionals had long been operating under a quota and central planning system, which explains their lack of enthusiasm for competition. An anonymous observer remarked that the chemists in the sector were not aware of or receptive to technological innovation (interview, August 2012). He also added that the owners were less interested in specializing in, for instance, sheepskin or cattle hides, crust production, or finished leather.

Some of the constraints in this sector could have been tackled through appropriate policies, institutions, and organization. This did not happen for several reasons. First, other than the broad definition of the strategy, no comprehensive roadmap was developed to chart how the sector could upgrade its position in the GVC. GVC analysis focuses on the 'dynamics of inter-linkages within the productive sector, especially the way in which firms and countries are globally integrated...' It also examines 'the full range of activities which are required to bring a product or service from conception, through the different phases of production (involving a combination of physical transformation and the input of various producer services), delivery to final consumers, and final disposal after use' (Kaplinsky and Morris 2000: 4). Most of the policy decisions have not been informed by an integrated approach and knowledge of the industry. For instance, data on the local or global outlook of the industry are not available to MOI. Most of the reports submitted to the NECC focused on export performance and urgent constraints rather than underlying structures. Nor was the design of a multimodal transport system informed by appreciation of the features of the global market in leather and related products. The policy decision to upgrade products, though important and long overdue, was not supported by coherent long-term plans.

Second, pressure from powerful lobbies (in particular tanneries) weakened policy coherence and consistency. Some policies appeared incompatible, for instance, those promoting live animal exports versus those promoting the meat processing industry. In addition, some decisions were not followed through and firm accountability and monitoring was lacking. For instance, the import of raw materials and semi-processed leather was raised as far back as 2004, but was never seriously addressed. This was mainly due to pressure from existing tanneries happy with the status quo, and policymakers who did not insulate themselves from this pressure. Even the upgrading of products was only implemented much later (in October 2012).

Third, the institutional setting did not effectively support the sector. There was no strong institution working on the input side, and there has been a failure to coordinate trade facilitation and logistics. This is critical to an industry needing to import accessories and components, and to export under tight delivery and cost schedules. Research and vocational training institutions have weak links to the industry. The lead institution for the sector was strengthened only after 2010. Overall, this lack of institutions has further solidified the inertia. This situation stands in stark contrast to Brazil, where research and development support is effective (see Di John, forthcoming).

Further evidence of inertia includes the inability to diversify the product range, in part because sub-contracting is almost nonexistent. For instance, Ethiopian footwear firms have focused on men's shoes, while foreign-owned firms produce women's shoes, for which there is a bigger and more rapidly changing market. Government has put insufficient effort into designing policy instruments and institutions to lead firms towards higher productivity and industrial upgrading. Rather, a perceived easy way out has been taken in the form of misguided and detrimental efforts to continue protection and restrict FDI, as well as the weak interest in exporting and industrial upgrading and lack of inter-firm linkages and specialization (see Section 6.4.2 for details). Porter (1998: 598) points to the wider significance of problems such as these by emphasizing that 'the most serious mistake is to support policies that will undermine true competitive advantage, reduce the impetus to improve and innovate, and create an attitude of dependence on government'.

In other countries, (for instance, the Sinos Valley footwear cluster in Brazil and central eastern Italian footwear clusters) industrial associations, firms, and local and national governments have played an active role in industrial upgrading. The Sinos Valley cluster employs 153,400 people in 1,821 firms (tanneries and footwear and leather article manufacturers). It exported 100 million pairs of shoes worth approximately $900 million in 1991. The dynamism of this cluster arose in response to international competition and increased costs. Cooperative and collective action was the key to this success (see Schmitz 1995a, 1995b, 1998; IDS 1997).

6.4.2 Backward linkages: neglected constraints and opportunity

The evidence shows that the quality, price, and shortages of raw hides and skins were the binding constraint on the leather and leather products industry. A number of observations support this finding.

INPUTS AS KEY CONSTRAINT ON PRODUCTIVITY
AND EXPORT COMPETITIVENESS
Most representatives of the firms surveyed stated that the major causes of low capacity utilization were shortages of working capital and the

shortage and poor quality of raw materials. These are obviously inter-related issues. In terms of constraints on export performance, close to 40 per cent stated that the delays, high prices, and poor quality of raw materials were the major constraint. In response to the question on the main cause of lack of competitiveness in terms of price and timely deliv-ery, the firms pointed to the prices and inadequate supplies of raw mater-ials as a prime reason. Most of the firms also identified these factors as the major cause of the lack of competitiveness in terms of quality. According to recent ELIA data, less than 20 per cent of skins and hides qualified as Grades 1–3, while Grade 4–6 account for above 80 per cent (MOI 2012a; ELIA 2012). This is consistent with the findings of other studies (see USAID 2008; Dinh et al. 2012; Global Development Solutions 2011). A comparative study on livestock development in Botswana and Ethiopia indicates that Ethiopia's cattle productivity is among the lowest in the world, and that the supply chain is dominated by 'numerous intermedi-aries and actors', a situation that increases transaction costs (UNECA 2012).

LINKAGE EFFECTS IN THE LEATHER SECTOR

The above evidence is consistent with the analysis of linkages, particularly the input and output side of tanneries and the input side of the leather products sub-industry. Tanneries and leather products have high material intensity. Based on the responses of thirty-eight firms, hides and skins are the key components in the input–output linkage. In tanneries (in 2011), 97 per cent of local raw materials were hides and skins, with sheepskin alone having a 69 per cent share. Similarly, in leather products, 79 per cent of local inputs are finished leather. Hides and skins account for the lion's share of the cost of inputs. In leather products, finished leather has a share of 56 per cent. Clearly, for tanneries, the supply, quality, and prices of hides and skins are crucial to their growth and competitiveness. The same is true of finished leather in the leather products industry.

The price of hides and skins has increased over time, constraining the growth and competitiveness of the industry. The cost of sheepskin increased twelvefold from ETB 7.71 to ETB 91.53 between 1993 and 2012, and threefold between 2010 and 2012 alone as the capacity of tanneries expanded. Similarly, although less spectacularly, goatskin prices increased sevenfold between 1993 and 2012, and by 183 per cent between 2010 and 2012. The corresponding figures for cattle hides are fivefold and

166 per cent. The quasi-census shows that over the same period, other input prices were fairly stable, although some showed less dramatic increases.

According to the CSA survey of livestock, Ethiopia had more than 52 million cattle (almost half of all livestock), 24.2 million sheep, and 22.6 million goats (CSA 2012a). Livestock is concentrated in the most populous regions of Oromia, Amhara, and Southern Nations, Nationalities, and Peoples' Region (SNNPR). There have been fundamental problems in livestock development. For instance, the level of commercialization (surplus to subsistence sold) ranges from 12 per cent for cattle to 25 per cent for sheep and 18 per cent for goats, and 10 per cent overall. The most extensive use of cattle was for draught, and in the case of sheep and goats, breeding. Livestock contributes up to 45 per cent of Ethiopia's agricultural GDP (25 per cent according to MOFED estimates) (Behnke 2010: 7). In low-income countries, livestock has broader social significance than as a financial asset or food source, and represents the basis of livelihood and cultural identity (Economist at Large 2011).

The number of slaughtered animals has been very low, and insufficient to supply tanneries. The off-take rate for Ethiopian livestock was also low, 40 per cent for sheep, 27 per cent for goats, and 14 per cent for cattle (MOA 2012). According to the CSA Agricultural Sample Survey, 61 per cent of skins and 48 per cent of hides were not marketed but used within producer households (2012a). Moreover, due to traditional animal husbandry practices, the estimated reproductive rate is 37 per cent (which means 28 million sheep produce only 9 million lambs), one of the lowest in the world. At the other end of the spectrum are New Zealand, Australia, and the UK, with a reproductive rate of 150 per cent. Improving the agricultural extension system and providing a stronger incentive package is essential, but not sufficient. This has to be supported by other interventions, such as specialized infrastructure development.

Further, the quality of raw hides and skins has deteriorated in the last twenty years. Although Ethiopian highland sheepskins (from so-called Abyssinian sheep) are of good quality, this quality is undermined by traditional slaughter methods and poor handling of raw hides and skins during collection. According to ELIA, in the 1980s and early 1990s 50 per cent of tanneries received Grades 1–3, a result of the compulsory dipping of animals, as opposed to 20 per cent in 2012. Studies show that the major reason for the defects is ectoparasites, also colloquially known as 'cockle' or '*Ekek*' (USAID 2008; MOA 2012; ELIA 2012). This widespread infestation, which can be controlled through appropriate veterinary services, damages skins and undermines the effects of improved rearing practices. These findings are consistent with interview responses by Ministry of Agriculture officials, tanneries, and leather products firms. Although traceability is difficult because of the inter-regional movement of animals and skins, sheepskins from Gojjam and Gondar are held to be of better quality and sell at a premium, while poor quality skins from Wollo sell at a lower price.

Poor livestock health, estimated to cost more than $2 billion per year in SSA in the 1980s, is a major constraint and requires government to take an active lead (de Haan and Umali 1994). Unfortunately, veterinary services and agricultural extension services in Ethiopia are poor and neglected (Embassy of Japan 2008; USAID 2008; UNIDO 2005), a situation that has been highlighted in various Ethiopian government documents (CSA 2012a; MOA 2012; MOI 2012a, MOFED 2010; see also Little et al. 2010 and Mahmoud 2010). Studies and pilot projects have been conducted by various organizations, including USAID and Pittards, which show that the technology is available to improve skin quality by up to 80 per cent, and that reproductive performance can be immensely improved.

The introduction and expansion of ranches should be explored as a complementary policy with medium-term relevance for the meat-processing industry and supply of raw hides and skins. There is limited experience of ranches in Africa, although they are common in Latin America. The type of ranches is related to political factors.[6] This policy option was, however, not considered in the development of the livestock sector in Ethiopia, possibly to avoid the risks that smallholder farmers might face by becoming more dependent on livestock.

Currently, the livestock sector is viewed as supplementary to crop production by smallholder farmers, rather than as a sustainable source of livelihood (which also contributes to structural transformation and industrialization). The necessary interventions, from livestock development to the leather products industry, require a coherent and integrated approach and high priority in terms of resource allocation. Evidence suggests that

---

[6] See Mwangi (2007) on the political factors that transformed property rights and the ranch system.

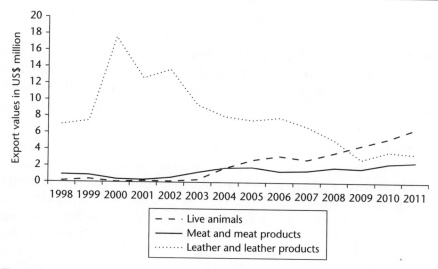

Figure 6.6. Export comparisons: live animals, leather, and meat processing, 1998–2011
Source: Own computation based on ERCA (2012a)

although there was a clear strategic articulation of this priority, no comprehensive policy approaches were formulated.

There is also a lack of compatibility in policies. As previously mentioned, one major policy contradiction regards exports of live animals, which grew faster than meat exports. The former's share of export earnings increased from a negligible 0.16 per cent to 6.57 per cent in fourteen years (see Figure 6.6). However, domestic slaughterhouses and meat exporters are on the verge of closure due to high prices and lack of supply. In November 2012, the association of meat processing plants and abattoirs requested the government to ban the export of live animals (MOI 2012a).

The structural problems related to smallholder livestock management need to be addressed with more effective and coherent policy instruments. Exploring the experiences of Brazil, Botswana, and South Africa can help in addressing these constraints. For instance, in Botswana there are still some 700 ranches, but their share of the national herd (3 million in 2010) has dropped from 30 to 10 per cent because of low returns. Feedlot operators face similar problems (FAO/GOB 2013). Ranches in some African countries have been increasingly constrained by overgrazing and lack of harmonization with pastoralist community norms (Behnke and Scoones 1992; Ash, Bellamy, and Stockwell 1994). In Ethiopia as well, periodic environmental disasters erode livestock numbers and productivity, and the effects of overgrazing are considered to be immense (Hardin 1968; Economists at Large 2011; Aklilu and Wekesa 2002). It is noteworthy that there is no inherent conflict between continued smallholder production and the development of, or experiments with, larger scale arrangements such as ranches: the answer is not 'either/or', but leveraging complementarities.

To conclude, the meat and meat processing industry and the supply of hides and skins are complementary and could have induced the rapid development of a new industry. This is a typical example of Hirschmann's 'neglected problem':

> ...I have distinguished between *privileged* and *neglected* problems. I defined as 'privileged' those problems whose victims have adequate access to the policymakers so that the latter are obliged to pay attention, for the sake of political stability in general and of their own political survival in particular. 'Neglected' problems, on the other hand, do not enjoy this direct access, but they can be brought to the attention of policymakers in various indirect ways...How privileged a problem is depends on answers to such questions as: how numerous and how concentrated are the problem's victims, how important is the issue to them, and how much influence do they have? (Hirschman 1981: 150)

6.4.3 *Political economy of value-addition and industrial upgrading*

An important illustration of the policymaking process is the experience of trying to promote greater value addition in leather. Upgrading may refer to process upgrading, product upgrading, or chain upgrading. Studies suggest that product and process upgrading can happen within the GVC, including under multinational corporations. However, it is unlikely that chain upgrading can develop under the existing global governance system for value chains (Humphrey and Schmitz 2004; Gereffi et al. 2005; and Kaplinsky and Morris 2000). This governance system mirrors the relative power of actors and their ability to assert their interests, and it is the global retail chains that are at the apex of the industry, with their reach extending right down to the tanneries. The value addition is closely associated with the technological level of the industry. For instance, Italy's leather and leather products industry is much more advanced than Kenya's or Ethiopia's (see Table 6.4).

Ethiopian raw hides and skins were exported during the imperial period and under the Derg (1974–91) before being banned in 1983. After 1983,

Table 6.4. Value chain comparator of Ethiopia, Kenya, and Italy

Comparative factors	Kenya	Ethiopia	Italy
Availability of raw hides and skins	Abundant	Abundant	Low
Quality of raw hides and skins	Generally poor	Low–high	High
Sustained capital investment	Low	Low	High
Technological sophistication of facilities and equipment	Low–medium	Low–medium	Very high
Process skills	Limited	Limited	Very high
R&D	Limited	Limited	Very high
Product development	Limited	Limited	Very high
Unique skills within the sector	Rare	Rare	High
Degree of vertical integration	Low	Low	High
Product perception by the global market	Poor	Poor (high for sheepskin)	Very high

Source: Adapted from UNECA and AU (2013)

wet-blue and pickle hides and skins dominated exports, predominantly to Italy, where they were processed into finished leather. The export of pickle and wet-blue hides and skins was prohibited in 2007. Exportable products then had to be processed up to the higher crust level. In September 2008, Proclamation No. 567 imposed an export tax on enterprises 'exporting hides and skins without adding significant value' (FDRE 2008a). The tax rate was 150 per cent of the value of raw hides and skins and 5–20 per cent for wet-blue and pickle. In November 2011, MOFED Directive No. 30 increased the rate to 150 per cent of the value of all raw hides and skins and semi-finished leather. It was only in December 2011 that crust exports were also discouraged through a high export tariff (MOFED 2011b). At present, exportable products need to be processed up to the level of finished leather to avoid these steep taxes. MOI states that thorough discussion and consultation with the industry (through ELIA) preceded the decision on crust exports. However, although it may seem straightforward to induce domestic value addition in this sector, in fact several fundamental changes are required.

Upgrading within the semi-processed stage is important, but the key leap occurs in upgrading to finished leather. This requires upgrading of the industry in terms of skills, technology, quality and supply of inputs, market channels, and of the mentalities of firms and industrial actors. The decision to ban semi-processed leather exports was discussed at NECC meetings from 2005 onwards. For instance, at its eighteenth and twenty-second meetings, it was decided that tanneries would not receive incentives and access to loans if they did not produce finished leather. At the

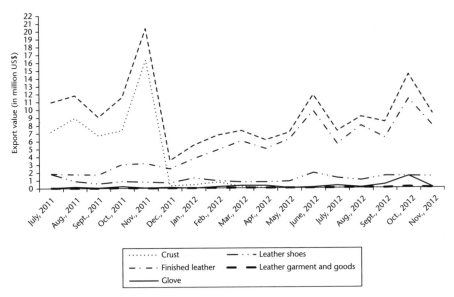

Figure 6.7. Monthly exports of leather sector ($ million), July 2011–November 2012
Source: Own computation based on LIDI data, 20 December 2012

thirty-first meeting, it was also decided to tax tanneries that did not start producing finished leather.

The final decision to ban crust exports was made in August 2011, with December 2011 given as the cut-off date. When firms realized this decision was irrevocable, they maximized their crust exports between September and November 2011, temporarily increasing export revenues (Figure 6.7). On the other hand, prices of raw hides and skins had been increasing rapidly even before, but now skyrocketed. After January 2012, however, finished leather exports dropped for many months, reflecting the industry's lack of readiness to make such exports. Many of the preparations were incomplete, and a comprehensive package was not yet in place. Many in the industry also resisted the change. In short, although the policy was important, its implementation resulted in resource wastage and havoc.

DEVELOPING THE LEATHER PRODUCTS INDUSTRY
Another aspect of upgrading is development of the leather products industry. In the early 1990s, there were only two footwear firms. As NECC meeting minutes reveal, the government was committed to building up the leather products industry by attracting new actors to the sector

(mainly after 2008) and by developing the capacity of domestic footwear firms through a benchmarking programme. Among the foreign firms attracted, a few (for instance, ARA from Germany and Huajian from China) were industry leaders. Since 2008, government had made special efforts to attract such firms, and has since cleared some of the obstacles in their way.

Between 1992 and 2001, most investment was in tanneries (91.5 per cent). From 2002 to 2011, investment trends and numbers of firms changed. Up to 2006, 50 per cent of firms in the industry invested in leather products. This number peaked at 106 firms between 2007 and 2012, accounting for 80 per cent of all investment. This clearly demonstrates the focused investment promotion of the leather products sub-industry. Indeed, NECC minutes reveal that of the 348 issues discussed after 2004, 90 per cent focused on leather products, as did thirty-five of its thirty-nine (on average) annual decisions. Although gradual and limited, value addition has increased recently. In the tanning sub-industry, the value of local raw materials and semi-processed products showed a bigger increase than imported inputs.

VIEWS OF TANNERIES AND LEATHER PRODUCTS FIRMS
ON THE BAN OF CRUST EXPORTS
It should be clear that the ban of crust exports affected different actors differently and their responses mirror their divergent interests (UNIDO 2003). During interviews, it became apparent that many foreign-owned tannery firms that also owned tanneries in their home countries preferred to export crust and add value at home. Their interests did not match those of the Ethiopian government. Many of the domestic firms disliked the decision because their interlocking interests with buyers (foreign tanneries) were jeopardized and they were unable to compete in the changed circumstances. The majority of the firms stated that the preparation time was too short, and only half indicated that the policy has had positive effects on tanneries. By contrast, 88 per cent of the leather products firms maintained that the policy had positive effects, as it allowed them to buy finished leather on more favourable terms. This may have been based on the assumption that the tanneries would be unable to meet export standards of finished leather. In fact, the price of finished leather continued to rise between 2012 and 2013, thanks to the continuing mismatch between supply and demand.

VIEWS OF FIRMS ON TEMPORARY BAN ON LICENSING
NEW TANNERIES

In response to the shortage of raw hides and skins, domestic tanneries put increasing pressure on government to ban new investment in tanneries. Although MOI did make this decision, the Leather Industry Development Institute (LIDI) did not agree on the need for it. LIDI was concerned that such a ban would reduce domestic competition, affecting the leather products industry. In this it appears that LIDI was right, as the decision mainly benefited existing tanneries. Government could have provided information on the circumstances in the industry and left the decision on whether to invest to firms. This decision also undermines the expansion of capacity for future growth, in response to supply once the input problem is addressed. On the effects on firms, more than 70 per cent of tanneries agreed it was positive, as did 53 per cent of leather products firms. Experience elsewhere shows that the outcome of such decisions is contingent on specific conditions (for instance, domestic competition and processing capacity). It is evident that the policy decision was not based on a comprehensive sectoral study.

In conclusion, the policy decisions seem to have had some positive effects, in that exports of finished leather gradually increased. Nevertheless, the process was painful in terms of reduced capacity for almost a year, and the finished leather capacity still does not match the soaked capacity. This has two policy implications: industrial policies could work in this sector, but success is not automatic. It entails extensive planning, monitoring, negotiation, sanctioning, as well as temporary pain. Moreover, such a policy would have been more successful if it had been supported by richer analysis of the sector and a comprehensive package with a longer term perspective at a much earlier stage.

6.4.4 *Binding constraint: Logistics and trade facilitation*

Particularly for landlocked countries, international trade requires efficient logistics and trade facilitation. This is very much the case for Ethiopia. World Bank studies point out that the logistics and trade facilitation constraint has become more significant in the last few years. For instance, customs and trade facilitation is the major problem encountered by Chinese FDI in Ethiopia (World Bank 2012a). Other major obstacles are trade regulation, tax administration, access to finance, tax rates, macroeconomic instability, labour regulation, and electricity. According to *Doing Business 2011, 2012,* and *2013* (World Bank and IFC 2011, 2013), Ethiopia was ranked 152 in 2009, 157 in 2010, and 161 in 2013 in cross-border trade. Arguably, compared with Ethiopia, other countries have made more improvements that are appropriate. In the survey responses, the firms not surprisingly identified import–export logistics and trade facilitation as major constraints. In relation to export delivery times, 55 per cent stated that logistics were the foremost constraint.

In short, external trade is much more costly in Ethiopia than in many countries, and it takes much longer to import and export. One twenty-foot container costs $2,160 to export and $2,660 to import. In terms of delivery times, it takes forty-two days on average to export and forty-seven days to import such a container. The current industrial norm for delivery of footwear and other leather products is less than forty-five days from the date of order. This clearly highlights the challenge. Due to intense competition and the dominance of GVCs, an export market has to be carved out in conditions of stiff competition from Asian manufacturers. The most successful exporting economies (Korea, Germany, and Singapore) have the shortest delivery times and lowest costs (as low as four days and $439 per container). Examples of developing countries include Vietnam (twenty-one days and $600), and Egypt (twelve days and $625/755). It is also believed that inland costs can be significant in landlocked countries, depending on mode of transport.

Experience elsewhere shows that successful logistics and trade facilitation policies involve an integrated or multi-modal transport system, economical rail transport, enhanced competition among logistics providers, and harmonization of customs and transport among neighbouring countries. Single windows linked electronically, automation, and factoring risks have also been adopted in many countries. The key ingredient in this exercise is effective institutions.

Many efforts have been made by government to improve logistics. These include establishment of dry ports, a multi-modal transport system in 2011, industrial zones, and economic operators authorized by the customs authority. Not all these efforts have been effective, and logistical obstacles remain. According to many in the industry, the failed introduction of the multi-modal transport system had adverse effects on manufacturing firms. This system, found to be effective in many countries, was unsuccessfully implemented in Ethiopia. It proved impossible to trace containers, and shipments took up to four months (double the earlier period). The new system failed from the very beginning for many reasons. First, it was designed without sufficient knowledge or study of fundamental issues such as the problems associated with inland freight transport and port related aspects. Second, the implementation agency was a merger—still incomplete—of three SOEs: ESL (shipper), Ethiopian Maritime and Transit Service, and the Ethiopian Dry Port Authority. Moreover, none of these individual entities had good track records.

Third, there was no proper piloting of a complex system involving new technology, which would have enabled officials to learn by experimenting and partial execution, and nor was there sufficient consultation with customers, industrialists, and other actors. For successful policy implementation, timing is important. For instance, it has been argued that the system's introduction should have been linked to the commencement of the new Djibouti–Addis rail corridor. Fourth, hiring experienced partners or consultants or adopting a management contract was not considered. Fifth, in the middle of the project, all transit and clearing agents were forbidden to pursue their activities. This may have reflected the government's broader economic and political concerns about middlemen, market intermediaries, and traders.

A related issue was the monopoly rights granted in May 2000 to ESL to ship all import cargoes, except where the line does not have the capacity or serve the route. This directive, written in the form of a letter, has significant policy implications. First, while ESL was granted a monopoly, no government office was named to regulate the company. This flies in the face of Stiglitz's argument in the mid-1990s that privatization should not proceed without prior establishment of effective regulatory bodies (Stiglitz 1998). Second, ESL was insulated from competition, and the outcome was negative. Even after enjoying a monopoly for twelve years, ESL was still uncompetitive and weak in capacity. This was in stark contrast to state-owned EAL, which had to contend with stiff international competition. EAL has grown and expanded to become one of the leading airlines in Africa. Third, manufacturers and exporters experienced delayed deliveries, as ESL had a limited number of vessels capable of calling all ports of origin. Such delays resulted in missed orders and increased costs, eroding the leather/leather products industries' already thin margins.

6.5 Policy instruments in leather and related industry

This section discusses direct policy instruments, including export and investment promotion, industrial financing, and privatization.

6.5.1 *Investment and export promotion instruments*

EXPORT PROMOTION SCHEMES

The export promotion schemes include foreign exchange retention for all exporters, and other manufacturer-targeted schemes such as duty-draw-backs, vouchers, and bonded warehouses. Of these, only foreign exchange retention seems to have been remotely effective. This is confirmed by 73 per cent of the firms surveyed, which also reported no major implementation problems. By contrast, 85 per cent of firms stated that the voucher system was ineffective and entailed enormous bureaucratic difficulties. According to the unpublished report of the Taskforce on Export Promotion Incentives Review, 187 firms were registered as beneficiaries of the voucher system, of which fifty-two (28 per cent) are in floriculture, forty-two (23 per cent) in leather and leather products, thirty-eight (20 per cent) in textiles/garments, and twenty-eight (15 per cent) in agro-processing. Only forty-two firms (about 60 per cent of all firms in the leather sector) were registered as beneficiaries, showing the low interest in the scheme by manufacturers in this sector. Even those which were registered did not benefit from the scheme. Duty-drawbacks and bonded warehouses were also ineffective. The reasons for these failures lie in the weak design of the instruments and low implementation capacity of government agencies.

EXCHANGE RATE POLICY

Ethiopia devalued its currency in 2010–11 by about 25 per cent. The government has used exchange rate policy to promote exports, and, as already noted, leather/leather goods were prioritized for export. In this case, the policy clearly failed, as the interviews with firms and export data for 2005–11 confirm. Only 43 per cent of survey respondents indicated that devaluation had a positive impact, in contrast to two-thirds of floriculture firms. This deviates from the expectation that devaluation should have a significant positive effect on exporters. A possible explanation is that most of the firms failed to work at full capacity and mainly sold

Table 6.5. Domestic-owned firms' share of export and local sales (by volume), 2005–11

Year	Export sales (in %)	Domestic sales (in %)
2005	95.73	4.27
2006	97.41	2.59
2007	71.23	28.77
2008	50.52	49.48
2009	67.71	32.29
2010	62.14	37.86
2011	62.47	37.53

Source: Oqubay (2012)

locally, resulting in smaller export earnings. Firms are increasingly producing for the domestic market, which is more profitable. For instance, the quasi-census results show that the share of exports in total sales decreased by 33 per cent between 2005 and 2011 (Table 6.5). This implies that the policy instruments and incentives have not been calibrated to influence the behaviour of industrialists, and to link export promotion with exploitation of the domestic market.

INVESTMENT PROMOTION INSTRUMENTS

Initially investment incentives were designed to attract any type of new investment, a practice that continued until 2012. The incentives were neither designed to monitor reciprocity, nor to attract the best industrial performers, who would advance Ethiopia's technological and marketing base. The total number of investment certificates issued between 1992 and 2012 was 220. However, of those registered between 2003 and 2007, only 12 per cent became operational, 7 per cent were at the implementation phase, while 81 per cent were still in the pre-implementation phase. Investment increased gradually after 2002, peaking after 2007. Between 1992 and 2001, more than 86 per cent of investors were domestic, and they were primarily interested in tanneries. The primary reason for investing in this sub-sector was its familiarity in Ethiopia (see Table 6.6).

After 2005, the government began to target investment promotion. Of the thirty-one investment certificates provided to FDI, 68 per cent were registered between 2007 and 2011. Moreover, increased labour costs in many emerging economies (including China) may have served as a pull factor. There was also an investment shift away from tanneries, which had dominated in the 1990s, towards leather products after 2007 (see

230

Table 6.6. Domestic-owned firms' reasons for investing

Reasons	Ranked first	
	No. of firms	Share in %
Natural resources	16	30.2
Experience and knowledge of the sector	14	26.4
Family background	12	22.6
Cheap labour	5	9.4
Growing domestic market	2	3.8
Others: Availability of incentives, political stability, cheap land, ease of access to USA/Europe market	4	7.6
Total	53	100

Source: Oqubay (2012)

Table 6.7. Investment certificates in leather and leather products (1992–2011)

Period	All firms	Average firms/Year	Foreign firms (FDI)		Tanneries sub-sector		Leather products sub-industry	
			Firms	In %	Firms	In %	Firms	In %
1992–2001 (10 years)	47	4.7	4	13	43	91.5	4	8.5
2002–2006 (5 years)	40	8	6	19	20	50	20	50
2007–2011 (5 years)	133	26.6	21	68	27	20	106	80
Total 1992–2011(20 years)	220	11	31	100	90	41	130	59

Source: Own computation based on unpublished FIA data (July 2012)

Table 6.7). Consequently, the share of investment in leather products increased to 80 per cent. In terms of geographical distribution, more than 50 per cent of the investments targeted Addis Ababa and 34 per cent the Oromia region.

Despite the increased number of investments, the administration was cumbersome and there were difficulties in acquiring land and other services. Profit-tax holidays were easier to implement, as the firms confirmed. More than 55 per cent of firms complained that customs duties and land deliveries were problematic, causing delay and additional costs. Two-thirds of the firms complained about poor coordination among federal agencies as well as among federal, regional, and local administrations.

6.5.2 Industrial financing in leather and leather goods

DBE has provided industrial financing to various industries in the manufacturing sector (DBE 2012a, 2012d). Major beneficiaries were textiles and

Table 6.8. Summary of DBE's industrial financing (in ETB million)

Sector	Number of loans	Beneficiaries in %	Average loan amount	Total portfolio	Loans in %
Textile	32	10	156	4,995	46.2
Non-metallic mineral	16	5	238	3,816	35.2
Food processing and beverage	221	71	4	869	8.1
Chemicals and chemical products	22	7	30	669	6.2
Leather and leather products	21	7	22	465	4.3
Total manufacturing sector	312	100	35	10,814	100

Source: DBE (2012d)

garments (46 per cent share), non-metallic minerals (35 per cent), and food processing and chemicals (close to 15 per cent). With a share of 4.3 per cent of the total loans to manufacturing, less than half a billion ETB went to leather and leather products (Table 6.8). The average size of loans to firms in this sector was ETB 22 million, while the average for the manufacturing sector was ETB 35 million. The limited share and loan size for leather and leather products was partly a function of the lower investment requirements, but does also raise the important question of whether the sector got what it required to fulfil its export and employment creation potential.

Eighty-eight per cent of firms in the sector indicated that inadequate credit facilities posed major challenges, and pointed to the gap between working capital requirements and available industrial financing. Working capital plays an important role in this sector, as firms are usually forced to carry a large inventory. This is due to the high material intensity of the sector, inefficient trade and logistical infrastructures, and inefficient management within firms. The period for holding stock and inventory is double that of the overall manufacturing sector (CSA 2012c). The leather and leather products sector's poor performance may have discouraged banks from extending loans to the sector. For instance, in an interview with the author in 2012 (Oqubay 2012), a senior CBE official, it was indicated that the bank was unwilling to provide working capital because the firms would not repay within the stipulated twelve months. Thus, financing policy seems to have been ineffective in promoting this sector. The leather and leather products industry was also unable to benefit from the export credit guarantee scheme (Table 6.9).

Table 6.9. Export Credit Guarantees, 1 September–30 November 2011

Commodities or products	No. of loans	Amount (ETB million)	Share %
Oil seeds	17	316	61
Cereals pulses	6	88	17
Textile and garments	4	64	12
Livestock	3	37	7
Gum, incense, bee products	2	14	3
Total	32	519	100

Source: DBE (2012d)

6.5.3 *Privatization in leather sector*

Another government policy in the leather and leather products industry was privatization. All nine large state-owned firms were privatized and remain in operation. The previous Derg regime had made major investments to expand the capacities of these firms. Privatization in this sector was implemented over fifteen years, and was guided by the government's pragmatic interests rather than ideology. Domestic firms were given priority and more favourable loans (the central bank's saving rate). Accordingly, three-quarters of the firms went to domestic buyers (PPESA 2012). Valuations were revised when the exaggerated estimates became less attractive to investors. There is no evidence that privatized factories were transferred to interest groups connected to the ruling party. Even the regional endowment funds were not among the buyers: for instance, EFFORT established a new tannery in Tigray under the name Sheba Tannery. In addition, the government used two transfer modalities: most of the firms were sold by open tender, while the biggest tannery, Ethiopian Tannery, was transferred to Pittards through direct negotiated sale. Pittards, which initially opted for contract management, improved productivity, made an additional investment, and strengthened production management. In 2011, it also established a glove factory, with a second leather products factory following in 2012.

Between 2007 and 2011, additional investment of ETB 234 million was made by the new owners to equip the privatized firms. Capacity utilization of privatized tanneries and footwear factories stood at 69 per cent and 56 per cent respectively in 2011, which were not below the industry's low average capacity utilization. This does not allow us to conclude that all privatized firms have improved their performance. For that, a more detailed study is required. Measuring the outcomes of privatization raises

Table 6.10. Major problems of privatized firms

Problems	Percentage
Shortage, high price, poor quality of raw materials	49
Shortage of skilled personnel and capacity	20
Shortage of finance	9
Logistics, customs, and trade facilitation	13
Others	9
Total	100

Source: Oqubay (2012)

several methodological issues, including differentiating direct and indirect factors. Some of the privatized firms were still among the best performing top five exporters in the sector in 2011. Privatized firms faced problems similar to those faced by other firms (see Table 6.10).

6.5.4 Summary

In sum, first, the policy instruments were only partly successful and were not comparable in scale to the support provided to the cement or floriculture sectors. Second, many of these instruments suffered from design deficiencies, insufficient implementation capacity, as well as coordination problems. Third, the firms in this sector played a largely passive and insignificant role in the process, an issue with deeper implications.

6.6 Drivers of transformative change: specialized institutions

This section focuses on three relevant institutions, namely export coordination institutions, the lead organization for the leather and leather products industry, and intermediary institutions.

6.6.1 Export coordination and NECC

Some of the most significant NECC decisions included the decision to privatize state-owned tanneries (May 2004) and that to prohibit new tanneries from receiving government incentives (February 2006). Other equally important decisions were, for instance, the one stipulating that tanneries be supported in producing finished leather (September 2005) and that DBE loan allocations be guided by this decision and not be made to new investors in tanneries (October 2005). Moreover, in January 2007, it was decided to impose the new tax on tanneries that did not start producing finished products. However, in May 2007, it was decided to encourage Turkish investors in the tanning sub-industry, thereby reflecting inconsistency in policy decisions. There were clearly other policy inconsistencies, including the decisions to export live animals while also importing raw hides and skins to alleviate shortages. Similar decisions were repeatedly made, suggesting that government institutions were complacent and unresponsive, or lacked accountability or capacity.

Although NECC did treat this sector as a priority, there were problems in the decision-making process. First, reports to government lacked depth and a strategic analytical perspective, and were limited to tackling immediate constraints. Consequently, policies and decisions were not well informed. For instance, discussions on input constraints were not based on detailed study and a comprehensive approach to the development of this strategic sector. Second, decisions were not effectively implemented. Third, the producers, enterprise owners, and trade unions were not engaged in the decision-making process, an approach that exacerbated the information gaps and divergences in the implementation of decisions. Moreover, an opportunity to build trust between state and the industry was missed. Government should play a role in promoting active private sector involvement, as the industrialization process depends on such activism.

6.6.2 LIDI as lead agency

The lead agency for the leather and leather products industry is LIDI. Its precursor, the Leather and Leather Products Technology Institute, had been established in 1998 by the Council of Ministers. Its main tasks focused on training and information services and improved productivity and quality standards. In addition to the resources allocated by the Ethiopian government, the Italian government, the Common Market for Eastern and Southern Africa's Leather and Leather Products Institute, and UNIDO provided technical assistance and financial support. Building of the Leather and Leather Products Technology Institute facilities took more than five years. In June 2010, this institute was re-established with expanded responsibilities and duties as LIDI. The new organization's mandate included:

...to study and recommend policies to the government; conduct research; promote and support investment in leather and leather products sector; provide training services; enhance technological and know-how transfer; provide laboratory services; assist in market development; promote input-output linkages; provide design and product development services; network with all potential stakeholders and institutions. (FDRE, Council of Ministers, Regulation No. 181, 2010)

Led by a director-general, there were directorates for leather manufacturing technology; footwear manufacturing technology; leather garments and goods manufacturing technology; market support; research; and investment support (project engineering). The institute has 265 personnel, almost equally divided between line and support staff. Among line staff, 64 per cent were professionals and 32 per cent had technical certificates and diplomas. Among the technologists and technicians, 34 per cent were in leather manufacturing, 31 per cent in footwear manufacturing, and 34 per cent in garment and goods manufacturing.

LIDI is equipped with state-of-the-art technology and modern facilities. The latter included models of a tannery, a footwear factory, and a leather garment and goods factory. It also has an effluent treatment plant, fully equipped laboratories, a computer-aided design/manufacture centre, a library, computer facilities, and training halls. LIDI's main deficiency was its lack of capacity to use these facilities to support the industry. In 2011, government made an agreement with two Indian institutes, the Central Leather Research Institute to support the leather sector, and the FDDI to support the footwear and leather products industry. There is evidence that the twinning arrangement is contributing to improvement in LIDI's capacities and those of the leather and leather products industry (LIDI 2012a, 2012b, 2012c).

Eighty-four per cent of firms agreed that LIDI has made a valuable contribution in supporting the sector, and affirm that the institute works closely with industry (86 per cent). Eighty-one per cent of firms agreed that the institute focuses more on supporting firms than on regulation, a higher rating than that for EHDA in floriculture. Evidence does not suggest that learning had been rapid or to the required level. Lack of capacity remains LIDI's single greatest challenge (see Table 6.11). Moreover, coordination among government institutions was weak, contributing to LIDI's ineffectiveness. According to the survey results, 69 per cent of the firms view coordination among federal government institutions as

Table 6.11. Firms' response to 'What is the key limitation of LIDI?'

Key limitations	Per cent
Lack of skilled personnel	24.6
Lack of implementation power	22.9
Lack of focus on domestic market	13.1
Poor training support	9.8
Limited mandate	9.8
Lack of technological up gradation	8.2
Others	11.5
Total	100

Source: Oqubay (2012)

poor, while 60 per cent regard coordination among federal, regional, and local administrations in the same light.

A review of firms' requests to LIDI highlights the coordination challenge. A review of 316 letters (LIDI 2012e, 2012f) showed that 40 per cent of those from foreign-owned firms related to permit requests for expatriates from the labour affairs office. Delegating authority to provide these permits to LIDI on behalf of the labour office would have eased this problem. Domestically owned firms' most frequent requests (37 per cent) related to sending sample shoes or raw skins overseas, which should not have required such permission to begin with. Again, a simple directive would have solved this problem. This also shows how administrative hurdles that should never have arisen in the first place can overwhelm an agency, weakening its focus on key aspects of the industrial policies to promote the development of the sector.

The data also show that these problems became more frequent over time (eight in 2010, fifty-five in 2011, eighty-eight in 2012). Usually two to four weeks are lost because of such administrative bottlenecks, significantly delaying delivery times and increasing costs. This conclusion is also supported by the author's survey results (Oqubay 2012): the majority of firms indicated that they spend significant management time on government-related issues, and even more than firms in floriculture and cement (Table 6.12).

This shows the failure of such government agencies as MOI and LIDI in providing coordinated and effective support. During interviews, most firms regarded LIDI and the ministry as 'toothless lions'. This in turn shows the limitations of NECC in guiding the parties and enforcing decisions. It also confirms that logistics and trade facilitation, as well as government bureaucratic procedures, continued to be critical constraints.

Table 6.12. Time spent on government-related issues

Management time (%)	Floriculture		Leather		Cement		Total	
	Firms	In %	Firms	In %	Firms	In %	Firms	In %
≤15	19	35	19	34	5	31	43	34
16–30	22	41	23	41	6	38	51	41
>30	13	24	14	25	5	31	32	25
Total	54	100	56	100	16	100	126	100

Source: Oqubay (2012)

In the long-term, it is perhaps the competitiveness of domestically owned firms that is most affected by such constraints.

6.6.3 *Effectiveness of ELIA as intermediary institution*

ELIA is the industrial association of the sector and the main intermediary institution. It was founded in 1994 as Ethiopian Tanners Association and reorganized itself in 2004 into Ethiopian Tanners, Footwear and Leather Products Manufacturing Association. In 2004, the association had twenty members, mainly tanneries. In 2007, it became ELIA and had forty-four members, more than 60 per cent of which were tanneries. This group continues to dominate the association. By contrast, in Vietnam it is the leather products (footwear, bags etc.) manufacturers that dominate the national industrial association.

Twelve of the fifty-five survey respondents were not members. Although ELIA's capacity mirrors the capacity of its members, responding firms admit the association is ineffective. They said it played a weak role in market development (61 per cent), in target setting and monitoring (78 per cent), and in investment promotion (66 per cent). Regarding its role in training and knowledge transfer, 90 per cent of the firms gave it a poor rating. Less than 60 per cent were satisfied with ELIA's role in policy development and government lobbying (see Table 6.13).

Although members rate the dialogue between government and the industry as satisfactory, they recommended more discussion forums, improved participation by stakeholders, and further government support. Many of these views, however, are based on exaggerated expectations concerning government's role. Significant parts of the industry are comfortably locked into the status quo and are unwilling to engage. Sixty-four

Table 6.13. Views on ELIA's role

Degree of ELIA's role	Lobbying government		Market development		Training/ know-how transfer		Target setting/ monitoring		Policy initiations		Investment promotions	
	No.	%	No.	%	No.	%	No.	%	No.	%	No.	%
Excellent	1	2	–	–	–	–	–	–	4	9	2	5
Satisfactory	25	58	17	39	4	10	9	22	23	52	11	29
Poor	17	40	27	61	36	90	32	78	17	39	25	66
Total	43	100	44	100	40	100	41	100	44	100	38	100

Note: No. represents the number of firms
Source: Oqubay (2012)

per cent of firms admitted that the association's members do not play an active role. Furthermore, the association does not include recent entrants into the industry, including foreign-owned firms. In addition, hides and skins suppliers are not part of ELIA or any other association, which further compounds the challenges. All of this indicates that government has failed to address important institutional aspects of the sector.

6.7 Conclusions

The disappointing performance of the leather and leather products sector in Ethiopia is a reminder that industrial policy can fail. A number of conclusions stand out from the research into this industry. First, in terms of policy outcomes, sector performance was characterized by erratic and sluggish growth throughout. Compared to cement or floriculture, performance was very disappointing. Notably, massive animal resources were not productively used. The evidence strongly suggests that comparative advantage in natural endowments does not automatically lead to sustained competitive advantage. Moreover, potential linkage effects are converted into actual linkage promotion through effective policies, which were lacking. Nonetheless, the sector is not quite the abject failure it is sometimes made out to be. In recent years, there have been signs of recovery and positive initiatives such as benchmarking. Policies did achieve some value-adding in existing tanneries (from semi-finished to finished) and in attracting new entrants into the leather products subsector. Furthermore, it should also be emphasized that one of the most important macroeconomic conditions for maximizing linkages may be ensuring a competitive exchange rate.

Second, in terms of policymaking and policy capabilities, it is evident that policy improvements and huge investment in institutional development were made. The policies and institutions rightly identified the key constraints: inputs and logistics, for instance. Nevertheless, they could not address them due to problems in operationalizing policies and, in some cases, inappropriate policy choices. The institutional deficit in input development (livestock development and marketing chain for raw materials) was a significant failure. In fairness, dealing with small, scattered producers/input suppliers is always more difficult than dealing with a few 'modern' enterprises, such as in the cement industry.

Third, the main economic actors in the sector are not well organized and have conflicting interests. As a result, they played a much less prominent part than in other sectors, contributing to the industry's slow growth and lack of competitiveness. Unlike the intermediary institution in floriculture, ELIA played an insignificant role, and lacked internal cohesion and a jointly developed agenda. Firms suffered from inertia, preferring to limit themselves to the domestic market and shy away from exports. This also shows that the incentives partly failed to induce the required behaviour and export discipline. Thus, government–industry dialogue forums need to be institutionalized more effectively.

Finally, it is noteworthy that this experience is associated with path dependence in the leather and leather products industry. Path dependence influences and shapes understanding, problem solving, policy design, and implementation. Instituting desired changes in a long-established sector with an accumulated network of interests is more difficult than in newer sectors. Path dependence in this old sector at least partly explains the long history of stagnation, the limited deepening of the value added, the inertia among actors and their intermediary institutions, and the ineffectiveness of policies. Operationalization of policy was insufficient or policies were followed for far too long. There are two possible policy responses to change the sector. One is to allow foreign investment in tanneries; the other is to continue to protect them but to introduce a reciprocal control mechanism, with clear targets as the condition for the protection.

7

Failing Better

Political Economy and Industrial Policy in Ethiopia

*Diversity notwithstanding, all late industrializers have in common industrial-
ization on the basis of learning, which has conditioned how they have behaved.*

Alice Amsden, *Asia's Next Giant* (1989)

7.1 Comparative performance

7.1.1 *Performance, policy learning, and Ethiopian 'anti-fragility'*

Without wishing to provoke charges of policymaking hubris, I believe
there is evidence of 'anti-fragility' in Ethiopian industrial policy. Anti-
fragility is the term coined by Nicolas Taleb (2012) to describe the ability
of a system to be strengthened by stress rather than collapsing under its
weight (fragility). This is distinct from robustness, defined by Taleb as the
ability to fend off threats and remain unchanged. To understand the
sources of anti-fragility in policymaking, one must appreciate policy processes based on learning-by-doing and adaptability, characteristics rarely
explored in studies of policy and performance in developing countries.[1]
Through sector case studies, previous chapters have shown examples of
these policy dynamics. It is also important to understand the conditions
that allow for anti-fragility rather than robustness or fragility. In Ethiopia,
these conditions seem to include the ruling party's experiences as a

[1] For a discussion of 'adaptive capacity' in decision-making in 'mega-projects', see Giezen et al.
(2014).

liberation movement and in the protracted military struggle to oust the Derg regime. In the post-liberation period, the EPRDF has survived under enormous external threats; succeeded in developing a cohesive ideology and mechanisms for resolving internal differences; often revitalized itself after internal crises; and blended experiment, pragmatism, and long-term vision and principles. By contrast, many other successful liberation movements have degenerated after assuming power, often plunging their countries into destructive violence (see EPRDF 2011b; Young 1997; Clapham 2009; Tareke 1990, 1991).

At first glance, it is easy to identify successes and failures in the case studies explored earlier in this book, but this is not, per se, a study about success or failure, a too simplistic binary evaluative framework to be useful. At the very least, the evidence in preceding chapters shows how frail the categories of success or failure can be when applied on an aggregated sector-wide basis. For example, despite disappointing overall performance in leather and leather products, there have nonetheless been important advances in this sector from which lessons may be learnt (for instance, value addition). Floriculture appears to be an obvious and clear success (UNIDO-UNCTAD 2011: 63), yet there are areas of failure and emerging challenges that necessitate new policy responses. The emphasis is better placed on challenges and problems and the logic behind them, an approach that is also a healthy safeguard against self-congratulation. While success brings new problems and challenges, problems have the potential to generate new and unexpected opportunities. Reinvigorating growth ultimately depends on leveraging learning in policymaking, and having the political resolve to take decisive action and ensure coordination among multiple actors.

Earlier chapters have shown that the outcomes of Ethiopian industrial policy have been distinctly uneven. This is a puzzle for policymakers and scholars alike and requires explanation. As the discussions in Chapters 4–6 illustrate, floriculture, cement, and leather and leather products feature prominently in national development and industrial development strategies. Likewise, the broader context has affected general conditions in each of these sectors in similar ways. This book has argued that the Ethiopian state has played an important developmental role within a market economy, a role that goes beyond merely 'facilitating' comparative advantage, as has been advocated by some. The country's political landscape is shaped by a federal and nascent multiparty system, and also the continuing dominance of the ruling party since 1992. These factors are believed to have been favourable to the growth of all three sectors, and for the first time in its history, the country has witnessed a decade of rapid economic growth. What has not thus far been explained is why, within this broader context, there has been such marked variation in performance.

This chapter provides a comparative overview of the three sectors before outlining such explanations as have been put forward. These are more or less standard explanations—that outcomes must be a function of comparative advantage; are a product of neopatrimonialism; or are a product of a 'discovery process'. While not without some value, none of these explanations is sufficiently convincing empirically or logically. Instead, the chapter goes on to argue that the Ethiopian experience of policy and performance is better understood in light of Albert Hirschman's insights into 'linkages' and the unevenness of developmental processes. From this perspective, bottlenecks and constraints can be creative. As Samuel Beckett put it in *Worstward Ho*: 'Ever tried. Ever failed. No matter. Try again. Fail again. Fail better.'[2]

7.1.2 Comparative analysis of the three sectors

Performance across the three sectors reveals several facts. First, *sectoral performance* was markedly *uneven*: disappointing and erratic growth in the leather and leather-working industry, and higher growth in both the cement and floriculture sectors. This can be seen in the comparative growth in production, employment, and exports (see Figure 7.1).

Second, output growth was much stronger after 2002 than between 1992 and 2002. This coincides with and may to a significant extent be attributed to the government's policy learning and the refinement of its development strategies and industrial policies after 2003. This in turn signals the importance of a relatively stable political settlement since the removal of the Derg in the early 1990s. It has to be noted that this initial phase was also characterized by economic transition from a command economy to a free market economy, the imperatives of postwar reconstruction with exceedingly scarce resources, and political reform. This transition served as a springboard for economic stability and recovery

---

[2] And indeed as the 2013 Australian Open tennis champion Stanislaw Wawrinka had tattooed on his forearm.

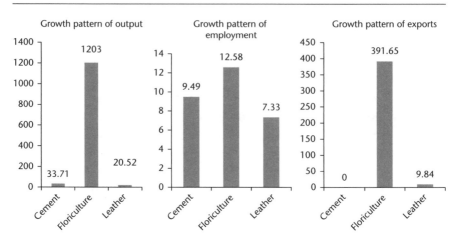

Figure 7.1. Comparative performance in three sectors (2003–12)
Source: Summarized from previous chapters (all in per cent)

after the late 1990s. It is also evident that growth in post-1991 Ethiopia was much faster than in pre-1991 Ethiopia. Learning by doing is as much a feature of policymaking as of a firm's management and production techniques. Arguably, a key feature of the overall policymaking context (and its effectiveness) was the combination of relative political stability/continuity and a sharp political shock. On one hand, political stability and continuity since 1991 created an environment conducive to learning by doing, similar to that allowed by industrial protection. On the other, the 2005 elections produced a 'shock'. The unexpected political challenge in 2005 acted almost as a 'hiding hand' by prompting a renewed developmental imperative and refreshing the coherence of policy commitments.

The significance of policy learning by doing or an evolving adaptive capacity (Giezen et al. 2014) is not commonly emphasized in the literature on the political economy of industrial policy in Africa. But in another respect, the Ethiopian evidence does confirm the findings of Whitfield (2011) and Buur et al. (2012), who argue that political continuity and coalition stability matter greatly for the outcomes of productive strategies. Whitfield (2011), for example, argues that support for Ghana's potentially strong horticultural export sector was undermined by the incentive structure built into the political settlement after the advent of democracy. Effectively, elites were not compelled to support new productive sectors, however great their long-term potential: on one hand, emerging horticultural producers were not strong enough to represent a threat; on the other, the returns to government would not flow quickly enough to warrant state support. In Mozambique, where there has been greater political and party continuity since independence, there are nonetheless factional divisions that have undermined the coherence and stability of state support for particular sectors (Buur et al. 2012), although in other sectors, such as sugar, support has been more sustained and effective.

The record in Ethiopia suggests that a development-oriented state indeed performed better over time than states without an activist industrial policy and that its industrial policy has contributed to higher growth. The facts regarding the policy measures, institutional changes, and sectoral performance underpin this assertion. The important implication is that an appropriate industrial policy can work even in a very poor African country like Ethiopia. Moreover, this growth and industrial expansion took place in a landlocked economy in a 'bad neighbourhood', thereby distinguishing the experience even more clearly from the predictions and typologies of some influential analysts (Collier 2006, 2007, 2009; Collier and Gunning 1999; Easterly 2002; Easterly and Levine 1997; Fosu 1992, 2012).

Third, despite higher growth during this period (1992–2013), the outcome in terms of structural transformation was underwhelming, indicating the limitations of industrial policy. The share of manufacturing in the economy and in export earnings remained low throughout. This reflects an inherent weakness in current industrial and other related policies in Ethiopia, which, as noted in earlier chapters, can be contrasted with the policies adopted to transform Korea economically from 1960 to 1980 and China between 1985 and 2005. The implication is that industrial policy capability in Ethiopia remains rudimentary, and needs further development. Nonetheless, the relatively strong performance of the overall economy and some parts of industrial production underscores the importance of the Ethiopian government's efforts to maintain policy independence, since the policies pursued often represented a direct challenge to Bretton Woods prescriptions, prescriptions routinely followed by most African countries.

7.2 Conventional arguments and standard explanations

7.2.1 Comparative advantage

One influential explanation views factor endowments (particularly cheap labour and natural resources) as the most influential determinants of the success of industrial policy. A World Bank publication (2012), based on this approach, tried to demonstrate how light manufacturing could be promoted in Africa, by taking Ethiopia as one of the African case studies, with Vietnam as a comparator, and China as benchmark. Justin Lin, former chief economist of the World Bank, champions this approach (Lin and Chang 2009). The key argument is that countries such as Ethiopia can successfully industrialize if they stick to their comparative advantages and focus on light manufacturing, such as leather and apparel, and on taking the prescribed actions to address key constraints identified in the value chain. This approach fails to consider the political economy determinants of industrialization, such as the nature and role of the state and the role of policies in determining or avoiding path dependency. It falls into the all too common trap of casting economic development as a largely technical challenge. Buur et al. (2012) and others in the Elites, Production and Poverty programme at the Danish Institute for International Studies provide one alternative exploration of productive success and failure that is much more realistic in its appreciation of the political economy of productive expansion (or stagnation).

While factor endowments are clearly important, there are difficulties with a policy approach that relies exclusively on them. According to Lall (1999: 9) 'the traditional theories of comparative advantage that are noted as the foundations of government policy are based on highly simplified models of "perfect" markets with no scale economies, costless and full information flows, no risk and so on.' Not only are the assumptions unrealistic, often in the extreme, but many regression analyses provide no convincing empirical evidence for the postulates of comparative advantage theory. Indeed, as has been noted, one renowned macroeconomist, Greg Mankiw 'was not surprised by the lack of robustness in the cross country results, given the large number of candidate variables relative to the number of country observations. He conjectured that economists support free trade because they believe Ricardo, not because they have been convinced by regressions.'[3] In other words, there is a strong element of faith among economists in Ricardian comparative advantage theory, but this does not make it the best guide for policy. The assumptions in the theory are a gross oversimplification of real

---

[3] Rodriguez and Rodrik (2001:338).

economies that are characterized by ubiquitous market and information 'imperfections' (as they appear, at least, to neoclassical economics). These circumstances in turn require active industrial policies in order to accelerate industrialization and structural transformation of economies. *However, industrial policies should be based on market realities, rather than on abstract models of 'perfection'.* Korean and Taiwanese economic transformations, for example, were possible because they successfully moved up the ladder from simple products to advanced skills and technology using active industrial policies, rather than merely specializing in their traditional comparative advantages (Lall 1999; Chang 1999; Singh 2011).

Factor endowment provides an inadequate explanation of the puzzle at hand for many reasons, and factor endowments alone do not account for the success or failure of industrial performance across sectors in Ethiopia. The comparative advantage argument might predict that Ethiopia would be competitive in basic leather production but not necessarily in leather products (in particular, higher-end gloves, accessories, etc.), or in high productivity flowers. This is because some versions of comparative advantage thinking (Owens and Wood 1997) look more at the ratio of skills to cultivable land—evidently higher in Holland (a high-productivity flower producer) or in Italy's leather products sector. Yet there has been a sharp rise in productivity and skills in some of these sectors in Ethiopia, whereas even in the more obvious area of basic production of leather from hides and skins, Ethiopian performance has historically been very poor (under a variety of different policy regimes). Further, there is plenty of evidence from a range of countries of their accelerating their growth and structural change by challenging factor endowment constraints.

Likewise, growth in the Ethiopian cement industry did not depend on factor endowments. The cement industry is a capital-intensive heavy or basic industry, with large economies of scale and dependence on professional management. In Ethiopia, it is also a strategic import-substitution industry that was driven by a fast-growing domestic market. It was neither a light industry nor labour-intensive, and was not based on the country's endowment of cheap labour or natural resources. Further, expansion in this sector was dominated by domestically owned firms and indeed by state-owned and EIGs, thereby deviating from international trends in which cement is typically dominated by massive global firms. This evidence suggests that the advice to sub-Saharan Africa to focus on light industry and to avoid building up such capital-intensive industry is based on unwarranted assumptions.

Of course, there is some common sense in adopting the 'Ricardian' comparative advantage approach, at least partially, as almost all developing countries have done at some stage of their development. A 'Ricardian' strategy essentially follows and supports existing comparative advantage. It effectively means, for a low-income country, specializing in the export of primary commodities and perhaps some light manufacturing that is technologically undemanding and requires little skilled labour. Such a strategy typically will be supported by a 'light touch' state and by liberalized trade, which indeed will provide the price signals to illuminate comparative advantage. Nevertheless, historical facts also show that 'Ricardian' strategies can create self-sustaining growth only by shifting to a second type of strategy, namely, the 'Kaldorian' strategy (Schwartz 2010).[4] A 'Kaldorian' strategy is more complicated and prioritizes the expansion of manufacturing, given the idea that manufacturing plays a unique role in the growth and structural change process. Such a strategy also rests on the premise that it is not possible to accelerate industrialization and to speed up the gains from economies of scale and learning-by-doing in manufacturing without protective policies.

In the Ethiopian context, static comparative advantage was not the key driver of industrial policy or performance in any of the three sectors featured in this book. For instance, despite abundant Ethiopian livestock resources, the leather and leather products industry has remained stagnant: this suggests a form of impotent or unrealized comparative advantage. The government has long failed to upgrade the industry or attract dynamic private investors into it; and the strategy has lacked coherence and remained largely ineffective. By contrast, leather industries in Brazil, China, and Italy have continued to play a major economic role, and not without significant state intervention to support their growth or, in the case of Brazil, resurgence. In Ethiopia, the sector has continued to be uncompetitive internationally. Even cheap labour has not helped reverse the industry's stagnant and falling productivity, though the latter may have begun to change with recent inward investment by a major Chinese women's shoe producer, as well as other foreign investors.

---

[4] On Ricardian and Kaldorian strategies, see Chapter 2, Section 2.3.2.

By the same token, in floriculture, despite the existence of natural endowments (water, soil, land, climate, relative market proximity, etc.), the industry did not flourish until the early 2000s. What facilitated the rise of this new industry were the government's readiness to 'pick' this industry (and to allow it to be 'picked' by entrepreneurs in line with the government's overall development strategy) and to implement appropriate policy and policy instruments, combined with the readiness of investors (foreign and national) to participate in this industry.

These examples also suggest another area where political economy, rather than abstract technical economic principles, is critical. As Buur et al. (2012) argue in regard to sectoral variation in Mozambique, one factor that matters is sustained political support and another is the organizational capacity within a given sector or industry. Further, foreign investment can raise such organizational capacity, as in the recent cases of foreign investment in the Ethiopian leather sector. The flower sector is a very good example of both domestic sector organization and a huge contribution to this by foreign investors.

7.2.2 Patronage and neopatrimonialism

Another version of industrial policymaking is propounded by the neopatrimonial school. The patronage and neopatrimonial interpretation has enjoyed much currency in the donor community and neoliberal circles since the early 1990s and comes in several shades. A key inspiration in this interpretation is Weber's identification of three 'ideal' or 'pure' types of legitimacy, namely traditional, charismatic, and legal. According to Clapham's (1985: 48) widely used definition, 'neopatrimonialism is a form of organization in which relationships of broadly patrimonial type pervade a political and administrative system which is formally constructed on rational-legal lines.' Thus neopatrimonialism is a system of government that is a mix of the rational-legal Weberian-type state, with separation of powers and impersonal rules, and surviving personal relations that guide decisions, resource allocation, appointments, etc. Weber (1947) applied the term to traditional authority in 'the Orient, Near East, and Medieval Europe'. However, on the basis of Clapham's definition and personal observation of political processes and behaviour in advanced industrial countries, including the US, UK, and France, neopatrimonialism is a globally pervasive and enduring feature of governance. This would seem to reduce even further the concept's analytical value for understanding African economic policy and performance.

However, it is to precisely the enduring and pervasive 'chronic failure' of economic growth in Africa until recently that current proponents of neopatrimonialism apply the concept. According to this pessimistic view, there is no foundation or scope for developmental states in Africa. Industrial policy, this school holds, cannot succeed in Africa, since it will only reinforce, and be confounded by, neopatrimonialism. According to Altenburg (2011: 8):

> Industrial policy plays an important role in stabilizing neopatrimonialism as it creates political space for politicians and bureaucrats to allocate government resources to specific groups of beneficiaries. These can be employed to strengthen ties of loyalty between individual politicians or bureaucrats and private beneficiaries, but also to buy political support from specific social and ethnic groups that are considered important for the survival of the incumbent regime.... Consequently, politicians and bureaucrats who want to employ industrial policy for patronage and clientelism can easily find technical justification to mask their political objectives.

Successes in some African countries are seen as exceptional or unsustainable, and generate a supplementary literature on 'developmental neopatrimonialism'. Kelsall et al. (2010: 28) argue that 'centralized, long-horizon rent-seeking, when combined with broadly pro-capitalist policies, can generate dynamic growth'.

Industrial policy is thus viewed as a vehicle to benefit party members and supporters; party-affiliated businesses, such as endowment funds; and specific ethnic groups. Ethiopian government programmes such as the micro and small enterprises development programme are seen as a channel for consolidating the ruling party's position. Influential NGOs, the donor community, political parties, and vocal dissidents very much subscribe to this view (Kelsall 2013). Nonetheless, no strong theoretical grounds or empirical evidence are adduced to explain how this is different from other political systems, for instance in the UK and US.

Conceptually, the neopatrimonial view has fundamental flaws and cannot offer a solid analytical approach. First, it reflects *Afro-pessimism* and is imbued with an entrenched prejudice that views African culture or Africans as incapable of making progress (Mkandawire 2001; Padayachee 2010). All ills are attributed to the failures of African leaders or societies. Consequently, it is blind to country-specific peculiarities and the diversity among (and within) African countries. Yet, historical evidence shows that many African countries had the vision and capacity to secure high economic growth, for instance, during 'the golden period of Africa from 1960 to 1980' (Soludo et al. 2004). Even after the 1980s, Mauritius and Botswana succeeded in sustaining growth, and since 2000 a dozen countries, including Ethiopia, have achieved high economic growth.

Second, it is a *static*, simplistic view that ignores how economic and political forces are in constant motion, and the complexity of policy-making. According to Ottaway (2003), neopatrimonialism is 'an ill-defined code word for the political ills that afflict the continent', and for Clapham (1996: 820) '... explanation in terms of culture should be regarded as deeply offensive'. Mkandawire further refutes the notion in conceptual and analytical terms.

> [a] ... while providing descriptions of the styles of exercise of authority ... the concept has little analytical content and no predictive value with respect to economic policy and performance ... [b] Economic policymaking is a highly complex process involving ideas, interests, economic forces and structures, 'path dependence' and institutions, and cannot be reductively derived from the 'logic of neopatrimonialism'. It will require serious attempts to understand the ideas, interests and structures, which shape or hinder Africa's development efforts. The neopatrimonial approach is too simplistic and too formulaic to help in understanding the complex drama of development taking place in Africa.

Furthermore, Altenburg (2011) relied on a limited number of selective interviews, which may not lead to objective observations. For instance, individuals do not—as Altenburg suggests—own endowment funds, and the law on endowment funds does not allow resource channelling to political parties. The presence of political leaders on the boards of state-owned or endowment fund–owned firms does not necessarily support this conclusion. Moreover, loans have been available to most floriculture firms, including foreign-owned firms (some of whom have 'over-picked' the state). The beneficiaries of the biggest DBE loans were private firms with no political ties or connections, including foreign firms. If supporting the *chaebols* in Korea was not neopatrimonialism, how can support for regional, publicly owned endowment funds in Ethiopia be counted as such? The evidence on the allocation and performance of concessionary loans to the floriculture sector, where there was at first little or no discipline (Amsden's 'reciprocal control mechanism') on borrowers, suggests, if anything, naivety on the part of state agencies rather than calculated patrimonial misallocation.

Despite neopatrimonial assertions, state-owned enterprises have also not necessarily or uniformly nurtured predatory groups and clienteles. The Mugher Cement Enterprise was a pioneer and played a leading role in the cement industry. As we have seen, other state-owned enterprises such as EAL and DBE have served as key vehicles of industrialization and change in the political economy of Ethiopia. Indeed, international evidence suggests that ownership—state versus private—is not the key factor in enterprise performance, and that, if anything, state-owned enterprises have most often been fundamental to industrial catch up (Musacchio and Lazzarini 2014a, 2014b).[5] Support to the private sector in Ethiopia's priority industries does not demonstrably produce the patronage predicted by neopatrimonial theory. Again, there is nothing exceptional in the blurred lines between government-controlled state enterprises and private sector enterprises. As Milhaupt and Zheng (2014: 8) argue: 'The... response to the 2008–2009 financial crisis in the United States illustrates that even in countries where private ownership of enterprise has strong ideological and historical roots, the boundary between government control and private control' can be blurry. In addition, the focus of state-owned and endowment fund enterprises on large-scale manufacturing and strategic projects shows their developmental role in overcoming 'market failures'. Getting prices and property rights wrong (Amsden 1989) has, as the evidence suggests, been critical to the, albeit inchoate, process of structural change in Ethiopia. Endowment funds made critical investments—and took or socialized fundamental risks—in cement, beverages, leather and leather products, textiles and garments, and transport. In sum, claims by proponents of the neopatrimonalist approach appear in large part to be unfounded and not empirically grounded.

7.2.3 *Limits of 'industrial policy as a process of discovery'*

Another approach to industrial policy and performance that has had some influence in recent years is 'industrial policy as discovery process'. This hypothesis would attribute success in the floriculture sector to collective

---

[5] Musacchio and Lazzarini (2014b: 16) highlight '...thanks to SOEs Brazil developed large sectors that initially were not funded by the private sector alone, such as steel, airplane manufacturing, telephony, national oil, gas, petrochemicals, mining, and an integrated electric grid...Most applied innovation efforts were also essentially executed by state agencies (such as Embrapa in agriculture) as well as large SOEs such as Petrobras and Embraer.'

learning and the discovery process. Industrialization *is* very much about learning. And the idea of a discovery process captures something relevant, something not dissimilar to the emphasis in this book on adaptation, on Hirschman-like dynamics of creative problem-solving. This is, therefore, a relevant and interesting perspective, though one that like so many mainstream perspectives seems strangely unaware of a whole tradition of development economics and engagement with industrial policy. At the same time, it seems to be an over-simplistic, descriptive, and *post hoc ergo propter hoc* approach. The level of private sector development, existing and potential tensions between conflicting interests, the risk of political capture by sector interests, etc., are important variables that are given little attention in this kind of approach. The predictions of this framework are also slightly fatalistic, calling for a less proactive or more passive industrial policy until after a new and promising industry is discovered. This is fully consistent with the pessimism Rodrik (2014) has expressed elsewhere: 'I come down on the pessimistic side, due to what I think are poor prospects for industrialization.'[6] But if everything boils down to a mysterious process of discovery, how are policymakers to operate? Should they simply sit and wait for discoveries to unfold?

This so-called discovery framework also fails to consider that the private sector may not, left to itself, always represent the best interests of the broader economy. Its entrepreneurs may be inclined to make 'discoveries' that are not really in the interests of overall transformation or welfare improvements or, without appropriate government intervention, may be a realm of rentier opportunity (Mazzucato 2013a). It is more likely that the private sector focuses on short-term returns rather than the long-term interests of industry; just as, on the flipside, governments may be so beset with factional divisions or frequent democratic turnover they too focus excessively on the short run and fail to 'facilitate' investors in promising new sectors (Whitfield 2011).

The nascent private sector in Ethiopia has in the past demonstrated a tendency to focus on short-termism and on the temptations of engaging in speculative activities rather than productive sectors, and to prefer light industry over riskier intermediate or heavy industry. This should not be taken as evidence of uninformed judgements or hasty decisions.

---

[6] <https://www.sss.ias.edu/files/pdfs/Rodrik/Research/An_African_growth_miracle.pdf> 'An African Growth Miracle?', Institute for Advanced Study, Princeton, April 2014 (p. 2).

Rather, it is a product of their experience and resources, and of prevailing incentive structures. Given the high risks involved in investing in the manufacturing sector, and high rents in services and trading, there is nothing 'wrong' or surprising in this preference. Specific sectoral features and, indeed, broader political economy factors also shape interests and investment patterns. Unlike in floriculture, the government was the pioneer and key player in the development of the cement industry throughout its initiation and growth stages (through its state-owned enterprise). The government gradually induced the private sector to play an active role in the industry, through the demonstration effect of the state-owned enterprise and the inducement or linkage effect of the rapidly expanding market for cement (principally in the construction sector). The government had to 'show' the sectoral prospects to private sector investors rather than wait for them to 'discover' these for themselves. In a nutshell, the narrative in the cement industry shows that its development required an active and leading role by government, despite the prompts and hints given by an industrial strategy that favoured large-scale infrastructure investments, and by the rapid growth of the construction sector.

Although industrial policymaking is indeed a learning process, and there is a need for state and private sector to communicate (and often industrialists will know better), the 'discovery process' approach (Rodrik 2004) reduces the process to an unrealistic fable whose moral is that everyone should be nice and listen to each other, the typical charm of liberal assumptions. Nor is it always just a matter of the kind of creative imbalance that Hirschman (1958) emphasized, though that is important: it is also a matter of conflicting interests and tensions. Often these conflicts are too intense and the scarcity of resources compounds the tension. Hence, states have sometimes to be more interventionist. The South Korean state, in the period of early rapid industrialization, was far from 'nice' and infamously put people in jail when they did not perform. Although this might not be a 'lesson' to encourage, it is an indication of the intensity of conflicts of interest. For instance, it is precisely in the leather and leather goods sector where these conflicts have created an obstacle to sectoral expansion and transformation.

The 'discovery process' interpretation was also based, in its application to Ethiopia, on biased and incorrect evidence, as is shown in earlier chapters. What mattered in floriculture was not dialogue per se, but the decisive government response to the constraints of the industry. The government took swift political decisions to make land available, to make loans accessible, and to ensure that air transport and logistics infrastructure were provided. In view of the resource constraints and political sensitivity, the state showed its capability to manage rents, to socialize risk, and to make critical political choices. There was almost inevitably some corruption and wastage in this process, and some individuals had clearly taken advantage of incentives without adequate 'reciprocal control mechanisms' in place, especially early on. But over-all, the evidence suggests a net gain in terms of foreign exchange earnings, employment creation, structural changes, and (unevenly) the development of enterprise governance capabilities. The government's readiness to listen to the private sector was an outcome of its strong political commitment and strategic orientation to develop this sector. Land provision was a highly contested political issue, and the political decision to subsidize air transport at a time when government had withdrawn subsidies on kerosene and fertilizer was potentially dangerous, as were concessional loans in the context of very scarce credit. These key decisions could not have been made but for the state-owned development bank, the state-owned air transport firm, and publicly owned land (including former state-owned farms). These issues say a lot about a developmental state and the policy independence of the government, rather than its capture by patronage. The backdrop was that in contrast to many countries in sub-Saharan Africa, the Ethiopian government resisted privatizing the development bank and held land under public ownership, despite pressure from international financial institutions and strong neoliberal prescriptions (what Joseph Stiglitz calls 'market fundamentalism'). These were not primarily matters arising out of a dialogue process, but rather out of political constraints and political economy.

In addition, the frequent narrative is that the private sector pioneered the floriculture industry. This narrative is associated with the implicit assumption that foreign investors were the key drivers of this sector. This is far from the truth. For instance, the state explicitly encouraged the development of sectoral organizational capacity by advising the two Ethiopian pioneers to establish their association EHPEA in order to over-come obstacles and voice their interests. EHPEA is now one of the most effective intermediary institutions, and an example to other industries.

Therefore, development of this sector was mutual and complementary, rather than one-directional.

7.3 Linkage approach to policymaking

7.3.1 *Unfolding of linkage effects in the three sectors*

As discussed in previous chapters, from a linkage perspective the pace of development in general and industrialization in particular depends on industries with strong backward and forward linkages. What the evidence from the research suggests, though, is that there is considerable variety in the way in which apparently obvious 'pressure mechanisms' or 'pacing devices' (Hirschman 1992) unfold, or fail to unfold. There is nothing automatic about linkage effects. They depend on policy, but they also depend on politics, and on the structure and particularities of specific sectors.

LINKAGES ARE NEITHER HOMOGENEOUS NOR AUTOMATIC
The linkage approach should not be taken to mean that linkages seamlessly reveal themselves (perhaps a version of the 'discovery process'), automatically generating new productive activities, and taking effect in a uniform way. Nor should it be assumed they reveal themselves in similar shape and scale and with similar dynamism. This is not the case in the real world, as the sectoral chapters show. In fact, the diversity among linkage effects has been striking, and there was no instance in this research where they repeated themselves or where they appeared in one form. The first important distinction is whether the linkages emanate from inside the industry or from outside. Some linkages may initially originate in another industry, sector, or activity to create the conditions for the activity under observation. A typical example is the backward linkage from the construction industry to the cement industry that enticed the growth of cement production. In contrast, in floriculture, the linkages were 'transplanted' from elsewhere (notably from the export market, not from domestic market dynamism). There was clearly already a latent, readily accessible source of autonomous export demand. But that of itself did not stimulate investment. A combination of regional demonstration effect (Kenyan success), exploratory contacts with potential investors, and a raft of policies was required to generate momentum in the flower industry, which in

turn developed its own logic of opportunity and linkage to other investors and to other related activities like packaging and logistics.

A second aspect of linkage effects is that the direction and dynamism of the linkages may change gradually. At the initial stage, the prime linkage for the leather sector may have been the forward linkage from livestock, that is, raw hides and skins, to tanning and leather manufacture. The push from this linkage became too weak, and the linkage feedback loop shifted in the opposite direction from the leather sector back to the development of raw skins and hides production, in short, a backward linkage. But this linkage in turn only (and for a long time very slowly and fitfully) unfolded because of the identification of the sector's potential by successive governments (supported by a string of external consultancy reports).

The third aspect is that exploitation of potential linkage effects depends not only on policy design and execution, but also on politics. Arguably, one of the key lessons of this study is that almost all linkage effects required government policy to be effectively exploited, and the outcome mirrored the quality and effectiveness of the adopted policy and institutional response. It is noteworthy that some policy responses depended on the state's posture on addressing the issue. The linkage to air transport and cargo logistics in floriculture, the linkages to the energy sector, and those from the construction industry to cement, and the critical financing of the expansion of all three sectors by the state-owned development bank, were possible because of the *decision-making of the state* (in the form of political imperatives and cohesion, policy design, and institutional settings) at that particular time.

In some cases, such as the development of a packaging industry initially to service floriculture, the key was the emergence of new entrepreneurs induced to invest by the rapid growth of flower exports, but even they were supported by government policies. Yet in the cement industry, manufacturers directly diversified into a backward linkage to the manufacture of cement bags (economies of scope). In the leather sector, the response to linkage possibilities was left to smallholder livestock owners, but without fundamental structural and social transformation they were not in a position to take advantage of the opportunities created by an emerging leather sector. Developing a dependable input industry based on many and scattered producers is perhaps more difficult than supporting a few modern manufacturers.

257

FAILURES AND SUCCESSES IN FACILITATING
LINKAGE MECHANISMS

It is therefore sensible to suggest that an important explanation for the variability in policy outcomes was the differences in policy approach to developing the linkage effects. The evidence so far shows the following:

a) In *the floriculture sector*, downstream (forward) linkages were more important than upstream linkages. The industry's growth would have been arrested if the solutions in cold chain logistics and dependable air services were not put in place. This binding constraint was removed primarily through state support. EAL was there to fully exploit the opportunity created. It made strategic moves including expensive aircraft purchases to modernize its fleet, and subsidizing its services when necessary. The government also, through EHDA, successfully supported the corrugated packaging industry, and improved the local availability of inputs, thereby contributing to the sector's competitiveness. These efforts helped not only address binding constraints but also to fully exploit opportunities to develop new industries. In addition, government made land available and provided close to ETB 1.5 billion to the majority of firms in the flower sector, including foreign firms. Even realizing a competitive advantage based, in part, on factor endowments (land and agro-climatic conditions) required political and policy intervention in the form of land policy, leases in particular. This was also symbolic in terms of demonstrating the government's commitment to the sector, as well its readiness to welcome FDI.[7]

b) In *the cement industry*, the backward linkage (from the construction boom) was strong and effective. The growth of the construction industry was itself an outcome of government policy intervention, including macroeconomic policies that produced sustained economic growth and programmes such as housing and infrastructure development and capacity building in the construction industry. Sustaining this rapid growth was important politically (the 2005

---

[7] The demonstration effect of this commitment should not be underestimated. Arguably, it helped reveal fresh opportunities in other sectors and hence to build momentum for FDI flows into Ethiopian manufacturing. In this sense, there may be a form of global intersectoral linkage, where the obstacles and pressure points include multinational firms' challenges in finding reliable manufacturing and assembly suppliers.

election revealed narrow latitude for failure). This is similar to the situation where internal and external threats provoked 'political will' in industrialization policies in East Asia (Doner et al. 2005). Housing development was the flagship programme in urban centres. This drive (with its direct effect on cement demand and on political commitment to resolve key constraints of the cement industry) was instrumental in the exponential growth of this sector. Energy and freighting constraints were addressed through large-scale government resource allocation to infrastructure development. The capital-intensive character of the industry, and its scope for economies of scale, also required government investment in the sector through the state-owned Mugher Cement Enterprise.

c) The analysis of *the leather and leather products sector* clearly showed that linkage effects are not always automatic or as compelling as they would appear to be. The growth of the sector depended on a sustainable supply of cheap and good-quality hides and skins, something that would appear possible given the huge livestock numbers in Ethiopia. The strategy in this sector was built on comparative advantage (cheap labour and livestock resources), and this sector was singled out for promotion in the overall development strategy, i.e. Agricultural development-led industrialization (ADLI) and Industrial Development Strategy of Ethiopia (IDSE). Nevertheless, livestock resources are scattered across the country and agricultural transformation is required to meet the growing demand and requirements of the leather and related products sector. Considering that livestock herds are dispersed among a large population of often very low-income smallholder farmers, it may be a long time before livestock production and husbandry is fully commercialized and transformed. Traditional agriculture has diminishing returns, but the feedback loop from leather manufacturing was too weak to exert the necessary pressure on traditional farming. The government's capacity to mobilize its own resources (directly through the state-owned enterprises) in shaping this linkage was too limited, which is surprising in light of the country's ADLI strategy. Hirschman, in *The Strategy of Economic Development* (1958), refers to backwardness in agriculture by quoting Gerschenkron's hypothesis that 'the more backward it is, the more the state intervention is needed'. Yet, in Ethiopia, what has happened is the reverse: the leather and leather products sector should have enjoyed a much more forceful and effective industrial policy. This does not, however, preclude the possibility of promoting a more realistic policy option, namely modern ranches and modern slaughter and meat-processing firms.

7.3.2 Linkages as coping mechanisms and policy learning

It is useful to draw out the parallels and direct connections between linkages, in the sense of one economic activity 'calling forth' or making viable another, on the one hand, and the policymaking and institutional process, on the other. The core of the linkage and 'unbalanced growth' approach is the recognition that bottlenecks and imbalances can be creative—they can induce recognition of a problem that requires an innovative solution, and signal incentives to provide such a solution.[8] However, this does not always happen. When it does happen in economic activities, it is called a linkage. In policymaking, this response is more about learning by doing, adaptation, and so on. In addition, the learning and accumulation of policy experience can, of course, be applied to other problems as they arise. It is difficult for outsiders to see this clearly. Instead, they come as external experts (Hirschman's 'visiting economic expert syndrome') with blueprints, models, and best practices, which are often limited and inappropriate, undermining the scope for institutional/ policymaking innovation (they may divert Hirschman's 'pressure mechanisms' and clog up the 'pacing devices').

Clearly, this situation becomes very interesting where the institutional/ policymaking process takes place at the point where an economic linkage does or does not materialize, or a sector does or does not undergo its own development and learning by doing. One example is cheap loans to flower farms. Subsidized loans were made available, with two negative results: some of them were diverted into very different uses by some investors (possibly including transfer abroad through over-invoicing and so on) and some of them were invested, but in unnecessarily expensive equipment

---

[8] Here there is a direct parallel between Hirschman's idea of linkages and his (1967) idea, in *Development Projects Observed*, of the principle of the 'hiding hand', whereby underestimation of the costs and difficulties of a large project are necessary for the project to be begun at all, but then, once these problems arise, they often provoke creative problem-solving adaptations.

and technology. Part of the problem lay in DBE's lack of appropriate and effective mechanisms either to choose between borrowers or to monitor or discipline them. But it seems that there was at least partial learning here: the development bank started imposing more *ex ante* discipline by, for instance, forcing borrowers to put up cash rather than just a fence around the land. Monitoring was also strengthened (involving joint action with EHDA, the lead government agency in floriculture) and measures included transferring assets and loans to a third party. This indicates that there has been adaptation, but only partially. One concludes that a reciprocal control principle and monitoring/disciplining have not been fully developed.

Another such example is the interactions between the EHPEA, EAL, the government, and the massive Dutch-owned flower farm. Here, too, government adapted. At first, government subsidized rent for no good reason or purpose, allowing the firm to monopolize forwarding of output to the airport for other flower producers in Ziway. However, there have been changes since then, including direct service provision to all growers by EAL. Here, the question arises: to what extent and how is business decision-making and 'soft' technology or knowledge of running a capitalist enterprise developing among Ethiopian producers? And how is it spreading (if it is spreading) from Ethiopians who play a lead role to others, and from foreign investors (such as the relatively small French-owned Gallica or Sher-Ethiopia) to Ethiopian owners? In addition, how does government influence this 'soft' technology transfer? Evidence suggests that farm productivity has improved and the gap with Kenya is narrowing, while changes in terms of product and market development and technological advancement are insignificant. This requires further research.

Against this backdrop, it is possible to suggest that part of the explanation for the failure in the leather and leather products industry was that government policy lacked adequate appreciation of, or responsiveness, to the scope for and challenges to stimulating linkages, despite the many studies conducted (for instance, UNIDO, Japanese, and Cramer). The challenge of profoundly transforming agriculture (the time needed, scale, and politics of intervention) was beyond the scope of the policy response. This can also be associated with the view that agriculture, unlike manufacturing, has fewer linkage effects. The challenge was compounded by the institutional inertia of, in particular, the Ministry of Agriculture

and regional extension services, and the intermediary institution, especially ELIA, the industrial association for the leather industry, and the
absence of institutions that equally represented the interests of all firms
and stakeholders in the input chain. In view of the structural rigidities in
agriculture, alternative solutions focused on development of modern
ranches and strengthening modern slaughterhouses might have helped
address input constraints.

7.3.3 Path dependence in leather and leather products

Lall (1999, 2003) emphasizes that learning is 'path dependent', and adds:
'Once embarked on, technological trajectories are difficult to change
quickly, as specialization patterns tend to persist over long periods.' This
is particularly true of the Ethiopian leather and leather products industry.
This industry has been characterized by low-value products for many
decades. Tanneries were dominant and they have been interlocked in
mutual interest with Italian tanneries, an unholy alliance whereby Ethiopian tanneries supply semi-finished leather. This created a comfort zone
and a false shield for the sector. These circumstances were a reflection of
the long tradition of Ethiopian tanneries under the command economy,
where tanneries did not have to compete among themselves or with
others. In the footwear sub-sector, the moribund, stagnant productivity
equilibrium was suddenly disturbed by liberalization and the subsequent
competition from imported goods and entry of new firms. The sub-sector
faced fierce competition from imported Chinese footwear (from the mid-
1990s to the mid-2000s in particular), and almost all the footwear firms
were on the verge of shutdown, as they were uncompetitive even in the
Ethiopian market. Most firms then embarked on investment in technological and skills accumulation. The entry of many new firms has positively reinforced this transition to a better path.

In the leather sub-sector, however, no such exogenous shock arose, as
liberalization did not automatically lead to the inflow of imported semi-
processed hides and skins. Even privatization of state-owned tanneries did
not break old path dependence. Consequently, the old equilibrium
remained undisturbed. Since 2005, the tendency to sell only to the domestic market and shy away from exports has become dominant in the sector.
Further, some key players in tanneries had backgrounds in the speculative
skins and hides trade. Hence, these tanneries did not face input shortages,

and were less interested in fundamental transformation of the input chain. Tannery interests dominated ELIA, making the association less receptive to new government policies focused on exports. Efforts to deepen the industrial structure met passive resistance, forcing the government to postpone many policies for a long time. In addition, existing firms perceived new investments in the tannery sub-sector as a threat, and lobbied policymakers concertedly and with some success. In this sector, piecemeal intervention and changes that depended solely on existing actors did not bring about the required change.

Different policy decisions may have had varying results in breaking path dependence and the development of a new growth path. For instance, the government pursued and strongly adhered to a policy of developing the leather products sub-sector (such as footwear and garments). Leather products provide narrower scope for poor performance, as their production forces firms to confront global competition. The presence of new actors with such experience enhances the chances that interventions will bear fruit, and contributes to breaking the inertia and forging a new path. This may compel backward linkage activities, for instance, in the leather sub-sector. The ban on exporting semi-finished leather and the requirement for increased value addition may also have a transformative effect in breaking path dependence. In addition, the import of inputs (raw skins and hides, semi-processed, and finished leather) could have helped break path dependence.

Yet, the banning of new tanneries (despite the government's good intentions to strengthen domestic firms) may further solidify existing inertia, as it reduces competition within the leather sub-sector and reduces pressure to transform the input value chain. Arguably, given the strength of path dependence in this sector, the best policy option would have been a targeted promotion of firms based on their past successes, rather than on the origin of investment. Moreover, the introduction of performance standards (including ex-post) could be more effective in channelling the dynamics in the right direction.

7.4 Variations in industrial structure and policy implications

Industrial structure by itself is not everything. Nevertheless, the findings suggest that industrial structure and industry-specific factors were important for performance variation and policy effectiveness across sectors. Knowledge of industrial structure aids selectivity and targeting in industrial policies, guides understanding of the roles and characteristics of economic actors, and highlights the economic and technological characteristics and requirements of the specific industry and the opportunities they afford. Industrial structure reveals the underlying forces and basic characteristics of sectors, the 'type of the economic activity defined by a combination of capital intensity, economies of scale, production flexibilities, and asset/factor flexibility' (Evans 1997: 61–87). The three aspects that have significant implications for industrial policymaking in Ethiopia are the characteristics of firms and investors, the latitude for performance standards, and the stage of industrialization.

7.4.1 *Economic actors and policymaking*

The characteristics and behaviour of firms and producers vary across sectors. For instance, the cement and floriculture sectors have been dominated by a few medium and large firms. This makes it easier for government to support and interact with sector leaders. In the leather sector, actors are heterogeneous, with varying sectoral interests: tanneries (mostly medium and large firms), leather products (dominated by many small enterprises, in addition to medium and large firms), unorganized input traders, and small, scattered skins and hides producers. These actors operate under varied institutional settings, and often have conflicting interests.

Until late 2003, efforts to attract FDI were driven by the need for capital investment and, hence, there was no selective sectoral targeting or stringent monitoring of the process. There have been some shifts towards selectivity in the three sectors more recently. In floriculture, investment promotion targeted industrial leaders, for instance the Netherlands, which plays a dominant role internationally. The majority of foreign-owned firms had the marketing and technological capability needed to secure Ethiopia a foothold in the global market. The government arranged finance, which added to its leverage on foreign investors. Local firms were supported with training interventions (by government, the industrial association, and the Dutch embassy) that facilitated expertise and skills transfer. This is an example of how aid, foreign policy, and multinational interests partly converge; of how a bilateral state agency (the Dutch embassy), acting primarily in the interests of Dutch capital, smoothed entry for Dutch firms, and subsequently provided assistance and technology transfers to Ethiopia, probably beyond what Dutch firms themselves would have done; and at the same time, an example of how multinationals depend on their country of origin to promote their global reach. The foreign-owned floriculture firms were family-owned and medium-sized, as well as quick to adapt. It appears that the political risks and pressures that come with these firms have not been unmanageable. There *have* been political challenges in the flower sector relating to compensation issues, the environment, and labour, all of which required government responses. This situation has shaped the pattern and momentum of the sector throughout its history (2004–12), as has the active role played by industrialists (domestic and foreign) and their intermediary institutions (the sector's industrial association and the Dutch embassy).

The leather and leather products sector continued to be dominated by domestic firms with institutional interests that created hostility to competition and a strong dependency on government. Until after 2008, designs to target investment promotion were inadequate. Domestic enterprise owners were less interested in seeing significant FDI or in learning from counterparts. After 2008, the government took important steps to engage firms such as Pittards (in 2009), Huajian (in 2011), ARA (in 2010), and New Wing Addis (in 2010) through a managed privatization process and promotion of FDI. Nonetheless, it appears that government acted only after a long stalemate and when the damage had been done. *In this industry, the policy approach promoted inertia, while in floriculture it produced a dynamic state–business partnership that enhanced collective action and collective learning.*

In cement, state-owned Mugher, and later Messebo, played a leading role in terms of taking risks and being first-movers. Others then followed, facilitating collective action. Further, there is a lesser presence of FDI in the Ethiopian cement sector than in the corresponding sectors in any other African and many other non-African economies. This may well have been important to the domestic evolution of firm and technology capabilities, but thus far has undoubtedly come at the cost of efficiency. The point is that policy, and indeed the larger issue of industrial policy and the 'developmental state', is not independent of either industry structure or the pattern of interests among investors and other relevant actors in specific sectors. Just as 'governance capabilities' may vary across sectors within a country, so too will the degree of 'state autonomy' vary across sectors and over time.

Finally, the industrial structure of the cement industry permitted and called for the government's direct role through state-owned enterprises. This has allowed the sector to benefit from the critical role played by the state. This was not the case with the other two sectors, which were more favourable to small and medium, family-owned firms. The role given to and played by state-owned enterprises in Ethiopia has been driven by the belief that they are essential to industrialization, which requires an activist role by the state. The neoclassical view emphasizes that markets would function efficiently and that state intervention is bad. For instance, according to World Bank (2013), 'Private sector-led activities appear to be constrained by the policy choices favouring public investment'. This view rejects the state's role in direct economic activities through large state-owned enterprises (World Bank 1995; Shirley 1997) and holds that the state should confine itself to protecting private property rights and reducing transaction costs (North 1990). Consequently, privatization of state-owned enterprises has been included as a key component of the Washington Consensus (Williamson 2008) and its successors. The neoclassical view fails to see that markets are neither always superior to states, nor immune themselves from politics (Stein 2006; Chang 2006). Bureaucratic decision-making in state-owned enterprises is wrongly blamed, although bureaucracy is a feature of all large firms, private or state-owned (Chang and Singh 1997; Chandler 2004).

State-owned enterprises are founded with multiple aims, for instance, economic transformation or catch up (Amsden 1989; Chang 1994). There are also no grounds for assuming that state-owned enterprise performance is weak because of the size of the enterprise or state ownership (Chang and Singh 1997; Jalilian and Weiss 1997). Indeed, the research does not support the argument that privately owned firms are more efficient than comparable state-owned enterprises (Mühlenkamp 2013). There is certainly huge variation in the performance of state-owned enterprises, which is still poorly understood (Musacchio and Lazzarini 2014a, 2014b), but so is there variation among private firms. The differences between large private and large state-owned enterprises often evaporate on close inspection: 'Large, successful firms—regardless of ownership—exhibit substantial similarities in areas commonly thought to distinguish SOEs from POEs: market dominance, receipt of state subsidies, proximity to state power, and execution of the state's policy objectives'

(Milhaupt and Zheng 2014). A good example is Brazil, where 'thanks to SOEs Brazil developed large sectors that initially were not funded by the private sector alone, such as steel, airplane manufacturing, telephony, national oil, gas, petrochemicals, mining, and an integrated electric grid...' (Musacchio and Lazzarini 2014b: 16). Moreover, most applied innovation efforts were also developed either by state agencies like Embrapa in agriculture or by large state-owned enterprises such as Petrobras and Embraer (Musacchio and Lazzarini 2014a).

7.4.2 Latitude for performance standards

The prevailing incentive structure for private sector actors, including the persistence of rent-seeking opportunities and lack of incentive to accelerate learning and accumulate technological capabilities, creates intense pressure on a society or government seeking to speed up structural transformation. Hirschman (1967: 87) notes that latitudes for performance standards are 'the propensities and pressures to which the decision makers are subject', and that some projects or activities are 'so structured that latitude is severely restricted or completely absent: in these cases I shall speak of lack of latitude or positively, of the presence of "discipline" imparted by the project.' However, such pressure mechanisms or disciplining opportunities are not equally realized in all sectors. For instance, developing countries typically have better advantages in process-centred production (such as refineries or cement manufacture) than in product-centred production.

Technological and economic characteristics impose different latitudes on performance standards in the three studied sectors in Ethiopia. Floriculture's narrow latitude for failure arises from the perishability of the product, and the care it requires from farm to points of consumption. This is reinforced by constant pressure from supply-side technological uncertainties. This is one reason why there is a concentration of family-owned medium-sized firms in the sector. The exclusive orientation to export markets imposes the need to cope with international competition. This has had an important disciplining effect, in particular, on the many domestic firms that were new entrants into the industry. It also helped to liquidate at an early stage the exclusively rent-seeking firms that were unwilling to change.

The same was true of the cement industry, whose economies of scale, capital intensity, high entry and exit barriers, and continuous production process acted as a positive force to improve capacity utilization. The risk of failure was too great. This was reinforced by the nature of the product, which is perishable and bears immense risks and legal implications if quality standards are not met. In contrast, in the leather sector such pressures did not exist, particularly in the tanning and basic leather sub-sector. The industry was built on the dominance of tanneries and not on the leather products sub-industry. By contrast, the leather products sub-industry has much narrower latitude for failure. Producers in this sector also 'exploited' the loophole of being able to supply the domestic market, rather than the much more competitive export market. This wide latitude interacted with the inadequate and inconsistent policy approaches in the sector.

According to Lall (1999), the 'domestic market plays an important role in national capabilities', as local demand affects the development of products, quality, etc. This is crucial in countries like Ethiopia, where the domestic market is, given population size, potentially large. This requires intensification of competition in domestic markets, which helps to dissipate rents not based on performance. Porter (1998: 119–20) argues that

> domestic rivalry not only creates advantages but also helps to avoid some disadvantages ... The stock of knowledge and skill in the national industry accumulates as firms imitate each other and as personnel move among firms. Domestic rivalry not only creates pressures to innovate, but also to find ways that upgrade the competitive advantages of firms. Toughened by domestic rivalry, the domestic firms are equipped to succeed abroad.

Where really open and fair competition is unlikely, other devices need to be instituted by the state, such as reciprocal control mechanisms or other disciplining measures.

The role of the domestic market in building national capabilities also suggests that there should be no dichotomy between export-led industrialization and import substitution: the value of exporting does not preclude nurturing production for the domestic market. This is opposite to the view associated with the approach that undermines import substitution, hindering integration between both strategies to maximize their complementarities. In the three Ethiopian sectors, export discipline and competitive pressure seem to have played a critical role, especially in flower production. Lack of intense competition in the domestic market for leather and leather products, and the weakening of export discipline are major factors in the sector's disappointing growth. The disparity between the success of state-owned EAL (unlike many other state-owned airlines), which has had to compete in the international aviation industry, and the disappointing performance of the state-owned Ethiopian Shipping Lines, which has enjoyed a monopoly and unjustified rents, is a typical example of the critical role of competition in industrial performance and competitiveness. Competition is not a magic ingredient, as it may not breed success (as witness the failed airlines around the world). Though it is rarely 'perfect' and is neither the only nor always the most effective means of promoting learning, adaptation, or productivity, competition is, nonetheless, one 'disciplining' mechanism that narrows the latitude for failure.

7.4.3 Stage of industrialization

Variation in outcomes of industrial policy across the three sectors is partly a function of the challenges and opportunities that come with the level of development of the industry. It appears that, in some ways and contrary to what one might expect, initiating a new industry is easier than stimulating an existing industry. For instance, Hirschman (1968) highlighted how the challenge in the early stages of import substitution is much easier than in the second stage of industrialization, when the interlocking interests of different groups and political structures have become established. There may also be a problem if there is insufficient capacity among policymakers to follow and understand changes in industrial structure over time and to adapt to the sector's dynamic challenges. For example, floriculture, after a decade of initial growth, appears to have entered a new industrial stage since 2010, but the state has largely maintained the existing policies. There is evidence that the slower growth of the flower industry after 2009 reflected policies that have 'run out of steam', requiring new policies suitable for the next growth stage. The same risk seems to confront the cement industry, which has entered a new phase since 2012. Each industrial stage brings its own constraints, challenges, and opportunities that call for appropriate responses. Arguably, initial success in an industry may create the illusion of wider latitude for failure, and entrench institutional patterns of behaviour and sets of interests, all of which pose fresh challenges for policymakers. This highlights the need for policy capabilities that include the ability to sustain a long-term vision and constant monitoring.

7.5 Unevenness of policy instruments and organizations

Policymaking is a dynamic and complex process beset by dilemmas, tensions, and uncertainties. It involves diagnostic policy design, implementation, and evaluation of impacts. For instance, if policy outcomes are not monitored, how can policymakers or others know whether there are blockages or what the concrete policy effects are? Policies are also the product of negotiations between conflicting interests, rather than merely technical endeavours or the seamless translation into action of higher-level visions or strategies. This implies that policies adopted as feasible and relevant may not necessarily be the most effective ones.

It is often difficult to separate the outcome of a policy from other relevant variables, and policy outcomes may need a long time horizon for their full effects to become clear. Successful policies would make themselves redundant over time, due to emerging constraints, challenges, and opportunities. Although plans are necessary elements of industrial policy, their effectiveness is undermined by the uncertainty of data and the reality of constant change. Within this complex context, it is likely that mistakes will be made. Policy-learning capabilities may help reduce mistakes and improve the pace and scope of policy learning. Ultimately, what matters is that benefits outweigh costs, and that lessons are learned to minimize future mistakes and develop the capacity to adapt to and recover from mistakes.

More importantly, the choice of policy instruments reflects political choices and political constraints (domestic and international). While the same instrument may be used for different aims, divergent instruments can be used to achieve a specific goal. For instance, privatization or FDI policy may serve different purposes, and many incentives can be used with an inbuilt reciprocity principle. In Ethiopia, the government's cohesive strategic direction and political orientation has infused most specific policy instruments, contributing to a consistency. Federalism, the relative weakness of the state bureaucracy and stronger institutional strength of the party, the relatively underdeveloped private sector, and the state's activist orientation, have all shaped political choices. For instance, active use of state-owned enterprises where 'the market' was reckoned unlikely to lead to the most productive and developmental outcomes was compatible with the government's approach to privatization. This can be contrasted with policies followed in other African countries such as Mozambique and South Africa (see Cramer 2000). The policy on FDI has been consistent, given the relative weakness of the domestic private sector and the government's priority to strengthen it. The political commitment to strengthen the DBE and provide subsidized long-term loans to key industries was made possible by the cohesiveness of the governing coalition and by the political pressures that helped cement this cohesion. Nevertheless, the disparity in the coherence and concentrated use of the design and implementation instruments has generated varied results.

7.5.1 Inconsistency in applying the reciprocity principle

Although most of the instruments (for instance, investment promotion, export promotion, exchange rate policy) were applied across the three sectors, their outcomes, importance, and applicability varied from sector to sector. Export promotion required huge administrative capacity, while investment incentives were easier to administer. The evidence shows that uniform incentives were easier to implement than sector-specific instruments, and applying a 'reciprocal control mechanism' was difficult: incentives were linked very weakly to performance standards. The principle of reciprocity depended upon a more sophisticated capacity to administer the incentives than incentives without such a requirement. Export promotion policy was less effective in leather and leather products, as it partly failed to shape the behaviour of actors. The policy to attract FDI into the leather sector had limited effect until 2006. In the absence of a strong link between incentives and performance, outcomes have depended partly on the nature of actors, export discipline, and competitive pressure. The message is that *reciprocity* and performance-driven instruments have a central function in industrial development.

In Korea, 'the reciprocity principle operated in almost every industry' and 'in return for protection in the domestic market, the government required the enterprises to export part of their production' (Amsden 2007a: 96, 2001: 151). However, the political setting in Ethiopia is different from Korea's. Unlike Korea, where the political economy allowed for a concentration of intermediate assets among national champions

(Amsden 2001), the requirements of federalism and a political commitment to equitable regional growth make such resource concentration difficult in Ethiopia. Amsden argues in *The Rise of the Rest* that where there is broad equality, it is easier to concentrate intermediate assets, because there is less political risk. Ironically, where there is high initial inequality (as in Latin America), risk-averse leaders do not dare to concentrate these assets. The Ethiopian experience suggests that, despite low initial inequality, the federal system constrains the scope for concentration of intermediate assets and necessitates a wider dispersal than may be optimal for industrial policy. The endowment funds may contribute to narrowing regional disparity, but also arouse envy in regions where no strong endowment funds exist.

An important condition for the reciprocal mechanism to work is the introduction of export discipline, as it constantly forces firms to improve their productivity. Ocampo (2007: 2), for instance, emphatically argues that '...a successful export strategy is highly dependent on how the export sectors are integrated with other domestic economic activities, not least in terms of employment generation'. Export discipline must be supplemented by increased competition and rivalry in the domestic market. According to Porter (1998: 119–20), toughened by domestic rivalry, it is more likely that 'domestic firms are equipped to succeed abroad'. When imposing reciprocal control mechanisms or equivalent forms of discipline becomes too difficult, governments are left with the ruthless discipline of export competition as the chief mechanism to promote adaptation (or to destroy its prospects). That is why it is suggested that competition policy be an integral part of any industrial policy (see also Roberts 2004). In contrast to the mainstream approach, these authors argue that

> competition policy ought to be seen as the set of measures providing incentives as well as the "sticks" fostering innovative behaviours.... In short, competitive pressures on individual firms must be strong enough not only to dissipate monopolistic rent but, more importantly, to induce firms to adopt active competitive strategies instead of just profiting from the incentives provided by industrial and technology policies' (Possas and Borges 2009: 450)

Domestic rivalry within the leather and leather products industry continues to be low, allowing firms to operate in a comfort zone while undermining the incentive to improve competitiveness and export orientation. In contrast, competition in the cement industry has latterly intensified, while competitive pressure has been high throughout in floriculture. This does not mean that designing and implementing competition policy is easy, as it is usually captured by specific interests.

Export target-setting and monitoring were put in place after 2006, but the evidence shows this has not been highly successful. The most significant reasons for this failing have been lack of reliable data and of effective participation by relevant actors in the planning process. Nonetheless, it would be a mistake to dismiss target-setting as a complete failure, for the research also shows that in some ways there have been 'policy linkage' and 'institutional linkage' effects. For instance, target-setting has helped reveal bottlenecks in capability, calling forth responses, though unevenly. As an example, the export earnings target for leather and leather goods, which is set each year, was $0.5 billion in 2014–15. Although actual implementation lagged badly, investigation of causes and bottlenecks resulted.

7.5.2 Compatibility and cohesiveness of policy instruments

There was variation in the use of generic and sector-specific instruments. Other than the generic policy instruments used in multiple sectors (for instance, exchange rate policy and investment incentives), there are instruments that have been used to address sector-specific constraints. The varied approaches pursued to solve cold storage constraints and packaging inputs in the flower sector, and the approach to solve the raw materials constraints in the leather sector (supply, price, and quality of raw hides and skins) are classic examples not only of specific needs, but also of the variable success in addressing them. Capacity to address such constraints is influenced by the priority given by the top political leadership, depth of analysis, and institutional strength. In general, sector-specific instruments were more effective than the generic incentives in addressing the constraints in each sector, and their effectiveness is easier to assess. Integrated and coordinated use of instruments also enhanced policy effectiveness. In the flower and cement industries, there was better governance of policies than in leather. The heterogeneity and scattered nature of the actors and the diverse sub-industries in leather and leather goods have thus far over-taxed existing policy capabilities.

There were also disparities in the speed of application of instruments, and in how much they were concerted. Instruments that were implemented swiftly and in concert had better effects than those implemented piecemeal. The support provided to the flower sector was swift, coordinated, and concentrated, and had a clear impact. Loans were provided in high density without fundamental mistakes being made. Mistakes were indeed made, but the cost was much lower than the benefits. In cement, support in accessing mineral deposits and energy supplies (electricity, heavy fuel oil, coal), and the design of regulations were directly related to the requirements of the industry. It became easier to identify the progress and drawbacks of sector-specific instruments. In floriculture, the critical requirements were serviced land (with transportation and energy access and proximity to the airport), availability of air transport, cold storage facilities, and packaging options. Support has been focused on these issues, enabling the sector to grow. In the leather and leather products industry, sector-specific interventions were not evident until 2010, when benchmarking and upgrading value addition were introduced. It is clear that sector-specific instruments deserve greater focus and are more challenging. Policy decisions related to leather were sometimes inconsistent (for instance, the export of live animals and import of inputs), which further undermined policy effectiveness. Some of the decisions were not taken at an early stage, as was evident in floriculture.

High-level political commitment was crucial in developing the floriculture sector. The same was true of the cement industry, as there was strong political pressure on government to support the construction sector. The state was able to exert strong pressure and make bold decisions to meet requirements. In the leather sector, despite its priority in government policy, this was not the case. The measures were too fragmented and incoherent, producing minimal synergy. Industrial loans (investment and working capital) were not easily available in sufficient amounts.

7.5.3 Quality and appropriateness of policy responses

The quality of industrial policy depends on the ability to make adequate analysis of the situation, participation of concerned actors in the policy-making process, and transparency and accountability in decision-making. This book shows that the quality of policies has been mixed. The multimodal transport intervention is a typical example of insufficient study or preparation and minimal involvement by industrialists and other stakeholders. This failed initiative created additional disruption in the trade logistics of the leather industry. Insufficient analytical work was observed in many decisions across all sectors, although the effects were felt less in industries with active enterprises and intermediary institutions (mainly in floriculture) and larger firms that leveraged the advantage of their size (mainly in cement). The major victim was the leather sector, as key stakeholders were passive and the intermediary institution was weak.

7.5.4 Coordination and insufficient organizational competence

a) *Insufficient institutional capacity:* Implementation failure has mirrored implementation capacity (in terms of attitude, skills, and structure) in various government agencies. For instance, LIDI (in the leather sector) had better organizational capacity than EHDA (in the flower sector) in terms of facilities and staffing. Nevertheless, the challenges and constraints in both sectors were different, and the capacity of LIDI was inadequate and focused on administrative tasks. This was further compounded by the relative weakness of the fragmented actors in the value chain. There was no strong intermediary institution of input suppliers, and the agency working on livestock development was weak.

b) *Institutional tensions and poor coordination:* The coordination requirement differed among instruments and sectors. Coordination among federal government agencies (horizontal) and among governments (vertical: federal, regional, local) has in most cases been deficient. This has been especially important for the leather and leather products value chain. Federal and regional priorities are not necessarily the same, a factor compounded by capacity constraints, which are even more visible at lower levels. Further, rigid bureaucratic practice and hierarchies in government agencies (another example of path dependency but also the product of particular political history, see Lefort 2007, 2013) acted as constraints on learning and adaptation.

c) *Intermediary institutions and state–business relations*: Intermediary institutions are important in enhancing an industry's capacity in terms of market development, training, and technological advancement, or representing the interests of economic actors. They facilitate policymaking by improving the flow and quality of information, communication of intentions, and joint actions. There has been major variation in the roles played by intermediary institutions among the three sectors.

EHPEA has played an active role throughout the history of the floriculture industry. Communication with the highest level of policymakers and government agencies was open, facilitating the timely resolution of problems and improving coordination. In the cement industry, the absence of intermediary institutions did not hamper communication, due to the large size of the firms. This does not necessarily imply that this will be the case in the future though. In the leather and leather products industry, ELIA, which mainly represented tannery interests, was weak and passive with respect to influencing policymaking, and members lacked a common vision. Moreover, economic actors in the input supply chain were not organized into any association.

7.6 Conclusions

The country's political landscape, rapid economic growth, and development strategy have been conducive to the growth of all three of the sectors studied. What has not thus far been effectively explained is *why* and *how*, within this broader context, there has been such marked variation in performance. The dilemma here is why a common industrial policy foundation produced different outcomes in different sectors. Existing literature provides limited empirical evidence and research, as the more typical comparisons in industrial policy and developmental state literature are between countries rather than between sectors within individual countries.

This chapter has synthesized the conclusions and analyses in the various case studies and sought to identify comparative insights, thereby generating a unique picture of the patterns of policymaking and performance. The discussions have also shown that industrial policy outcomes in Ethiopia have been distinctly uneven in recent years. The research suggests there are three main factors shaping this variation, with significant policy implications and a wider relevance beyond Ethiopia. First, industry-specific factors, in particular the nature of economic actors, the industry's latitude for performance, and the stage of development of the industry were the key determinants of the pace and scope of policy outcomes. Second, the varying scope for linkage effects in different sectors, and the appropriateness of policies in promoting creative linkage effects, were crucial factors, with path dependence and low-value traps acting as impediments in one sector. An additional point is that past sectoral experience proved to be more of a constraint than a boost to industrial prospects: the main example here is the largely stagnant and mainly export-oriented leather and leather products sector, where a form of path dependence thwarted policy objectives and interventions.

Third, the disparity in political commitment to, compatibility between, and consistency of policy instruments and institutions was significant. Political factors (for instance, the post-2005 election period and urban development programmes, such as housing and infrastructure) played an important role in promoting the cement industry. Political pressure from scattered producers in leather inputs and processing played an equally important, but opposite role. The quality of policy decisions and institutional capacity varied among the sectors. The particular tensions and trade-offs that arise in policymaking across individual sectors, ministries, and organizations are also very relevant. Overall, what matters for the evolution and effectiveness of industrial policy is the way these three factors—industrial structure, linkage dynamics, and (broadly) politics—interact.

Finally, the contribution of this research, and perhaps its most original policy implication, is that it has unequivocally shown the importance for policymakers of understanding and engaging with the *interaction of industrial structure, linkage potential*, and *politics/political economy*. The interrelational dynamics among these variables have significant implications for policy design and implementation; and for the type of selective intervention chosen to promote industrialization, as well as for how to guide the design of reciprocal control mechanisms and assess their viability. It is often pointed out that selectivity is critical to industrial policy: this research provides a way of guiding thinking regarding that selectivity.

8

Lessons from Industrial Policy in Twenty-First-Century Africa

This chapter ties together the book's findings and arguments on industrial policy and performance across three sectors in Ethiopia and highlights future research areas. After summarizing the previous chapters and focusing on policy learning and lessons for Africa and other developing economies, the chapter concludes with a discussion of Africa's catch up and activist industrial policy in light of the theoretical perspectives and empirical findings presented in the book. This final section reinforces the link to the basic premise of the book—that industrial policy should be the vehicle for catching up and structural transformation. As has often been noted in earlier chapters, this is a departure from the more 'market-friendly' interventions favoured by conventional economists, including those who have rediscovered industrial policy in recent years.

8.1 Summary

8.1.1 *Main findings and theoretical implications*

This book has examined industrial policymaking in Ethiopia between 1991 and 2013, and has sought to shed light on why outcomes have been uneven across industries, despite a common foundation in industrial development strategy and industrial policy. This puzzle has received little attention in existing literature, since most studies generalize at the national and international levels, and not at the level of cross-sectoral comparison. Above all, the research for this book supports the argument that industrial policies can work and indeed thrive in a low-income African country such as Ethiopia, and that the state can play an activist developmental role, with policy independence an important factor. The pretentions, lapses, setbacks, and failures of the 'developmental state', far from indicating its uselessness, should be viewed, the book argues, as part and parcel of the real-world process of accelerating structural change and development. Industrial policymaking in Ethiopia is a work in progress, and the examples discussed in the book illustrate the colossal challenge of catching up and industrializing in twenty-first-century Africa.

In Chapter 2, the cardinal concepts of industrial policy, structural transformation, catch up, the developmental state, and linkage effects are examined, and the African context is briefly laid out. In addition, debates on industrial policy and development are presented, and the economic structure in developing countries (especially SSA countries) and historical growth trends are outlined. Industrial policy has always been the subject of ideological contention, and the dominant perspectives are strongly averse to such policy in developing countries and have been better at accounting for its failures than its evident successes. This book has deployed structuralist and political economy perspectives (more pluralist than the 'mono-economics' prevailing in the discipline since the late 1970s) to investigate the rationale for and recent experiences with industrial policy in Ethiopia.

Ethiopia is a low-income, landlocked economy in a 'bad neighbourhood', and has the second largest population in Africa, and yet it is also one of the few developing countries to record rapid economic growth in the early twenty-first century. Chapter 3 maps out the history and foundations of policymaking in Ethiopia, including the industrial development strategy of the current government and the associated institutional framework, information that is not available elsewhere in the literature. The policy instruments include industrial financing, investment and export promotion, trade protection, the state as direct economic actor/industrial player, and privatization. The chapter sets out the roles of the overall export coordinating institution and specific institutions designed to develop priority sectors, intermediary institutions (such as industrial associations), and investment administration institutions. This descriptive analysis highlights government adaptations of international experience and practice, particularly in East Asian countries. Industrial policy instruments relating to specific sectors are further discussed in subsequent chapters.

Chapter 4 examines growth patterns, linkage effects, and industrial policy and policymaking in the cement industry. Cement production is a strategic industry in many countries. The Ethiopian cement industry has undergone major changes throughout the period under consideration, growing faster than in most developing countries. This growth, although characterized by swings, has been dramatic and has been driven by the expansion of the domestic market and the construction boom. The book demonstrates how the government's industrial policies shaped the development of the cement industry through direct and indirect interventions. Some policies were more effective than others. Similarly, the incentives yielded different outcomes, some more desirable than others. The cement sector has absorbed a large share of scarce resources, involving a number of trade-offs, tensions, and learning experiences. Also demonstrated in the chapter is the synergy between industrial and other public policies, the interplay between economic and political factors, as well as the dynamics of policymaking and the significance of the narrow latitude for poor performance. In sharp contrast to the overall African cement industry, where multinationals preponderate, domestically owned firms continue to dominate the industry in Ethiopia. SOEs have played a pioneering role through spill-over effects, and continue to make an important contribution. Overall, the cement industry in Ethiopia has been a binding agent of economic development and transformation in multiple ways.

Chapter 5 explores floriculture, whose economic success has attracted international interest and policy debate. This sector shares many characteristics with manufacturing. Emerging in Ethiopia in 2004, it has since experienced sustained growth, making Ethiopia one of the leading producers and exporters of cut flower in the world. The standard explanations for this success are comparative advantage, factor endowments, a discovery process, and developmental patrimonialism, rather than the role of the state. A detailed analysis of the drivers of the growth in the industry is undertaken in the chapter, yielding a more comprehensive explanation than has been available before. Government policy has been critical in nurturing and expanding the sector, as have the interplay between policymaking and institutions, the dynamics of industrial structure, and interest groups. Ethiopian floriculture classically demonstrates how unemployed labour and underutilized local entrepreneurial potential, as well as natural endowments, can be mobilized for economic development, but do not just bloom automatically under the warm sun of comparative advantage. State commitment to develop the sector and its use of policy instruments was exceptionally clear and coherent. Collective learning was also impressive, with the industry 'picking the state' and the state 'picking the firms'. Floriculture also benefited from the narrow latitude for poor performance and export discipline. The chapter also shows how policies that helped bring about successful take-off became insufficient as the industry matured and confronted new challenges, which call for new policy responses. The chapter demonstrates an ongoing 'learning by making policy', in spite of these new challenges.

Chapter 6 focused on the underperformance of the leather and leather goods industry and the reasons for the disappointing outcomes. The 'joint production' of outcomes in this case involved policy design, the structure of the industry, and, very much, the sector's political economy. What the chapter clearly shows is that factor endowment arguments are grossly inadequate explanations for the failings in this sector. In contrast to cement and floriculture, the performance of the sector has been disappointing and characterized by erratic and sluggish growth. Industrial policy has been unable to reverse this poor performance, or to fully exploit potential linkage effects and insertion into the GVC. The main puzzle is that there has been prolonged manufacturing experience in the sector and there is a plentiful endowment of livestock. Yet the policies failed to generate the required behaviour and export discipline among firms. The main economic interests in the sector have been fragmented and often conflicting. Tanneries have dominated, while the leather products industry (which is integrated into GVCs) has failed to exert much influence. This demonstrates how linkage effects are not necessarily automatic, and how the policy instruments and institutions also lacked the dynamism to promote them. Policy also failed to address strategic input problems, while trade and logistical constraints further weakened the sector's competitiveness. Dependence on small-scale livestock husbandry is also part of the explanation, as is the wide latitude for poor performance in the sector. The sector has experienced path dependence that has perpetuated a low-value trap. Despite these failings, recent policy on value addition and new entrants is helping to break the logjam in the sector. Moreover, there is recent evidence of more investment, better quality, and increased exports of higher-end products.

8.1.2 *Implications for policymaking in Ethiopia*

It is in Chapter 7 that the insights from previous chapters are synthesized and developed. While sectoral performance has been uneven, the development-oriented state performed better over time (especially after 2002) and its industrial policy has contributed to higher growth. That said, manufacturing output remains extremely low.

One thing the case studies reveal is that learning by doing is as much a feature of government policymaking as of firms' or organizations' performance. Comparative advantage/factor endowments and neopatrimonial arguments do not provide sufficient explanation for the unevenness of policy outcomes, and cannot account for such dynamics as learning by doing, learning by failing, or 'failing better'. The book demonstrates that there are three main factors shaping the variation in sectoral performance, and suggests that these may have wider relevance for other developing countries. First, industry-specific factors, in particular the nature of the economic actors, the industry's latitude for performance, and its stage of development, matter greatly. Second, success in promoting creative linkage effects was crucial, while path dependence and low-value traps act as impediments. Third, the depth of political commitment to, consistency of policy instruments, and compatibility of policy institutions was significant to the success of a sector. Overall, what matters for the evolution and effectiveness of industrial policy is the way these three factors interact.

The book also shows that even in successful economic sectors, the seeds of failure were and are present, while there are signs of productive policymaking evident even in the disappointing leather and leather goods sector. This has significant policymaking implications for these three sectors, the wider manufacturing sector, and for overall economic development in Ethiopia and possibly beyond. As the book repeatedly shows, there are many important issues requiring policy responses. In the cement sector, the key policymaking challenges are sustaining the sector's dynamism through linkages to construction and infrastructure development, and the development of coal mining. There is also the promotion of the manufacturing of other building materials. Although domestic market growth is the primary driver of this sector's performance, different instruments are essential to expanding the industry's market horizons and to improving its productivity and competitiveness. Furthermore, technological development, a neglected area, needs policy focus, as it could serve as the foundation for equipment manufacturing.

The leather and leather goods sector deserves special mention, because of its apparently wider scope for linkages, its contribution to export earnings and employment generation, and indeed its potential for poverty reduction in rural areas. Promotion of multiple linkage effects, especially backward linkages, is vital. A comprehensive review of policies is required, as is devising policies that break the sector's path dependence and a constant focus on upgrading the industry. These efforts need to be augmented by the development of market and technological capability by attracting foreign firms that are key players in the GVC. While inadequacies and limitations in research and knowledge are often obstacles to effective policy design and prioritization in Ethiopia, this is less the case in this sector. However, what became clear is that the policy challenge in this sector is at least as much political as technical.

Meanwhile, floriculture is in a critical transition phase to a new stage of development. Specifically, the development of domestically owned firms, technological deepening of the industry, and the development of linkages to the wider horticulture sector in various growth corridors have emerged as new challenges that the government needs urgently to address.

Although this book focused on three specific sectors, it has wider implications for manufacturing. First, a detailed study of the remaining sectors is necessary, although they may generally resemble these three sectors. The textile and garment sector, for instance, has been long established in Ethiopia, and is an export priority. It faces major constraints, and its growth has not been impressive until very recently. Linkage effects with agriculture are significant, and the domestic market is growing. Both domestic and export markets are key drivers of its growth. Moreover, agro-industries are playing an insignificant role in export earnings, despite their large potential. Among import-substitution industries, pharmaceuticals, steel, and beverages have divergent characteristics. More broadly, the point is that policymakers cannot design a cookie-cutter policy in the expectation that it will work uniformly across sectors. Instead, they need to design policy and to assess performance on the basis of detailed knowledge of the sector and its political economy. This stricture applies both to state departments and development banks.

Second, there are also cross-cutting issues affecting all manufacturing industries that require a policy response. For instance, in view of global competition and the global business revolution (Nolan 2003), redefining the role of national champions is required. Present policy has been insufficient to maximize the synergies between the export and domestic markets. Furthermore, industrial clustering and industrial parks have played an insignificant role till now, but could play a much bigger future role in overall industrial development strategy. Again, some of these issues point to dilemmas that the government will need to address. For instance, there is the tension between industrial clustering and agglomeration and the political commitment to spreading resources and opportunities across federal regions. Meanwhile, the effect of joining WTO would need to be considered within this broader strategic and policy context, and with an understanding of its implications for the industrialization process and for preserving 'policy space' (UNCTAD 2014).[1]

Third, there is a need to promote policy capabilities and adaptive capacity, including developing multiple policy institutions. The availability of reliable data is a major problem in Ethiopia, as research institutions are too few and too thin. Policy learning has to be supported by analysis based on reliable data. Many government agencies lack full knowledge of the industry they are responsible for and their plans rely on insufficient research. Furthermore, industrial policymaking is intertwined with the federal political framework, and each needs to reinforce the other. Considering the limited and unique experience of federalism in Ethiopia, it is important that the interplay of policymaking, institutions, and federalism be properly researched. Other countries such as Korea, Taiwan, or China, having unitary government systems, yield little information of direct relevance, although clearly, given China's massive regional differences, there may be something to learn from Chinese policy experience. Such research in Ethiopia might yield unique insights of value to Ethiopia and other countries.

Finally, perhaps the most original policy implication of this book is its unequivocal demonstration of the importance for policymakers of understanding and engaging with the *interaction among industrial structure, linkage potential,* and *politics/political economy.* The dynamics among these variables have significant implications for policy design and

---

[1] *Policy space* refers to the 'various tensions between national policy autonomy, policy effectiveness and international economic integration' UNCTAD (2014: vii). Globalization, market internationalization, and legal agreements (multilateral, regional, and bilateral) create obligations that undermine the scope of national policy.

implementation, for the type of interventions to be instituted to promote industrialization, and for the design of reciprocal control mechanisms and assessment of their viability.[2]

8.2 Lessons for policy learning in twenty-first-century Africa

As argued above, industrial policy can be effective in Africa, notwithstanding the conventional wisdom among development agencies, economists, and IFIs. One consequence of the weight of this conventional wisdom has been the diversion of research attention elsewhere: it is important that this be reversed. There is a need for more research into African industrial policymaking, particularly its intersection with structural change and its relationship with politics and political settlements in individual countries. This would improve understanding of how industrial policies can promote structural transformation and foster economic catch up. The author hopes to have made the case throughout for engaging in further comparative research within specific countries. Such research should focus on country-specific understanding of, and practices in, policy development and implementation, as theoretical concepts and constructs have ultimately to be based on empirical evidence and experience. Much work has been done on African industrial sectors, but it is often either narrowly technical or too shallow, the product of 'quick and dirty' studies. And it is important to encourage pluralism in research and evidence collection. The lesson after decades of enormous amounts of research—especially into rural economies—to support the global poverty reduction campaign is that significant gaps in perspective and evidence are still all too common. These are arguably the result of ideological blind spots and of the influence of entrenched, but insufficiently questioned, research assumptions.

Three key issues of policy learning in Africa emerge from this book: the critical role of policy independence in policy learning; the role of learning-by-doing as the main thrust of capacity-building in policymaking; and the intelligent use of signals and mechanisms (such as

---

[2] While much evidence has been presented in previous chapters, additional evidence of possible value to researchers and policymakers may be provided by the author. Much of this evidence would have been more difficult, even impossible, for 'outsiders' to assemble.

latitude for performance, hiding hand, and linkage effects) to steer and enhance policy learning.

8.2.1 *Policy independence*

Policymaking is a pattern and mode of action geared, in this case, to economic development. Policy choice influences shifts in political economy, and is constrained by the existing political economy. In other words, no state is wholly autonomous from the wider political economy of a society. Policy independence above all means the right, and political space, to make policy choices free of political pressure or, at any rate, without succumbing to particular interests. From a slightly more unusual perspective, it means reserving the right to make mistakes and, in the process, to learn from them. Policy independence also means the freedom to make major policy decisions that entail risks and bold experiments. Without this dimension, policy decisions will only sustain the status quo. In terms of industrial policy, this may effectively mean abandoning hopes of anything other than the very slowest and most modest structural change. Major policy decisions will only achieve more ambitious results if they are made within a long-term perspective. So, policy independence also entails the right to chart long-term perspectives for development. This independence, however, has its limits. Unlimited protection against the consequences of 'mistakes' may reinforce a pattern of failure, with massive social and political consequences. Policy independence is unlikely to generate constructive experimentation and learning from errors if applied without discipline. This discipline comes in various highly context-contingent forms, but is fundamentally a matter of political viability.

Policymaking in Ethiopia has reflected policy independence, including occasional pressure from IFI and some donors, usually in the form of economic threats. For instance, the government has refused to yield to pressure to open up the finance sector to foreign banks, to privatize utilities and telecom, to reform public land ownership, to freeze public investment, and not to expand universities. The events in the late prime minister's office described in Chapter 2 show the lengths to which the Ethiopian government is willing to go to maintain policy independence. Ethiopia has also embarked on building the Grand Renaissance Dam on the Blue Nile, depending entirely on domestically mobilized resources, and despite the threat and withdrawal of support by external forces. In areas of common interest, it has collaborated with external forces and accepted assistance. The government has been able to develop its own policies because of domestic political support, and by capitalizing on the country's important role in the geopolitics of the region.

Policy independence is a major concern in many African countries. Some countries, despite independence from colonial rule, have little freedom to make their own policy choices or, at any rate, have not been highly effective in using what freedom they have. They are obliged to 'consult' on their policy proposals to get a green light, and receive backing for being 'good students'. Economic embargoes are enforced against those who would set a bad example. As one diplomat said to a friend: 'One of the unique things about working as a diplomat in Ethiopia is that all feel equal, as Ethiopia has never been ruled by colonial masters, as was the case in many other countries.' Another European diplomat remarked that Ethiopia is fortunate in not having to get the green light for major policy decisions, and that it can make them without having to consider the reaction of former colonial masters. It is difficult to believe that such practices continue in some African countries into the twenty-first century, after half a century of independence. It is important that African countries be able to make their own policy choices and bold experiments. This can only be achieved if African countries individually and collectively resist such intrusions, and if the international community condemns them. But it is also incumbent on those, like Ethiopia, with greater room for manoeuvre to use this effectively, thus to signal to others what is possible and sensible.

8.2.2 *Learning by doing, emulation, and role models*

Learning by doing is the prime means of mastering production among late developers. This concept is equally valid for policymaking. We also know that almost all late developers catch up by emulation, learning by copying. According to Reinert (2010: xxiii), emulation means 'imitating in order to equal or excel ... [this], rather than "comparative advantage" and "free trade", lies at the heart of successful development ...' As the history of economic development shows, development almost by nature is about copying and emulation.[3] However, there is a balance between

---

[3] Indeed, it may even be driven by something akin to the 'mimetic envy' that is at the core of Girard's work (see, for example, Girard 1977).

copying and learning by doing that is difficult to define. On one hand, early catching up involved trying to repeat things that happened in the UK in the ways they happened, although as Gerschenkron (1962) pointed out, the solutions became different because the game had changed. This is what China and East Asian Tigers have pragmatically done: copy technology, copy policies, etc. But, on the other hand, copying and learning are not straightforward, and it is not always obvious which lessons are more important or applicable.

Some lessons may be quite straightforward, but most are more complex and less easy to 'carry across' from one context to another. The 'best practices approach' that focuses on reviewing and applying detailed lessons to other contexts may not be helpful, as the conditions in different countries vary in terms of history, culture, political economy, the role of the domestic market, and exposure to international trends. For instance, Ethiopia has always been an independent country and was never colonized. And its history shows that fundamental political and economic changes have occurred during regime changes, sometimes by violent means. At the moment, the country's ethnic federalism is the only such experiment on the continent, and the country's ruling party has a history of focusing on its rural political base. So, there is much that works (or doesn't) because of political factors that are not the same across African countries. To adopt the currently fashionable randomized controlled trials approach to development, or rather the critique of this approach, we cannot be at all sure that 'what works here' will also and equally 'work there' (Cartwright and Hardie 2012).

However, this does not mean there are *no* lessons applicable to certain other contexts. Without dwelling on detailed practices, some broad lessons may be drawn. For instance, understanding the *industrial structure* of different sectors, and leveraging *latitudes for performance* are valuable in industrial policymaking. Hirschman's *linkage* concept (the favouring of industries with strong backward and forward linkages as well as supporting activities with greater employment linkages through indirect and induced mechanisms) is essential in bringing dynamics and impetus to new activities and increasing returns and in creating economic space in developing economies. The principle of *reciprocity* is important in almost all conditions, despite the challenges of implementation and its dependence on the state's political clout. As East Asia shows, reciprocity has been indispensable in promoting exports and fighting rent seeking. According to Amsden (2007a: 94, 96):

> The guiding principle of the best bureaucracies—politics permitting—was to give nothing away for free. *Reciprocity was ideal.* . . . The reciprocity principle in Korea operated in almost every industry. . . . Reciprocity helped governments. If projects succeeded, they got more power. The elitist development banks, flagship of the 'developmental state', subjected their clients to monitorable conditionalities. (my emphasis)

Despite the efforts made, the rudimentary application, and the mixed results of reciprocity in Ethiopia, the government needs to continue experimenting with and mastering reciprocity.

In addition, many scholars highlight the importance of role models for late developers. Amsden particularly showed their relevance for learning, based on the economic histories of Argentina, Chile, and the Philippines in contrast with the experiences of Korea and Indonesia. Amsden (n.d.) argues that:

> A problem in Argentina and Chile was the absence of any hands-on role model to guide them. . . . [T]hey could emulate nothing regional. Nor did . . . multinational investment from Europe or the US, offer much guidance. . . . Overall, the Philippines . . . had good students but no teacher to guide it when an opportunity presented itself . . . Off-setting the costs of emulation, role models provide hands-on knowledge to emulators. . . . Korea and Taiwan . . . used many of the same agents, policies, institutions and tactics [as Japan] to build their own heavy industries. . . . Africa's disappointing economic performance in the presence of rich raw materials may be attributed to . . . a continuity in foreign ownership of mines and plantations, and the absence of a concrete role model to emulate other than abstract theory.

Applying these approaches requires trial and error (rather than the quasi-scientific notion of experiment in the randomized controlled trial literature) and learning by doing. It also requires adaptive capacity in decision-making (Giezen et al. 2014). If learning by doing is important in manufacturing, it is even more so in policymaking, where it depends on a pragmatic approach, curiosity in learning, and the boldness (including political commitment) to experiment and make mistakes. There will be no learning without mistakes, and the aim should be to improve the pace of learning and to narrow the scope for and of mistakes. Ethiopian patterns of policymaking show attempts at experimenting on mini and grand scales, often with mixed outcomes. Learning by doing is probably a good lesson for other African countries to learn in making industrial policy work.

In sum, what is important is not simply the fact of having a role model, but the matter of which role model presents itself or is chosen. There are some indications in the basic policy documents of the ruling party and the government that the latter has been looking to East Asia (in particular, newly industrializing Korea, China, and Taiwan) for role models. There are also close links with Japanese and Korean scholars on industrial policy and frequent visits to China by policymakers. The Japanese *kaizen* concept has been chosen to lead the productivity and quality improvement movement in the manufacturing sector; while vocational education and training and higher education have been organized on the German model.

8.2.3 *Applying Hirschman's supporting devices and mechanisms*

Although learning by doing, emulation, and having the right role models are central to policy learning, they may not be sufficient. As Hirschman highlights, the biggest problem in underdeveloped economies is the inability to make decisions, and he underlines that devices and mechanisms which induce investment and policy decisions are essential. One such device might be institutionalizing a sensibility among policymakers to linkage effects—as important to policymaking as to production or industrialization. Some industrial policy decisions and instruments will force government to take steps to mitigate negative outcomes or exploit the opportunities that arise. In Ethiopia, DBE took important policy decisions to offset the failure of loans to the floriculture sector, and this experience was applied to loans to other sectors.

Another factor that may enhance policy learning is the latitude for performance and Hirschman's 'law of the hiding hand'. According to Hirschman (1967: 28), the hiding hand is 'essentially a transition mechanism through which decision makers learn to take risks; and the shorter the transition and the faster the learning, the better'. According to this concept, the scope for creativity and energy is usually underestimated, just as much as project risks and difficulties are systematically underestimated. This law gives us important insights into the psyche of many policymakers, who will not take bold decisions on large projects that may involve big risks. The mechanism of the hiding hand—where it operates, and perhaps too little is known about the conditions under which it is more (or less) effective—can help developing countries in making such decisions. Hirschman (1968: 129) highlights this unorthodox approach as follows:

> It could be argued that a country without much experience in solving technological problems should stay away from [such] projects . . . But the opposite course can also be defended: how will the country ever learn about technology if it does not tackle technologically complex and problem-rich tasks? . . . [A] certain 'unfitness' of the project for a country becomes an additional and strong argument for undertaking it; . . . *if it is successful*, [the project] will be valuable not only because of its physical output but even more so because of the social and human changes it will have wrought. [Emphasis added]

This approach stands in dramatic opposition to the much more common advice from development economists and aid organizations that interventions should be tailored to current 'capacity'; that while South Korea or China might effectively have made bold interventions, low-income countries should not 'try this at home'. Again, for Hirschman, the benefits go beyond the physical outcome in a fundamental way, in the shifts that new projects may bring about in attitudes to development and readiness to take risks. The Ethiopian narrative shows that government has been undertaking extraordinarily challenging projects. The Grand Renaissance Dam project and the integrated housing programme are typical examples. Such big projects would have detrimental political costs were they to fail, pushing government to make extraordinary efforts to ensure success. The hiding hand concept is also associated with the concept of latitude for performance, as many economic activities have narrow or wide latitude, depending on the technological and structural nature of the industries. This concept of latitude for performance forces us to accept that underdeveloped countries can succeed in capital intensive industries, the airline industry being a typical example. Industries such as airlines have narrow latitude for failure, as they need to be run right or not at all. Latitude for performance also applies to policymaking and political latitude. According to Hirschman (1968: 139): ' . . . latitude and lack of latitude can both be valuable in facilitating learning or acquisition of needed skills and traits . . . latitude is attuned to gradual learning, whereas lack of latitude has a special affinity for the changes that take place through discontinuous commitments to new values and types of behaviour.' Understanding the latitude for performance can help shape and accelerate learning and skills development.

8.3 Can Africa catch up?

Contemporary scholarly debate has focused on the prospects for Africa's catching up, and the avenues for achieving this. This is an even more critical agenda for African policymakers and Africans in general. Most views on this subject focus on external factors (resource booms and prices, FDI flows, cost of borrowing, etc.) or on the unconditional convergence that is supposed to flow merely by liberalizing trade. This book is premised on the argument that external factors are relevant only if the internal dynamics are supportive. Despite global excitement about 'Africa Rising', 'Lions on the Move', and so on, strong strains of pessimism persist about the prospects for African industrialization and catch up. One strain comes from the long tradition, evident in some UNCTAD publications, for example, that emphasizes binding international constraints. In this, it harks back to variants of the Prebisch–Singer hypothesis about the adverse terms of trade for exports from low-income countries. Another strain, noted in Chapter 7, comes from economists like Dani Rodrik, who otherwise acknowledge the role that industrial policy has played elsewhere but are pessimistic about the chances for successful industrialization in Africa.

Although economic history does not provide all the answers, it does provide a clue as to future trends, and may even provide (partial) answers to current challenges. The history of industrialization shows that some late developers have indeed caught up with advanced capitalist economies in terms of income levels, productivity, and technical prowess. The most notable nineteenth-century examples are the US and Germany. Both these late developers have sustained their leadership into our own century. During the first half of the twentieth century, nobody imagined that the greatest catch up and late industrialization would take place in East Asia. Japan was devastated during the Second World War and Korea crumbled after the Korean War, which in turn followed decades of deeply resented colonial oppression by Japan. Taiwan seemed to many to be little more than a backward refuge for the corrupt losers in China's political upheavals. But after a few decades, Japan succeeded in becoming a leading industrialized economy in the world. By the end of the twentieth century, (South) Korea and Taiwan had undergone the fastest industrialization in history to reach the upper rungs of the ladder. In three decades, China has emerged as the second biggest economy, built the biggest sovereign wealth fund, and become a global manufacturing powerhouse.[4] These are economic 'miracles' of the not so remote past. Despite the successes of these countries, history has shown that only a few such countries forged ahead, while most countries struggled as economic laggards.

It is highly probable that the fate of Africa will not be different from this trend. Africa (with more than fifty countries) is heterogeneous, with diverse political economies, histories, cultures, and geopolitics. Many African countries (including the most populous, such as Ethiopia and Nigeria) have great internal diversity. Most of them have not enjoyed even moderate economic growth for many years, and have suffered because of the colonial legacy, misguided IFI prescriptions, weak states and fragmented political economies, and plain bad policy. Globalization has been a major challenge, with Asian giants offering stiff competition even in labour-intensive industries. Market fragmentation and weak infrastructure represent additional challenges. Nonetheless, Africa has a chance to exploit trade, financing, and investment opportunities with emerging countries. Increased labour costs in China and other emerging economies are also an opportunity. This suggests some African countries can catch up, while many may fail to seize the new opportunities.

The specific policies that are required are neither automatic nor the same, as contexts differ. But even those who succeed will have to surmount the huge challenge of low levels of industrialization and technology and the backwardness of their economies. While East Asian countries had some industrial basis when they embarked on rapid industrialization, most African countries have none. On the other hand, the experience of the leather and leather goods industry discussed in this book suggests that a manufacturing past does not automatically pave the way for success. According to Hirschman (1958: 109), 'The lack of interdependence and linkage is...one of the most typical characteristics of underdeveloped economies...Agriculture in general, and subsistence agriculture in particular, are...characterized by scarcity of linkage effects.' This necessitates an economic development strategy that induces sustained forward movement. Hirschman (1958: 63, 66, 88) emphasizes that:

---

[4] Indeed, in mid-2014 the International Comparison Project and IMF growth projections suggested the Chinese economy would outgrow the US economy sooner than earlier forecasts (for instance, see *Huffington Post* (2014)).

293

The real scarcity in underdeveloped countries is not the resources themselves but the ability to bring them into play...If the economy is to be kept moving ahead, the task of development policy is to maintain tensions, disproportions, and disequilibria...The investment that is induced by complementarity effects may help to bring about a real transformation of an underdeveloped economy...[O]ne disequilibrium calls forth a development move which in turn leads to a similar disequilibrium and so on ad infinitum...Once economic progress in the pioneer countries is a visible reality, the strength of the desire to imitate and follow suit, to catch up obviously becomes an important determinant of what will happen among non-pioneers.

Such a possibility gives hope to latecomers from Africa, and can provide opportunities for neighbours as well as being a source of motivation and experience.

8.3.1 *The 'soul' of industrial policy and catching up*

Successful catching up has depended on active industrial policy. What distinguishes industrial policy is its '*soul*', that is, the purpose and underlying pattern of industrial policy. The basic pattern of active industrial policy is essentially the same, although the tools change to fit the domestic and international context. Similar instruments may be used for different purposes, and the nature of the industrial policy is what determines the outcome of the policy. Reinert (2010: 34) highlights that 'any policy recommendation will depend totally on context and structural issues, and therefore on specific knowledge'. As witnessed in many African countries, industrialization continues to play a minor role, and the economic reforms promoted by IFIs have done little to promote new industries (Watanabe and Hanatani 2012). To achieve catch up (and take-off), African governments will have to successfully address the key challenges of late development, that is, to promote institutional innovations that create and concentrate investment and foster productivity and learning (creating Verdoorn effects).

An active industrial policy, while initially dependent on and overlapping with a Ricardian strategy (relying on comparative advantage in agricultural exports and low-value light manufacturing), will eventually shift its focus to a more Kaldorian strategy. A Ricardian strategy on its own can neither bring structural change to the economy nor achieve catch up.[5] Ultimately, it is a Kaldorian strategy (which partly ignores factor disadvantages or advantages, focuses on manufacturing exports, and is investment-driven) that can address the challenges of catch up in terms of investment concentration, learning, and innovation.

As discussed in Chapter 2, Kaldor's growth laws emphasize manufacturing as an engine of growth, the strategic role of exports, and the fundamental importance of the balance of payments (Thirlwall 2002). But history repeatedly demonstrates that realizing the benefits of these 'laws' and managing the structural balance of payments constraint on low-income countries can only be achieved by an activist or developmental state. The biggest advantage of latecomers is Gerschenkron's 'relative degree of backwardness' vis-à-vis industrial forerunners. According to Gerschenkron, 'a point will be reached at which the advantages implied in rapid economic development will more than offset those obstacles to economic progress, which are inherent in the state of economic backwardness' (Gerschenkron 1955: 13; Hirschman 1958: 8). In contrast to neoclassical thinking, he emphatically stressed that the degree of state intervention increases with the relative degree of backwardness between latecomer and forerunner. The experience of the Asian forerunners is a great example for many African countries, and has gradually inspired many African policymakers, not least in Ethiopia.

The above discussion reinforces the argument that active industrial policies and an activist state go hand in hand, and that an active industrial policy must essentially focus on manufacturing and exports (because of the dynamics of increasing returns, learning by doing, spill-over, and linkages). It is also worth mentioning that cheap labour is no guarantee of sustained economic growth, while sustaining productivity in line with international competition is. Continuously upgrading the technological basis of industries and diversifying into new activities and industries is the essence of an active industrial policy. This is what climbing the ladder means.

---

[5] The availability of cheap labour is repeatedly raised, while the centrality of labour productivity is ignored in most debates. For instance, Japan has been able to sustain labour productivity, matching increased labour costs for almost fifty years. In contrast, evidence suggests that in many countries (such as Vietnam) labour costs have exceeded productivity growth, resulting in the relocation of some factories to other countries with cheap labour. So, the only guarantee of sustained competitiveness is a focus on productivity growth.

Both economic theory (within a particular tradition) and, arguably more important, economic history suggest that there is no reason for African countries not to catch up with more advanced economies. The external environment is unpredictable and often hostile, even when prices and foreign capital flows and so on appear favourable. Successful catching up has to rely fundamentally on internal changes and policies that push structural change, whatever the state of the external environment. This book has, hopefully, shown that there is evidence of 'developmentalism' at work in the specific context and conditions of Ethiopian manufacturing. In one of the poorest countries of the world where manufacturing accounts for one of the smallest shares of total economic activity, processes of structural change are under way, and they owe a great deal (more than is typically understood or predicted) to ongoing learning by doing and learning by copying in policymaking.

Furthermore, the Ethiopian experience shows that development policy is complex and highly contested, and that industrial policy is no different. Carefully thought-through policies are necessary but not sufficient to produce desired results. Policies often yield intended outcomes only when driven by 'transformative' institutions, and where there is strong state capacity (and adaptive capacity) to pursue goals and enough flexibility to allow for course changes when things go wrong. These attributes have to become embedded in institutionalized policy learning. Policymaking is a hotbed of conflicting interests and groups jockeying to achieve narrow sectoral objectives. Thus, the state is constantly involved in reconciling intersectoral and intra-group competition without sacrificing the most sacred politic goal, the 'national project' of structural transformation.

Will Africa forge ahead in the twenty-first century? As Hirschman always stressed, a realistic but optimist perspective is essential to 'prove Hamlet wrong' (Adelman 2013). And there may be greater scope for African governments to prove the many doubting Hamlets of development economics wrong if they are able to carve out greater policy space, and then use it more effectively. As Thirlwall highlights (2002: 77–8):

> Ajit Singh tells how Nicholas Kaldor taught him three things. 'First, the only way for a country to develop is to industrialise; second, the only way for a country to industrialise is to protect itself; and third, anyone who says otherwise is being dishonest! The developed economies do preach double standards.' They preach free trade for developing countries, yet protect their own markets.

Bibliography

General bibliography

Abramovitz, Moses (1994) 'Catch-up and convergence in the growth boom and after'. In *Convergence of productivity: Cross-national studies and historical evidence*, edited by William Baumol, Richard Nelson, and Edward Wolff. Oxford: Oxford University Press.

Adelman, Jeremy (2013) *Worldly Philosopher: The Odyssey of Albert O. Hirschman*. Princeton: Princeton University Press.

AfDB (2011) *African Economic Outlook 2011: Africa and its emerging partners*. African Development Bank.

AFP (Agence France-Presse) (2003) 'Ethiopia rejects IMF proposal to privatize loss-making state firms'. 31 August.

Aghion, Beatriz Armendariz (1999) 'Development banking'. *Journal of Development Economics* 58(1):83–100.

Aklilu, Yakob, and Mike Wekesa (2002) *Drought, livestock and livelihoods: Lessons from the 1999–2001 emergency response in the pastoral sector in Kenya*. London: Humanitarian Practice Network, Overseas Development Institute.

Aktouf, Omar (2004) 'The false expectations of Michael Porter's strategic management framework'. *Revista Universidad & Empresa* 6(6):9–41. Available at <http://essay.utwente.nl/65339/1/D%C3%A4lken_BA_MB.pdf>

Aktouf, Omar (2005) 'The False Expectations of Michael Porter's Strategic Management Framework'. *Revista Gestao e Planejameto* Ano 6, 1(11) (January–June 2005):75–94. Available at <http://www.revistas.unifacs.br/index.php/rgb/article/view/199/207>

Altenburg, Tilman (2010) Industrial Policy in Ethiopia. Discussion Paper, Bonn.

Altenburg, Tilman (2011) Industrial Policy in Developing Countries: Overview and Lessons from Seven Country Cases. Discussion Paper 4/2011. Bonn, German Development Institute. Available at <http://www.die-gdi.de/en/discussion-paper/article/industrial-policy-in-developing-countries-overview-and-lessons-from-seven-country-cases/>

Altenburg, Tilman (2013) 'Can Industrial Policy Work under Neopatrimonial Rule?'. In *Pathways to Industrialization in the Twenty-First Century: New Challenges and Emerging Paradigms*, edited by Adam Szirmai, Wim Naudé, and Ludovico Alcorta. Oxford: Oxford University Press.

Amsden, Alice (n.d.), 'Chapter Four: Getting Property Rights "Wrong"', in Developing from Role Models. Unpublished. Available at <http://ubuntuatwork.org/wp-content/uploads/2010/02/Developing-From-Role-Models-Alice-Amsden.pdf> (accessed 5 May 2014).

Amsden, Alice H. (1989) *Asia's Next Giant: South Korea and Late Industrialization*. Oxford: Oxford University Press.

Amsden, Alice H. (1990) 'Third World Industrialization: "Global Fordism" or a New Model?'. *New Left Review* I(182):5–31. Available at <http://newleftreview.org/I/182/alice-h-amsden-third-world-industrialization-global-fordism-or-a-new-model>

Amsden, Alice H. (2001) *The 'Rise of the Rest': Challenges to the West from Late-Industrializing Economies*. Oxford: Oxford University Press.

Amsden, Alice H. (2007a) *Escape from Empire: The Developing World's Journey through Heaven and Hell*. Cambridge MA: MIT Press.

Amsden, Alice H. (2007b) *Nationality of Firm Ownership in Developing Countries: Who Should 'Crowd Out' Whom in Imperfect Markets?* Momigliano Lecture 2007.

Amsden, Alice H. (2008) 'The Wild Ones: Industrial Policies in the Developing World'. In *The Washington Consensus Reconsidered*, edited by Narcis Serra and Joseph E. Stiglitz. Oxford: Oxford University Press.

Amsden, Alice H. (2009) Grass Roots War on Poverty. Available at <http://werdiscussion.worldeconomicsassociation.org/wp-content/uploads/Amsden-Poverty-reformatted.pdf>

Amsden, Alice H., and Wan-Wen Chu (2003) *Beyond Late Development: Taiwan's Upgrading Policies*. Cambridge MA: MIT Press.

Amsden, Alice H., and Takashi Hikino (1994) 'Staying Behind, Stumbling Back, Sneaking Up and Soaring Ahead: Late Industrialization in Historical Perspective'. In *Convergence of productivity: Cross-national studies and historical evidence*, edited by William Baumol, Richard Nelson, and Edward Wolff. Oxford: Oxford University Press.

Ancharaz, Vinaye D. (2003) Trade Policy, Trade Liberalization and Industrialization in Mauritius: Lessons for Sub-Saharan Africa. November. Department of Economics and Statistics, University of Mauritius. Available at <http://www.docin.com/p-67824501.html>

Anderson, Benedict (1991) *Imagined Communities: Reflections on the Origins and Spread of Nationalism*. London: Verso.

Ash, A.J., J.A. Bellamy, and T.G.H Stockwell (1994) 'State and transition models for rangelands: Application of state and transition models to rangelands in northern Australia'. *Tropical Grasslands* 28:223–8.

Austin, Ian Partick (2009) *Common Foundations of American and East Asian Modernisation: From Alexander Hamilton to Junichero Koizumi*. Singapore: Select Publishing.

Balema, Adis Alem (2014) *Democracy and Economic Development in Ethiopia*. Trenton NJ: Red Sea Press.

Bayliss, Kate (2006) 'Privatization theory and practice: A critical analysis of policy evolution in the development context'. In *The New Development Economics: After the Washington Consensus*, edited by K.S. Jomo and Ben Fine. New Delhi: Tulika Books.

Bayliss, Kate, and Ben Fine (2008) *Privatization and alternative public sector reform in Sub-Saharan Africa: Delivering on Electricity and Water.* New York: Palgrave Macmillan.

BBC (2003) 'Ethiopia Hits Out at IMF'. BBC News, 1 September 2003.

Behnke, Roy (2010) The Contribution of Livestock to the Economies of IGAD Member States. Study Findings, Application of the Methodology in Ethiopia and Recommendations for Further Work. IGAD LPI Working Paper No. 02. United Kingdom: Odessa Centre. Available at <http://www.fao.org/fileadmin/user_upload/drought/docs/IGAD%20LPI%20WP%2002-10.pdf>

Behnke, Roy, and Ian Scoones (1992) *Rethinking Range Ecology: Implications for Rangeland Management in Africa.* Dryland Networks Programme, Overseas Development Institute, Issues Paper No. 33, March.

Bhagwati, Jagdish (1989a) 'US Trade Policy at Crossroads'. *World Economy* 12(4): 439–80.

Bhagwati, Jagdish (1989b) *Protectionism.* Cambridge MA: MIT Press.

Bhowon, Veeping, Narainduth Boodhoo, and Pynee A. Chellapermal (2004) 'Mauritius: Policy making in Africa'. In *Politics of Trade and Industrial Policy in Africa: Forced Consensus?*, edited by Charles Soludo, Osita Ogbu, and Ha-Joon Chang. Trenton NJ: Africa World Press.

Brautigam, Deborah (2011) *The Dragon's Gift: The Real Story of China in Africa.* Oxford: Oxford University Press.

Brautigam, Deborah, and Tania Diolle (2009) 'Coalitions, Capitalists and Credibility: Overcoming the crisis of confidence at independence in Mauritius'. April 2009. Available at <http://publications.dlprog.org/Coalitions,%20Capitalists%20and%20Credibility.pdf>

Brian.Carnell.com (2003) 'Ethiopia and the International Monetary Fund at Loggerheads Over Privatization'. Available at <https://brian.carnell.com/articles/2003/ethiopia-and-the-international-monetary-fund-at-loggerheads-over-privatization/> (accessed 22 February 2015).

Buur, Lars (2014) The Development of Natural Resource Linkages in Mozambique: The Ruling Elite Capture of New Economic Opportunities. DIIS Working Paper No. 03. Available at <http://rucforsk.ruc.dk/site/files/48177968/Buur_The_development_of_natural_resource_linkages_in_Mozambique_December_27.docx>

Buur, Lars, Obede Baloi, and Carlota Mondlane Tembe (2012) Mozambique Synthesis Analysis: Between Pockets of Efficiency and Elite Capture. DIIS Working Paper No. 01. Available at <http://transparentsea.co/images/f/fe/WP2012-01-Mozambique_web.pdf>

Cartwright, Nancy, and Jeremy Hardie (2012) *Evidence Based Policy: A Practical Guide to Doing it Better.* Oxford: Oxford University Press.

CBI (2002) 'Cut flower and Foliage', EU Strategic Marketing Guide. Centre for Promotion of Imports from Developing Countries, Ministry of Foreign Affairs, The Netherlands. Available at <http://www.cbi.eu>

CBI (2013) Cut flower market information. Centre for the Promotion of Imports, Ministry of Foreign Affairs of the Netherlands. Available at <http://www.cbi.eu/market-information/cut-flowers-foliage>

Chabal, Patrick, and Jean-Pascal Daloz (1999) *Africa Works: Disorder as political instrument*. Oxford: James Currey.

Chandler, Alfred (2004) *Scale and Scope: The dynamics of industrial capitalism*. Cambridge MA: Harvard University Press.

Chandler, Alfred, Franco Amatori, and Taksashi Hikino (eds.) (1997) *Big Business and the Wealth of Nations. Historical and Comparative Contours of Big Business*. Cambridge: Cambridge University Press.

Chang, Ha-Joon (1994) *The Political Economy of Industrial Policy*. London: Macmillan.

Chang, Ha-Joon (1999) 'The Economic Theory of the Developmental State'. In *The Developmental State*, edited by Meredith Woo-Cumings. Ithaca: Cornell University Press.

Chang, Ha-Joon (2003a) *Globalisation, Economic Development and the Role of the State*. London: Zed Books.

Chang, Ha-Joon (2003b) *Kicking Away the Ladder: Development Strategy in Historical Perspective*. London: Anthem Press.

Chang, Ha-Joon (ed.) (2006) *Rethinking development economics*. London: Anthem Press.

Chang, Ha-Joon, and Ajit Singh (1997) 'Can large firms be run efficiently without being bureaucratic?'. *Journal of International Development* 9(6):865–75.

Chenery, Hollis (1960) 'Patterns of Industrial Growth'. *American Economic Review*, vol. L, No. 4, September:624–54.

Chenery, Hollis, Sherman Robinson, and Moshe Syrquin (eds.) (1986) *Industrialization and growth: A comparative study*. Oxford: Oxford University Press.

China Cement Association (2013) 'The development of China cement industry'. Presentation of Lei Qlanzhi, President of China Cement Association in Izmir, Turkey, in October 2011. <http://www.tcma.org.tr/images/file/Cin%20Cimento%20Birligi%20Baskani%20Lei%20QIANZHI%20.pdf>

China Leather Industry Association (2012). Available at <http://www.chinaleather.org/eng/>

Clapham, Christopher ([1985] 2004) *Third World Politics: An Introduction*. Taylor and Francis e-Library.

Clapham, Christopher (1996) 'Governmentality and economic policy in sub-Saharan Africa'. *Third World Quarterly* 17(4):809–24.

Clapham, Christopher (2009) 'Post-war Ethiopia: The trajectories of crises'. *Review of African Political Economy* 36:120, 181–92. Available at <http://www.tandfonline.com/doi/abs/10.1080/03056240903064953#.Ui4wKMaTiSo>

Collier, Paul (2006) *Africa: Geography and growth*. Centre for the Study of African Economies, Oxford University, July 2006. Available at <http://users.ox.ac.uk/~econpco/research/pdfs/AfricaGeographyandGrowth.pdf>

Collier, Paul (2007) 'Growth Strategies for Africa'. Paper prepared for the Spence Commission on Economic Growth, Centre for the Study of African Economies, Oxford.

Collier, Paul (2009) The political economy of state failure. Revised March 2009. Available at <http://www.iig.ox.ac.uk/output/articles/OxREP/iiG-OxREP-Collier.pdf>

Collier, Paul, and Willem Gunning (1999) 'Why has Africa grown slowly?' *Journal of Economic Perspectives* 13(3):3–22.

Commission for Africa (2005) *Our Common Interest: Report of the Commission for Africa.* Available at <http://www.commissionforafrica.info/wp-content/uploads/2005-report/ 11-03-05_cr_report.pdf>

Cramer, Christopher (1999a) 'Can Africa Industrialize by Processing Primary Commodities? The Case of Mozambican Cashew Nuts'. *World Development* 27(7):1247–66.

Cramer, Christopher (1999b) The Economics and Political Economy of Conflict in Sub-Saharan Africa. Centre for Development Policy and Research, Discussion Paper 1099. Available at <http://www.soas.ac.uk/cdpr/publications/papers/file24327.pdf>

Cramer, Christopher (1999c) Privatisation and the Post-Washington Consensus: Between the lab and the real world? Centre for Development Policy and Research, Discussion Paper 0799.

Cramer, Christopher (1999d) Consultancy study on Ethiopian leather sector, conducted for the Government of Ethiopia, 1999. Unpublished.

Cramer, Christopher (2000) Privatisation and Adjustment in Mozambique: A Hospital Pass? SOAS Department of Economics Working Paper Number 111.

Cramer, Christopher (2006) *Civil War is Not a Stupid Thing: Accounting for Violence in Developing Countries.* London: Hurst.

Cramer, Christopher (2012) 'East Africa between tragedy and hyperbole'. Unpublished presentation, SOAS.

CSTEP (2012) *A study of energy efficiency in the Indian cement industry.* Bengalaru: Center for Study of Science, Technology and Policy.

De Waal, Alex (2012) 'The theory and practice of Meles Zenawi'. *African Affairs* 112 (446):148–55.

Di John, Jonathan (2006) *The Political Economy of Taxation and Tax Reform in Developing Countries.* WIDER Research Paper 2006/74. Helsinki: UNU-WIDER.

Di John, Jonathan (2008) 'Why is the Tax System so Ineffective and Regressive in Latin America?' *Development Viewpoint,* No. 5, June.

Di John, Jonathan (2009) *From Windfall to Curse? Oil and Industrialization in Venezuela, 1920 to the Present.* University Park: Penn State University Press.

Di John, Jonathan (forthcoming) *Manufacturing Brazil: Social Order and Industrialization, 1990 to the Present.*

Diamond, William (1957) *Development Banks.* Washington DC: Mimeo: AFD. Economic Development Institute, International Bank for Reconstruction and Development.

Diamond, William, and V.S. Raghavan (eds.) (1982) *Aspects of development bank management.* London: Johns Hopkins University Press.

Dinh, Hinh T., Vincent Palmade, Vandana Chandra, and Frances Cossar (2012) *Light Manufacturing in Africa: Targeted policies to enhance private investment and create jobs.* Washington DC: World Bank.

Doner, Richard, Bryan Ritchie, and Dan Slater (2005) 'Systemic vulnerability and the origins of developmental states: Northeast and Southeast Asia in comparative perspective'. *International Organization* 59(2):327–61.

Dos Santos, Paulo (2011) 'A Policy Wrapped in Analysis: The World Bank's Case for Foreign Banks'. In *The Political Economy of Development: The World Bank, Neoliberalism and Development Research*, edited by Kate Bayliss, Ben Fine, and Elisa Van Waeyen-berge. London: Pluto.

Drucker, Peter (1999) *Management: Tasks, Responsibilities, Practices*. Oxford: Butter-worth-Heinemann.

Earle, Edward Mead (1986) 'Adam Smith, Alexander Hamilton, Friedrich List: The Economic Foundations of Military Power'. In *Makers of Modern Strategy from Machia-velli to the Nuclear Age*, edited by Peter Paret. Oxford: Clarendon Press.

Easterly, William (2002) *The Elusive Quest for Growth: Economist's Adventures and Misad-ventures in the Tropics*. Cambridge MA: MIT Press.

Easterly, William, and Ross Levine (1997) 'Africa's growth tragedy: Policies and ethnic divisions'. *Quarterly Journal of Economics* 112(4):1203–50.

EEA (2013) *Ethiopia financial sector performance review. Proceedings of the Third Inter-national Conference on the Ethiopian Economy*. Ethiopian Economic Association. Addis Ababa: Ethiopian Economic Association. Available at <http://www.eeaecon.org/node/4944>

Embassy of Japan (2008) *A Series of Studies on Industries in Ethiopia*. Addis Ababa: Embassy of Japan. Available at <http://www.et.emb-japan.go.jp/Eco_Research_E.pdf>

Evans, Peter (1995) *Embedded Autonomy: States and Industrial Transformation*. Princeton: Princeton University Press.

Evans, Peter (1997) 'State structures, government-business relations and economic transformation'. In *Business and the state in developing countries*, edited by Sylvia Maxfield and Ben Schneider. London: Cornell University Press.

FAO (2008) *Global hides and skins market: Review of 2004–2007 and prospects for 2008*. Food and Agriculture Organization of the United Nations. Available at <www.fao.org>

FAO (2009) *Global hides and skins markets: A review and short-term outlook* (As of Novem-ber 2009). Food and Agriculture Organization of the United Nations. Available at <http://www.fao.org/economic/est/est-commodities/hides-skins/en/>

FAO (2011) *World statistical compendium for raw hides and skins, leather and leather footwear 1992–2011*. Food and Agriculture Organization of the United Nations. Avail-able at <http://www.fao.org/fileadmin/templates/est/COMM_MARKETS_MONITOR ING/Hides_Skins/Documents/AA_COMPENDIUM_2011.pdf>

FAO (2013) *World Statistical Compendium for raw hides and skins, leather and leather footwear 1993–2012*. Food and Agriculture Organization of the United Nations. Avail-able at <http://www.fao.org/fileadmin/templates/est/COMM_MARKETS_MONITOR ING/Hides_Skins/Documents/COMPENDIUM2013.pdf>

FAO/GOB (2013) *Botswana agrifood value chain project: Beef value chain study*. Food and Agriculture Organization of the United Nations and the Government of Botswana.

FDDI (2012) Presentation on leather products industry. Unpublished Notes, Indian Footwear Design and Development Institute, Addis Ababa, Ethiopia.

Fine, Ben (1996) 'Introduction: State and development'. *Journal of Southern African Studies* 22(1):5–26.

Fine, Ben (2006) 'The developmental state and the political economy of development'. In *The New Development Economics: After the Washington Consensus*, edited by K.S. Jomo and Ben Fine. London: Zed Books.

FloraHolland (2010) Abridged 2010 Annual Report. Available at <http://www.floraholland.com/media/168711/Jaarverslag%202010%20Eng.pdf>

FloraHolland (2012) Annual Report 2011. <http://www.floraholland.com/media/477979/jaarverslag_floraholland_2011_engels.pdf>

FloraHolland (2014) 'FloraHolland books small profit in turbulent year for the floriculture industry'. Press Release. Available at <https://www.floraholland.com/en/speciale-paginas/search-in-news/v20291/floraholland-books-small-profit-in-turbulent-year-for-the-floriculture-industry/>

Fosu, Augustin K. (1992) 'Political instability and economic growth: Evidence from sub-Saharan Africa'. *Economic Development and Cultural Change* 40(4):829–41.

Fosu, Augustin K. (2012) 'The African economic growth record, and the roles of policy syndromes and governance'. In *Good growth and governance in Africa: Rethinking development strategies*, edited by Akbar Noman, Kwesi Botchwey, Howard Stein, and Joseph E. Stiglitz. Oxford: Oxford University Press.

Frank, André Gunder (1967) *Capitalism and underdevelopment in Latin America: Historical studies of Chile and Brazil*. New York: Monthly Review Press.

Gebreeyesus, Mulu, and Michiko Iizuka (2010) Discovery of the flower industry in Ethiopia: Experimentation and coordination. UNU-MERIT Working Paper Series No. 25.

Gereffi, Gary (1994) 'The organization of buyer driven global commodity chain: How US retailers shape overseas production networks'. In *Commodity Chains and Global Capitalism*, edited by G. Gereffi and M. Korzeniewicz. London: Praeger.

Gereffi, Gray, and Karina Fernandez-Stark (2011) Global Value Chain Analysis: A Primer Centre on Globalization, Governance and Competitiveness. 31 May. Available at <http://www.cggc.duke.edu/pdfs/2011-05-31_GVC_analysis_a_primer.pdf>

Gereffi, Gary, John Humphrey, and Timothy Sturgeon (2005) 'The governance of global value chains'. *Review of International Political Economy* 12(1):78–104.

Gerschenkron, Alexander (1962) *Economic Backwardness in Historical Perspective*. Cambridge MA: Harvard University Press.

Gerschenkron, Alexander (1955) 'The Problem of Economic Development in Russian Intellectual History.' In *Continuity and Change in Russian and Soviet Thought*, ed. E. J. Simmons. Cambridge, MA: Harvard University Press.

Giezen, Mendel, Luca Bertolini, and Willem Salet (2014) 'Adaptive Capacity within a Mega Project: A Case Study on Planning and Decision-Making in the Face of Complexity'. *European Planning Studies*. Available at <http://www.tandfonline.com/doi/pdf/10.1080/09654313.2014.916254#.VFK6jFdBeE8>

Girard, Rene (1977) *Violence and the Sacred*. Baltimore: Johns Hopkins University Press.

GIZ (2009) *Leather and footwear industry in Vietnam: The labour markets and gender impact of the global economic slowdown on value chains*. Eschborn: Deutsche Gesellschaft für Internationale Zusammenarbeit.

Global Cement (2012) Top global cement companies. 17 December. Available at <www.globalcement.com>

Global Development Solutions (2011) The Value Chain and Feasibility Analysis; Domestic Resource Cost Analysis. Background paper, World Bank, Washington DC. (Light Manufacturing in Africa Study). Available at <http://econ.worldbank.org/africamanufacturing>

Goodrich, Carter (1965) *The Government and the economy, 1783–1861*. New York: Bobbs-Merrill.

Grabel, Ilene (ed.) (2003) 'International Private Capital Flows and Developing Countries'. In *Rethinking development economics*, edited by Ha-Joon Chang. London: Anthem Press.

de Haan, Cornelis, and Dina Umali (1994) 'Public and private sector roles in the supply of veterinary services'. *World Bank Research Observer* 9(1):71–96.

Hagmann, Tobias, and Jon Abbink (2012) 'Twenty years of revolutionary democratic Ethiopia, 1991–2011'. *Journal of Eastern African Studies* 5(4):579–95.

Hagmann, Tobias, and Jon Abbink (eds.) (2013) *Reconfiguring Ethiopia: The politics of authoritarian reform*. London: Routledge.

Hall, Peter (1987) *Governing the Economy: The politics of state intervention in Britain and France*. Cambridge: Polity Press.

Hamilton, Alexander (1934) *Papers on Public Credit, Commerce and Finance*, ed. Samuel McKee. New York: Columbia University Press.

Hardin, Garrett (1968) 'The Tragedy of the Commons'. *Science*, new series, 162 (3859):1243–48.

Henderson, Vernon (1974) 'The sizes and types of cities'. *American Economic Review* 64 (4):640–56.

Henderson, Vernon (2003) 'Marshall's scale economies'. *Journal of Urban Economics* 53:1–28.

Herring, Roland J. (1999) 'Embedded particularism: India's failed developmental state'. In *The Developmental State*, edited by Meredith Woo-Cumings. Ithaca: Cornell University Press.

Hirschman, Albert O. (1958) *Strategy of Economic Development*. New Haven and London: Yale University Press.

Hirschman, Albert O. (1963) *Journeys toward Progress: Studies of economic policy-making in Latin America*. New York: Twenty Century Fund.

Hirschman, Albert O. (1967) *Development Projects Observed*. Washington DC: Brookings Institution.

Hirschman, Albert O. (1968) 'The Political Economy of Import-Substituting Industrialization in Latin America'. *Quarterly Journal of Economics* 82(1):1–32.

Hirschman, Albert O. (1971) *A Bias for Hope: Essays on development and Latin America*. New Haven: Yale University Press.

Hirschman, Albert O. ([1981] 2008) *Essays in Trespassing: Economics to politics and beyond*. Cambridge: Cambridge University Press.

Hirschman, Albert O. ([1986] 1992) *Rival views of market society and other recent essays*. Cambridge MA: Harvard University Press.

Hirschman, Albert O. (1991) *The Rhetoric of Reaction: Perversity, Futility, Jeopardy.* London: Harvard University Press.

Hirschman, Albert O. (2013) *The Essential HIRSCHMAN,* edited and with an introduction by Jeremy Adelman. Princeton and Oxford: Princeton University Press.

Hobday, Michael (1995) 'East Asian latecomer firms: Learning the technology of electronics'. *World Development* 23(7): 1171–93.

Hobday, Mike (2013) 'Learning from Asia's success: Beyond simplistic "lesson-making"'. In *Pathways to Industrialization in the Twenty-First Century: New Challenges and Emerging Paradigms,* edited by Adam Szirmai, Wim Naudé, and Ludovico Alcorta. Oxford: Oxford University Press.

HSRG (2012) Human security report 2012. Human Security Research Group. Available at <http://www.hsrgroup.org/human-security-reports/2012/overview.aspx>

Huffington Post (2014) 'China To Have World's Largest Economy This Year: World Bank', 5 March. Available at <http://www.huffingtonpost.ca/2014/05/03/china-worlds-largest-economy_n_5255825.html>

Humphrey, John, and Hubert Schmitz (2004) 'Chain governance and upgrading: Taking stock'. In *Local Enterprises in the Global Economy,* edited by Hubert Schmitz. Cheltenham: Edward Elgar.

IDS (1997) Collective Efficiency: A Way Forward For Small Firms. IDS Policy Briefing. Issue 10, April. Available at <http://www.ids.ac.uk/files/dmfile/PB10.pdf>

Imara (2011) Imara African cement report: Africa, the last cement frontier, February. Available at <http://www.cgmplc.com/content/assets/pdf/imara_201102_african_cement_report.pd>

International Cement Review (2012) Cemnet.com (South Africa's PPC invests in Ethiopian cement firm, By ICR Newsroom, Published 26 July 2012 <http://www.cemnet.com/News/story/150263/south-africa-s-ppc-invests-in-ethiopian-cement-firm.html>

ITC (2012) Market news service. International Trade Centre. Available from <http://www.intracen.org>

Jackson, Patrick (2006) *Civilizing the Enemy: German Reconstruction and the Invention of the West.* Ann Arbor: University of Michigan Press.

Jalilian, Hossein, and John Weiss (1997) 'Bureaucrats, business and economic growth'. *Journal of International Development* 9:877–85.

Jalilian, Hossein, and John Weiss (2000) 'De-industrialisation in Sub-Saharan Africa: Myth or Crisis?'. *Journal of African Economics* 9(1):24–43.

Jerven, Morten (2010a) Accounting for the African Growth Miracle: The official evidence—Botswana 1965–1995. *Journal of Southern African Studies,* 36(1):73–94. Available at <http://www.tandfonline.com/doi/abs/10.1080/03057071003607337>

Jerven, Morten (2010b) African Growth Recurring: An Economic History Perspective on African Growth Episodes, 1690–2010. Simons Papers in Security and Development, No. 4, June.

Jerven, Morten (2011) 'The quest for the African Dummy: Explaining African Postcolonial economic performance revisited'. *Journal of International Development* 23 (2):288–307.

Jianhua, Zhong (2013) *China's special representative on African affairs on Trade, Aid and Jobs*. Africa Research Institute, 6 August. Available at

Johnson, Chalmers (1982) *MITI and the Japanese miracle: The growth of industrial policy, 1925–1975*. Stanford: Stanford University Press.

Johnson, Chalmers (ed.) (1984) *The Industrial Policy Debate*. San Francisco: Institute for Contemporary Studies.

Jomo, K.S., and Rudiger von Arnim (2012) 'Economic liberalization and constraints to development in Sub-Saharan Africa'. In *Good growth and governance in Africa: Rethinking development strategies*, edited by Akbar Noman, Kwesi Botchwey, Howard Stein, and Joseph E. Stiglitz. Oxford: Oxford University Press.

Jourdan, Paul, Gibson Chigumira, Isaac Kwesu, and Erina Chipumho (2012) *Mining Sector Policy Study*. Zimbabwe Economic Policy Analysis and Research Unit. December.

Kaldor, Nicholas (1966) *Causes of the Slow Rate of Economic Growth of the United Kingdom*. Cambridge: Cambridge University Press.

Kaldor, Nicholas (1967) *Strategic Factors in Economic Development*. Ithaca: New York State School of Industrial and Labour Relations, Cornell University.

Kaplinsky, Raphael (2005) *Globalization, poverty and equality: Between a rock and a hard place*. Cambridge: Polity Press.

Kaplinsky, Raphael, and Mike Morris (2000) *A handbook for value chain research*. Prepared for the IDRC. <http://www.ids.ac.uk/ids/global/pdfs/VchNov01.pdf>

Kay, Cristobal (2002) 'Why East Asia Overtook Latin America: Agrarian Reform, Industrialisation and Development'. *Third World Quarterly* 23(6):1073–102.

Kelsall, Tim (2013) *Business, politics and the state in Africa: Challenging the orthodoxies on growth and transformation*. London: Zed Books.

Kelsall, Tim, David Booth, Diana Cammack, and Frederick Golooba-Mutebi (2010) Developmental patrimonialism? Questioning the orthodoxy on political governance and economic progress in Africa. Working Paper No. 9, July. Africa Power and Politics. Available at <http://r4d.dfid.gov.uk/PDF/Outputs/APPP/20100708-appp-working-paper-9-kelsall-and-booth-developmental-patrimonialism-july-2010.pdf>

Khan, Azizur Rahman (2012) 'Employment in Sub-Saharan Africa: Lessons to be Learnt from the East Asian Experience'. In *Good growth and governance in Africa: Rethinking development strategies*, edited by Akbar Noman, Kwesi Botchwey, Howard Stein, and Joseph E. Stiglitz. Oxford: Oxford University Press.

Khan, Mushtaq H. (2000a) 'Rents, efficiency and growth'. In *Rents, rent-seeking and economic development: Theory and evidence in Asia*, edited by Mushtaq Khan and K.S. Jomo. Cambridge: Cambridge University Press.

Khan, Mushtaq H. (2000b) 'Rent-seeking as process'. In *Rents, rent-seeking and economic development: Theory and evidence in Asia*, edited by Mushtaq Khan and K.S. Jomo. Cambridge: Cambridge University Press.

Khan, Mustaq H. (2006) 'Corruption and governance'. In *The New Development Economics: After the Washington Consensus*, edited by K.S Jomo and Ben Fine. London: Zed Books.

Khan, Mushtaq H., and Stephanie Blankenburg (2009) 'The Political Economy of Industrial Policy in Asia and Latin America'. In *Industrial Policy and Development: The Political Economy of Capabilities Accumulation*, edited by Mario Cimoli, Giovanni Dosi, and Joseph E. Stiglitz. Oxford: Oxford University Press.

Khan, Mushtaq H., and K.S. Jomo (eds.) (2000) *Rents, rent-seeking and economic development: Theory and evidence in Asia*. Cambridge: Cambridge University Press.

Kitching, Gavin (1982) *Development and underdevelopment in historical perspective: Populism, nationalism and Industrialization*. London: Methuen.

Kohli, Atul (2004) *State-Directed Development: Political Power and Industrialization in the Global Periphery*. Cambridge: Cambridge University Press.

KOICA (2013) Project for Establishment of the Detailed Action Plans Strategy to Implement Ethiopian National Economic Development Plan Strategy (Growth and Transformation Plan, GTP). Korea International Cooperation Agency, Korea International Development Institute, and Dalberg. August. Addis Ababa, Ethiopia.

Kolli, Ramesh (2010) A Study on the determination of share of the private sector in Ethiopian Gross Domestic Product. Addis Ababa: Addis Ababa Chamber of Commerce and Sectoral Association.

Kornai, Janos (1980) *Economics of shortage*. 2 vols. Amsterdam: North Holland.

Kornai, Janos (1990) *The road to free economy: Shifting from a socialist system. The Example of Hungary*. New York: Norton.

Krueger, Anne (1974) 'The political economy of rent-seeking society'. *American Economic Review* 64(3):291–303.

Krueger, Anne (1980) 'Trade policy as an input to development'. *American Economic Review* 70(2):288–92.

Krueger, Anne (1990) 'Government failure in economic development'. *Journal of Economic Perspectives* 4(3):9–23.

Lall, Sanjaya (1992) 'Technological Capabilities and Industrialization'. *World Development* 20(2):165–86.

Lall, Sanjaya (1996) *Learning from the Asian Tigers: Studies in Technology and Industrial Policy*. London: Macmillan.

Lall, Sanjaya (1999) Promoting Industrial Competitiveness in Developing Countries: Lessons from Asia. Commonwealth Secretariat, Commonwealth Economics Paper Series, Economic Paper 39. October.

Lall, Sanjaya (2000a) Selective Industrialization Trade Policies in Developing Countries: Theoretical and Empirical Issues. QEH Working Paper No. 48.

Lall, Sanjaya (2000b) The Technological Structure and Performance of Developing Country Manufactured Exports, 1985–1998. QEH Working Paper No. 44.

Lall, Sanjaya (2003) 'Technology and industrial development in an era of globalization'. In *Rethinking development economics*, edited by Ha-Joon Chang. London: Anthem Press.

Lall, Sanjaya (2004) Reinventing Industrial Strategy: The Role of Government Policy in Building Industrial Competitiveness. UNCTAD, G24 Discussion Paper Series No. 28, April. Available at <http://unctad.org/en/Docs/gdsmdpbg2420044_en.pdf>

Lall, Sanjaya (2005) Is African Industry Competing? QEH Working Paper Series Paper No. 121. Available at <http://213.154.74.164/invenio/record/18469/files/lall.pdf>

Lavopa, Alejandro, and Adam Szirmai (2012) Industrialization, employment and poverty. 2012-081. UNU-MERIT Working Paper Series, 2 November 2012. Available at <www.merit.unu.edu/publications/wppdf/2012/wp2012-081.pdf>

LEFASO (2004) Vietnam leather and footwear industry: Opportunities and challenges on the way Vietnam entering WTO. Presentation by Secretary General of the Vietnam Leather and Footwear Association, Nguyen Thi Tong. Available at <http://siteresources.worldbank.org/INTRANETTRADE/Resources/WBI-Training/288464-1139428366112/Session6-NguyenThiTong-Footwear_EN.pdf>

LEFASO (2012) *Decision on permitting to rename Vietnam Leather - Footwear Association to Vietnam Leather, Footwear and Handbag Association.* Available at <http://www.lefaso.org.vn/default.aspx?ZID1=240&ID1=2>

Lefort, René (2007) 'Powers—*mengist* —and peasants in rural Ethiopia: The May 2005 elections'. *Journal of Modern African Studies* 45(2):435–60.

Lefort, René (2013) 'The theory and practice of Meles Zenawi: A response to Alex de Waal'. *African Affairs. Journal of the Royal African Society* 112(448):460–70.

Lin, Justin Y. (2009) *Economic Development and Transition: Thought, Strategy and Viability.* Cambridge: Cambridge University Press.

Lin, Justin and Ha-Joon Chang (2009) 'Should Industrial Policy in Developing Countries Conform to Comparative Advantage or Defy it? A Debate between Justin Lin and Ha-Joon Chang'. *Development Policy Review* 27(5):483–502.

Lindbeck, Assar (2007) Janos Kornai's contributions to economic analysis. IFN Working Paper No. 724.

List, Friedrich (1827) *Outlines of American Political Economy, in Series of Letters. Letter VII. Reading.* 22 July 1827. Philadelphia: Samuel Parker.

List, Friedrich ([1841] 2005) *National System of Political Economy. Volume 1: The History.* New York: Cosimo.

List, Friedrich (1856) *National System of Political Economy.* Vol. I–IV. Memphis: Lippincott.

Little, Peter, Roy Behnke, John McPeak, and Getachew Gebru (2010) Future Scenarios for Pastoral Development in Ethiopia, 2010–2025. Report No. 2. Pastoral Economic Growth and Development Policy Assessment, Ethiopia.

Mahmoud, Hussein (2010) *Livestock Trade in the Kenyan, Somali and Ethiopian Borderlands. Africa Programme.* September. AFP BP 2010/02. Chatham House, London. Available at <https://www.chathamhouse.org/sites/files/chathamhouse/public/Research/Africa/0910mahmoud.pdf>

Mahoney, James (2000) 'Path dependence in historical sociology'. *Theory and Society* 29(4):507–48.

Mano, Yukichi and Aya Suzuki (2011) *The case of the Ethiopian cut flower industry.* Hermes Ir, Japan. Technical report. Hitotsubashi University Repository Available at <http://hermes-ir.lib.hit-u.ac.jp/rs/bitstream/10086/25583/1/070econDP13-04.pdf>

Markakis, John (2011) *Ethiopia: The last two frontiers.* New York: James Currey.

Marshall, Alfred (1920) *Principles of Economics.* London: Palgrave Macmillan.

Mazzucato, Mariana (2011) *The Entrepreneurial State*. DEMOS, Open Research Online, London. Available at <www.demos.co.uk/publications/theentrepreneurialstate>

Mazzucato, Mariana (2013a) *The entrepreneurial state: Debunking public vs. private sector myths*. London: Anthem Press.

Mazzucato, Mariana (2013b) 'Lighting the innovation spark'. In *The Great Rebalancing: How to Fix the Economy*, edited by Andrew Harrop. Fabian Society, London. Available at <http://www.fabians.org.uk/wp-content/uploads/2013/01/FABJ320_web.pdf>

McMillan, Margaret and Dani Rodrik (2011) Globalization, structural change and productivity growth. NBER Working Paper No. 17143, June. Available at <http://www.nber.org/papers/w17143>

Meek, James (2014) *Private Island: Why Britain Now Belongs to Someone Else*. London: Verso.

Meisel, Nicolas (2004) Governance and development: A different perspective on corporate governance. OECD Development Centre Studies, May.

Melese, Ayelech Tiruwha, and A.H. Helmsing, (2010) 'Endogenisation or enclave formation? The development of the Ethiopian cut flower industry'. *Journal of Modern African Studies* 48(1):35–66.

Milhaupt, Curtis, and Wentong Zheng (2014) Beyond Ownership: State Capitalism and the Chinese Firm. Available at <http://papers.ssrn.com/sol3/papers.cfm?abstract_id=2413019>

Mkandawire, Thandika (2001) 'Thinking about Developmental States in Africa'. *Cambridge Journal of Economics* 25(3):289–313.

Mkandawire, Thandika (2010) 'From maladjusted states to democratic developmental states in Africa'. In *Constructing a Developmental State in South Africa: Potentials and challenges*, edited by Omano Edigheji. Pretoria: HSRC Press.

Mkandawire, Thandika (2013) Neopatrimonialism and the political economy of economic permormance in Africa: Critical reflections. Institute for Future Studies. 22 April. Available at <http://www.iffs.se/wp-content/uploads/2013/05/2013_1_thandika_mkandawire.pdf>

Mühlenkamp, Holger (2013) *From state to market revisited: More empirical evidence on the efficiency of public (and privately-owned) enterprises*. Munich University Library, Munich. Available at <http://mpra.ub.uni-muenchen.de/47570/>

Musacchio, Aldo, and Sergio, Lazzarini (2014a) *Reinventing State Capitalism: Leviathan in Business, Brazil and Beyond*. Cambridge MA: Harvard University Press.

Musacchio, Aldo, and Sergio, Lazzarini (2014b) 'State-owned Enterprises in Brazil: History and Lessons'. Paper prepared for OECD Workshop on State-owned Enterprises in the Development Process, Paris, 4 April. Revised version, 28 February.

Mwangi, Esther (2007) *Socioeconomic Change and Land Use in Africa: The Transformation of Property Rights in Maasailand*. London: Palgrave Macmillan.

Nico, de Froot (1998) 'Floriculture World Trade: Trade and Consumption Patterns'. Agricultural Economics Research Institute (LEIDCO), The Netherlands.

Nolan, Peter (2003) 'Industrial policy in the early 21st century: The challenge of the Global Business Revolution'. In *Rethinking development economics*, edited by Ha-Joon Chang. London: Anthem Press.

Nolan, Peter (2012) *Is China Buying the World?* Cambridge: Polity Press.

Noland, Marcus, and Howard Pack (2003) *Industrial policy in an era of globalization: Lessons from Asia*. Washington DC: Institute for International Economics.

North, Douglass C. (1990) *Institutional changes and economic performance*. Cambridge: Cambridge University Press.

O'Brien, Patrick K. (1991) *Power with Profit: The State and the Economy 1688–1815: An Inaugural Lecture Delivered in the University of London*. London: University of London.

Ocampo, José A. (2005) 'The quest for Dynamic Efficiency: Structural Dynamics and Economic Growth in Developing Countries'. In *Beyond Reforms, Structural Dynamics and Macroeconomic Vulnerability*, edited by José A. Ocampo. Palo Alto: Stanford University Press and ECLAC.

Ocampo, José A. (2007) 'Introduction'. In UN-DESA (2007) *Industrial Development for the 21st Century: Sustainable Development Perspectives*. United Nations Department of Economic and Social Affairs, New York. Available at <http://www.un.org/esa/su stdev/publications/industrial_development/full_report.pdf>

Ocampo, José A. (2008) 'Introduction'. In *Industrial Development for the 21st century*, edited by David O'Connor and Monica Kjollerstrom. London: Zed Books.

Ocampo, José A., Codrina Rada, and Lance Taylor (2009) *Growth and policy in developing countries: A structuralist approach*. New York: Columbia University Press.

OECD (1975) *The Aims and Instruments of Industrial Policy: A Comparative Study*. Paris: Organisation for Economic Co-operation and Development.

OECD (1976) *The footwear industry: Structure and governmental policies*. Paris: Organisation for Economic Co-operation and Development.

Ottaway, Marina (1999) *Africa's new leaders: Democracy or state reconstruction?* Washington DC: Carnegie Endowment for International Peace.

Ottaway, Marina (2003) 'African priorities: Democracy isn't the place to start'. *New York Times*, 23 May. Available at <http://www.nytimes.com/2003/05/23/opinion/23iht-edmarina_ed3_.html>

Owens, Trudy, and Adrian Wood (1997) 'Export-oriented industrialization through primary processing?'. *World Development* 25(9):1453–70.

Oya, Carlos (2010) Rural inequality, wage employment and labour market formation in Africa: Historical and micro level evidence. International Labour Organization, Working Paper 197, August.

Oya, Carlos (2011) 'Agriculture in the World Bank: Blighted Harvest Persists'. In *The political economy of development: The World Bank, neoliberalism and development research*, edited by Kate Bayliss, Ben Fine, and Elisa Waeyenberge. London: Pluto.

Oya, Carlos (2012) 'Combining Qualitative and Quantitative Methods: Issues, Tools and Challenges'. Unpublished notes.

Padayachee, Vishnu (ed.) (2010) *The Political Economy of Africa*. New York: Routledge.

Page, John (2011) 'Can Africa industrialise?' *Journal of African Economies* 21, Supplement 2, AERC Plenary Session. Available at <http://jae.oxfordjournals.org/content/21/suppl_2/ii86.full>

Page, John (2013) 'Should Africa Industrialize?' In *Pathways to Industrialization in the Twenty-First Century: New Challenges and Emerging Paradigms*, edited by Adam Szirmai, Wim Naudé, and Ludovico Alcorta. Oxford: Oxford University Press.

Page, John, and Mans Söderbom (2012) Is small beautiful? Small enterprise, aid and employment in Africa. United Nations University World Institute for Development Economics Research, Working Paper No. 2012/94.

Palma, Gabriel J. (2003) 'The "Three Routes" to Financial Crises: Chile, Mexico and Argentina [1]; Brazil [2]; and Korea, Malaysia and Thailand [3]'. In *Rethinking Development Economics*, edited by Ha-Joon Chang. London: Anthem Press.

Palma, Gabriel J. (2009) 'Flying geese and waddling ducks: The different capabilities of East Asia and Latin America to "demand-adapt" and "supply-upgrade" their export productive capacity'. In *Industrial Policy and Development: The Political Economy of Capabilities Accumulation*, edited by Mario Cimoli, Giovanni Dosi, and Joseph E. Stiglitz. Oxford: Oxford University Press.

Palma, Gabriel J. (2011) How to create a financial crisis by trying to avoid one: The Brazilian 1999-financial collapse as 'Macho-Moneterism' can't handle 'Bubble Thy Neighbour' level of inflows. Cambridge Working Papers in Economics (CWPE) 1301. Available at <http://www.econ.cam.ac.uk/research/repec/cam/pdf/cwpe1301.pdf>

Palma, Gabriel J. (2012) How the full opening of the capital account to highly liquid financial markets led Latin America to two and half cycles of 'mania, panic and crash'. Cambridge Working Papers in Economics (CWPE) 1201. Available at <http://www.econ.cam.ac.uk/research/repec/cam/pdf/cwpe1201.pdf>

Pankhurst, Richard (1996) 'Post-World War II Ethiopia: British military policy and action for the dismantling and acquisition of Italian factories and other assets, 1941–2', *Journal of Ethiopian Studies* 29(1):35–77.

Pasinetti, Luigi (1981) *Structural Change and Economic Growth: A theoretical essay on the dynamics of the wealth of nations*. Cambridge: Cambridge University Press.

Pasinetti, Luigi (1993) Structural economic dynamics: A theory of the economic consequences of human learning. Cambridge: Cambridge University Press.

Peres, Wilson (2013) 'Industrial policies in Latin America'. In *Pathways to Industrialization in the Twenty-First Century: New Challenges and Emerging Paradigms*, edited by Adam Szirmai, Wim Naudé and Ludovico Alcorta. Oxford: Oxford University Press.

Polanyi, Karl (1944) *The Great Transformation: The Political and Economic Origins of our time*. Boston MA: Beacon Press.

Porter, Michael E. (1998) *The Competitive Advantage of Nations*. New York: Palgrave Macmillan.

Porter, Michael E. (2008) The five competitive forces that shape strategy. *Harvard Business Review*. January. Reprint No. R0801E, Harvard Business Review. Available at <http://www.exed.hbs.edu/assets/documents/hbr-shape-strategy.pdf/>

Possas, Mario, and Heloisa Borges (2009) 'Competition Policy and Industrial Development'. In *Industrial Policy and Development: The Political Economy of Capabilities Accumulation*, edited by Mario Cimoli, Giovanni Dosi, and Joseph E. Stiglitz. Oxford: Oxford University Press.

Prebisch, Raúl (1950) *The economic development of Latin America and its principal problems*. New York: UN Department of Economic Affairs.

Reinert, Erik S. (2009) 'Emulation versus comparative advantage: Competing and complementary principles in the history of economic policy'. In *Industrial Policy and Development: The Political Economy of Capabilities Accumulation*, edited by Mario Cimoli, Giovanni Dosi, and Joseph E. Stiglitz. Oxford: Oxford University Press.

Reinert, Erik S. (2010) *How Rich Countries Got Rich and How Poor Countries Stay Poor*. London: Constable.

Reuters (2009) 'Ethiopia says recession hits Dutch flower sales'. Available at <http://af. reuters.com/article/investingNews/idAFJOE5210BX20090302>

Rhee, Yung Whee, Bruce Ross-Larson, and Garry Pursell (2010 [1984]) *How Korea did it? From economic basket case to successful development strategy in the 1960s and 1970s*. Seoul: Random House Korea.

Ricardo, David ([1817] 2004) *The Principles of Political Economy and Taxation*. New York: Dover Publications.

Riddell, Roger (1990) *Manufacturing Africa: Performance and Prospects of Seven Countries in Sub-Saharan Africa*. London: James Currey.

Rikken, Milco (2011) *Global Competitiveness of the Kenyan Flower Industry*. Technical Paper for Kenya Flower Council and the World Bank Group. Available at <http:// www.euacpcommodities.eu/files/2.ESA_.D02_KFC_Seminar_Issue_-_Global_Com petitiveness.pdf>

Roberts, Simon (2004) The role for competition policy in economic development: The South African experience. Trade and Industrial Policy Strategies (TIPS) Working Paper 8. Available at <http://crdi.ca/EN/Documents/The-Role-of-Competition-Policy-in-Economic-Development.pdf>

Rodrik, Dani (1997) Trade Policy and Economic Performance in Sub-Saharan Africa. Harvard University-Harvard Kennedy School, Centre for Policy Research, NBER Working Paper No. 6562.

Rodrik, Dani (2004) 'Industrial Policy for the 21st Century'. September. Available at <http://www.hks.harvard.edu/fs/drodrik/Research%20papers/UNIDOSep.pdf>

Rodrik, Dani (2008a) 'A practical approach to formulating growth strategies'. In *The Washington Consensus Reconsidered: Towards a New Global Governance*, edited by Narcis Sera and Joseph E. Stiglitz. Oxford: Oxford University Press.

Rodrik, Dani (2008b) 'Notes on the Ethiopian economic situation: Refining Ethiopian Industrial Policy Strategy'. Unpublished.

Rodrik, Dani (2008c) Normalizing Industrial Policy. Commission on Growth and Development Working Paper No. 3, Washington DC.

Rodrik, Dani (2011) The Future of Economic Convergence. National Bureau of Economic Research Working Paper 17400. Available at <http://www.nber.org/papers/w17400.pdf>

Rodrik, Dani (2012) *The Globalization Paradox: Why Global Markets, States, and Democracy Can't Coexist*. Oxford: Oxford University Press.

Rodrik, Dani (2014) An African Growth Miracle? April. Available at <https://www.sss. ias.edu/files/pdfs/Rodrik/Research/An_African_growth_miracle.pdf>

Rodriguez, Franscisco, and Dani Rodrik (2001) *Trade Policy and Economic Growth: A Sketpic's Guide to the Cross-National Evidence.* Available at <http://www.nber.org/chapters/c11058.pdf>

SaKong, Il, and Youngsun Koh (eds.) (2010) *The Korean Economy: Six Decades of Growth and Development.* The Committee for the Sixty-Year History of the Korean Economy. Seoul: The Korean Development Institute (KDI).

Schmitz, Hubert (1995a) 'Collective Efficiency: growth path for small-scale industry'. *Journal of Development studies* 31(4):529–66.

Schmitz, Hubert (1995b) 'Small shoemakers and Fordist giants: Tale of a super cluster'. *World Development* 23(1):9–28.

Schmitz, Hubert (1998) Responding to Global Competitive Pressure: Local Co-operation and Upgrading in the Sino's Valley, Brazil. IDS Working Paper 82. Available at <https://www.ids.ac.uk/files/Wp82.pdf>

Schmitz, Hubert (1999) 'Global competition and local cooperation: Success and failure in the Sinos valley, Brazil'. *World Development* 27(9):1627–50.

Schmitz, Hubert (2004) 'Local Upgrading in Global Chains: Recent Findings'. Paper presented to DRUID Summer Conference 2004 on Industrial Dynamics, Innovation and Development. Elsinore, Denmark, 14–16 June. Available at <http://www.druid.dk/uploads/tx_picturedb/ds2004-1422>

Schmitz, Hubert (2007) 'Reducing complexity in the industrial policy debate'. *Development Policy Review* 25(4):417–28.

Schmitz, Hubert, and Peter Knorringa (2000) 'Learning from global buyers.' *Journal of Development Studies* 37(2):177–205.

Schwartz, Herman (2010) *States versus markets: The emergence of a global economy.* New York: Palgrave.

Seguino, Stephanie (2000) 'The effects of structural change and economic liberalisation on gender wage differentials in South Korea and Taiwan'. *Cambridge Journal of Economics* 24(4):437–59.

Selim, Tarek, and Ahmed Salem (2010) *Global Cement Industry: Competitive and Institutional Dimensions.* MPRA_paper_24464, Munich, Munich University Library. Available at <http://mpra.ub.uni-muenchen.de/24464/2/MPRA_paper_24464.pdf>

Selwyn, Ben (2012) *Workers, state and development in Brazil: Powers of labour, chains of value.* Manchester: Manchester University Press.

Sender, John (1999) 'Africa's Economic Performance: Limitations of the current consensus'. *Journal of Economic Perspectives* 13(3):89–114.

Sender, John (2003) 'Rural Poverty and Gender: Analytical Frameworks and Policy Proposals'. In *Rethinking development economics,* edited by Ha-Joon Chang. London: Anthem Press.

Sender, John, Christopher Cramer, and Carlos Oya (2005) Unequal prospects: disparities in the quantity and quality of labour supply in sub-Saharan Africa. World Bank, Washington DC, World Bank Social Protection Discussion Paper Series 0525. <http://siteresources.worldbank.org/SOCIALPROTECTION/Resources/0525.pdf>

Sender, John, Carlos Oya, and Christopher Cramer (2006) 'Women working for wages: Putting flesh on the bones of a rural labour market survey in Mozambique'. *Journal of Southern African Studies* 32(2):313–33.

Sender, John, and Sheila Smith (1986) *The Development of Capitalism in Africa*. London: Methuen.

Shin, Jang-Sup (1996) *The Economics of the Latecomers: Catching-up, technology transfer and institutions in Germany, Japan and South Korea*. London: Routledge.

Shirley, Mary (1997) 'The economics and politics of government of ownership'. *Journal of International Development* 9(6):849–64.

Simon, Bereket (2011) *The tale of two elections* (in Amharic). Addis Ababa: Mega Printing Enterprise.

Singh, Ajit (2011) Comparative advantage, industrial policy and the World Bank: Back to first principles. March. Available at <http://www.cbr.cam.ac.uk/pdf/WP418.pdf>

Söderbom, Mans (2011) 'Firm size and structural change: A case study of Ethiopia'. *Journal of African Economies* 21, Supplement 2, AERC Plenary Session, May. Oxford Journals, Oxford: Oxford University. Available at <http://jae.oxfordjournals.org/content/21/suppl_2/ii126.full.pdf+html>

Soludo, Charles, Osita Ogbu, and Ha-Joon Chang (eds.) (2004) *The politics of trade and industrial policy in Africa: Forced Consensus?* Trenton NJ: Africa World Press.

Sonobe, Tetushi, and Keijiro Otsuka (2006) *Cluster-based industrial development: An East Asian Model*. New York: Palgrave Macmillan.

Stein, Howard (2006) 'Rethinking African Development'. In *Rethinking development economics*, edited by Ha-Joon Chang. London: Anthem Press.

Stein, Howard (2012) 'Africa, industrial policy, and export processing zones: Lessons from Asia'. In *Good growth and governance in Africa: Rethinking development strategies*, edited by Akbar Noman, Kwesi Botchwey, Howard Stein, and Joseph E. Stiglitz. Oxford: Oxford University Press.

Stewart, Frances (2002) Horizontal Inequalities: A Neglected Dimension of Development. QEH Working Paper Series. Working Paper No. 8. Available at <http://www3.qeh.ox.ac.uk/pdf/qehwp/qehwps81.pdf>

Stewart, Frances (2008) *Horizontal inequalities and conflict: Understanding group violence in multiethnic societies*. New York: Palgrave MacMillan.

Stiglitz, Joseph (1998) 'More Instruments and Broader Goals: Moving Towards the Post-Washington Consensus'. WIDER Annual Lecture, Helsinki, 7 January 1998.

Stiglitz, Joseph E. (2002) *Globalization and its discontents*. London: Penguin.

Stiglitz, Joseph E. (2011) The Mauritius Miracle. Project Syndicate. Available at <http://www.project-syndicate.org/commentary/the-mauritius-miracle>

Studwell, Joe (2013) *How Asia Works: Success and Failure in the World's Most Dynamic Region*. London: Profile Books.

Sutton, John, and Nebil Kellow (2010) *An Enterprise Map of Ethiopia*. International Growth Centre.

Szirmai, Adam, Wim Naudé, and Ludovico Alcorta (2013) *Pathways to Industrialization in the 21st century: New Challenges and Emerging Paradigms*. Oxford: Oxford University Press.

Taleb, Nassim N. (2012) *Antifragile: Things that gain from disorder*. London: Penguin.

Tareke, Gebru (1990) 'Continuity and discontinuity in peasant mobilization: The cases of Bale and Tigray'. In *The Political Economy of Ethiopia*, edited by Marina Ottaway. New York: Praeger.

Tareke, Gebru (1991) *Ethiopia: Power and Protest: Peasant Revolts in the Twentieth Century*. Cambridge: Cambridge University Press.

Tekeste, Abarham (2014) *Trade Policy and Performance of Manufacturing Firms in Ethiopia*. Saarbrücken: Scholars' Press.

The Economist (2008) 'Kenya's flower industry'. 7 February. Available at <http://www. economist.com/node/10657231>

The Economist (2009) 'Dutch flower auctions'. 8 April.

The Economist (2013) 'The entrepreneurial state: A new book points out the big role governments play in creating innovative businesses'. 31 August. Available at <http:// www.economist.com/news/business/21584307-new-book-points-out-big-role-gov ernments-play-creating-innovative-businesses>

The Economist Intelligence Unit (2012) Ethiopia: At an economic crossroads. 21 August. Available at <http://country.eiu.com/article.aspx?articleid=659462850& Country=Ethiopia&topic=Economy>

The Guardian (2011) 'Ethiopia's partnership with China: China sees Ethiopia as a land of business opportunities, but the African country remains in charge of any deals'. 30 December. Available at <www.theguardian.com/global-development/poverty-mat ters/2011/dec/30/china-ethiopia-business-opportunities>

Thirlwall, Anthony (1980) *Balance-of-Payments Theory and the United Kingdom Experience*. London: Macmillan.

Thirlwall, Anthony (2002) *The nature of economic growth: An alternative framework for understanding the performance of nations*. Cheltenham: Edward Elgar.

Thirlwall, Anthony (2011) *Economics of Development*, 9th edn. London: Palgrave Macmillan.

Thirlwall, Anthony, and Stephen Bazen (1989) *Deindustrialization*. Oxford: Heinemann.

Tregenna, Fiona (2008a) 'The contributions of manufacturing and services to employment creation and growth in South Africa'. *South African Journal of Economics* 76(S2): s175–s204.

Tregenna, Fiona (2008b) 'Sectoral engine of growth in South Africa: An analysis of services and manufacturing'. UNU-WIDER Research Paper No. 98. November.

Tregenna, Fiona (2012) 'Sources of subsectoral growth in South Africa'. *Oxford Development Studies* 40(2):162–89.

Tregenna, Fiona (2013) 'Deindustrialization and Reindustrialization'. In *Pathways to Industrialization in the Twenty-First Century: New Challenges and Emerging Paradigms*, edited by Adam Szirmai, Wim Naudé, and Ludovico Alcorta. Oxford: Oxford University Press.

UN COMTRADE (2012) United Nations Commodity Trade Statistics, Statistics Division.

UNCTAD (2000) Tax Incentives and Foreign Direct Investment: A global survey. ASIT Advisory Studies No. 16. Geneva: United Nations Conference on Trade and Development.

UNCTAD (2006) LDC Report. United Nations Conference on Trade and Development. Available at <www.unctad.org>

UNCTAD (2008) Trade and Development Report, 2008. Domestic Sources of Finance and Investment in Productive Capacity, Chapter IV. Available at <http://unctad.org/en/docs/tdr2008ch4_en.pdf>

UNCTAD (2011) UNCTAD Least Developed Countries Report 2011. United Nations Conference on Trade and Development.

UNCTAD (2014) Global governance and policy space for development, Trade and Development Report, 2014. New York and Geneva.

UNCTAD-UNIDO (2011) Economic Development in Africa Report 2011: Fostering Industrial Development in Africa in the New Global Environment. United Nations Industrial Development Organization, New York and United Nations Conference on Trade and Development, Geneva.

UN-DESA (2009) World Population Policies 2009. United Nations Department of Economic and Social Affairs, New York.

UN-DESA (2013) World Population Prospects: The 2012 Revision, New York.

UNECA and AU (2011) *Economic Report on Africa 2011. Governing Development in Africa: The Role of the State in Economic Transformation.* Economic Commission for Africa and Africa Union. Available at <http://www.uneca.org/sites/default/files/publications/era2011_eng-fin.pdf>

UNECA (2012) Report on livestock value chains in Eastern and Southern Africa: A regional perspective. United Nations Economic Commission for Africa, Addis Ababa. November.

UNECA and AU (2013) Making the Most of Africa's Commodities: Industrializing for Growth, Jobs and Economic Transformation. Economic Report on Africa 2013. Available at <http://www.uneca.org/publications/economic-report-africa-2013>

UNECA and AU (2014) Dynamic Industrial Policy in Africa: Innovative Institutions, Effective Processes and Flexible Mechanisms. Economic Report on Africa 2014. <http://www.uneca.org/publications/economic-report-africa-2014>

UN-HABITAT (2010) The Ethiopia Case of Condominium Housing: The Integrated Housing Development Programme. United Nations Human Settlements Programme, Nairobi.

UNIDO (2003) A blueprint for the African leather industry: A development, investment and trade guide for the leather industry in Africa. United Nations Industrial Development Organization, Vienna.

UNIDO (2005) A Strategic Plan for the Development of Ethiopian Leather and Leather Products Industry. Volume I and II. United Nations Industrial Development Organization, Vienna.

UNIDO (2012) Ethiopia: Technical assistance project for the upgrading of the Ethiopian leather and leather products industry. United Nations Industrial Development Organization, Vienna.

USAID (2008) Success Story: Ethiopians Learning to Fight Ectoparasites. United States Agency for International Development, Washington, DC.

USGS (2010a) *2010 Minerals Yearbook, Ethiopia (Advance Release)*. US Geological Survey and US Department of the Interior. June.

USGS (2010b) Hydraulic Cement African Production, by Country. US Geological Survey.

USGS (2011a) Mineral Commodity Summaries: Cement. US Geological Survey. January.

USGS (2011b) USGS Mineral Program Cement Report. Available at <http://minerals. usgs.gov/minerals/pubs/commodity/cement/mcs-2011-cemen.pdf>

USGS (2013) Mineral Commodity Summaries: Cement. US Geological Survey. January. Available at <www.minerals.usgs.gov/minerals/pubs/mcs/2013/mcs2013.pdf>

Vaughan, Sarah, and Mesfin Gebremichael (2011) Rethinking business and politics in Ethiopia: The role of EFFORT, The Endowment Fund for the Rehabilitation of Tigray. APPP Research Report 2.

Vergne, Jean-Philippe, and Rodolphe Durand (2010) 'The Missing Link between the Theory and Empirics of Path Dependence: Conceptual Clarification, Testability Issue, and Methodological Implications'. *Journal of Management Studies* 47(4):736–59.

Wade, Robert ([1990] 2004) *Governing the Market: Economic Theory and the Role of the Government in East Asian Industrialization*. Princeton: Princeton University Press.

Warren-Rodriguez, Alex (2008) 'Uncovering dynamics in the accumulation of technological capabilities and skills in the Mozambican manufacturing sector'. Available at <http://www.soas.ac.uk/economics/research/workingpapers/file43193.pdf/>

Warren-Rodriguez, Alex (2010) 'Industrialisation, state intervention and the demise of manufacturing development in Mozambique'. In *African Political Economy*, edited by Vishu Padayachee. New York: Routledge.

Warwick, Ken (2013) Beyond Industrial Policy: Emerging Issues and New Trends. OECD Science, Technology and Industry Policy Papers No. 2.

Washington Council for International Trade (2013) <http://wcit.org>

Watanabe, Matsuo, and Atsushi Hanatani (2012) 'Issues in Africa's Industrial Policy Process'. In *Good Growth and Governance in Africa: Rethinking Development Strategies*, edited by Adam Szirmai, Wim Naudé, and Ludovico Alcorta. Oxford: Oxford University Press.

Weber, Max (1947) *The Theory of Social and Economic Organization*. New York: Free Press.

Weiss, John (2013) 'Industrial Policy in the Twenty-First Century: Challenges for the Future'. In *Pathways to Industrialization in the Twenty-First Century: New Challenges and Emerging Paradigms*, edited by Adam Szirmai, Wim Naudé, and Ludovico Alcorta. Oxford: Oxford University Press.

Whitfield (2011) Growth without Economic Transformation: Economic Impacts of Ghana's Political Settlement. DIIS Working Paper No. 28. Available at <http://subweb.diis.dk/graphics/Publications/WP2011/WP2011-28-Growth-without-Economic-Transformation-Ghana_web.pdf>

Williamson, John (2008) 'A short history of the Washington Consensus'. In *The Washington Consensus Reconsidered: Towards a New Global Governance*, edited by Narcis Sera and Joseph E. Stiglitz. Oxford: Oxford University Press.

Woo-Cumings, Meredith (ed.) (1999) *The Developmental State*. Ithaca: Cornell University Press.

Woo-Cumings, Meredith (1999) 'Introduction: Chalmers Johnson and the Politics of Nationalism and Development'. *The Developmental State*, edited by Meredith Woo-Cumings. Ithaca: Cornell University Press.

World Bank (1995) Bureaucrats in Business: The Economics and Politics of Government Ownership. Policy Research Report. World Bank, Washington DC.

World Bank (2008) Reshaping Economic Geography, 2009 World Development Report, Washington DC.

World Bank (2009a) Cement sector in Africa and CDM: Investing in clean technologies and energy savings. Key sheet. May.

World Bank (2009b) Cement Sector Program in Sub-Saharan Africa: Barriers analysis to CDM and solutions. World Bank/CF Assist. April.

World Bank (2009c) Ethiopia: The Employment Creation Effects of the Addis Ababa Integrated Housing Program. Report No. 47648-ET. March 2009.

World Bank (2010) Africa's Infrastructure: A time for transformation. African Development Forum.

World Bank (2012a) 'Chinese FDI in Ethiopia: A World Bank Survey'. Draft, unpublished. World Bank, Poverty Reduction and Economic Management, Africa Region, AFTP2, October, Addis Ababa.

World Bank (2012b) Diagnosing corruption in Ethiopia: Perceptions, Realities, and the way forward for key sectors, edited by Jannelle Plummer. Washington DC: World Bank.

World Bank (2013) Life expectancy at birth, total (years). Available at <http://data.worldbank.org/indicator/SP.DYN.LE00.IN>

World Bank and International Finance Corporation (2011) *Doing Business 2011: Making a difference for Entrepreneurs*. Washington DC: World Bank.

World Bank and International Finance Corporation (ed.) (2013) Doing *Business 2013: Smarter Regulation for Small and Medium Enterprises*. Washington DC: World Bank.

Wrong, Michela (2005) *I didn't do it for you: How the world used and abused a small African nation*. London: Harper Perennial.

Wu, John C. (2004) *The mineral industry of the Republic of Korea*. Reston, VA: USGS. Available at <http://minerals.usgs.gov/minerals/pubs/country/2004/ksmyb04.pdf>

Young, Allyn (1928) 'Increasing returns and economic progress'. *Economic Journal* 38 (152):527–42.

Young, John ([1997] 2006) *Peasant Revolution in Ethiopia: The Tigray People's Liberation Front 1975–1991*. Cambridge: Cambridge University Press.

Zenawi, Meles (2012) 'States and Markets: Neoliberal Limitations and the Case for a Developmental State'. In *Good growth and governance in Africa: Rethinking development strategies*, edited by Akbar Noman, Kwesi Botchwey, Howard Stein, and Joseph E. Stiglitz. Oxford: Oxford University Press.

Zewde, Bahru (ed.) (2002a) *The History of Modern Ethiopia 1955–1991*. Athens: Ohio University Press.

Zewde, Bahru (2002b) *Pioneers of Change in Ethiopia: The Reformist Intellectuals of the Early Twentieth Century*. Oxford: James Currey.

Selected local references

AACG (2003) Housing stock and demand in Addis Ababa. Unpublished. Housing Development Agency.

CBE (2011) Special truck loan and pre-shipment export credit facility guideline. Letter of Commercial Bank of Ethiopia's president to all branches, district, and head office organs. P/BZ/08/11. Addis Ababa, Ethiopia.

CBE (2012) Summary of performance progress on grand initiatives, priority sector financing, and FCY inflow. Commercial Bank of Ethiopia. Unpublished. Addis Ababa, Ethiopia.

Chemical Industry Development Directorate, MOI (2012) Letters and minutes (Nos. 1–80) compiled by Ministry of Industry from 2009–12. Addis Ababa, Ethiopia.

CSA (1988) *Results of the survey of manufacturing and electricity industries* (1984/85). Central Statistical Authority, February 1988, Addis Ababa, statistical bulletin 58.

CSA (1990) *Results of the survey of manufacturing and electricity industries* (1986/87). Central Statistical Authority, January 1990, Addis Ababa, statistical bulletin 75.

CSA (1991) *Results of the survey of manufacturing and electricity industries* (1987/88). Central Statistical Authority, January 1991, Addis Ababa, statistical bulletin 87.

CSA (1992) *Results of the survey of manufacturing and electricity industries* (1988/89). Central Statistical Authority, April 1992, Addis Ababa, statistical bulletin 97.

CSA (1993) *Results of the survey of manufacturing and electricity industries* (1989/90). Central Statistical Authority, April 1993, Addis Ababa, statistical bulletin 112.

CSA (1994) *Results of the survey of manufacturing and electricity industries* (1992/93). Central Statistical Authority, August 1994, Addis Ababa, statistical bulletin 126.

CSA (1995) *Results of the survey of manufacturing and electricity industries* (1993/94). Central Statistical Authority, August 1995, Addis Ababa, statistical bulletin 136.

CSA (1996) *Results of the survey of manufacturing and electricity industries* (1994/95). Central Statistical Authority, September 1996, Addis Ababa, statistical bulletin 158.

CSA (1997) *Report on large scale manufacturing and electricity industries survey.* Central Statistical Authority, October 1997, Addis Ababa, statistical bulletin 178.

CSA (1998) *Report on large scale manufacturing and electricity industries survey.* Central Statistical Authority, October 1998, Addis Ababa, statistical bulletin 191.

CSA (1999) *Report on large scale manufacturing and electricity industries survey.* Central Statistical Authority, September 1999, Addis Ababa, statistical bulletin 210.

CSA (2000) *Report on large scale manufacturing and electricity industries survey.* Central Statistical Authority, October 2000, Addis Ababa, statistical bulletin 231.

CSA (2001) *Report on large scale manufacturing and electricity industries survey.* Central Statistical Agency, February 2001, Addis Ababa, statistical bulletin 248.

CSA (2001, 2002, 2007, 2008, 2010, and 2011b) Statistical Abstracts of 2001, 2002, 2007, 2008, 2010, and 2011. Central Statistical Agency, Addis Ababa, Ethiopia.

CSA (2002) *Report on large scale manufacturing and electricity industries survey.* Central Statistical Agency, October 2002, Addis Ababa, statistical bulletin 265.

CSA (2003) *Report on large scale manufacturing and electricity industries survey.* Central Statistical Agency, October 2003, Addis Ababa, statistical bulletin 281.

319

CSA (2004) *Report on large scale manufacturing and electricity industries survey.* Central Statistical Agency, November 2004, Addis Ababa, statistical bulletin 321.

CSA (2005) *Report on large scale manufacturing and electricity industries survey.* Central Statistical Authority.

CSA (2006) *Report on large scale manufacturing and electricity industries survey.* Central Statistical Agency, November 2006, Addis Ababa, statistical bulletin 380.

CSA (2007) *Report on large scale manufacturing and electricity industries survey.* Central Statistical Agency, October 2007, Addis Ababa, statistical bulletin 403.

CSA (2008) *Report on large scale manufacturing and electricity industries survey.* Central Statistical Agency, October 2008, Addis Ababa, statistical bulletin 431.

CSA (2009) *Report on large scale manufacturing and electricity industries survey.* Central Statistical Agency, December 2009, Addis Ababa, statistical bulletin 472.

CSA (2010) *Report on large scale manufacturing and electricity industries survey.* Central Statistical Agency, November 2010, Addis Ababa, statistical bulletin 500.

CSA (2011) *Report on large scale manufacturing and electricity industries survey.* Central Statistical Agency, August 2011, Addis Ababa, statistical bulletin 531.

CSA (2012a) *Agricultural sample surveys (from 2005 to 2012),* Vol. II, Statistical Bulletins 331, 361, 388, 417, 446, 468, 505, and 532. Central Statistical Agency, Addis Ababa, Ethiopia.

CSA (2012b) List of firms involved in the 2012 survey of manufacturing sector, leather and leather products sector. Central Statistical Agency, Addis Ababa, Ethiopia.

CSA (2012c) *Report on large scale manufacturing and electricity industries survey.* Central Statistical Agency, August 2012, Addis Ababa, statistical bulletin 532.

CSA (2013) Population size of towns by sex, region, zone, and wereda. July. Central Statistical Agency, Addis Ababa, Ethiopia.

CSO (1977) Results of the survey of manufacturing industries in Ethiopia (1976). Statistical Bulletin 17. June. Provisional Military Government of Socialist Ethiopia, Central Statistical Office, Addis Ababa, Ethiopia.

CSO (1983) Ethiopia Statistical Abstracts of 1968, 1980, and 1982. Central Statistical Office, Addis Ababa, Ethiopia.

CSO (1987) Results of the surveys of manufacturing industries (1976/77 to 1983/84). Statistical Bulletins 23, 29, 30, 38, 48, and 53. Central Statistical Office, Addis Ababa, Ethiopia.

CSO and MCIT (1969) Survey of manufacturing and electricity industry (1964/5–1966/7). Statistical Bulletin 2. June. Central Statistical Office and Ministry of Commerce, Industry and Tourism, Addis Ababa, Ethiopia.

DBE (2009) The priority area projects of the DBE. As approved by the Board of Directors of the Development Bank of Ethiopia, Addis Ababa, Ethiopia.

DBE (2012a) *A Guide to Development Bank of Ethiopia.* Development Bank of Ethiopia, Addis Ababa, Ethiopia.

DBE (2012b) Loan portfolio concentration report as of December 2011. Unpublished. Development Bank of Ethiopia, Addis Ababa, Ethiopia.

DBE (2012c) Monthly Report on Status of Flowers Projects. Assistant President, PO/241/12, Development Bank of Ethiopia, Addis Ababa, Ethiopia.

DBE (2012d) Third Quarter Performance Report 2011/12. Unpublished. Development Bank of Ethiopia, Addis Ababa, Ethiopia.

DLV (2012) Quantitative unified information. DLV consultancy to Ethiopian horticulture sector <http://www.dlvplant.nl/uk/content/projects-africa.html>. Addis Ababa, Ethiopia.

EAL (2012) Freight data. Unpublished. Ethiopian Airlines. Addis Ababa, Ethiopia.

EEPCO (2012) Detailed Information of EEPCO. Supplementary data for interview with CEO of Ethiopian Electric Power Corporation, Addis Ababa, Ethiopia.

EFFORT (1995) Memorandum of Foundation. Endowment Fund for the Rehabilitation of Tigray.

EFFORT (2010) EFFORT Corporate Strategy. Endowment Fund for the Rehabilitation of Tigray.

EFFORT (2011) EFFORT Performance Report. Endowment Fund for the Rehabilitation of Tigray.

EHDA (2011a) Export performance report of 2011. Amharic version. Ethiopian Horticulture Development Agency, Addis Ababa, Ethiopia.

EHDA (2011b) Guideline on the value chain of floriculture export. Ethiopian Horticulture Development Agency, Addis Ababa, Ethiopia.

EHDA (2011c) The 2011 horticulture sector report. Ethiopian Horticulture Development Agency, Addis Ababa, Ethiopia.

EHDA (2012a) EHDA Statistical Bulletin 01, October. Ethiopian Horticulture Development Agency, Addis Ababa, Ethiopia.

EHDA (2012b) Report to National Export Coordinating Committee. Unpublished. Ethiopian Horticulture Development Agency, Addis Ababa, Ethiopia.

EHDA (2012c) New Approach to Market Ethiopian Flowers in the Russian Federation. Ethiopian Horticulture Development Agency, Addis Ababa, Ethiopia.

EHDA (2012d) Minutes of meetings (Numbers 1–25 of EHDA from 2009–12). Unpublished. Archives of Ethiopian Horticulture Development Agency. Addis Ababa, Ethiopia.

EHDA (2012e) Correspondence from firms and other stakeholders (Numbers 1–35), 2009–12. Archives of Ethiopian Horticulture Development Agency, Addis Ababa, Ethiopia.

EHDA (2013) Labour records of firms and summary review. May. Addis Ababa, Ethiopia.

EHPEA (2007) A Guide for new investors. Ethiopian Horticulture Producers and Exporters Association. Available at <http://www.EHPEA.org.et>

ELIA (2012) Letter submitted to the Prime Minister at the government-private sector dialogue on 24 October 2012. Unpublished.

EPRDF (2011a) *Five Years Growth and Transformation Plan and Ethiopian Renaissance*. Addis Ababa: Ethiopian People's Revolutionary Democratic Front and Mega Printing.

EPRDF (2011b) *The EPRDF from founding to the present*. Amharic version. Addis Ababa: Ethiopian People's Revolutionary Democratic Front and Mega Printing.

EPRDF (2011c) *Ethiopia's Renaissance and EPRDF Lines*. In Amharic. Addis Ababa: Mega Printing.

EPRDF (2013a) *EPRDF reaffirmed its commitment to the renaissance of Ethiopia and the construction of the Renaissance Dam*. Addis Ababa: Ethiopian People's Revolutionary Democratic Front.

EPRDF (2013b) Meles's Portrait: Sketch of who he is. Ethiopian People's Revolutionary Democratic Front, Addis Ababa. Available at <www.eprdf.org.et>

EPRDF (2013c) *New Vision* (bimonthly editions). Ethiopian People's Revolutionary Democratic Front, Addis Ababa <www.eprdf.org.et>

EPRDF (2013d) Report of 9th EPRDF Congress, Ethiopian People's Revolutionary Democratic Front. Bahirdar, Ethiopia.

EPRDF (2013e) EPRDF Renaissance Path and Ethiopia's Future. In Amharic, March 2013. Office of EPRDF, Addis Ababa, Ethiopia.

ERCA (2012a) Export revenues and volume. Unpublished data. Ethiopian Revenues and Customs Authority, Addis Ababa, Ethiopia.

ERCA (2012b) Data on the imports of textile and apparel imports 1998–2012. Ethiopian Revenue and Customs Authority, Addis Ababa, Ethiopia.

FDRE (1992) *Public Enterprises Proclamation No. 25/1992*. House of Peoples' Representatives, Addis Ababa, Ethiopia.

FDRE (1994) *An Economic Development Strategy for Ethiopia*. Federal Democratic Republic of Ethiopia, Addis Ababa, Ethiopia.

FDRE (1995) *Constitution of the Federal Democratic Republic of Ethiopia*. House of Representatives, Addis Ababa, Ethiopia.

FDRE (1996) *Ethiopia's Development Strategy (ADLI)*. Federal Democratic Republic of Ethiopia, Addis Ababa, Ethiopia.

FDRE (1998a) *Ethiopian Export Promotion Agency Establishment Proclamation*. Federal Democratic Republic of Ethiopia, Addis Ababa, Ethiopia.

FDRE (1998b) Export Promotion Strategies (Export Development Strategies), Number 5/Decision 159/1998. Amharic version. Federal Democratic Republic of Ethiopia, Addis Ababa, Ethiopia.

FDRE (2002) *The Industrial Development Strategy of Ethiopia*. Federal Democratic Republic of Ethiopia Information Ministry, Addis Ababa, Ethiopia.

FDRE (2008a) *Raw and Semi-processed Hides and Skins Export Tax*. Proclamation Number 567/2008. FDRE House of Representatives, Addis Ababa, Ethiopia.

FDRE (2008b) *The Regulation for the establishment of Ethiopian Horticulture Development Agency*. Regulation No. 152/2008. FDRE Council of Ministers.

FDRE (2012) The Strategy of the Development of Micro and Small Enterprises. Federal Democratic Republic of Ethiopia, Addis Ababa, Ethiopia.

FIA (2012a) Investment certificates provided to FDI and domestic investors. Unpublished. Federal Investment Agency, Addis Ababa, Ethiopia.

FIA (2012b) Consultations with business community; and the historical evolution of FIA and investment law (1992–2013). Unpublished. Federal Investment Agency, Addis Ababa, Ethiopia.

FIA (2012c) Minutes of meetings of the board of FIA (2008–12). Archives of the Federal Investment Agency, Addis Ababa, Ethiopia.

GOE (1960) *The Civil Code of Ethiopia Proclamation of 1960.* Proclamation Number 165/1960. Government of Ethiopia, Addis Ababa, Ethiopia.

LIDI (2011) Draft on the ban of crust and export of leather products. Unpublished. Leather Industry Development Institute, Ministry of Industry, Addis Ababa, Ethiopia.

LIDI (2012a) Interim Audit Report as per Requirement of Leather and Leather Products Sector Best Practice Standard for 18 tanneries and footwear firms. Leather Industry Development Institute, Ministry of Industry, Addis Ababa, Ethiopia.

LIDI (2012b) Minutes of meetings of Tanning and Footwear Industries Benchmarking, Number 1–7. Leather Industry Development Institute, Ministry of Industry, Addis Ababa, Ethiopia.

LIDI (2012c) Minutes of meetings of the twinning programme, Number 1–6. Leather Industry Development Institute, Ministry of Industry, Addis Ababa, Ethiopia.

LIDI (2012d) Draft profile of the leather sector, organized for research interview by LIDI. Director general's notes. Leather Industry Development Institute, Ministry of Industry, Addis Ababa, Ethiopia.

LIDI (2012e) Letters from firms (Number 1–330) in the leather and leather products sector, 2010–12. Leather Industry Development Institute, Ministry of Industry, Addis Ababa, Ethiopia.

LIDI (2012f) Facilitation Supports Requested by Firms in Leather Sector. Leather Industry Development Institute, Ministry of Industry, Addis Ababa, Ethiopia.

LIDI (2012g) Performance data. Unpublished. Planning and MIS Directorate, Leather Industry Development Institute, Ministry of Industry, Addis Ababa, Ethiopia.

MOA (2012) Review of animal resources. Unpublished. Ministry of Agriculture, Addis Ababa, Ethiopia.

MOFED (1999) Survey of the Ethiopian Economy: Review of Post-Reform Developments (1992/3–1997/98). Ministry of Finance and Economic Development, Addis Ababa, Ethiopia.

MOFED (2002) Sustainable Development and Poverty Reduction Program (SDPRP). Ministry of Finance and Economic Development, Addis Ababa, Ethiopia.

MOFED (2006) Ethiopia: Building on Progress: A Plan for Accelerated and Sustained Development to End Poverty (PASDEP) 2005/06–2009/10. Volume I. Ministry of Finance and Economic Development, Addis Ababa, Ethiopia.

MOFED (2010) Growth and Transformation Plan 2010/11–2014/15. Volume I, Main Text, and Volume II, Policy Matrix. Ministry of Finance and Economic Development, Addis Ababa, Ethiopia.

MOFED (2011a) A Study to improve tariff incentives. Ministry of Finance and Economic Development, Ministry of Industry, and Ethiopian Revenue and Customs Authority, Addis Ababa, Ethiopia.

MOFED (2011b) Raw and Semi-processed Hides and Skins Export Tax Amendment Directives. Directive No. 30/2011. Ministry of Finance and Economic Development, Addis Ababa, Ethiopia.

MOFED (2012a) *Macroeconomic Developments in Ethiopia. Annual Report 2010/11.* Ministry of Finance and Economic Development, Addis Ababa, Ethiopia.

MOFED (2012b) Ethiopia's macroeconomic data. Unpublished. National Economic Accounts Directorate, Ministry of Finance and Economic Development, Addis Ababa, Ethiopia.

MOFED (2012c) Ethiopian Tariff Amendments (1993–2011). Unpublished. Ministry of Finance and Economic Development, Addis Ababa, Ethiopia.

MOFED (2013a) Annual GTP performance report. Unpublished. Ministry of Finance and Economic Development, Addis Ababa, Ethiopia.

MOFED (2013b) A Directive to implement the export tariff incentive system. Amharic version. Ministry of Finance and Economic Development, Addis Ababa, Ethiopia.

MOFED (2014) Brief Note on the 2013 National Accounts Statistics. Unpublished. 25 October. Ministry of Finance and Economic Development. Addis Ababa, Ethiopia.

MOI (2012a) Summary of consultations between government and industrialists on 25 October 2012 at Sheraton-Addis. Unpublished. Ministry of Industry, Addis Ababa, Ethiopia.

MOI (2012b) Global cement consumption. Unpublished. Chemical Industry Development Directorate, Ministry of Industry, Addis Ababa, Ethiopia.

MOI (2012c) Industrial zone development strategy study. Amharic version. Unpublished. Ministry of Industry, Addis Ababa, Ethiopia.

MOI (2013) Directives to implement Proclamation 768/2012 on export tariff promotion. Amharic version. Ministry of Industry, Addis Ababa, Ethiopia.

MOM (2012) Report on mining and exploration licences. Ministry of Mines, Addis Ababa, Ethiopia.

MoTI (2008) Directive on Petroleum Cost Absorption for Air Freight of Floriculture. 14 April 2008.

MUDC (2013) Data on housing development, cement demand and consumption. July. Unpublished. Ministry of Urban Development and Construction, Addis Ababa, Ethiopia.

Mugher (2013) *Updated data on firm status*. July.

MWUD (2007) *Plan for urban development and urban good governance, PASDEP 2005/06–2009/10*. Addis Ababa: Ministry of Works and Urban Development and Berhanena Selam Printing.

MWUD (2009) Reports on capacity building of construction industry. Ministry of Works and Urban Development, Housing Development Office, Addis Ababa, Ethiopia.

MWUD (2010) Logistics Review and Plan of Housing Development Programme. Unpublished. Ministry of Works and Urban Development, Housing Development Office, Addis Ababa, Ethiopia.

MWUD (2013) Housing Development Programme Updated Data. Unpublished. Ministry of Works and Urban Development, Housing Development Office, Addis Ababa, Ethiopia.

Nazret (2010) 'Ethiopia-Derba Cement to buy 1000 Volvo trucks'. Available at <http://nazret.com/blog/index.php/2010/01/15/ethiopia_s_derba_midroc_cement_to_buy_10>

NBE (2011) *Annual Report 2009/10*. Addis Ababa: Domestic Economic Analysis and Publications Directorate, National Bank of Ethiopia.

NBE (2012a) NBE Letter to all banks, List of Flower Exporters with Outstanding Commitment From May 12, 2008 to April 30, 2012. FEMRMD/745/12. National Bank of Ethiopia, Addis Ababa.

NBE (2012b) Unpublished data. National Bank of Ethiopia Research Department, Addis Ababa.

NBE (2013) Regulations and directives of National Bank of Ethiopia. Addis Ababa. Also available at <www.nbe.gov.et>

NECC (2010) Study on Export Sector Development, Leadership, and Coordination. Unpublished draft. National Export Coordinating Committee, Prime Minister's Office, Addis Ababa, Ethiopia.

NECC (2012) Minutes of meetings (Number 1–92) of the National Export Coordinating Council, 2004–12. Addis Ababa, Ethiopia.

Oqubay, Arkebe (2012) Quasi-census (Number 1–150), site observations (Number 1–50), and interviews (Number 1–200) with selected firms in cement, floriculture, leather and leather products sectors, and related stakeholders. Unpublished. Addis Ababa, Ethiopia.

PPESA (2012) Privatization performance and reports. Unpublished.

Royal Netherlands Embassy (2012) Surveys of on Dutch Flower Firms in Ethiopia 2010–12. Unpublished, Addis Ababa, Ethiopia.

Index

Introductory Note
References such as '178–9' indicate (not necessarily continuous) discussion of a topic across a range of pages. Wherever possible in the case of topics with many references, these have either been divided into sub-topics or only the most significant discussions of the topic are listed. Because the entire work is about 'Ethiopia', the use of this term (and certain others which occur constantly throughout the book) as an entry point has been restricted. Information will be found under the corresponding detailed topics.